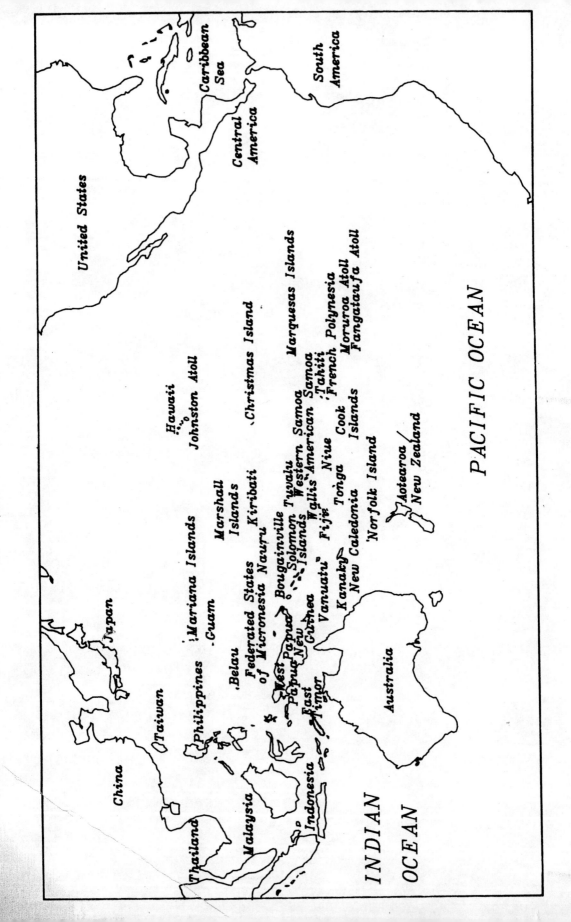

Sustainable Development
or
Malignant Growth?

Sustainable Development
or
Malignant Growth?

Perspectives of
Pacific Island Women

Edited by
'Atu Emberson-Bain

Marama Publications,
Suva, Fiji,
1994

Published in 1994
by Marama Publications,
Suva, Fiji

Design and Layout: 'Atu Emberson-Bain, Steven Vete, Roslyn
Sharpe, Jacqueline Ah Kee and Sashi Kumar

Cover design: Sashi Kumar

Editing Assistance: Roslyn Sharpe

Typsetting: Jacqueline Ah Kee

ISBN 982-326-001-X

Front cover photograph: Fiji Times

Back cover photograph: Litiana Waqalevu

Printed by Star Printery Ltd, Suva, Fiji

This publication was funded by the Australian International
Development Assistance Bureau (AIDAB).

Dedication

For my sister,

Vivian Nan Tatakiama Bain

Each bird
each one of us
bringing twigs
leaves
bits of blue
plastic
whatevah!
to make a new nest
together
a leafy womb
enfolding out progeny
the ovum we will make
together
born from our union
born from our struggle
born from communion.

Our leaves and twigs
made of heart
muscle
and bone.
Our song
born in ocean and
weaned on struggle.
Strong clear voices
singing:
we have arrived!

we are here.
we declare ourselves
we announce our presence.
we tell our own stories...'

Caroline Sinavaiana
Excerpt from Village of Hope:
By the River of Babylon

(Dedicated to the people of Barbados and the Caribbean on the occasion of the NGO Islands Forum, the United Nations First Global Conference on the Sustainable Development of Small Island Developing States, Barbados, April 1994.)

Acknowledgements

This collection of writings by Pacific Island women has been made possible by generous funding from the Australian International Development Assistance Bureau (AIDAB) in Canberra. The International Women's Development Agency (IWDA) in Melbourne sponsored the project. The book was conceived following the Pacific Regional Meeting of DAWN (Development Alternatives with Women for a New Era) in Suva in late 1992. Its completion is testimony to the enthusiasm and willing cooperation of the contributors which enabled us to overcome the tyranny of distance. In this regard, I would like to express my sincere thanks to the authors and poets who responded to my call for contributions. I owe a special gratitude to Claire Slatter for encouraging me to run with the idea, and for helping me to conceptualise the project and to see it through. Her advice, intellectual and practical support (not to mention hospitality) have helped me in significant ways to persevere against what, at times, have seemed like insuperable odds.

Two other special people who have shared their production skills and creative energy, and given me practical support, friendship and humour, are Roslyn Sharpe (who came to my rescue in Noumea and assisted in the early stages of editing) and Steven Vete (who has tolerated the difficulties of being a solo parent to four children in my long periods of absence). To my children, I would also like to say a heartfelt thank you.

Many other generous people have helped. I am grateful to Jacqueline Ah Kee for working long and late hours to accomplish the typesetting, to Sashi Kumar for assistance with the cover design and graphics, to Petelo Ioane for crafting the map at short notice, and to Ms Rahiman Kutty for her kind assistance in the Fiji Times Library. Vanessa Griffen graciously helped over the photographs and together with Arlene Griffen gave me much needed support and hospitality. Samantha Magick and Helen Sutherland were two other wonderful women who came to my aid, along with Claire Slatter, in the frenzied latter stages of the project. Samantha kindly assisted with proof-reading.

I am grateful to all those people and organisations who gave photographs for inclusion in the collection. In particular, I would like to thank Asaele Lave, Fiji Times, for his support and generosity; Litiana Waqalevu, Media Unit, University of the South Pacific; the Ministry of Forests, Fiji; the Women's Bureau of the South Pacific Commission, Noumea; the Pacific Concerns Resource Centre (PCRC), Suva; the Kanak and Exploited Workers Union (USTKE), Noumea; Mari Sasabe, Pacific Regional YWCA, Suva; Kerrie Strathy, SPACHEE, University of the South Pacific; Roman Grynberg, University of the South Pacific; and Rita Narayan, Suva. Other people who kindly supplied data and documentation include Brian Doyle (Statistics), Deveni Temu (Library), Hugh Walton (Fisheries), all of the South Pacific Commission in Noumea.

Contents

Part Five

Political Frameworks
and Perversions

Part Six

Rethinking Sustainability in the Pacific:
Women's Perspectives

Introduction:

Sustaining the unsustainable?

I remember
seeing you rise to lead and guide
while the world cried for equality
I remember that
in the global awakening of womanhood
development for you was already
a passing tune

Noumea Simi

     In the Pacific region - which has a population of close to 6.5 million - an intimate relationship has traditionally existed between people and their natural environment. Natural resources like the land and sea are crucial to human survival in more than just physical respects, forming the foundations of whole social and cultural systems as well as sources of subsistence and production for distribution and exchange. Nature is respected for its spiritual sanctity as well as its material value, and the physical environment is closely associated with still resilient polytheistic religious ideologies and traditional kinship systems. This interaction between Pacific Islanders and their physical environment has, however, been complicated, in many respects jeopardised, by the process of Western development which has directly intruded, often in quite harmful ways, upon people's lives, the natural environment and the relationship between them. In something of a cruel irony, the rich physical and human resources we possess have at times proved to be a curse: a sentence to some of the most destructive and unsustainable human activities imaginable, rather than a source of prosperity and well-being for our people. The natural riches we possess, along with other attractions like low-cost labour and militarily strategic locations, have been irresistible bait for the buccaneers of an omnipotent global system.

    The development 'wisdom' emerging in our region during the last decade stresses a number of major threats to the Pacific environment. Prompted by developments in the international arena, high population growth and rising sea levels have emerged amongst the most persistent preoccupations of regional meetings. 'Wall-of-death' driftnet fishing, toxic waste disposal, deforestation and nuclear testing are amongst other problems claiming the attention of Pacific governments, although rather more sporadically. Yet in many ways, the pattern of development politics that is reflected in debate and policy making today at the national, regional and international levels is discouraging. Development discourse and the search for solutions are conducted within fairly limiting parameters. Overpopulation is increasingly targeted as the culprit for environmental degradation; the links between government 'development' policies and environmentally destructive practices escape close scrutiny; specific problems (and their prescribed solutions) are analysed in isolation from the broader socio-political context (which would seem to offer a more instructive, holistic picture); and surface rather than root causes are commonly investigated. But perhaps the most contentious characteristic of current development trends is that the future of the region's people continues to be fashioned by an economic (market) model whose ideological foundations and purported development value have been accepted with few, if any, questions or reservations.

As Pacific Island states claimed the reins of political independence during the 1970s, some genuinely reflective and impassioned questions emerged - not only amongst students and non-government organisations (NGOs) but also from within the ranks of government leadership. At the heart of these was a very basic question about the kinds of philosophical principles that should underlie regional development in an independent Pacific. There was a search for a development framework that would enhance the material conditions of life for the majority of people; a recognised need to correct the problem of 'uneven' development by encouraging the allocation of resources to the disadvantaged rural sector; and a concern to forge an independence that would transcend the boundaries of political sovereignty by building the foundations of self-reliant economies and truly 'national' development. Import-substitution and state investment in the economy, aimed at strengthening our capacity for self-sufficiency and encouraging national (as opposed to foreign) control represented two prominent strategies, notwithstanding their limitations as an 'alternative' form of development. In terms of political structures, there was a general acceptance of, and belief in, the state's role as caretaker or provider of social services.

Today, as we find our small island states being sucked ever more deeply into the whirlpool of the global market-driven economy, our natural resources and environment are being plundered on a scale like never before, and the social consequences of continuing down what is essentially the old colonial road are making themselves felt. Pacific governments may not be indifferent or approving, but they are typically acquiescent or, at least, demure. On one level, there would appear to be a heightened sensitivity to our development and environment crisis. The gravity of its social consequences and political implications (for example the disturbing incidence of urban crime) is reason enough for constructive responses from the state. But unlike the leaders and opinion shapers of the 1970s, our governments do not appear to be addressing what we might call the 'fundamentals' of our development experience: they are not engaging in critical discussion on what regional development is, or should be, about, thus leaving its philosophical premises essentially undisputed territory.

In particular, there is little questioning (at the official level at least) of the purpose and ramifications of the free market ideology being peddled by the new-look colonial 'missionaries' of the 1990s - the powerful global financial institutions like the World Bank and the International Monetary Fund (IMF) which are the effective ghost-writers/directors of regional development policy. The

World Bank's development wisdom is not being scrutinised for the simple reason that it is perceived by many of our leaders as an infallible truth. Although economic growth is no longer assumed to be a sufficient condition for development, it is still seen as a crucial prerequisite (i.e. necessary condition), just as certain economic restructuring measures (such as private sector investment, deregulation and export-driven production) are regarded as the guaranteed means of achieving that growth. At its most basic level, the growth model involves the sanctification of the market and the principles of wealth generation, accumulation and profit. But as with all forms of self-proclaimed wisdom, there are generally flaws to be discovered beneath the confident surface. A moot point here is the 'Pacific paradox', a tag awarded to our region by the World Bank itself, which acknowledges that appropriate growth levels have not occurred in Pacific member countries in spite of indulgent levels of investment, aid and other resource flows during the past few years. The research and diverse experiences of Pacific women that form the basis of this book offer a critical response to some of this dominant thinking.

The inspiration for the collection comes from the pioneering work of a number of women scholars and activists from Asia, the Caribbean and Latin America - founding members of the third world feminist network known as DAWN (Development Alternatives with Women for a New Era) which was formed in 1984. At the Women's NGO Forum in Nairobi in 1985, DAWN contributed a feminist critique of development from the vantage point of poor women in the economic South. It called for

> a world where inequality based on class, gender and race is absent from every country and from the relationships among countries ... where poverty and all forms of violence are eliminated... and where the massive resources now used in the means of destruction will be diverted to areas where they will help to relieve oppression both inside and outside the home (Sen & Grown 1987:80).

DAWN's critique of the dominant 'development' model (globally promoted by multilateral lending agencies like the World Bank and the IMF) has been the basis for its continuing contributions to global meetings such as the 1992 Earth Summit in Rio and the 1994 United Nations International Conference on Population and Development in Cairo. Its research analysis and advocacy work remain committed to influencing development thinking and practice globally, regionally and nationally.

In December 1992, DAWN sponsored a Pacific regional meeting on women, environment and development in Suva, Fiji. The meeting brought together for the first time in many years women from different countries of the region. Women researchers, academics and activists from Fiji, Kiribati, Palau, Tonga, Papua New Guinea (PNG), Solomon islands, Vanuatu, Cook Islands and New Caledonia came together to share their perspectives and concerns about Pacific development issues and problems. Amongst the papers in this volume are two critiques of key regional development documents which embody much of the current development wisdom in the Pacific. They were specifically prepared for the DAWN meeting.

The papers in this collection provide evidence of some of the least desirable (although perhaps unanticipated) by-products of growth-based development and suggest that the dislocation being experienced by Pacific peoples raises doubts about the suitability of the 'chosen' development model. Growth does not appear to be resulting in enhanced livelihoods for the majority of people, particularly the poor. Quite the reverse, there are signs of serious development 'perversions': greater social inequalities, declining living standards, environmental degradation and community fragmentation and violence. Despite the 'gender-sensitivity' and professed commitment to gender equality reflected in official statements, the formation of women's ministries or departments, the allocation of public funds, the higher levels of women's employment, and, in some cases, the sponsorship of women as election candidates, women remain marginalised from development decision making - virtual bystanders of policies that continue to be overwhelmingly influenced by patriarchal structures and values. Now, more than ever, this anomaly needs to be corrected, for in their joint capacity as productive and reproductive workers, women are carrying much of the burden of the 'new' economic order as well as paying the price for its social and environmental 'fall-out'. In a number of ways, traditional gender relations are being ably instrumentalised into the march for growth. This is no more apparent than in the new labour-intensive export manufacturing industries which have successfully mobilised women's cheap labour as a means of securing a place in a highly competitive world market.

Other anomalies can be found in the concept of sustainable development (which embraces sensitivity to the environment) and the professed concern to 'humanise' development. The concepts of sustainable and human development take on board the reassuring (politically correct) language of the international community but do not appear to have inspired fundamentally new development approaches. They continue to be guided by the sacrosanct principles of the market and economic growth. For this reason, human development remains conceptually problematic in spite of the attention to factors like life expectancy, literacy and income levels. So too, it is possible to see that official (even World Bank) recognition of the wealth of traditional resource management practices and knowledge in the region (including the contribution of women) is leading to some accommodation of them within our own home-grown definitions of sustainable development. Yet, there is little, to date, to suggest that the perceived 'worth' of, say, the traditional subsistence economies, goes beyond an instrumental value for the market/growth paradigm, including their useful functions as buffers or 'safety nets' when the supposedly infallible market fails.

The cushioning role that traditional socio-economic systems of the Pacific are being asked to play has been played many times in the past - a successful rationale of early colonial capitalism that enabled the market economy to be conveniently subsidised by the pre-existing, so-called 'affluent' subsistence economy. But the current incarnation of a monolithic market system has the potential to threaten even more severely the resilience and life-sustaining capacity of the Pacific's subsistence economies. Ironically, they are being required to act as 'safety nets' for the mistakes and misdemeanours of the market economy. Falling world prices for traditional agricultural exports are putting the squeeze on many agricultural sectors and productive land (like labour) resources are being increasingly lost to export cash crops. The prioritisation of export agriculture is typical of regional agricultural policies today, reflecting the fact that 'household food [has become] of secondary importance to commercial food production' (Kofe 1993). This inevitably affects access to food land and in turn food production levels and health (including nutritional) and living standards. It is also raising the

iv

work burdens of women who are the main subsistence food producers in many countries around the region. According to the South Pacific Commission, food imports as a proportion of total imports and gross domestic product (GDP) are increasing across the region, with some countries habitually using up over 20 percent of their GDP to finance imported food.

The situation in the remaining colonial territories appears to be worse with French Polynesia, for example, importing around 85 per cent, and American Samoa some 80 per cent, of food requirements. For French Polynesia, the large claims on public revenue made by France's military and nuclear test programme during the past three decades (ranging from 57% of the territorial budget in 1988 to 90% in 1984 according to Blanchet 1991:36-38) underlie the territory's development distortions and explain the paltry proportion (0.9%) of the civil budget (which itself claimed only 31% of the territorial budget in 1986) allocated to agriculture (Henningham 1989:52). The deteriorating food security situation in most Pacific Island states is now recognised as a development issue that needs urgent attention (Kofe 1993).

Recent developments in the agricultural sector foreshadow greater threats to traditional subsistence economies in the future. For example, the view that customary land tenure is obstructive to both 'development' and 'more rational, sustainable land use' is leading to creative ways of harnessing traditional tenure systems and practices to the market-directed development process. Somewhat disingenuously, this development is accompanied by rhetoric about 'the relatively wise management of scarce land and sea resources' of traditional Pacific societies and an implied concern over the fact that 'traditional mechanisms for resource management are being undermined by the modern legal system and are in decline' (World Bank 1993:73). In a number of ways, the outward-oriented 'development' advocated by the World Bank works to the disadvantage of Pacific Island countries: it undermines traditional subsistence production; competes with domestically-oriented commercial agriculture; siphons off public funds; and promotes greater economic dependence because of its high foreign capital and import (technology/food etc.) requirements.

There are other disturbing outcomes of economic restructuring and the obsession with finding a competitive niche in the international market place which also expose the contradictions inherent in notions of sustainable and human development that remain primarily guided by market and economic growth principles. Amongst these are the relinquishment by Pacific Island states of their long-held responsibilities for providing basic educational, health and welfare services; the weakening of both modern democratic and traditional cultural institutions by the imposition of market or adjustment policies without community consent, and often in spite of popular resistance (for example in the cases of tax reforms in Fiji and Western Samoa, resource exploitation in Papua New Guinea and the Solomon Islands, and labour market deregulation in Fiji); the emergence of a 'new' culture of conflict and violence that embraces state-sponsored militarism, coercive labour practices, and community conflict over resource-revenue benefits; and the openings for greater foreign domination of Pacific Island economies created by privatisation and deregulation policies[1]. The cooption of liberal language and imagery ('free' trade, 'free' market etc.) has helped to mask the less-than-liberating features of market-driven development which magnanimously offers a fairly 'free' rein (or 'free' ride) to the powerful corporate and institutional barons of the 'free' world. The net outcome of more outward- (or wayward-?) oriented 'development' is that we are being pressured by the forces of the new colonialism into greater dependence on an unequal and capricious global market economy.

A critical component of economic adjustment policies, the limited and declining resources allocated to social services, particularly health, are also symptomatic of the 'malignancy' of current development trends. As a proportion of gross national product (GNP), health expenditure claims only 3.7 per cent in the Solomon Islands, 1.7 per cent in Fiji, 2.4 per cent in Vanuatu, 3.8 per cent in Tonga, 5.9 per cent in Kiribati, and 10 per cent in the Marshall Islands. Papua New Guinea, probably the richest Pacific Island state in terms of natural resources - and which has a staggering 40 per cent of its children under the age of five suffering from malnutrition (*Daily Post* 15 September 1992)[2]- allocates a mere 1.3 per cent of its GNP to health. (UNDP 1994:78) Attributed to 'the pressures associated with low economic growth', declining health budgets (as a % of total expenditure) are a related cause for concern in parts of the region such as Papua New Guinea, the Solomon Islands, Vanuatu and Kiribati (UNDP 1994:39-40). In the Solomon Islands, health expenditure has fallen by more than 100 per cent in just five years, from over 12 per cent of the national budget in 1986 to barely six per cent in 1991 (Siloko 1991). In Fiji and PNG, surges in military expenditure (in Fiji's case rising from $FIJ 16.3 million to $31 million between 1986 and 1991 in the wake of the 1987 military coups and in PNG on account of military offensives against Bougainville) have been an additional factor in diverting scarce resources away from health. Disturbingly, government health cuts are taking place at a time when preventable communicable diseases 'continue to affect a major proportion of the population' (UNDP 1994:21) and other, non-communicable, development-related and more expensive diseases (euphemistically termed 'lifestyle diseases') like diabetes, cardiovascular disease and cancer, as well as child malnutrition, are on the increase. Pacific countries have some of the highest rates of diabetes and Vitamin A deficiency amongst children in the world[3]. The pressures on regional World Bank-member countries to apply a user-pays principle - based on the rationale of cost recovery - may well mean that health care will increasingly become the privilege of the wealthier members of society while health standards for the poor will deteriorate.

Deforestation and soil erosion will also probably intensify in response to the dual pressures of export agriculture and, to a lesser extent, subsistence farming on marginal land. Although data on deforestation is limited, the damage caused by large-scale logging is already assuming crisis proportions. The World Bank acknowledges that 'there are indications of serious deforestation in many locations' of the region like PNG, the Solomon Islands, Vanuatu, Western Samoa and Fiji (World Bank 1993:73-74). In PNG, foreign loggers are ripping through the forests at devastating speed, causing incalculable destruction to the land, rivers, and food sources of customary landowners. In Western Samoa, as much as one-third of the forest area on the island of Savai'i has been lost to logging, agriculture and other forms of 'development'. Between 1986 and 1991, the deforestation rate for the country as a whole averaged 3.5 per cent a year (as much as 6% if only commercial forest is taken into account). In the Solomon Islands, logging operations in 1993 stripped the country of four per cent of its commercially exploitable forest. These (official) rates are especially worrying when compared to the much lower (0.9%) global rate of tropical deforestation estimated by the World Bank (ibid). At the community level, the loss of productive land resources encourages greater dependence on bought food items, lower health and nutritional standards and higher levels of rural out-migration and poverty.

Small or subaltern?

The physical hazards of the Pacific landscape, to some extent shared by other island regions around the world like the Caribbean, are conventionally featured as a handicap. More significantly, they commonly serve as an explanation for our economic dependence and are a perceived obstacle to 'development'. Our island environments are said to be especially vulnerable because of their smallness and limited resources. Many are inflicted with perennial destruction from natural disasters like hurricanes. The fragility of our ecosystems and the isolation created by vast expanses of ocean create quite special problems of communication, transportation and trade within the global economy[4]. The Pacific Islands are unquestionably small by global territorial standards; they are isolated; and many have limited land and other natural resources (including water). A notable exception is PNG, the largest Pacific economy whose land area totals nearly 0.5 million sq km and population is 3.6 million, and which is endowed with abundant natural resources. PNG has one of the four largest rainforests in the world and one of its most spectacular fisheries.

Although the issue of smallness, as an ideological concept, has been critically debated in the region and found by some Pacific scholars to be problematic or misplaced[5], our objective condition of smallness (and this extends to our isolation, ecological frailty etc.) would appear to be highly significant within the Pacific's political economy. The smallness of Pacific Island states has contributed to their subordinate position within the global economic system, underlying their position of relative powerlessness that persists today, and in turn influencing the welfare of their populations. Our smallness has been a liability exploited by predators. One alarming consequence has been our selection and continuing status as a 'nuclear [and military] playground'[6] in spite of strong and longstanding popular resistance. Indeed, the systematic militarisation and nuclearisation of the region have meant that 'the "peaceful" Pacific Ocean is arguably one of the most highly militarized environments, and, in per capita terms, some of its individual islands are among the most highly militarized areas on earth' (Thaman 1986:1). Another example of our vulnerability as small island states relates to the huge expanses of sea which, in contrast to the much larger land masses around the world, deprive us of what Morrison calls the '"fall-back" option': being able to rely on other ecosystems 'to fill the gap' if one ecosystem is damaged (Morrison 1988:1-8). For the hundreds of Pacific atolls (tiny, low altitude coral formations) whose people are dependent on the sea for food, poor resource management has the potential to do serious, even irreversible damage to the physical environment and life-sustaining capacity of islands. To this extent then, smallness is significant precisely because the consequences of environmental mismanagement or abuse are amplified.

If sustainable development is to translate into sustainable livelihoods for Pacific people, we need to be aware of the underlying politics of the global development-environment debate, for these continue to shape our conceptualisation of 'development' and 'environment'. Just as development has been critically influenced by a belief in the virtues of economic growth, the environment has been typically seen as a narrow physical entity, thus precluding more than a passing concern for the broader human impact of development policies. It is the recent 'humanising' of development (rather than the environment) that has fortuitously brought people back into the picture, although as noted earlier, this has not displaced economic growth as the preeminent development 'ethic'. Ironically, as this adjustment of the development equation has taken place, debate at the global level has taken another political turn to address issues of 'population' - above all to make the link between the problems of overpopulation in the economic South or 'developing' world (of which the Pacific is a part) with environmental degradation. This has strengthened the pressure for **more** economic growth and **less** population growth (with a continued focus on controlling women's fertility). Despite the complexities of population issues in the Pacific region[7] and the considerable variations in growth rates, the theory has met with hospitable responses at both government and inter-government levels. At times, articulation of the new 'wisdom' at regional meetings has displayed the conviction of the born-again fundamentalist. Yet however well crafted, development theories which focus on the damaging effects of high population growth and density on the environment simply do not provide all the answers to the most pressing questions that face us.

There would seem to be a real need for our working definitions of the environment and development to be guided more intimately by social and cultural considerations - above all by a desire for social equity - and by the human/social implications of what occurs in the twin domains of the economy and physical environment. At its most fundamental level, the search for sustainable development and a healthy environment confronts 'the relationship of humanity [or human economy] with nature [or ecology]' (Pietila 1990:64) Artificial distinctions between the physical and social spheres of the environment fail to take account of this. Equally deficient is conceptualising development without some notion of social justice, or defining population as a homogenous concept undifferentiated by mediating factors like social class, gender or ethnicity, since it is workers and particularly the poor, a disproportionate number of whom are women, who have been the chief victims of environmental degradation, entrenched models of economic development, and overconsumption by the rich. While the notion of sustainability has nudged development along in the direction of a more people-conscious concept, the dominant growth ideology continues to measure development by quantitative variables like GDP or export earnings. Cultural definitions of sustainability may vary, but development must surely imply minimum standards in the quality of people's lives and a fairer distribution of resources, if it is to deliver socially relevant outcomes and socially just solutions.

*Fundamentally a focus on human development as **the** goal of economic and social processes reaffirms the centrality of people realizing their potential to be creative, useful and fulfilled members of society; the acquisition of material wealth is a means to that end, not an end in itself. It harks back to earlier (pre-capitalist) values of self-realization through creativity, reciprocity, and a rich spiritual life. A society that gives such values short shrift by raising material acquisition from the status of means to the position of dominant end impoverishes itself in many ways, and lets loose forces of social disintegration and violence. Social disintegration and social pathologies are not so much results of extreme poverty (except in so far as poverty and marginalisation go hand in hand with the breakup of communities and value systems) but of a search for material acquisition as an end in itself bereft of human values.*

Gita Sen 1994

The papers that follow examine some of the specific features and negative outcomes of the current development model as well as the political and other forces influencing the development process and the lives of today's Pacific Islanders. They have a constructive and instructive intent. At a crossroads in our development experience, we have not yet reached the point of no return. We thus need to seize the opportunity to ask some legitimate and important questions about whose interests are really being served by the market-growth system. Economic restructuring has been presented to us as a panacea. But can the market really deliver social development, environmental protection, sustainable and healthy livelihoods for the poor, and equality for women? Can the arguments of 'efficiency' (which underpin the push for private sector development and economic deregulation) translate into 'human' development? Should we continue to press the growth accelerator if this is at the expense of equity, food security and basic needs? Is the Pacific 'state' really such a liability to development, as the World Bank would have us believe, or does it offer us a more reliable avenue to development than the market (assuming reform of its undemocratic and patriarchal features)? If the Pacific is such a 'paradox', does the fault really lie with the region's once sustainable subsistence economies?

There is no shortage of questions and the search for answers will doubtless continue. An encouraging sign is that critical thinking is not only being expressed in plaintive cries from the political wilderness. The comments of Vanuatu's Prime Minister, Maxime Carlot Korman, in his opening address to the Pacific Regional Ministerial Conference on Population and Sustainable Development in September 1993, point to a healthy cynicism emerging in official circles:

> What kind of economic policy should our small island nations opt for to ensure over the next decade or two an annual growth of at least 7%, which in real terms means only 4% given the population growth rate? ... Some Asian countries are managing to maintain this level at present, but what can we tell our people to whom economic growth still stands for breakdown of traditional social relationships, urban problems, pollution, destruction of the environment, foreign investment? (Carlot Korman 1993)

As Pacific Islanders, we need to come up with our own vision of development: to ask ourselves whether our development direction should continue to be determined by foreign institutions and ideologies which promote economic ethics (like wealth accumulation, profit, and resource plunder) that have little relevance to - in some respects directly contradict - our own heritage of development knowledge and practices. Traditional ideologies about the environment in the Pacific, primarily people's relationship to the land and their land management systems, may in fact offer an answer to our search for more sustainable models of development. In spite of the scarcity of our resources and the cultural constraints on equitable distribution inherent in some of our more stratified chiefly societies, successive generations of Pacific islanders traditionally enjoyed relatively high levels of economic self-reliance in harmony with their environment. At the time of European contact, sustainable or rational land management, including food preservation, was practised, along with systems of food production and consumption based on principles of communalism and reciprocal exchange. In other words, 'sustainable development' flourished prior to colonial conquest, military occupation, the imposition of a cash economy, and the fostering of Western 'development' - i.e. long before the concept was 'invented' by the North and then sold back to the South. But the rules of the current 'development' game and its overarching economic system would in many ways appear to be stacked against us. As an editorial of the *New Internationalist* has evocatively observed:

> Someone has to be the loser of the modern economic game, for it is a game whose rules demand losers as well as winners. It is inherently predatory, and predators can't survive without

victims. In fact, like a hungry alligator, it needs a lot of victims to keep it fed. The environment is among its prey, as are the poor - and the smallest and most vulnerable fish are the children of the poor (*New Internationalist* 1992:23).

It is perhaps timely, then, that we look back into the past for clues as to how to build a self-reliant, sustainable future: a time to wake up some of the friendly ghosts of yesteryears. Whatever the cynical views of the World Bank about 'inward-looking' development, there would seem to be some merit in reconsidering this option. One of the potential outcomes could be greater participation by, and empowerment of, local communities, including women, within development planning. This would inject fresh perspectives, and arguably more relevant priorities, into the development process. It could produce more accountable and socially just development that captures the unique strengths and values of our traditional cultures and reorientates production towards meeting people's needs. Whatever their shortcomings, the Pacific's traditional production and social systems took as their driving force the economic and social well-being of people. The clash with today's market-driven 'development' would seem to be obvious.

At the same time, the factors and processes which have historically mediated population/environment/development issues within the Pacific region emphasise the importance of broadening the development debate beyond the narrow, and in many respects misleading, preoccupation with population growth. They highlight the implications of continuing colonial and neo-colonial domination and the need to recognise as fundamental the structures of power and control that critically shape the destinies (including the environmental welfare) of the region's small island states. Once the focus of the debate shifts to tackling some of the more sensitive political 'realities' of regional development, the way will surely be cleared for building a new development edifice. The essays that follow represent an attempt to do just this. We hope they will be thought-provoking.

'Atu Emberson-Bain
Suva, Fiji, October 1994

Notes

1. For example, about 97 per cent of logging operations in Papua New Guinea are conducted by foreign companies.

2. It is pertinent to note here that according to the World Bank 'absolute poverty is virtually nonexistent' amongst its Pacific member countries'. The Bank acknowledges only that wide disparities exist in income distribution and that 'relative poverty is still a concern, particularly in Kiribati, Solomon Islands and Vanuatu (World Bank 1991:4).

3. Another sober reminder of the health problems we continue to face is the alarming incidence of infant deaths in countries like Vanuatu, the Solomon Islands, Papua

New Guinea and Kiribati (43-63 per thousand live births in 1992). According to a 1992 estimate of the United Nations Children's Fund (UNICEF), as many as 9,000 babies under the age of one year are dying each year from mostly preventible deaths including diet-related illnesses and malnutrition that are linked to the fact that 'traditional food production systems are being substantially altered in the process of development, urbanisation and cash cropping'.

4. The Marshall Islands, for example, has its total land mass of just 70 sq miles carved up amongst 35 low-lying atolls and islands that are spread over close to 400,000 sq miles of ocean.

5. See Hau'ofa et al. (1993) for a wide ranging collection of responses to Epeli Hau'ofa's critique of the 'smallness' complex.

6. 'Nuclear playground' is a description used by Stuart Firth as the title of his book (1987) on nuclear colonialism in the Pacific.

7. For example, there would seem to be evidence that militarism is a contributing factor to escalating patterns of population growth in parts of the region. In Guam, the heavy expansion in military activity and installations (which include numerous naval bases and an airforce base) has been a major contributor to its rapid growth rate during the 1980s. Since the mid-1980s, Guam's 21,000 odd military personnel and their dependants have represented around 19 per cent of its population (Flores and O'Mallen 1991:38).

References

Carlot Korman, M. (1993) 'Opening address by the Prime Minister of the Republic of Vanuatu to the Pacific Regional Ministerial Conference on Population and Sustainable Development', 9-10 September, Port Vila, Vanuatu

Daily Post 15 September 1992

Firth, S. (1987) *Nuclear playground,* Sydney: Allen and Unwin

Flores, J. and O'Mallen, J. (1991) 'Trends and issues in the prevention of sexually transmitted diseases and AIDS' in Rubinstein, D.H. and Dames, V.L. (eds) *Uncle Sam and Micronesia: Social benefits, social costs,* Guam: Micronesian Area Research Centre, University of Guam

Hau'ofa, E. et al. (1993) *A new Oceania: Rediscovering our sea of islands,* University of the South Pacific 25th Anniversary publication, Suva: School of Social and Economic Development, USP in association with Beake House

Henningham, S. (1989) 'France and the South Pacific: Problems and prospects', working paper no. 62, Canberra: Peace Research Centre, Australian National University

Kofe, S. (1993) 'Human resource development: Development issues in the Pacific Island countries', paper presented to a Meeting of Senior Officials on Population and Sustainable Development in the Pacific, Port Vila, 6-8 September

Morrison, R.J. (1988) 'The fragility of some South Pacific ecosystems', *Ples* 4

New Internationalist (1992) 'Population: The pathological game', September

Pietila, H. (1990) 'Reflections on the Brundtland Report: Our common future' in *Ifda dossier,* May/June, pp. 61-70

Sen, G. (1994) 'Outline for the Social Summit', paper prepared for DAWN on the occasion of the Second Preparatory Conference for the Social Development Summit, New York

Sen, G, and Grown, C. (1987) *Development, crises, and alternative visions: Third world women's perspectives,* New York: Monthly Review Press

Siloko, S. (ed.) (1991) *Children first,* Honiara: The Solomon Islands National Advisory Committee on Children

Thaman, R. R. (1986) 'Militarism, nuclear pollution and the Pacific environment', paper presented to the Fiji Anti-Nuclear Group Solidarity Conference for a Nuclear-Free and Independent Pacific, 5-8 August, Suva, Fiji

UNDP (1994) *Pacific human development report: Putting people first,* provisional edition, United Nations Development Programme (UNDP), April

World Bank (1993) *Pacific Island economies: Toward efficient and sustainable growth,* vol.1, Overview

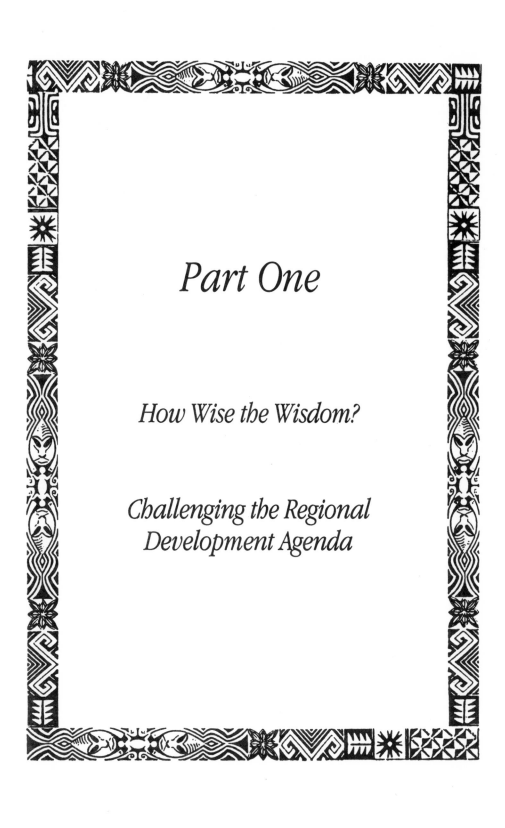

Part One

How Wise the Wisdom?

*Challenging the Regional
Development Agenda*

One

Blame it all on population:
Perceptions, statistics and reality
in the population debate in the Pacific*

Yvonne Underhill-Sem

Introduction

The interrelationship between population, environment and development is popularly based on the assumption that population growth is the leading cause of environmental stress and the major impediment to economic development. This simplistic and uni-dimensional view ignores the complexities of each component in this three-way interrelationship, and the subsequent complexities of their interactions. A more complete understanding also requires consideration of social, cultural and political factors. People have always modified their physical environment to provide for themselves and their families (Clark 1990). When these activities begin to threaten the ability of future generations to do the same, people's health and the well-being of their environment and livelihood systems also suffer. Because the causal factors in this closely connected system vary from place to place, and over time, effective remedies require a combination of in-depth knowledge of the particular determinants involved, as well as a clear understanding of the process of change in different situations.

This complex population, environment and development nexus has been addressed by scholars, politicians, religious leaders and human rights activists over many years. The earliest antecedents can be found among social and political philosophers, beginning with Confucius, whose arguments focus on the relationship between population size, the ideal political system and the best economic process. Despite many learned discussions concluding that population growth cannot be wholly blamed for all the environmental and economic problems in the world, there are still many who, in the absence of substantiating evidence, continue to believe that population growth is the main problem.

With the recent proliferation in the Pacific of population programmes and policies[1], matched by increasing aid funds, these interrelationships need to be spelt out clearly, carefully and repeatedly, so that we in the Pacific can avoid the problems experienced in other 'developing' regions of the world, problems which can to a significant extent be traced back to a poor understanding of the precise relationship between population growth, economic development and environmental change.

This paper begins by offering an overview of the population situation in the Pacific region. It will then briefly outline two of the common arguments in which population is blamed: the 'population growth is outstripping resources' argument[2] and the 'population growth is the cause of economic decline' debate[3]. The problem with both these arguments is that while they possess some elements of logic and truth, empirical evidence to support them is lacking. Despite this, population policies and programmes are developed as if the causal relationships between population change, economic development and environmental degradation are all clearly identified[4].

Before I am accused of being blind to the potential consequences of rapid population growth in the Pacific, I should state that I am well aware of the need to control environmental degradation, to raise standards of living to more equitable levels, and to ensure that women have access to quality care. My intention in writing this paper, however, is to provoke more critical questioning of the projects and policies which have been designed (explicitly or implicitly) to influence population trends in the Pacific.

The population situation in the Pacific

Comprising 0.1 per cent of the world's population, the Pacific region is notable for its smallness in terms of both land area and population size, and its location in the largest ocean. Because of these features, the region is best treated as a distinct entity, although it does share some of the population dynamics typical of other regions of small and vulnerable states. Although we do not experience the critical population problems of our larger neighbours, there is still a need for policies aimed at maintaining healthy, educated and productive populations.

It is important at the outset, however, to make a few clarifying points regarding the so-called 'facts' of the region's populations. First, there are many and varied difficulties facing anyone attempting to record, collect and analyse demographic data in the Pacific. It takes experienced population specialists to generate reliable facts about the population of each country - facts which take into account incomplete but important historical information, as well as the complexities of information collected in a rapidly changing economic, social and cultural environment. Reliable information on population characteristics within individual countries is a prerequisite for any regional population overview, but the poor quality of information about the populations of some countries severely compromises the reliability of any regional population review.

A second major point concerns the difficulties of generalising about the population trends of 22 countries in the Pacific. It is tempting for the sake of simplicity to look at groups of countries or sub-regions within the Pacific. However, there is little demographic evidence to justify such groupings, and new approaches in Pacific demography include analysis across national boundaries which supports other arguments disputing this questionable system of categorisation (Thomas 1989). In particular, the practice of dividing the region into the sub-regions of Melanesia, Polynesia and Micronesia, which originated with anthropologists and was perpetuated by colonial administrations, is misleading because it assumes that cultural factors are the central force in these processes. It ignores the fact that environmental, economic, social and political forces also have important influences on demographic processes. Given the tremendous variation in social, economic, political, religious and cultural features within countries of the region, national or regional 'facts' may not actually be found on the ground.

These two points are important to bear in mind throughout this paper. Data is drawn from the statistical bulletins of the South Pacific Commission. While each country in the region must be sure of the characteristics of its own population, crude indicators of regional demographic characteristics are useful for comparative purposes. Infant mortality rates (IMR) are low in Polynesia and Micronesia, but notably high in the Western Pacific, although still not as high as West Africa and South Asia (United Nations 1988). As a result, life expectancy is comparable to levels in so-called 'more developed countries', except again for countries in the Western Pacific (ibid). The total fertility rate (TFR) is slightly higher than the rate in 'less developed countries' as a whole, but much lower than West Africa and South Asia (ibid). In general, the Pacific region does not have the glaring population problems faced by other regions in the world. However, there are localised problems which require immediate attention, such as infant mortality rates in the Western Pacific.

Size and growth of Pacific populations

The total population of the Pacific was estimated to be about 6.7 million in mid-1994. Over 60 per cent of this population is found in the large resource-rich country of Papua New Guinea, while a further 20 per cent is found on the two main high islands and numerous small islands of Fiji. Other large land masses of the Western Pacific comprise countries with populations in excess of 100,000, while in the northern, central and eastern parts of the Pacific, countries are smaller and more widely dispersed over volcanic islands and smaller atolls. This distribution is important to note in discussing regional population trends because the population of Papua New Guinea is so large in comparison to other countries that demographic trends in that country dominate the regional picture, concealing trends elsewhere as well as those within its own national boundaries. This is another reason to treat population analysis at the regional level with caution.

Closely related to the size of the population is the rate at which it is growing. Although there have been recent claims that the population growth rate is almost three per cent, this is hard to substantiate (Hayes forthcoming). For one thing, it is difficult to estimate a regional average annual growth rate because of the variable quality of data and problems of cross-country comparisons. Population estimates and projections are based on different assumptions of not only the direction in which fertility and migration rates will move, but also the level to which they will move. As members of small communities, we recognise the complex range of factors that influence people's decisions relating to fertility and migration. On another level, generalisations about population growth rates can hinder more instructive analysis and understanding of the region's population

3

problems. There has been a tendency to sensationalise the issue of growth (in isolation from other factors) in order to seize the attention of the general public, and perhaps divert attention from other more sensitive issues such as income inequalities, poverty and the mismanagement of public revenues.

Average annual population growth rates vary across the region, from an estimated 6.1 per cent in the Commonwealth of the Northern Mariana Islands, down from 8.8 per cent in the 1973-1990 period, to an estimated minus 5.3 per cent in Niue. Both these cases highlight the significance of international migration to population growth. Between these two extremes lie the other countries of the region (Table 1). Only the Marshall Islands and the Federated States of Micronesia (FSM) have estimated growth rates of over 4.0 per cent; and only the Solomon Islands and American Samoa over 3.0 per cent. Most countries in the region have estimated growth rates under 3.0 per cent, so an estimated regional average of 2.1 per cent seems more plausible (South Pacific Commission 1993).

Most populations in the Pacific will continue to grow, as they have in the past, although probably not as fast as in the last 50 years. Despite rapid population growth in the past, many Pacific countries have still attained high levels of literacy, increased levels of per capita income and higher life expectancies. Whether their populations will continue to be healthy, well-educated and productive will depend as much on the ability of governments to invest in health and education services and employment creation, as on the pace at which they will grow in the future.

Table 1   Population, growth rates, and natural increase

Country	Most recent census year	Population	Annual growth rate %(1)	Rate of natural increase %
American Samoa	1990	46 673	3.8	34
Cook Islands*	1991	18 552	1.1	19
Fed States Micronesia*	1990	100 520	4.0	27
Fiji	1986	715 375	1.9	21
French Polynesia	1988	188 814	2.5	24
Guam	1990	133 152	2.2	22
Kiribati*	1990	72 335	2.1	20
Marshall Islands	1988	43 380	4.2	40
Nauru*	1992	9 729	2.3	15
New Caledonia	1989	164 173	2.0	18
Niue	1989	2 267	-5.3	14
Northern Mariana Is.	1990	43 345	6.1	32
Palau	1990	15 122	1.8	18
Papua New Guinea*(2)	1990	3 560 308	1.5	23
Pitcairn	1991	66	0.0	0
Solomon Islands	1986	285 176	3.7	34
Tokelau*	1991	1 577	-1.3	15
Tonga	1986	94 649	0.5	23
Tuvalu	1991	9 043	2.3	20
Vanuatu	1989	142 944	2.4	29
Wallis and Futuna	1990	13 705	1.2	25
Western Samoa	1991	159 862	0.3	26

Notes:
*   Provisional figures
(1)   Average annual growth rate (%) 1974-91
(2)   Excludes North Solomons Province

Source: South Pacific Commission (1993)
South Pacific Economies Statistical Summary: SPESS, no.13

The age-sex structure of Pacific populations

Pacific populations are mostly youthful with considerable potential for future growth even if fertility rates dropped to replacement level. This built-in population momentum is evident in any youthful population, and is particularly evident in the large countries of Papua New Guinea and the Solomon Islands, as well as French Polynesia, Western Samoa and Vanuatu. High fertility rates are primarily responsible for this feature, but are to some extent offset by the out-migration of those aged 20-39 years, as in French Polynesia and Western Samoa. Countries like the Solomon Islands which do not have the same opportunities for migration bear the full consequences of high fertility. Kiribati, New Caledonia, Fiji and Guam are relatively less youthful, indicating lower fertility, while there is evidence of declining fertility in Tonga's population structure.

By analysing the age-sex structure of a population, it is possible to project when there will be a greater demand for particular services. The increasing numbers of young people evident in our populations in the mid-1980s are now needing primary education, and they will contribute to the growing pressure on employment and housing over the next seven to 10 years. These predictions can be fairly accurate, especially where international migration is not an option, and they can, for example, form the basis of detailed plans for providing employment opportunities for the emerging labour force.

Population distribution

Population distribution within countries in the Pacific varies tremendously. While Nauru is recorded as being totally urban, the more populous countries of Papua New Guinea, the Solomon Islands and Vanuatu have less than 20 per cent of their population living in urban areas. Rapid rates of urbanisation have been recorded only in the recent past in these countries due to the relatively recent emergence of centralised political and economic systems. However, these rates appear to be slowing down. In other countries, the proportion of the population living in urban areas appears to be falling, although discrepancies in the definition of 'urban' could be a cause of such a trend. It is clear though that the larger countries have lower urbanisation rates but greater potential for rural to urban migration.

Low-density areas generate problems because of the logistical difficulties of providing services to scattered populations, separated by miles of sea, rugged country, or both. Transportation is difficult to provide on a cost-effective basis, and markets are small, making commercial ventures unprofitable. At the other end of the density spectrum, many of the urban areas of the major islands suffer from problems of high density although, aside from the Marshall Islands, this is still well below that of other 'developing' countries. Considerable stress is put on the environment resulting in problems such as shortages of potable water and pollution, due to inefficient or non-existent systems of solid and liquid waste disposal. Basic services like health care, housing, education and transportation are also stretched. But urban densities do not create these problems on their own. Sluggish investment in the physical and economic infrastructure, compounded by difficulties in alienating customary land, are major problems in most countries.

Mortality trends

Mortality in the Pacific has undergone a rapid decline in a relatively short time (Taylor et al. 1989). Life expectancy has increased in all countries, although there is still an 18-year difference between the country with the lowest life expectancy (Papua New Guinea at 55 years) and the highest (Guam at 73 years). Infant mortality rates have also declined for all countries over the last 30 years, although Papua New Guinea and Kiribati still record rates of over 60 per thousand. Maternal mortality continues to be a problem in parts of the Western Pacific, where isolated populations are poorly served with primary health care.

Mortality is undoubtedly the easiest of the demographic variables to change because of the widely shared belief in improving the health status and life chances of communities. The demand for mortality reduction is relatively easy for governments to meet by supplying the services which will reduce premature mortality. Like other 'developing' countries, Pacific Island countries have benefited from the adoption of improved public health programmes, as well as imported medical technology, especially childhood immunisation.

Although there have been rapid declines in mortality, especially in the Eastern Pacific, there are important differences in mortality rates within countries. In particular, remote areas of Papua New Guinea and Kiribati have extremely high infant mortality rates. Most of the decline in mortality has occurred within the youngest age groups, with the result that more babies are surviving into childhood. Further rapid declines are difficult to foresee in many countries because of the need to use sophisticated medical technology to improve the survival chances of newly born infants suffering from congenital diseases that are not amenable to improvements in primary health care.

One of the main implications of this rapid decline in mortality is that rates of natural increase have risen. This is because there has not been a corresponding decline in fertility to offset the growing number of surviving babies. Accordingly, populations will continue to remain youthful even though the babies that survive now will live longer. We can therefore probably expect a greater number of older people in the next century. There are, however, also indications of an increase in premature mortality due to lifestyle diseases, such as cancer and heart disease, that are more commonly associated with industrialised or 'developed' countries. Careful targeting of health resources is necessary to ensure that the improvement and maintenance of primary health services and public health measures do not compete with the growing, mostly urban, demand for costly tertiary diagnostic and treatment services.

Fertility trends

Fertility rates in the Pacific are moderate, although some countries have high total fertility rates (TFR) which exceed 5.0, such as the Marshall Islands, the Solomon Islands, the Federated States of Micronesia, Vanuatu and Papua New Guinea. If such levels persist, they will result in further broadening of the base of population pyramids, adding to the existing growth momentum. However, there are indications that fertility is declining in FSM, Wallis and Futuna, Kiribati and elsewhere. Given the growing world-wide evidence of a fertility transition from high to low birth rates, as proposed by demographic transition theorists (Demeny 1992), it is likely that high-fertility populations in the Pacific will experience a

7

similar fertility decline. More research is needed, however, to gauge both the speed of this decline as well as the level to which fertility is likely to fall. Some countries in the Pacific are well advanced in their fertility transition (Fiji, Cook Islands, Tonga, Tuvalu), although levels have not fallen as low as expected.

There is a general correlation between high fertility and low life expectancy in the Pacific, so it is likely that the reduction of mortality (or the increase in life expectancy) will tend to reduce fertility rates. Once parents experience improved survival rates of their offspring, fewer births would be required to reach the desired family size. However, complex and divergent relationships between fertility and life expectancy are apparent in the region, highlighting the need for broader, more holistic perspectives on fertility (including measures to reduce it) as well for caution over generalising about the region as a whole. They emphasise the importance of more country-specific demographic research. For example, in contrast to the conventional high fertility/low life expectancy correlation, high fertility behaviour occurs in the Solomon Islands, Vanuatu and FSM, countries which already demonstrate high life expectancy. Another exception of the opposite kind is the situation in Tuvalu, which has the lowest fertility (2.7) in the region but also a relatively low life expectancy (59 years).

Changing fertility behaviour is problematic because fertility will not fall until couples actually want to reduce their family size. The challenge is to both promote smaller families and provide the means of doing this. This requires a more holistic approach to fertility reduction, including multi-sectoral programmes involving education, income generation and social security in old age. There are still many communities in the Pacific where the economic value of children is high. This makes it difficult to reduce fertility rates merely by providing the means of controlling them.

Trends in migration

Migration in the Pacific is difficult to generalise about because all the determining factors of this process vary both between and within countries. Current political and economic relationships with previous metropolitan powers, the accessibility of other islands, and the attraction of distant capital cities establish the direction of movement. Levels of socio-economic development and the existence of established kinship networks affect the means of migration. Furthermore, while movements across international borders can be monitored, it is more difficult to study internal mobility. There has always been a tradition of mobility in the Pacific. Indeed, the settlement of the Pacific is itself testimony to the extensive mobility of our forebears. While there is clear evidence of the movement from rural to urban areas, there is also significant movement between rural areas or small islands.

Tangible monetary benefits can result from migration. This is especially the case when one of the region's neighbouring metropolitan countries is the destination, because of the flow of remittances to home communities. In the long term, however, the viability of this cash flow is uncertain as second-generation Pacific migrants, with arguably less of a commitment to support family they may never have visited or met, replace their parents as the main income earners. This will have economic implications for communities experiencing high levels of out-migration. Extended economic recessions in the metropolitan countries will also affect the levels of remittances sent back to Pacific countries. If, however, people are able to return to their islands and villages of origin when they retire, bringing with them their life savings and superannuation, there will be fiscal benefits for Pacific countries.

The lone traveller
(for Jioji)

you've come back
only to leave again
to count, measure
perceive and pace
the unending road
to our becoming

you will discover the sea
and its secrets
the forgotten ships
of our ancestors
who rode the darkness and remoteness
of nature
guided only by the line
that is the link to the land

you will see wind and water
flowing
towards the fierce fabric
of time
you will see battles and ruins
minds throbbing, moving
from one sea to another
you will see castles, monuments
that endured endless years
of exile
and you will cross lands
that are not yours

and when you return
you will find that the earth
has given birth
to many different tunes
and when you call them
nobody replies

Konai Helu-Thaman

There will also be a marked change in the age-sex structure of populations - with more resident older people and older widowed women - because women generally have higher life expectancies than men. This will have direct implications for some services like health and transportation, as elderly people have different health needs and are at the same time less mobile. It will also indirectly affect the amount of money in circulation if returning Pacific Islanders have portable superannuation packages; and it will impinge upon social relationships as more family elders adjust to life in the Pacific having spent much of their adult lives in a metropolitan country.

'Population growth is outstripping resources'

There is little doubt that rapid population growth affects natural resources and therefore must be a focus of concern. However, there are divergent views on precisely how this occurs. Clearly, in a situation where the number of people increases but their access to crucial resources like arable land (which will permit them to produce more food) does not, people will suffer. But rarely is it the case, as some biologists would have us believe, that it is solely because of rapid population growth that available resources become insufficient. Resources are culturally defined and they therefore vary over time and space. They are threatened by both naturally occurring physical processes like droughts, floods and hurricanes[5], and by human-devised institutions with inequitably allocated powers. The problems of resource depletion as a result of both these natural and political processes also need to be a focus of inquiry and concern.

Much of the debate on population and the environment stems from the Malthusian theory (Malthus [1798] 1970) that proposed that 'population, when unchecked, increases in a geometrical ratio' while the means of supporting this population increases 'only in an arithmetical ratio'. The consequences of this imbalance between population numbers and physical resources, Malthus argued, would be 'misery and vice' (op.cit.:71-71). The choice for humanity, therefore, was either to accept these 'positive' determinants of increased mortality, or to adopt preventative measures like decreasing fertility through postponed marriage or sexual abstinence. Steeped in his own moral sensitivities, not untypical of his time, Malthus was, however, against birth control, and saw instead the need for 'moral restraint' as the means of reducing the misery arising from the 'mismatch' of population numbers with resources.

Neo-Malthusians continue to subscribe to this original logic, but steeped in the moral sensitivities of today (notably that women in 'developing' countries must take ultimate responsibility for the effect of rapid population growth on resources), they argue the case for population control in developing countries. Such views are contentious for a number of reasons, not least for their failure to recognise that factors such as unequal resource distribution, extremes of wealth and overconsumption by the rich, modern technology and global economic policies are also an important part of the equation, indeed demonstrating stronger links with the process of environment degradation than population size per se.

Closely related to Malthusian theory is the concept of carrying capacity. According to this view, there is a critical level of population density beyond which people will suffer. However, close empirical evidence of this argument has shown that little purpose is served by identifying the critical density levels beyond which populations should not grow. According to Blaikie and Brookfield

10

(1987:29), 'if carrying capacity changes with each turn in the course of socio-economic evolution, each new technological input or new crop introduction, and can vary markedly according to the bounty or otherwise of rainfall in a given year, of what use is the concept?' In the Pacific context, the carrying capacity of a particular country or region is also related to the level of external assistance (for instance see Lockwood 1992 for the case of French Polynesia).

Alternative hypotheses concerning the relationship between population and physical resources have been posited. The argument of Boserup (1965) is one of the more striking: rather than population growth being a hindrance to economic growth, she claims, it can actually be the prerequisite for agricultural development. Boserup proposes that without growing population pressure, there would be no incentive to develop labour-intensive agricultural techniques or technologically sophisticated agricultural systems. Evidence from Papua New Guinea, however, suggests that the adoption of new crop varieties can lead to the intensification of agriculture independently of population pressure (for example bananas in Milne Bay and sweet potato in the Highlands) (Graham Sem 1994, Port Moresby, pers. comm.). Other studies argue that the cause of intensified resource use can be linked to the pressure to maintain or raise social status (Brookfield 1972).

In spite of the continuing debate over the precise role that population growth plays in the depletion of resources or intensification of resource use, there are still many instances of depleted resources and degraded environments in the Pacific in places where growth rates are declining or stable. The Cook Islands is just one example (Sem & Underhill 1992). The problem for the Pacific of not exploring this issue more fully and empirically is that population alone becomes the focus of analysis, to the exclusion of all other factors in resource use and degradation. In particular, more attention should be given to changing technologies, changing patterns of consumption, inefficient bureaucracies, the inequitable distribution of wealth, and unequal access to resources.

'Population growth is the cause of economic decline'

Despite the considerable public exposure given to the adverse consequences of a population explosion, scholarly research since the 1980s has repeatedly argued for a modified assessment of the consequences of population growth for economic development in 'developing' countries. The culmination of much of this research is summed up in the report of the National Academy of Sciences (Working Group on Population Growth and Economic Development 1986). Notably, this report recognises four critical issues. First, that population growth can have both negative and positive effects. Second, that there are both direct and indirect linkages between population and development. Third, that severe problems previously attributed to population growth were probably due to other causes. And fourth, that population sometimes exacerbates more fundamental problems, rather than causes them directly. Kelley (1988) provides a well-framed discussion on the economic-demographic evidence supporting this modified position, showing that 'neither formal growth theory nor simulation models have provided a basis for making conclusive statements about the net impact of population on development' (1988:1690). Little empirical evidence can be found to support the proposition that population growth affects economic development by changing the propensity for, and form of, savings and capital formation because this argument is based on the erroneous assumption that it is personal savings which fuel economic growth. Hayes (forthcoming) has shown the many problems with this macroeconomic attempt to assign a role for population growth in economic development. The following summarises his argument[6].

There are three main points which discredit the argument about the critical role of capital formation through personal savings. First, it has become more widely acknowledged that personal savings are not the main fuel of the economy. Instead, changes in techniques of production play a more important role in raising productivity. Second, additional children do not necessarily mean fewer savings, but in fact can lead to greater economies within families. Furthermore, for many village-dwellers in Papua New Guinea, for instance, children are not only regarded with affection, but represent the only available 'superannuation' in their old age (McDowell 1988). Additionally, spending on health and education is an investment in human resource development in a way that military or defence spending is. not. Third, where people have no money to save, such as in the majority of subsistence households in the Western Pacific, they cannot divert their earnings. Instead, the main source of savings in many Pacific economies comes from governments, state-owned enterprises and foreign aid.

However, Kelley's conclusions (1988) suggest the need for some caution within the Pacific region. Population growth, he says, is more likely to affect economic development in countries where natural resources are scarce; where economies of scale are difficult to achieve; and where markets and other institutions, like governments, do not allocate resources in an efficient way over time and space. Pacific Island countries with extensive Exclusive Economic Zones (EEZs) or substantial mineral or terrestrial resources cannot rightfully be said to be resource-poor, although many have yet to exploit these resources as effectively as they might. Economies of scale are difficult to achieve and are rightfully a concern. However, the allocation of resources by government institutions, customary land tenure systems, and traditional fishing rights require more analysis.

On the basis of research findings, there would appear to be no firm evidence to support the theory that slower population growth will improve economic development: 'Slowing population growth is not a substitute for solving other problems, [although] it can reduce some of the extreme manifestations of these problems while they are being solved.' (Working Group on Population Growth and Economic Development 1986:89). Rather than uncritically accepting the established 'wisdom', which is frequently propagated by journalistic scaremongering, more effort should go into identifying the actual determinants and conditions of economic growth, and particularly the role that human-devised institutions play in controlling and allocating resources. This does not, however, mean disregarding the issue of population growth. Greater investment in maternal and family health - a direct outcome of this debate - is one of the most fundamental and desirable investments a 'developing' country can make.

Even though rapid population growth does have an impact on resource use and economic change, it is clearly a complex multi-causal relationship. Greater consideration needs to be given to the multifarious nature of change in population dynamics, 'developing' economies and physical environments. The challenge for those concerned with population-related issues in the Pacific is to be clear about what they are doing and for what reasons. Preston (1987 in Hayes forthcoming) has identified four distinct fields in which the impact of population can be analysed: the macroeconomic, the microeconomic, the environmental and the medical. It is useful to pay heed to these distinctions to ensure that population programmes and policies do not promote conflicting messages. Debate over the effectiveness of various policies can then be more clearly focused.

For instance, policy measures which instruct family planning workers to tell their clients (most of whom are women) about the problem of rapid population growth and how they have a responsibility to limit the number of children they have for the benefit of the country or the world, confuse macroeconomic concerns with medical or health concerns. Having a clearer idea of the relationship between the three population variables - fertility, mortality and migration - and the structure of our populations in the Pacific, would be a crucial beginning.

Conclusion: Assumptions, statistics and reality

The only real truth is that although there is only one reality, there are many ways of experiencing it, and there is no final authority. This is the case for the environment/development/population nexus in the Pacific. While some people draw on unsubstantiated assumptions to explain this complex multi-dimensional issue, others use statistics, and many use both. This is not a problem on its own. However, there is already a considerable body of knowledge about population processes in the Pacific, and because time and new perspectives on reality change all things, we need to keep up with our changing world. We cannot assume that mortality, fertility and migration behaviour are the same throughout the region; or that they are similar to patterns discernible in other developing countries. If we want to provide a better world for our children, detailed innovative studies are needed to look at past and current demographic behaviour, using both quantitative and qualitative data, and drawing on the insights of all social sciences. It is also useful to heed Kelley's conclusion that 'values must enter prominently into the population debate' (1988:1720).

*   An earlier version of this paper was delivered to the Meeting of Senior Officials on Population and Sustainable Development in the Pacific, Port Vila, Vanuatu, 6-8 September 1993

Notes

1. These include the Pacific Island Development Programme on Population and Development, the South Pacific Commission's Population Programme, the Population and Environment Programme of the South Pacific Regional Environment Programme (SPREP), and the Papua New Guinea Population and Family Planning Project.

2. See Blaikie & Brookfield 1987 for a more detailed discussion.

3. See Kelley 1988 for a more detailed discussion.

4. I owe the articulation of this point to my colleague Geoff Hayes.

5. While these processes are regarded as natural, the anthropogenic contributions to global environmental change are evident from the atmospheric warming due to the proliferation of greenhouse gases.

6. Much of this section draws from his recent analysis, see Hayes (forthcoming).

References

Blaikie, P. and Brookfield H. (1987) *Land degradation and society,* London: Routledge

Boserup, E. (1965) *The conditions of agricultural growth: The economics of agrarian change under population pressure,* London: Allen & Unwin

Brookfield, H.C. (1972) 'Intensification and disintensification in Pacific agriculture: A theoretical approach' in *Pacific Viewpoint,* 13:18-29

14

Clark, W.C. (1990) 'Learning from the past: Traditional knowledge and sustainable development' in *The Contemporary Pacific* 2 (2):233-253

Demeny, P. (1992) 'Notes and commentary - policies seeking a reduction of high fertility: A case for the demand side' in *Population and Development Review,* 18 (2):321-332

Hayes, G. (forthcoming) 'Population growth, economic development and environmental stress in Papua New Guinea' in *Proceedings of the 20th Woigani Seminar,* Port Moresby: University of Papua New Guinea

Kelley, A. C. (1988) 'Economic consequences of population change in the third world' in *Journal of Economic Literature,* 26:1685-1728

Lockwood, V. (1992) 'Welfare state colonialism in rural French Polynesia' in Lockwood, V., Harding, T.G. and Wallace, B.J. (eds) *Contemporary Pacific societies'* New Jersey: Prentice Hall

Malthus, T.R. (1970) 'An essay on the principle of population' in Flew, A. (ed.) *Thomas Malthus: An essay on the principle of population,* Middlesex, United Kingdom: Penguin

McDowell, N. (ed.) (1988) *Reproductive decision making and the value of children in Papua New Guinea,* Boroko, PNG: Institute of Applied Social and Economic Research

Preston, S.H. (1987) 'The social sciences and the population problem' in *Sociological Forum,* 2:619-644

Sem, G. and Underhill, Y.J. (1992) *Climate change preparatory mission: Report on the Cook Islands,* Apia, Western Samoa: South Pacific Regional Environment Programme (SPREP)

South Pacific Commission (1993) *South Pacific Economies Statistical Summary: SPESS,* no.13, Noumea, New Caledonia

Taylor, R., Lewis, N.D. and Levy, S. (1989) 'Societies in transition: Mortality patterns in Pacific Island populations', in *International Journal of Epidemiology,* 18(3):634-646

Thomas, N. (1989) 'The force of ethnology: Origins and significance of the Melanesian/Polynesian division' in *Cultural Anthropology,* 30 (1):27-41

United Nations (1988) *World demographic estimates and projections 1950-2029,* New York

Working Group on Population Growth and Economic Development (1986) *Population growth and economic development: Policy questions,* Washington D.C.: National Academy of Sciences

Two

Banking on the growth model?
The World Bank and market policies in the Pacific*

Claire Slatter

Introduction

The World Bank's second (March 1993) report on Pacific Island economies[1] opens with a discussion of what is dubbed 'The Pacific Paradox' - that is, the low growth and persistent stagnation of Pacific Island economies over the last decade, despite favourable natural resource endowments and high levels of external assistance. The Bank's insistence on higher economic growth rates in a region which it acknowledges has achieved (and is enjoying) 'a relatively high standard of living' (p.ix) might itself be said to be paradoxical. Yet, in the Pacific region, as elsewhere, the Bank's analysis of national economic problems and its prescriptions of policy solutions are acquiring the status of undisputed 'truths'. Indeed, many of the policies and strategies advocated in the World Bank's two economic reports (of 1991 and 1993) for its Pacific member countries (PMCs) are already being implemented although public awareness of their origin is generally very limited. National governments present the policies as their own inspiration and the restricted circulation and classified nature of Bank reports (which may not be 'disclosed without World Bank authorisation') have encouraged this fiction.

This article critically reviews the World Bank reports of 1991 and 1993, examining the arguments, exposing some of the ideas and values which lie behind the economic prescriptions for PMCs, and discussing the impact that these are already having in the Pacific region. The framework that the World Bank has developed for PMCs in the 1990s entails the classic elements of structural adjustment commonly prescribed for member countries of the Bank. It is to be expected that this paradigm will produce the same devastating social consequences that have occurred elsewhere. Growth at any cost will almost certainly entail Pacific Island countries risking their social development achievements, as well as eroding those institutions and structures which have not only stood the test of time, but which would continue to ensure their well-being, if not their increased prosperity, in the future.

Growth for its own sake: The World Bank's first Pacific report

Towards higher growth in Pacific Island economies: Lessons from the 1980s is the first economic report by the World Bank on its six Pacific member countries[2]. The report consists of two volumes. A regional overview examines their 'growth performance' in the 1980s, assessing the factors underlying their relatively weak performance, and developing a framework for achieving higher rates of growth in the 1990s. A compendium of country surveys provides the empirical basis for the regional overview. World Bank missions visited the region in November 1989 and again in May-June 1990 to carry out surveys for the report. All principal authors are non-regionals (probably visiting the region for the first time), although the report acknowledges the contribution of Western Samoan economist Te'o Fairbairn.

Unsurprisingly, the 88-page regional report is focused narrowly on the economy, with only three pages devoted to a perfunctory and inadequate overview of the region's more general physical, economic and social features - geography and society, climate, natural resources, population, emigration, population density, culture, 'endowment constraints' (e.g. 'persistence of traditional patterns of economic organisation') and living standards (i.e. incomes and welfare indicators). The vast differences in the historical, cultural, physical and demographic features of the six countries are acknowledged in a footnote, which seeks to justify the authors' scant attention to 'the nexus of country specific factors that may have effected particular development outcomes'. It is explained that the report focuses principally on issues that 'cut across' all of the island economies: four chapters thus specifically deal with economic performance in the 1980s, the domestic policy environment of the 1990s, development challenges and growth prospects in the 1990s, and the need for improving aid performance.

The report begins by acknowledging that the six PMCs have achieved 'relatively high living standards in the face of many constraints' (p.i), noting that per capita gross national product (GNP) 'is at the upper end of the low income to middle income range' and that social indicators 'compare favourably with developing countries at the same **or higher** levels of income' (my emphasis; p.i). It then records the 'disappointing aspect' that economic performance has been 'sluggish' (GNP grew at only 0.6% per annum), compared with 'the more dynamic island economies of the Caribbean (5%) and Indian Ocean (7%)' (p.i). It emphasises that this has occurred despite 'some of the highest inflows of per capita development assistance'[3]. According to the report, poor growth performance in the 1980s, together with an annual average 2.2 per cent population increase over the same period, were responsible for significantly reducing per capita incomes. Aside from factors such as natural disasters (which affected all PMCs except Kiribati) and recent political disturbances (in some countries) which are considered to have negatively impacted on economic performance, poor growth rates are attributed to the 'inability to stimulate private investment in productive sectors' (p.i).

Specifically, the report criticises the PMCs inward-oriented development' strategies (for producing unsatisfactory results) and their protection of local industries (for contributing to high-cost local economies 'unable to

18

compete in world markets') (p.ii). It highlights the burden placed on public finances by state enterprises, and the stifling of a 'dynamic private sector' by over-regulation (asserting that foreign investors had been lost to other countries 'where the environment [was] more conducive to doing business') as factors responsible for poor growth (ibid). The report's analysis of the growth problem for PMCs clearly suggests that if these countries want to enjoy economic growth, they need to become more export-oriented, deregulate their economies (i.e. remove protection/tariffs on imports), sell off (or corporatise) burdensome public enterprises and provide incentives to the private sector. Yet apart from arguing that more rapid growth is necessary for raising living standards in the PMCs, there is no discussion of the likely human development benefits of such growth, nor indeed of what social policies should be adopted to ensure that growth realises higher living standards. Growth for its own sake appears to be the idea.

The report argues that 'increasing the pace of development is an imperative for the 1990s': that in light of the poor prospects for primary commodities, PMCs need to 'develop new sources of growth' (p.ii). The six countries are considered to 'have the potential for more rapid growth on a sustainable basis'; indeed Fiji is believed to be already demonstrating its capacity for growth 'under a revised strategy and policies' (p.ii; see discussion below). The prognosis is that reasonable rates of economic growth (2.5% per annum) can be achieved in the first five years of the 1990s, and then maintained throughout the decade, if these countries rise to the challenge of finding new sources of growth.

A number of 'dynamic growth strategies' are proposed which entail abandoning inward-looking, import-substitution policies and promoting private sector investment and export production. The report advises a shift from producing primary commodities towards the production of processed products for export. It recommends specialised production for external markets and sees sustained growth being achieved through a 'leading sector approach in which public policy facilitates the private sector's search for profitable niches in domestic and world markets' (ibid). The private sector is clearly considered the engine of growth. PMCs are advised to concentrate on a few specialised areas where they have a 'clear comparative advantage' (p.61). The Maldives (tourism and fisheries) and Mauritius (sugar and garments) are held out as small island economic success stories. Fiji's adoption of growth-centred market policies is applauded, especially the spectacular success of its export-oriented, tax-free garment industry.

Specific recommendations for macroeconomic management, public sector management and private sector development are made. Among these are a recommendation for 'fiscal adjustment', especially in the Solomon Islands and Vanuatu, to reduce fiscal deficits (commonly between 20% and 40% of gross domestic product [GDP]) to more manageable levels, and the proposal that 'appropriate wage and exchange rate policies' should be adopted to maintain external competitiveness (p.iii). In particular, the report advises against the practice of linking wages to the cost of living, recommending instead that they should be kept in line with economy-wide productivity. It also encourages PMCs to broaden their tax bases, lower direct tax rates, eliminate 'trade-inhibiting taxes' and shift towards an indirect tax system that 'does not discriminate across productive sectors' (ibid). Corporate tax rates are recommended 'at rates conducive to private investment and growth' (p.iv).

A number of public sector management policies (required for higher growth) are recommended. These include reduction of the administrative budget (particularly public sector wages and salaries which are considered to have grown excessively and to have inflated wages throughout the economy); improvement of physical infrastructure; and introduction of a programme of privatisation (particularly for commodity marketing boards and other enterprises which 'crowd out private investment' or which 'could be more efficiently managed by the private sector'). Additionally, the report proposes the abandonment of five-year planning and the adoption of a new approach to national planning - one that 'emphasises macroeconomic assessment and the preparation of broad development strategies' (p.vii). It advises (with evident confidence) that a new pattern of aid allocation 'will be likely' in the future, with private entrepreneurs receiving a share of aid resources through 'financialisation', that is the channelling of resources through the commercial financial - i.e. banking - system (ibid).

The main growth strategy proposed by the Bank is unequivocally that of expanding private sector participation in investment and economic activity (p.iv). In the view of the report's authors, 'the provision of a policy environment that facilitates private investment is a primary challenge for the 1990s' (ibid). All six countries are advised to put in place an 'outward-oriented incentives regime', introduce 'greater flexibility in wages', and help develop 'entrepreneurial capacity'.

Forsaking development for growth? The emergence of market regimes in the Pacific

The dynamic growth strategies advocated by the World Bank in its first (1991) economic report are the standard market-oriented macroeconomic policies that the Bank and the International Monetary Fund (IMF) inflict on debt-ridden countries as part of enforced structural adjustment programmes. These policies - which are austerity measures -are imposed as conditionalities for their loans. The Bank's Pacific report and its recommendations do not, therefore, represent disinterested, friendly advice to PMCs but a compulsory set of policies which must be adopted if they wish to continue to receive Bank assistance in the form of development loans. Although the report does not say so, economic planning in these countries is being strongly directed by the Bank.

For instance, Pacific governments are under strong pressure to divest state-owned enterprises by selling these off to private interests (whether foreign or local) and to remove protection for local industries. State-owned enterprises 'in virtually all sectors of the [Solomon Island] economy' are considered to be excessive and a drain on the country's budget resources (5% of GDP transfers in the last five years). The report advises that the Solomon Islands government is 'considering' (following World Bank advice?) selling off or liquidating some of its enterprises. It notes that the formerly government-owned Mendana Hotel has already been sold to Japanese interests and that bids are being sought for Solrice (the government-owned rice trading enterprise) and National Fisheries Development (NFD) (a state-owned fishing company)[4].

The Solomon Islands is not alone amongst PMCs to implement privatisation programmes - Fiji, Kiribati and Western Samoa have already sold off or corporatised state-owned enterprises. Western Samoa is not only selling off non-plantation activities formerly run by the state-owned WESTEC Holdings but is also leasing estates to the private sector. It is 'rationalising' its commodity marketing boards so that they have an essentially information-providing role, rather than that of 'stabilising producer prices for specific export crops' through centralised purchasing and marketing operations (p.41). According to the report, Western Samoa is, in addition, phasing out subsidies on fertilisers and agrochemicals.

Fiji has been implementing other prescribed policies, including cutting back on public spending (which has meant reduced allocations to health, education, housing and other social services); introducing a 'user pays' principle (which has raised the costs of public housing, health and education); and applying taxation 'reforms' aimed at broadening the tax base, providing incentives for private investment and reducing or eliminating trade-inhibiting taxes (import duties). In both Fiji and Western Samoa, taxation 'reform' has been introduced in the face of strong public opposition, including a massive public demonstration in the case of the latter, and has transferred the tax burden onto the poor. Both countries have also embarked on new export-oriented manufacturing ventures (garments in Fiji and automotive wire assembly in Western Samoa for example) based on generous tax incentives to investors and the unmitigated exploitation of unorganised (and mainly female) workers.

Economic and labour market deregulation in Fiji have entailed the additional imposition of repressive anti-labour decrees which strip workers and unions of hard-won rights and openly favour employers. Like other structural adjustment policies being applied in the country, these so-called 'labour reforms' have been applied amid widespread controversy and opposition. In fact, Fiji's structural adjustment programme was introduced by a repressive (military-installed) interim government on a self-appointed mission to resuscitate an economy afflicted by capital flight, loss of investor confidence, an exodus of professionals and skilled labour, and crumbling public morale, all of which were the consequences of two military coups in 1987 and the forces of militarism and racism that these unleashed. The justification of the policy package as a panacea to restore investor confidence and stimulate economic growth was a successful 'confidence trick' that shifted attention from the far more serious political crisis to the economic one. Conveniently, the military was on hand to allay any hitches in implementing the economic 'cure'.

The strategy of wooing private investors to salvage Fiji's economy, based on overly generous tax incentives and a passive or disciplinable labour force/trade union movement, has been officially acclaimed as a great success, although boosted investment levels have subsequently subsided. But, significantly, the World Bank report makes no reference to the undemocratic and repressive political context in which the 'revised strategy and policies' that have enabled Fiji to 'demonstrate its capacity for growth' (p.ii) were introduced. Effectively, this political context is denied, as is the coercive hand of the Bank and the IMF in dictating economic adjustment. Nor does the report acknowledge the fact that income disparities and poverty have increased markedly in post-coup Fiji - a fact borne out by the findings of a 1990 study by Father Kevin Barr which should have been taken into account.

The 'rapid growth' formula that the Bank prescribes for its PMCs represents a major departure from regional development thinking in the last two decades, when development was equated with state control of key sectors of the economy and its provision of resources and services to the people. Indeed, there is little doubt that the old development model, based on an avowed state commitment to distributing the benefits of development, and supported by the 'safety nets' of traditional (kin-based) social security systems, strong subsistence bases, traditional resource-use practices, large remittance inflows from kin working and living abroad, and generous levels of development assistance, was successful in achieving relatively high living standards in PMCs.

By advising PMCs to put all their eggs in the private sector and global market basket (by deregulating their economies, providing inducements to the private sector, promoting export industries and selling off state-owned enterprises), the World Bank is ignoring the critical role of the state in achieving such living standards. It is also disregarding the wisdom of inward-oriented development strategies pursued over the past two decades. In Fiji, for example, considerable investment in education (close to 20% of the budget in the 1970s and 1980s and nearly 6% of GDP) and health (8% of total government spending and about 3% of GDP in the 1980s with real per capita spending rising by close to 20% between 1981 and 1984) has effectively meant state-subsidised services. Together with the provision of other social services and subsidies (e.g. low-cost housing and utilities), regulated wages and conditions, and price controls, these investments have indeed been crucial to achieving the relatively high living standards that the Bank commends.

In the Bank's proposed growth-oriented development strategy, however, the role of the state is effectively reduced to one of supporting the private sector. Markets, not states, PMCs are told, are the only route to economic growth. The state is encouraged to assist the private sector find 'niche' markets for specialised agricultural/fisheries products, and manufactured goods and services; provide incentives for private investment; and maximise returns by investing in quality control measures, product research and education and training in the specialised industries. But public expenditure, in the Bank's view, should primarily centre on the provision, operation and maintenance of essential physical infrastructure and services associated with human resource development.

22

Madame multinational
*(translated from the French original
Madame Multinationale)*

Madame Multinational
holds court in all four corners of the earth
a river of African diamonds
encircling her blood-red throat
She travels by Rolls-Royce on gold
from Brazil to Mauritania or Australia
She charters special Boeing jets
from London to New York, via Paris or Tokyo
She treats herself to royal cruises
from Corfu to the Balaeric Islands of Capri
They call her Lady Jet Set
Or Miss Casino
from Monaco to Las Vegas
She has her antennae in Moscow Warsaw or Budapest
Industrial espionage is for her a past-time

She has intercontinental tentacles

The jade-coloured nickel of a Pacific island
is just another toy
in her bag of tricks and financial crises

The hunt for petroleum
or witches
fishing for nodules
beneath neo-colonies
the race for uranium
or arms
the folly of plutonium
from state monopolies
the fluctuations of Wall Street
from her spheres of influence
are some of her favourite amusements

The 'threat of communism'
is her obsession

Madame Multinational
understands no earthly language

She only loves King Dollar.

Déwé Gorode

It goes without saying that more rapid growth in PMCs in the 1990s, following adoption of the Bank's narrow prescriptions, is likely to be achieved at the expense of the mass of their populations, whose living standards will undoubtedly be lowered by an intensified market approach to development. In 1989, Fiji's real per capita health budget reportedly dropped by about 40 per cent from its 1984 level, requiring the introduction of a 'user pays' principle to meet the budget shortfall and 'make health services more efficient' (UNICEF/ Government of Fiji 1991). The indictment of the state that is implicit in market policy rhetoric about improving 'efficiency' and 'productivity' and achieving growth ironically appears to be lost on political leaders who have taken up the refrain of market policy advocates.

Fallacies and fibs in the Bank's growth arguments

The Bank's argument that more rapid growth is imperative in PMCs in the 1990s is premised on certain 'facts'. Notable amongst these is the theory that population growth rates are excessive and that (coupled with poor economic growth) they have lowered per capita incomes. These premises need to be critically examined. First, annual average population growth rates for the six PMCs are widely varying, ranging from 3.5 per cent for the Solomon Islands to

0.1 per cent for Western Samoa (even more so if non-member countries of the World Bank are included). Although these variations are mentioned in the report (in 28 lines given to the issue), they are ignored in the conclusion. For instance, it is noted that growth rates are high for the Melanesian countries (Vanuatu and the Solomon Islands) but that population density in these countries, as well as in Fiji, is 'modest'. High population densities are correctly pinpointed as primarily an **urban** problem, particularly acute in Kiribati (Tarawa), while low growth rates in Tonga and Samoa are explained by high out-migration to Australia, New Zealand and the USA. Given the widely varying demographic features of the six countries, it is misleading, even mischievous, to average population growth rates out at 2.2 per cent, and then to use this figure to argue generally that growth rates are excessive.

Second, the suggestion that per capita living standards have been lowered in the last decade is at odds with the report's own findings. The authors make early mention of the fact that despite the constraints they have faced, Pacific Island states have achieved 'quite high levels of income' compared to other developing countries (p.4). Per capita GNP ranges from $US 1500 in the case of Fiji to $US 400-600 in the Solomon Islands and Kiribati. They also note, importantly, that this has resulted in Fiji's case from 'a fairly broad-based growth process involving agriculture, tourism and manufacturing'; and in the cases of Samoa, Tonga and Kiribati, from significant remittance inflows from nationals working abroad which subsidise incomes and consumption patterns of family members at home (ibid). The authors caution, in a footnote, that average income figures should not be taken at face value as a measure of welfare, since there are wide income disparities within countries. They acknowledge that higher-earning expatriate and educated urban-based indigenous (elite) populations, as well as unequal traditional allocations of resources, inflate the averages (ibid).

Another point conceded by the report is that living standards for Fiji, Tonga and Western Samoa have been raised quite substantially, with indicators for life expectancy, infant mortality, literacy, primary education and health service access, sanitation and transport/communications being generally good, and even comparable to many middle-income countries. For Kiribati, the Solomon Islands and Vanuatu, such indicators have not been as good, with high infant mortality rates, low life expectancy and, in the case of the two Melanesian countries, high levels of illiteracy, poor sanitation and endemic intestinal diseases and malaria being exhibited. But significant attempts to improve living standards in all three countries are recognised in the report. For instance, investment in education in both the Solomon Islands and Vanuatu is expected to soon raise literacy rates (ibid).

The contradiction between the report's acknowledgment of the achievements of PMCs (or at least three of them) in raising living standards and its (unsupported) claim that these have been lowered in the last decade is curious. There is also the astonishing remark that the 'moderately high standards of living' of PMCs have been achieved and maintained 'more through an adherence to good education and health administrations established during the colonial period than through recent economic development'(p.6). This is an arrogant claim which ignores the significant investments in health and education that have been made by socially oriented independent Pacific governments over the last two decades. The subsequent statement that 'further improvements in social indicators will depend upon what can be achieved in broad-based, more rapid growth' (ibid) not only overlooks the importance of continued state support for these services, but

25

erroneously suggests that private wealth accumulation will mean improved living standards for the mass of ordinary people.

The fallacy of achieving sustainable human development through the mechanism of the global market has already been exposed by Thaman et al. (1992) who, in an incisive critique of the United Nation's Development Programme's (UNDP) 1992 Human Development Report, argue that the emphasis on markets is not particularly relevant in a region where protection of community-based terrestrial and marine resource-use systems is fundamental to sustainability, and where 'isolation from markets, limited resource bases and small internal markets limit the scope for participation in both local and global open markets, even if they were truly open' (pp.8,10). Thaman et al. also point out that far from advantaging Pacific states, the lowering of trade barriers to free global markets will make Pacific Island economies even less competitive. Moreover, growth strategies which have focused mainly on export production have only led, they say, to increasing economic disparities within Pacific Island states (ibid).

In contrast to other countries of the South where structural adjustment programmes have been imposed, PMCs are neither (at least not at the time the report was written) heavily indebted nor struggling to meet debt service obligations. Their 'modest debt exposure', as the report itself calls it, is indicated by the fact that debt service obligations were a 'comfortable' 10 per cent of export earnings (for Fiji), eight per cent for Western Samoa and less than five per cent for other countries (p17). It is explained that this 'marked contrast' of PMCs to other low- and medium-income countries has emanated from 'a cautious fiscal and monetary stance, good access to external grant financing and increased worker remittances' (ibid). The problem for PMCs other than Fiji is not that they have a debt servicing problem, but rather a problem of constrained creditworthiness due to their 'narrow production and export base' and 'small size'.

In the next sentence, however, the report suggests that new criteria for creditworthiness (which have little to do with the factors of size, production and export base) will be applied to PMCs in the next decade. Creditworthiness, it is proposed, will now be assessed in relation to the adoption of initiatives aimed at achieving private sector-led growth since it would be 'difficult to justify commercial borrowing to finance public investment' given that past high levels of public investment (and, as noted elsewhere in the report, 'some of the highest inflows of per capita development assistance') have resulted in 'virtually no change in per capita GDP' (p.17).

The World Bank's first Pacific report is steeped in the market ideology it aggressively champions along with the IMF, and it is bereft of any genuine concern for improving living standards in Pacific Island countries. It represents a fraudulent exercise in objective economic appraisal and ignores both the structural causes of Pacific Island economic problems and the strengths of traditional lifestyles, values, resource-use and social support systems. It does not explain how advantaging private investors (whose primary motive is private profit) and facilitating the accumulation of wealth by local and, more particularly, foreign companies (who mostly stand to benefit from the privatisation of state assets/companies) will bring about improved living standards to Pacific Islanders. Presumably through the mythical 'invisible hand' or equally illusory 'trickle down' effect?

Beyond perfunctory references, the report shows little understanding or appreciation of Pacific Island living standards. If anything, living standards (or

26

certainly wages and salaries) are considered to be too high, in the sense of not having been earned through increased productivity, but rather enjoyed as a result of subsidisation by aid donors and migrant kin living abroad. Indeed, in Volume 2 (Country Surveys), the report revealingly notes the adverse effect of remittances on labour supply in Tonga, namely 'higher reservation wages' and a corresponding reduction in production of export crops' (p.139). The suggestion here of an indolent population spoiled by hand-outs from abroad totally ignores the redistributive values inherent in Pacific cultures which lie behind kinship remittances. It also fails to account for the principle of non-accumulation or sufficiency that is part of traditional resource-use ethics. Elsewhere the report resorts to similarly unflattering imagery to criticise the large inflows of resources (especially external assistance) to support what it dubs a 'bloated public sector' in Western Samoa. The message to aid donors - and Pacific Islanders - is clear. The 1990s should see much less aid flowing into PMCs; and what does flow in should be directed primarily to growth-promising (and private sector) initiatives.

The report does not offer any of the lessons that the Bank should have learned from the experience of other countries of the South which have had to adopt market policies in IMF-imposed structural adjustment packages at immense social, economic, environmental and even political cost. Nor does it offer PMCs a balanced appraisal of their development performance over the last decade. While claiming remarkable economic recoveries for both Fiji and Vanuatu following the implementation of market policies, as indicated by an upward movement in their GDPs in 1989 (12.5% for Fiji and 4.5% for Vanuatu), the report says nothing about growing evidence of poverty in both these countries, as reported in National Situation Analyses of Children prepared by the United Nations Children's Fund (UNICEF) (UNICEF/Government of Fiji 1991 & UNICEF/Government of Vanuatu 1991).

From paradox to partnership: The second World Bank report

The World Bank's second (1993) regional economic report, entitled *Pacific Island economies: Toward efficient and sustainable growth,* covers eight Pacific Island states with the Marshall Islands and Federated States of Micronesia now having been added to the World Bank fold. It comprises nine volumes: a regional overview and eight country economic reports. Like the 1991 report, the 1993 regional overview analyses economic performance and recommends specific action for sustaining economic growth. While certainly more holistic in its approach, and seemingly more mindful of the peculiar specificities of PMCs (claiming that the objective is 'not to impose some model derived elsewhere but to adapt approaches...'), this second report is little different in substance from the first. It similarly highlights public sector 'reform', efficiency in the use of foreign aid and the crucial role of the private sector in achieving sustainable growth. It presents showcase countries for emulation (this time the East Asian newly industrialising countries [NICs] as well as the Maldives and Barbados). However, the inclusion of comprehensive chapters on both human resource development and environmental issues[5] in the PMCs makes the 1993 regional report more sound, and infinitely more useful, than its predecessor. The country reports provide useful reviews of, and policy prescriptions for, the eight economies under review.

The report introduces two new concepts in the Bank's analysis of PMC economies and prescriptions for growth. The first of these is the concept of 'the Pacific paradox' which summarises its analysis of their problems:

Development performance in the PMCs during the last decade or so has been marked by a paradox: virtually no growth (0.1% annually) occurred in average real per capita income during this period despite a favourable natural and human resource endowment, high levels of aid, and reasonably prudent economic management (pp.ix,1)[6].

Elaborating on the Pacific Paradox, the report says:

While investment has been high and macroeconomic policy largely under control, the overall economic climate has favoured public sector interventions of low effectiveness, rather than more efficient private sector activity. Education and human resource programs have been strengthened substantially, but limited domestic opportunities have resulted in substantial emigration of skilled workers, partially compensated by technical assistance, foreign aid in human resource development, and worker remittances. The blend of customary practices and modern systems has both inhibited development and helped provide some stability and social safety nets. An alluring but fragile environment also contributes both to the potential for tourism and to limitations of modern sector growth (p.5).

Although the report suggests that these diverse factors have to be taken into account in analysing the economies of PMCs and making recommendations, the executive summary of the recommendations indicates no departure from the policy prescriptions of the 1991 report. In sum, the following is advocated: more effective economic engagement with the rest of the world (i.e. producing more exports for the global market, particularly in the areas of agriculture, fisheries and small-scale manufacturing and promoting tourism which are considered to hold the most promise); enhancing international competitiveness (by ensuring 'a stable political and economic environment, satisfactory economic and human infrastructure, and a business environment that is conducive to trade and foreign investment'); broadening trade and investment links (especially with the growth centres of East Asia); and reforming the public sector (specifically by restructuring, consolidating, privatising, 'down-sizing' through retrenchments and other cost-cutting measures including lowering public sector wages which are deemed in some PMCs to be 'well in excess of average national incomes') (pp.ix-x).

Like the 1991 report, the 1993 report sees private enterprise as the key to generating economic growth in PMCs and argues strongly for the creation of an economic environment more conducive to private sector development. While acknowledging the 'notable results' of state-led development efforts (namely the provision of infrastructure and improvement in welfare), the report criticises this strategy for failing to achieve economic growth. State investment in commercial activities is also disparaged for inhibiting private sector development. The report advises that there is potential for private sector-led growth but says 'tapping such potential will require supportive policies and investments on the part of Pacific Island governments' (p.37). It cites the examples of squash production in Tonga, automotive wire assembly in Western Samoa and small- and medium-scale hotels in other PMCs to demonstrate that 'a few private sector investments can make significant contributions in [their] relatively small economies'. The report also reiterates the importance of taxation reform (to spread the tax burden while reducing income tax rates), relaxation of minimum wage legislation (to encourage new employment in labour-intensive activities), developing agricultural and other niche export products (even though cautioning against reliance on niche market industries as they are unpredictable) and corporatisation or privatisation especially of transport service operations (pp.42, 46-7, 50).

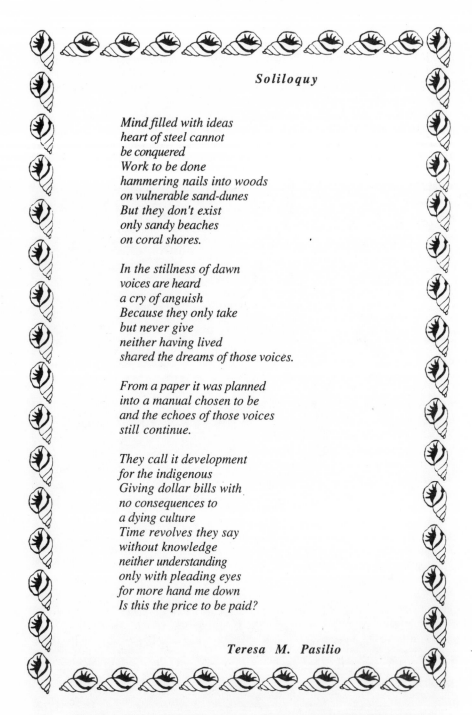

Soliloquy

Mind filled with ideas
heart of steel cannot
be conquered
Work to be done
hammering nails into woods
on vulnerable sand-dunes
But they don't exist
only sandy beaches
on coral shores.

In the stillness of dawn
voices are heard
a cry of anguish
Because they only take
but never give
neither having lived
shared the dreams of those voices.

From a paper it was planned
into a manual chosen to be
and the echoes of those voices
still continue.

They call it development
for the indigenous
Giving dollar bills with
no consequences to
a dying culture
Time revolves they say
without knowledge
neither understanding
only with pleading eyes
for more hand me down
Is this the price to be paid?

Teresa M. Pasilio

The second concept which encapsulates the Bank's essential prescription of a new economic model is that of a 'development partnership' between the state and the private sector. Brandishing the East Asian success story as a model, the report advocates a similar 'partnership', explaining that this will enable the state to become 'market-friendly' and 'complement rather than supplant the private sector' (p.37). In such a partnership, the state's function is reduced to ensuring macroeconomic stability and competitiveness through exchange rate, fiscal, monetary and wage policies; removing impediments to private (and especially foreign) investment[7]; promoting and disseminating information; and providing supportive physical and social infrastructure (pp.38-40). The island economies of the Maldives and Barbados are applauded for following the 'development partnership' model 'with heartening results' (p.37).

The report welcomes the adoption by both Fiji and Western Samoa (which have emerged as the Pacific region's front line 'market-friendly' states) of 'more flexible [strategic] planning processes' (p.27). These have replaced 'target-oriented, needs-based five year plans' which persist in Tonga, Vanuatu and Kiribati.

> The shift in emphasis towards strategic planning is consistent with a growth strategy that favours more of **a partnership between government and the private sector** [my emphasis]. In Fiji, for example, Economic Summits were held in 1989 and 1991 during which Government and the private sector jointly formulated sectoral growth strategies and defined a policy reform agenda. The benefits of such cooperation extend well beyond the preparation of a strategic plan: forging a consensus between Government and the private sector on strategy and policy has helped build credibility and speed adjustment to difficult reforms (ibid).

Implicit in the Bank's notion of 'partnership' then is an unabashed employer-state collusion in the implementation of employer-favouring (and worker-disadvantaging) market policies. Consequently, the post-coup partnership between government and employers in Fiji (reflected in the institution of the economic summit which endorsed the introduction of anti-labour decrees) is misleadingly termed a 'development partnership' by the Bank. The report makes no reference to the fact that economic summits have replaced the earlier tripartite consultative machinery (the Tripartite Forum) in which the Fiji Trades Union Congress participated during the pre-coup years of 1977-1986. Nor does it acknowledge that the post-coup 'development partnership' between the owners of capital and the state is marginalising and disempowering organised labour and denying fundamental worker rights.

In a chapter on human resource development, the report posits the importance of human resource development for growth and welfare, arguing that 'a part of the solution to long-run economic growth [in the PMCs] is an economy geared around efficient provision of services, for which the key factor of production is a healthy, well-trained labour force' (p.56). Yet it goes on to advise against increased budgetary allocations to education (currently at between 25% and 13% of recurrent expenditures for Vanuatu and Western Samoa respectively, which are considered 'very large'). Recording that government allocations to the education sector have declined in real terms over the last few years, the report advocates more efficient use of resources and a prioritising of primary, as opposed to post-secondary, education (pp.59-62). In the area of health services, the prioritisation of preventive and primary health care services is recommended in preference to curative, hospital-based care, to which a disproportionate amount of public expenditure on health in PMCs is already directed.

31

The Human Resource Development chapter also discusses the 'high reserve price of unskilled labour' in PMCs, where unskilled labourers command between three and seven times the wages paid to their South-East Asian counterparts (p.55). High wages are said to reflect the 'generally comfortable living conditions offered by semi-subsistence agriculture' (which are elsewhere (p.4) termed 'affluent subsistence'), rather than high productivity. Raising the level of productivity of the workforce and 'improving value for money' are advised as the 'only way' that PMCs can 'compete in the global marketplace' (p.56).

The fiction of environment-friendly growth

The inclusion of a special chapter on Economic Growth and the Environment in the 1993 report marks a significant departure from the World Bank's usual economic reports[8]. It suggests a novel 'environment-friendly' approach to the pursuit of growth. Such an approach is, however, in many respects at odds with the general thrust of the report and it is perhaps largely explained by the engagement of a well-known Fiji-based environment consultant on the World Bank team. Indeed the excellence of the environment chapter in the regional overview notwithstanding, attention to environmental issues appears very much like an extended 'footnote' to the main text. For instance, the chapter laments the tendency among some island decision makers 'to consider addressing environmental concerns as a luxury incompatible with growth and development' and it asserts in an admirably environmentally sensitive, if unWorld-Bankish, way that:

In fact, better environmental management is not merely compatible with economic growth, it is required for improved health standards, more equitable development, and often poverty alleviation. Failure to address environmental degradation will lead to a less pleasant physical environment, poorer health standards, eventually decreasing agriculture and forest yields, and worsening seafood quality and yields. The region's pristine environment is in considerable danger. Although pollution and environmental degradation are generally worsening, they are reversible if policies are improved and implemented and more appropriate mechanisms (regulations, incentives and price signals) are introduced (p.69).

Yet elsewhere in the report, the extent of environmental damage thus far suffered in Pacific Island countries 'compared with more industrialised and commercially oriented island states' appears to be played down (p.xv). The report also suggests, in the following oblique reference, that environmental management will become more of a problem in the future for PMCs, ironically as a consequence of the very growth policies that the Bank advocates!

New pressures and strains on the environment will arise, particularly to the extent that increased private sector activity contributes to a restoration of higher rates of economic growth. In the future, careful environmental management will take on an added importance **because practically all likely sources of economic growth will involve more intensive use of fragile natural resource bases** (my emphasis; p.xv).

Clearly this acknowledged connection between 'increased private sector activity' and 'new pressures and strains on the environment' admits no liability on the part of those who advocate the former as the only route to growth.

The drive for export revenue in PMCs is already intensifying both the search for new discoveries of minerals and the extraction of existing mineral and forestry resources, especially the latter. Rapacious logging in Papua New Guinea, the Solomon Islands and Vanuatu, way in excess of officially permitted levels, was recently reported as causing 'thousands of hectares of pristine forest [to be] destroyed weekly' (*Fiji Times* 14 July 1994)[9]. Ironically, it was the World Bank itself which reportedly sounded the alarm in the Solomon Islands where a dramatic increase in the rate of log exports in 1993 led it to warn that such a rate of exploitation, if continued, would 'see existing stocks depleted within eight years' (ibid). By presenting itself in this way as a defender of the environment, and treating the problem of environmental degradation as a discrete phenomenon unrelated to the growth strategies it advocates, the World Bank shows true genius. Profit-driven resource extraction by private, and usually foreign, interests is clearly a direct consequence of private-sector-biased, export-oriented free market economic policies, and the environment-friendly growth model suggested by the 1993 report is nothing less than a contradiction in terms.

Conclusion: To grow or not to grow?

Like other countries in the South that are in the pincers of multilateral lending agencies like the World Bank and the IMF, PMCs are currently in a Catch 22 situation - being damned if they do and damned if they don't follow the Bank's prescriptions for economic growth. As the Bank's 1991 report makes clear, a carrot-and-stick approach is being used. The Bank is holding out the promise of economic growth to PMCs if they follow the prescriptions laid down while, at the same time, advising them that there will be no economic support for their endeavours if they do not comply. Sadly, most Pacific Island governments and planners now appear to subscribe to the free market arguments of the World Bank. And similar analyses and prescriptions for growth are being trotted out by Pacific economists, in some cases under the sponsorship of agencies like the Australian International Development Assistance Bureau (AIDAB)[10].

The short-term economic growth prospects for PMCs following the World Bank framework may well be good and some people will undoubtedly benefit materially from them. But for the majority of people within the six countries, growth may prove extremely costly. Until recently, widening economic disparities resulting from growth-oriented development strategies based on export production have been moderated by major state involvement in key sectors of the economy, the provision of services, and the 'safety nets' of traditional (kinship-based) social security systems, the effective subsidisation of the market economy by the rural subsistence economy and the high level of remittances from Pacific Island emigrants residing abroad. These safety nets, which have effectively insured many thousands of Pacific Islanders against abject poverty and want, are being eroded at the same time as state responsibilities and roles in relation to achieving economic and social development are being drastically reduced in line with market-led development strategies.

The social price that PMCs may pay for growth might indeed be incalculable. Growth and development are not the same thing, and pursuing the former at the expense of the latter is a sure recipe for impoverishing the Pacific. The growth imperative is already fundamentally altering the meaning and nature of development in this region, threatening the material achievements made over the last two decades and, perhaps worst of all, undermining the redistributive ethic which lies at the heart of Pacific Island cultures.

---

*   An earlier version of this paper which critiques the 1991 World Bank Pacific regional report was presented to the Pacific Regional Meeting on Women, Environment and Development sponsored by Development Alternatives with Women for a New Era (DAWN), University of the South Pacific, Suva, Fiji, in December 1992.

Notes

1. World Bank (1993) *Pacific Island economies: Towards efficient and sustainable growth,* vol.1, Overview, 8 March.

2. The member countries in 1991 were Fiji, Kiribati, the Solomon Islands, Tonga, Vanuatu and Western Samoa.

3. In the Bank's view, massive aid flows have enabled PMCs to bridge their resource gaps and maintain high investment levels, but most investments have been in physical infrastructure and human resource development which have 'little immediate impact on economic growth'.

4. NFD has now been sold to British Columbia Packers (BCP), a Canadian company.

5. The chapter on economic growth and the environment provides a comprehensive discussion of the major environmental problems facing the island countries of the Pacific region. It expertly recounts the special vulnerability of island ecosystems and the serious threats posed by global warming (a problem beyond our capacity to control since this depends on reduced greenhouse gas emissions in industrialised states). It also covers the whole gamut of other environmental problems including water and sewerage, marine pollution, waste management, radiation, inappropriate land use, deforestation, biological diversity and species protection, over-harvesting of marine resources, tourism, and energy use. The chapter concludes with a discussion of responses to environmental issues.

6. Favourable natural resource endowment is explained as a high ratio of land per person and the possession of 'vast areas of ocean containing significant mineral and fishery potential', while advantageous human resource endowment arises from 'the comfortable living derived by the bulk of populations from subsistence activities'. As the report puts it: 'There is little hunger or poverty to speak of' (p.1). Official per capita development assistance to PMCs is rated as amongst the highest in the world - $US 225 compared with $170 in the Caribbean.

7. The report is, for instance, critical of both lengthy approval procedures for private investment (saying foreign investment tends to be attracted to countries offering short and clear-cut investment approval procedures), and ownership criteria for business licences that restrict foreign ownership to 49 per cent (arguing that a 'more flexible' arrangement is necessary, especially if foreign investors are unable to find a suitable local business partner (p.40). It also suggests that PMCs consider charging 'a single, lower income tax on all companies, domestic and foreign alike, which could help attract foreign companies' (p.42).

8. This point was made by well-known World Bank critic, Susan George, in a public lecture at the University of the South Pacific in Suva, Fiji in April 1994. In many respects, discussion of environmental questions by the World Bank was unavoidable in the post-UNCED Pacific. Since the Bank's completion of its 1991 economic report, national environmental management plans (NEMS), the product of inter-agency co-operation preparatory to UNCED, were developed for all PMCs under the auspices of the intergovernmental South Pacific Regional Environment Programme (SPREP). The Asian Development Bank (ADB), the United Nations Development Programme (UNDP) and the Australian International Development Assistance Bureau (AIDAB), among others, co-operated to support this endeavour, co-ordinating donor assistance through SPREP to both prepare submissions to UNCED (which was attended by nine heads of government) and to develop NEMS. Regionally, the concept of 'sustainable development in which environmental protection constitutes an integral part of the development process' was endorsed at the highest political level - the South Pacific Forum (p.82). And most Pacific countries also now have in place high-level environmental task forces which interlink regionally (p.79). The report's regional overview notes these developments in its environment chapter and commends them (pp.69, xv).

9. The *Fiji Times* reported that the PNG Minister of Forests had admitted that there had been illegal daily shipments of more than one million *kina* worth of logs; and that in Vanuatu, where rapacious logging had followed the lifting of a ban on log exports last year, the rate of logging was well in excess of the admissible 25,000 cubic metres. The Melanesian Spearhead Group, comprising the Prime Ministers of Papua New Guinea, the Solomon Islands and Vanuatu, had discussed the matter of logging in its 1994 meeting, the report said.

10. See for instance the series of national surveys of island economies written by Te'o Fairbairn and produced as part of AIDAB's International Development Issues Series. Two of these titles are Fairbairn 1991 & 1992.

References

Barr, K. (1990) *Poverty in Fiji,* Suva, Fiji: Fiji Forum for Justice, Peace and the Integrity of Creation

Fairbairn, T. (1991) *The Tongan economy: Setting the stage for accelerated growth,* International Development Issues, no.22, Canberra, Australia: AIDAB

---------- (1992) *The Kiribati economy: Development options and prospects for growth,* International Development Issues no.26, Canberra, Australia: AIDAB

Fiji Times 'Logging Worries Leaders', 14 July 1994

Thaman, R.R. et al. (1992) 'Human development in the Pacific Islands: The relevance and operationalisation of the UNDP human development initiative in the Pacific Islands', unpublished paper prepared for the United Nations Development Program (UNDP), Suva, Fiji

UNICEF/Government of Fiji (1991) *Situation analysis of the children in Fiji,* National Child Policy Committee, Suva, Fiji

UNICEF/Government of Vanuatu (1991) *Situation analysis of children and women in Vanuatu,* Port Vila, Vanuatu

World Bank (1991) *Towards higher growth in Pacific Island economies: Lessons from the 1980s,* vol.1, Regional Overview, and vol.2, Country Surveys

---------- (1993) *Pacific Island economies: Toward efficient and sustainable growth,* vol.1, Overview

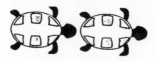

Three

Sanitising the regional environment crisis:
The politics of *The Pacific Way* report*

'Atu Emberson-Bain

Introduction

 The Pacific Way is a 52-page document on the environmental problems facing Pacific countries. It was prepared by the region's leading environmental agency, the South Pacific Regional Environment Programme (SPREP), on behalf of Pacific Island states for the 1992 UNCED Earth Summit in Brazil. The report is the product of several official statements emanating from regional environment and development meetings held during 1991 as well as SPREP's own Action Plan for Managing the Natural Resources and Environment of the South Pacific Region (1991-1995)[1]. It is attractively presented and enhanced by the use of Pacific-based artwork/graphics as well as photographs. It expresses the collective commitment of the 14 Pacific Island Developing Countries (PIDCs) which make up 50 per cent of SPREP's membership to tackling a wide range of increasingly serious environmental and development problems. These include global warming and associated sea-level rise, population growth, urbanisation, deforestation and toxic waste dumping.

 There are a number of reassuring messages that come through *The Pacific Way* and they offer some grounds for optimism to those organisations and individuals committed to promoting sustainable development in the region. One of these is the respect accorded to traditional systems (and knowledge) of resource management and conservation in Pacific societies, and within these the special role, experience and knowledge of women. The action priorities outlined in the final section of the report also contain plenty of promise, calling on Pacific governments to expand and develop existing National Environmental Management Strategies; to promote environmental education and training; and to encourage greater involvement by non-governmental organisations (NGOs) and indigenous communities in environmental decision making and the development process. There are calls for bans on nuclear testing, driftnet fishing and the dumping of toxic, hazardous and nuclear substances, and for the regulation of the activities of transnational corporations (TNCs) operating in the region (pp. 36, 45).

A radical charter?

All this might suggest that *The Pacific Way* is a sound, even radical, charter for sustainable development and environmental protection. Unfortunately, this is not the case, although one might be forgiven for thinking so if only selected parts of the last section (entitled Priorities for Further Action) were read. There is some strong content in *The Pacific Way*, but it is the generally rhetorical and ambivalent nature of the report, and its noticeable ideological leanings, that leave a more lasting impression. The report is short on critical analysis and it contains questionable assumptions about the relationship between economic growth and development, the desirable means of achieving 'sustainable development', and the causes of environmental stress. It also suffers from a conspicuous lack of statistical data (with the exception of natural disasters like hurricanes which are meticulously documented); and there is some strange organisation of material such as scattered commentary on a single issue through different sections which reduces the clarity of certain arguments.

There are other, equally serious, problems. One of these is the inconsistency between the body of the report and the Priorities for Further Action. This is reflected in the marked difference in the organisation and prioritising of issues, sometimes the absence of corresponding problems and concepts, and even contradictory arguments. Some inconsistency also appears within the Priorities section itself, for example in respect of nuclear testing where it curiously states that 'there are few data which can be used for decision-making in this area' and yet recommends that testing be stopped. In the section on climate change, the arguments are similarly weakened by the fact that diagnosis and prescription bear little relation to each other. The report boldly declares that it is the 'industrial countries [which] bear primary responsibility for reducing these [greenhouse gas] emissions'. However, none of its recommendations are directed towards these offenders from the economic North. In like fashion, a general call to regulate the activities of TNCs in the region is not supported by specific proposals. Indeed, there is little that suggests a genuinely critical position in the gentle request to these global giants to 'recognise two cultures - a commercial-style economy and a traditional society' (p.35).

Aside from these problems, the strategies section is perceivably stronger. It offers more incisive commentary, a less compromising position on certain (e.g. the nuclear) issues, and a more militant tone, although few details are given of the human and environmental horror story that has resulted from the use of the region as a 'nuclear playground', to use Stuart Firth's evocative term (Firth 1987). By contrast, simplistic generalisations and misleading platitudes are the order of the day in the main chapters. Coincidentally, editorial discretion appears to have been permitted a freer run in these: so much so in fact that one sometimes gets the impression of reading a tourist brochure or a flotsam and jetsam column rather than an official document. Along with the underpinning politics of *The Pacific Way*, this imbalance between the body and prescriptive section of the report raises doubts about its integrity and credibility as an 'independent' document.

How Pacific the perspective?

In many respects, *The Pacific Way* reflects the political realities of our region. Although the editors (both of whom are Australian) are at pains to point out that it 'does not represent the views of our developed partners in the region nor directly those of their territories', the fact remains that the 27-country membership of SPREP is heavily dominated (around 50%) by the colonial or ex-colonial industrialised powers of the North, either directly or through their territories, and the bulk of its work programme is financed by Australia, the United Nations (through its development and environment programmes [UNDP and UNEP]), the Asian Development Bank (ADB), the World Bank and New Zealand[2]. Moreover, the report concedes that 'they have all participated in the evolution of many consensus positions on sustainable development in our region' (p.7).

The metropolitan influence features in other ways too: in the membership of the ADB and UN agencies like the UNDP and the Economic and Social Commission for Asia and the Pacific (ESCAP) on the Pacific (UNCED) Steering Committee; in the use of expatriate (i.e. non-regional) consultants, including one (a principal contributor) from the ADB itself, for the writing of *The*

Pacific Way report; and in the generous funding provided by Australia, New Zealand and the heavily Japanese-funded ADB. The ADB's own report on 'economic policies for sustainable development', we are advised, provided the model format for *The Pacific Way*. In such circumstances, it would be something of a miracle for a genuine Pacific consensus to have emerged and been freely articulated.

The substantial strategic and economic importance of the Pacific region to colonial powers like France and the United States, as well as Pacific Rim 'partners' Australia, New Zealand and Japan, might explain the guiding metropolitan hand that has evidently been at work in the report to tone down some of its more radical content and less comprising sentiments. Not only a sizeable market for their exports, the region is rich in minerals and other natural resources like oil, fisheries and forestries. Through its combined Exclusive Economic Zones (EEZs), it boasts a fisheries-rich ocean of 30 million square kilometres, three times the size of the USA, and about six per cent of the earth's surface (pp.10, 43). In Papua New Guinea alone, a 2.3 million square kilometre exclusive fishing zone contains over 1,850 species of fish (Callick 1994). For France, there is a (currently suspended) nuclear test programme and military base in French Polynesia, a lucrative nickel industry in New Caledonia, and the general advantages of being a colonial power in a largely decolonised region. Little surprise then that the main sections of the report are silent (unlike the final section containing action recommendations) about the problems of nuclear testing, just as they are about the toxic waste dumping plans of Japan and the disposal of hazardous weaponry by the United States (an oblique reference to chemical weapons on Johnston Atoll). Nor indeed that they should have nothing to say about (French and US) colonialism and militarism as decisive causes of environmental, social, economic, and cultural devastation, even genocide, in the Pacific.

In respect of the region's mining industry which, with the exception of Nauru, is largely controlled by Australian, French and North American corporate interests, the report also fails to confront the unpalatable reality of environmental destruction and social dislocation, both of which have occurred as a consequence of mining 'development'. Mining has been increasingly identified with an uneven distribution of economic benefits and impoverishment, a general disempowerment of local communities, including the loss of land rights, and a scale of social conflict and violence that has reached devastating proportions in cases like Bougainville. The phosphate islands of Nauru and Banaba, the gold and copper regions of Papua New Guinea, nickel-rich New Caledonia, and the gold town of Vatukoula in Fiji all tell grim tales, but they are barely hinted at here.

Indeed, *The Pacific Way* even dispassionately describes as 'inevitable' the environmental degradation caused by mining and argues that the damage 'appears to be acceptable' in those (unspecified) instances where 'degradation is localised and the landowners consider they have been adequately compensated financially' because of the 'substantial' benefits brought by the industry (p.25). The report resorts to speculative language ('can' and 'possibly') about the social and environmental effects of mining, just as it does about nuclear pollution ('might'). In this respect, it is quite a shocking commentary, an insensitive understatement of the damage that has already occurred to the food grounds, homes and livelihoods of thousands of Pacific Islanders[3].

The power relations that underlie economic and political processes in the Pacific region hold the key to other analytical shortcomings and political leanings of *The Pacific Way* report. The North-derived and World Bank-promoted growth model of 'free' market development is peddled throughout the document, and rarely discreetly. At times, the concepts of (sustainable) growth and (sustainable) development are used almost interchangeably. On other occasions, their distinctiveness is ambiguously suggested by a reversible cause-and-effect relationship. Higher rates of economic growth are deemed necessary and, to a great extent sufficient, conditions for economic development and self-reliance. But conversely, the report states, 'long-term economic growth can only be achieved and maintained by following the principles of sustainable development' (p.36). Further, in order to 'implement sustainable development', we are told that 'it will be necessary to ... give greater emphasis to programmes and policies involving the [growth-based] private sector, including trade and investment'. Private sector initiatives aimed at 'sustainable economic growth' are tacitly supported by the structural adjustment programmes of the World Bank and the International Monetary Fund (IMF) (p.36).

Also echoing the 'wisdom' of the North is the contentious perception of population growth as the main environmental bogey facing the Pacific region, like the economic South generally. 'Many resource and environmental concerns', the report claims, 'can be traced to high population densities and the continuing high rate of population growth [as high as 5% in Wallis and Futuna]' (p.15). For Pacific atolls, the report argues, 'finding ways to stem or reduce overpopulation is fundamental to achieving sustainable development' (p.15). A revealing extension of the population growth argument - which captures little of the human sensitivities typical of the Pacific's communalist cultures - are the concerns expressed about urban youth unemployment for which no statistics are given despite the fact that it was rated in 1986 at over 50 per cent in the Marshall Islands and 30 per cent in Fiji (Slatter 1991: 25). The report makes no mention of the social consequences of current unemployment trends, such as their impact on people's livelihoods. It speaks only of their economic costs to the state, despairing of 'an ever-increasing proportion of government funds ... necessarily earmarked for social service needs, with less available for initiatives to stimulate economic development' (p.17).

A disconcerting feature of *The Pacific Way* is its spurious use of the language and symbols of the environment and 'sustainable development' discourses (even the paper is recycled). Culturally sensitive imagery of the 'Pacific Way' is woven deftly through the text and encapsulated in the title; and this cultural 'correctness' is supported by a number of popular myths about the Pacific. The subsistence and monetary economies, we are told, 'exist side by side throughout the Pacific' with the former 'predominating'. And it is the ever growing desire for the material benefits of the monetary economy (apparently by some amorphous mass of Pacific Islanders) rather than the production and consumption excesses of the North, that poses the 'risk' of 'diminish[ing] the ability of the subsistence economy to continue to provide basic foods and other needs traditionally obtained from forest, garden and sea' (p.12). In a diminutive (10-line) section on poverty, the well-worn myth of 'subsistence affluence' is used to discredit (unspecified) 'conventional economic and social indicators' of poverty and to point to, though not to tell, the 'real story' (p.18). Urbanisation and the transition from 'viable subsistence lifestyles' to the monetary economy are seen as 'part of the [poverty] problem', as is 'rapid' resource depletion resulting from 'over-exploitation'. But this recognition of the existence and causes of poverty in Pacific Island states, and the links between the growth-driven market economy on the one hand and environmental degradation and eroding subsistence livelihoods on the other, is just about as far as the deconstruction process goes. The growth ethic ultimately remains sacrosanct and the report reverts to the stereotypical view that poverty is an essentially exaggerated or inappropriate tag to give the Pacific region.

De-romancing the Pacific

This romantic imagery of the Pacific sits uneasily alongside the economic imperialism and underdevelopment that have featured prominently in its history. It is these processes, as opposed to high population growth rates, which have arguably had a more profound impact on the environment and living standards, and which have crippled traditional subsistence economies that were relatively sustainable and self-reliant in pre-contact times. The monetary economy, and specifically its export-driven industries like commercial agriculture, logging and mining, have had a predatory and destructive role in relation to its subsistence 'partner'. They have siphoned off land and labour resources, destroyed or contaminated food grounds, and lowered health and nutritional standards. The livelihoods of an increasing number of rural dwellers are more accurately described as impoverished than 'affluent', and a primary cause has been the 'free' market economy, ironically upheld as the ideal (even the only) road to regional development.

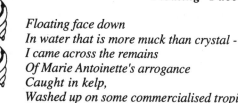

Floating Face Down

Floating face down
In water that is more muck than crystal -
I came across the remains
Of Marie Antoinette's arrogance
Caught in kelp,
Washed up on some commercialised tropical reef,
Tainted by radiation and foreign words.
The sharks tasted better fare
But those days were gone with the second invasion
By the sons of the Rising Sun.
This time the death weapons are far worse
Than the Pearl Harbour bombs and suicide honour.
Is greed an economic necessity?
The death of turtles dolphins whales seals shags
In a high tech death wall
Demarcates the invisibility
Of today's contrasts and society levels.
Who cares anyhow?
The canned fish from Thailand is still plentiful
Purchased aptly by Aid money.
Who wants to die for fish all day
In a lagoon befouled by toxic
Waste and dead coral?
The drinking water rots further north
Substituted by coca cola and budlite
Teeth rot, souls rot,
While the green back rolls in with the incoming tide;
It never quenched anyone's thirst for the nonsense
Of an idyllic tropical paradise -
Its all man made in BoraBora and Guam.
See any travel brochure.

Momoe Malietoa Von Reiche

The failure to discuss the thorny issues of militarism and colonialism also contributes to the sanitised snapshot we are given of the region's environment problems. It is not enough to mention the problems of nuclear testing in isolation from the colonial and neo-colonial structures that perpetuate the abuse of land, sea and human resources for military/nuclear-related activities in the islands of Micronesia and French Polynesia. The build-up of a military/nuclear capability by the industrialised colonial powers of France and the United States must surely be one of the most 'unsustainable' by-products of 'development' ever conceived. Although the pattern of militarisation has been historically forged by countries from the North, politically independent states like Papua New Guinea and Fiji must also bear responsibility for some of the social, economic and environmental destruction that has resulted from military activities in more recent years.

Certain contradictions (and ironies) are evident in the nostalgic celebration of 'tradition' in the report. Repeatedly, we are reminded of the rich value and sustainability of traditional management systems and cultural knowledge and of the need to preserve and use these, or at least what is left of them. On the other hand, the harmony that for centuries has characterised people's relationship with the physical environment and met their subsistence needs is now considered to be outmoded. Traditional resource management and conservation are said to be incapable of satisfying the greater material needs or improving the living standards of Pacific people in today's 'modern' world. In any event, as we are advised in one of several patronising statements, 'traditional controls ... were generally not applied with any specific higher conservation ethic in mind', but were merely 'practical management tools which had developed over many generations to ensure the supply of particular food stocks and medicines' (p.26). In respect of safeguarding biological diversity, the customary land system is even perceived as a hindrance to the implementation of protective environmental policies by Pacific governments (p.28). The challenge facing regional governments is therefore one of balancing the two 'absolutes' of environmental protection and 'the imperatives of economic development' to ensure that growth-led development is 'carried out in an environmentally sound and sustainable manner' (p.36). Ironically, it would seem, traditional production systems are celebrated for their (limited) instrumental value to Western development strategies, rather than as proof of their ability to offer a viable, and historically proven, development alternative.

Blaming the victim?

Ultimately, political factors ensure that many of the structural causes of the region's environmental, economic and social problems are circumvented. Blame and responsibility are inappropriately apportioned. Quite correctly, we are reminded of the fragility of Pacific Island economies and environments, including their small size, physical isolation, vast oceans and narrow resource bases; their vulnerability to natural disasters; and their shortage of appropriate technical and human resources. But in so far as human agency is identified as responsible for the environmental crisis, we are mostly given the impression of some nebulous 'human-induced' process at work, often without any indication that, more often than not, the 'human beings' involved are not in fact Pacific Islanders but foreigners, and the most destructive of them come in corporate form, as unharnessable transnational giants. There is little to be learnt about the region's development nightmares from references to: 'entire islands' having been 'rendered uninhabitable through environmental destruction by human beings'; or the 'human-induced' impacts on coastal areas and marine resources.

Certainly, physical and human resource factors may limit the capacity of Pacific Islanders to protect their environment and livelihoods. They may also hamper the effective integration of Environmental Impact Assessments (EIA) into national development planning. But, contrary to what the report argues, resistance to the use of EIA does not only come from 'some government administrations' (p.37), many of whose personnel have in fact been trained by international agencies like the World Bank and ADB. Private sector business interests have been more actively and consistently opposed to environmental controls, having more to lose from them. Moreover, some of the very agencies that now peddle the respectable 'sustainable development' agenda were themselves responsible for excluding environmental considerations in the past. It was they who set in place the review mechanisms for investment proposals and other development projects and, as a general rule, priority was attached to economic considerations with little, if any, account taken of EIA (p.37).

As for powerful institutions like the World Bank, whose economic vision is a major influence on Pacific Island governments and on the report, a professed sensitivity in recent years to environmental concerns (expressed in environmental assessments and safety clauses of Bank agreements as well as in novel staff and budget allocations) requires a circumspect, if not cynical, reading. According to development critic and writer Susan George, the Bank's environment agenda stems more from a concern about its image and the need to placate its critics, including NGOs in the lending (not the debtor) countries, than from a genuine change of heart. The Bank 'will always be dominated by the market approach, the rate of return approach, and an approval [i.e. project approval] culture, and this will continue in spite of the better rhetoric about the environment[4]'.

The 'blaming the victim' strain of *The Pacific Way* report is not only evident in the treatment of EIAs. It also comes through in the handling of the problem of biocides and other toxic/hazardous wastes[5], as well as in the disdainful asides about local ignorance or incompetence. It is curious that while space is taken up in bemoaning local skill and facility shortages, and the limitations of government regulation procedures, there is no suggestion that countries exporting toxic products like biocides (which include the Pacific's major trading partners like Australia and the United States) should be required to impose restrictions on the trade.

In general, the constraints which Pacific Island countries face in their struggle for sustainable development go much deeper than described in the report. Powerful interests have been the motor of much of the environmental destruction and the activities generated have often been beyond the control of Island countries. But because there are some sensitive nerves that have to be accommodated amongst the PIDC and SPREP membership, we find no discussion of the colonial legacy; no critical analysis of the current development model; no reference to the many inappropriate or environmentally damaging aid projects; and no acknowledgement of the power relations (including foreign control) that have persistently fashioned a subordinate status for Pacific states within the global economy.

For example, the only specific explanation offered for the high rate of internal migration and urbanisation (and the attendant problems of urban congestion, poverty and pollution) is the lack of social services in the outer islands and rural areas. Otherwise, this so-called 'demographic adjustment' is given all the romantic trappings of a travel guide, with people throughout the region simply 'on the move'. Similarly, the case of Ebeye Island in the Marshall Islands is singled out for its phenomenal population density of 23,200 per sq km - one of the highest in the world - but the reader is left completely in the dark about its root causes and devastating effects on people's welfare. The reality of Ebeye is that it is a particular kind of 'human-induced' catastrophe: an impoverished, polluted and disease-ridden 76 acres which has produced an 'unprecedented male suicide epidemic' along with rising rates of crime and violence. This 'ghetto' or 'slum' of the Pacific', as it has been generously termed, is the creation of the US military/defence industry. It is a labour reserve existing solely to service the plush Kwajalein missile base: 'home' to the 'mid-corridor' Islanders of Kwajalein Atoll who were forced out of their own homes so that the US, their United Nations Trust Administrator, could conduct its missile target practice from California (Alcalay 1990:9-10; Emberson-Bain 1992:12, 15-16).

The uncritical acceptance of economic models of the North results in a failure to acknowledge the links between the global economic system and its policies (e.g. structural adjustment and prioritising production for the export market) on the one hand and environmental destruction, deteriorating lifestyles and deepening social inequalities on the other. Discussion on land degradation outlines the pressures placed on food land by the cash crop export economy, with the result that subsistence farming must often be moved to marginal land (pp.24-25). But otherwise, we learn nothing about the connections between this particular environmental problem and the unsustainable livelihoods associated with it, including the negative outcomes for women who typically bear the primary responsibility for tending food gardens.

Treatment of health issues is another example. No comment is made about the relationship between phosphate mining and diabetes or cardio-vascular disease on Nauru; or between nickel mining and respiratory/lung disease (including lung cancer) in French-controlled New Caledonia. While the links are usefully made between the high incidence of nutrition-related non-communicable diseases and the shift to consumption of imported foods of dubious nutritional value and alcohol, and more sedentary lifestyles, the underlying causes of this transition (in particular land losses and forced resettlement, the destruction of food grounds, rural underdevelopment and other features of structural economic dependence and exploitation) are ignored. The rising dependence on imported foodstuffs and other costly and unhealthy consumer goods is at least partly a product of the very growth-led development model that is upheld as exemplary in the report.

Missed opportunities

A welcome feature of *The Pacific Way* is the recognition given to the primary role that women have traditionally played as 'day-to-day managers of many of the region's natural resources' and as environmental educators. It is therefore curious that discussion of women in the body of the report should be limited to a thin subsection of a section on Education and Public Awareness. Otherwise, women do not feature in the report, although they do appear in a few photographs! No mention is made of the critical role they play in the areas of family welfare, food production and economic and social development at the household and community levels. Overall, the report stops well short of advocating women's involvement as equal partners with men in development planning/policy making and resource/environmental management. It calls simply for their greater access to environmental information.

Be warned

O Fagaloa I weep for you
should you open your arms
to the dollar promises of greedy men
who will come with their poison
to build your dreams on

Be warned Fagaloa
that your ocean floors
will not belch forth death
that your guardian hills
will not cast ghostly shadows
to haunt you

Noumea   Simi

Will   you   survive?

I think of you
        dream about you
but in my heart
        is the pain
                of your survival
Will you live?

In my mind
        are the questions
forever wondering
        thinking
                wishing
                        praying
        for you to live
                to survive the
                        changes on
                                our shores

For in you
        lies my identity
                Will You Survive?

Teresa   M.   Pasilio

47

In many respects, the preparation of an official Pacific statement for the Earth Summit in Brazil on behalf of the region's six million people had the potential to open up a straining can of worms. Some fancy foot work by certain vested interests (or their proxies) appears to have saved the day for those who stood to lose from a more open and frank analysis. But for the silent majority of ordinary Pacific Islanders, the Pacific day (and, in the long term, the real Pacific Way) cannot be saved if political interests continue to intrude, so undermining the integrity of the environment/development debate. *The Pacific Way* is an ironic misnomer for what is a demonstrably un-Pacific political document, and the misinformation it contains does much to perpetuate the ignorance and myths about regional development problems. In this sense, the report missed a great opportunity to educate and mobilise Pacific youth, women and NGOs. While it might have made the UNCED and ADB establishments happy, as well as some of our Pacific Rim neighbours, it has limited value for Pacific Islanders themselves, largely because of its failure to confront the global structures and processes that represent the root causes of our environmental crisis and which continue to reproduce the instruments of regional underdevelopment. Unless these processes are themselves challenged and reformed, and unless Pacific people (at the community level) are permitted to speak for themselves, debates about sustainable development and official intergovernment documents like *The Pacific Way* will do little to stem the destructive tide.

Looking ahead

There are, however, some redeeming features of *The Pacific Way* report. As mentioned at the outset of this critique, encouraging statements include the call for a nuclear test ban and the recommendation that codes of conduct should be applied to transnational companies operating in our region. There are also some hard-hitting comments on the twin problems of global warming and sea-level rise which threaten the future survival of thousands of Islanders living on low-lying atolls. In this regard, *The Pacific Way* argues that the industrialised countries must shoulder the responsibility for reducing greenhouse gas emissions and it identifies the 'link between existing forms of energy production, consumption patterns and climate change'.

Other promising areas include development planning. National development planning and environmental management in most Pacific Island states have all too often tended to be top-down and patriarchal in approach; to be conceptualised and administered by urban (male) bureaucratic elites. There has been little consultation with rural communities or women in their capacity as food cultivators and custodians of family welfare. But there are definite possibilities for changing this and for overhauling the system. *The Pacific Way* expresses some welcome sentiments about the need for consultative and democratic decision making and specifically calls for local-level involvement in decisions about resource allocation and management (pp.34, 51). It also recognises the 'critical contribution of subsistence agriculture' - which continues to sustain over 80 per cent of the region's people - 'to the real incomes and quality of life of many South Pacific communities, and its role in providing a basis for self-reliance'. The report acknowledges the value of traditional patterns of land management and food systems including the long-tested methods of regulating hunting, cultivation, tree-felling and fishing practices (pp.40, 26). All told, the rhetoric can, and should, be translated into a real commitment, with concrete policies to build alternative (self-reliant and participatory) development models that meet the needs of the majority of people and which are accountable to them.

In fact, the greater involvement of the region's own human resources - its local communities, NGOs and women - would seem to be where the real (perhaps the only) hope lies for more sustainable and self-reliant forms of development. Part of this task would be to integrate traditional knowledge systems, but not for their instrumental value in advancing macroeconomic growth and strengthening the prevailing free market development model. Traditional knowledge and development ethics can, and should be, incorporated as fundamental, guiding principles of a genuinely 'Pacific Way' model of development. This would provide a sound basis for safeguarding and enhancing the long-term supply of food, (traditional) medicines, craft materials and other resources necessary for the reproduction of sustainable livelihoods. The problems faced by Pacific governments such as the shortage of information on national ecosystems, untrained or inexperienced staff, and the loss of traditional knowledge about the environment and resource management practices (all of which are lamented in the report) have a greater chance of being resolved if a more participatory development model is forged - one that is grounded in community perspectives and needs. Apart from the ethical considerations that justify this, it would seem to make practical sense to incorporate the views of those who are most directly (and often adversely) affected by development projects. It is they who are, in many ways, the real 'experts' on environmentally sound resource use.

*   An earlier version of this critique of the Pacific Island Developing Countries' Report to the United Nations Conference on Environment and Development (UNCED), 1992, was presented to the Pacific Regional Meeting on Women, Environment and Development sponsored by Development Alternatives with Women for a New Era (DAWN), University of the South Pacific, Suva, Fiji, in December 1992.

Notes

1. For a discussion of the SPREP Action Plan and a critical overview of SPREP's activities and orientation, see Bryant (1992).

2. SPREP's core budget for 1992 was reported to be $US 5,188,685, of which Australia contributed $1.4 million, UNDP - $950,000, ADB - $0.56 million, New Zealand - $0.47 million and UNEP - $0.35 million (SPREP 1992/93). In April 1993, a five-year South Pacific Biodiversity Conservation Programme was financed to the tune of $US 10 million by the Global Environment Facility, a joint initiative of the World Bank, UNDP and UNEP.

3. One of a number of Marshall Island communities affected by the US nuclear weapons-testing programme in the 1950s - the people of Rongelap Atoll - have lodged a claim for $US 100 million in compensation for radiation-induced health disorders and other damages. The Nuclear Claims Tribunal set up in the Marshall Islands by the United States has approved $US 20.8 million for personal injury claims although, to date, only a portion of this amount has been paid up (Fraser 1993a).

4. George expressed these views in a public lecture at the Suva-based University of the South Pacific, in April 1994.

5. According to the United Nations Environment Programme (UNEP), an annual 400 million tonnes of hazardous waste are generated globally, 98 per cent of which is produced by the industrialised countries. Since 1986, 'developing' countries (including countries in the Pacific region) have been targets of repeated attempts to dump over 163 million tonnes of this waste (Fraser 1993b).

References

Alcalay, G.H. (1990) Submission to the 57th Session of the United Nations Trusteeship Council, New York

Bryant, J. (1992) 'The South Pacific Regional Environment Programme - Changes in perspective or pragmatic response to global realities? A critique of the SPREP Action Plan', background paper prepared for the DAWN Regional Meeting on Women, Environment and Development, Suva, Fiji, 1-4 December

Callick, R. (1994) 'Fishing for a break from Moresby' in *Islands Business,* February

Emberson-Bain, 'A. (1992) 'Perilous pursuits: The environmental and social impact of the mining and nuclear industries in the Pacific', paper presented to the Social Science Research Council (New York)/DAWN Workshop on Population and the Environment, Mexico, January-February

Firth, S. (1987) *Nuclear playground,* Sydney: Allen and Unwin

Fraser, H. (ed.) (1993a) *Pacific Report,* vol.6, no.8

---------- (1993b) *Pacific Report,* vol.6, no.6

Slatter, C. (1991) 'Situation analysis of Pacific children: A regional perspective', paper prepared for the United Nations Children's Fund (UNICEF), Pacific Office, Suva, Fiji

South Pacific Regional Environment Programme (1992/93) Annual Report, Apia, Western Samoa

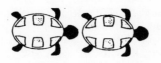

Four

The Pacific aid regime:
Continuity and change*

Premjeet Singh

Introduction

The South Pacific Islands are recipients of multilateral, bilateral and non-governmental aid, and more (per capita) foreign aid dollars are probably poured into the South Pacific region than into any other part of the developing world (UNCTAD 1985; Hoadley 1992:29). The total volume of official grant aid inflows into the region is estimated to be an annual $US 250 million in the 1990s; this includes country programmes, overseas training, payments to managing agents and other direct payments. Aid is a key source of investment financing in the South Pacific region, contributing at least 20 per cent of gross domestic product (GDP) except in Fiji where it accounts for just five per cent of GDP (World Bank 1993:9). The region's major donors are Australia, Japan, the European Community (EC) and the Asian Development Bank (ADB) which together account for 60 per cent of total aid inflows. Australia is the largest single donor, contributing 25 per cent of total assistance.

According to Hoadley (1992), high levels of aid in the Pacific region can be attributed to its greater creditworthiness, that is, its ability to assure overseas lending agencies of the security of their loans. He takes aid to be inclusive of World Bank-type loans, arguing that creditworthiness in the region is illustrated, firstly, by the fact that no Pacific Island country has so far defaulted on its loan repayments (although Western Samoa asked for a rescheduling of repayments in the 1980s); and, secondly, by the low debt service burdens in the region by third world standards[1]. Hoadley proposes that levels of borrowing are conditioned by the ability to utilise funds and not by the availability or willingness of lenders. This theory ignores the political and economic considerations that have determined the volume of financial resource flows into the Pacific region. This paper attempts to demonstrate how political and economic factors continue to influence official development assistance (ODA) and commercial loans from international financial institutions like the World Bank. In the following discussion, ODA is taken to refer to official development assistance grants as well as soft or low-interest loans.

Conventional (aid) wisdom

Amongst the establishment views about aid in the region are concerns about an aid-dependence 'mentality' and the artificially high living standards that are held to have resulted from high levels of aid (Fairbairn 1985 & 1986; Pollard 1988). According to Pollard (1988), current levels of welfare for South Pacific nations could not be maintained without continued aid. In turn, Hoadley (1992:29) argues that aid enables South Pacific people to have a satisfactory standard of living in spite of scarce resources and limited export earnings. Economic and social progress in the region are also seen by the World Bank to be linked in some measure to continuing aid inflows, although the Bank notes the lack of growth in Pacific Island economies despite the massive injection of aid funds. The use of aid funds on non-growth-creating projects and their inefficient management are suggested reasons for this (World Bank 1993:10-12). Calls for greater efficiency and accountability, and criticism of the 'Pacific Way' style of managing aid funds have even come from regional intergovernmental institutions like the South Pacific Commission (SPC) (Sokomanu cited in Waqa 1992:25).

There are a number of responses that can be made to these criticisms. First, patterns of aid distribution raise questions about the 'trickle down' of benefits to Pacific Island people. Aid is not distributed equally amongst island states. Smaller Polynesian and Micronesian states generally receive more per capita assistance than their Melanesian counterparts (Hoadley 1992:29) although Australian aid to Papua New Guinea (PNG) is disproportionately high (Jackson Committee 1984 & Canberra Times 7 May 1991). The unequal distribution of aid funds is also evident within countries where, as a general rule, only a minimal amount of aid reaches the poorer and disadvantaged sections of the community. As Sevele (1985:4) argues, these marginalised categories are

> the people who are under-served by health, housing, community, transport and administrative facilities. Little aid reaches them because the development policies of the recipient countries generally favour urban-based projects and activities in which poor people cannot participate owing to their peculiar circumstances.

High aid allocations to the military and defence issues (for example, $AUS 50 million is given to PNG by Australia every year) also mean that fewer aid resources are available for improving the living standards of the majority of people.

On foreign aid

Nobody understands why
there is no joy
when the dollars roll
from year in year out
with pledges of goodwill
inviting

Nobody understands for
it is easy to sink into
the comforts of Jap-made boats
and speedy journeys
on Aussie-paved highways
blinding

Nobody understands that
independence was a noble effort
to break from the strongholds
and hands-tied alliances forever
stamping our future on Kiwi plaques
reminding

Nobody understands because
we have sold our national pride
and dreamt for our children
destinies in foreign lands
feeding the bloodline of dependency
hooking

We understand but we will not
for like addicts we no longer feel
the pains of our achievements
the joys of our toils
the stigma of asking
dawning

Will we ever?

Noumea Simi

Second, a 'hand-out' mentality has been ascribed to aid-receiving Pacific Island states. It is probably true to say that Pacific leaders have generally proved receptive to aid overtures, on occasion even demanding more than donors have been willing to provide. The angry response of PNG Prime Minister Michael Somare, when informed of an imminent decrease in Australian aid in line with recommendations by the 1984 Jackson Committee (*Pacific Islands Monthly* May 1994), and the suggestion of Tuvalu's Prime Minister Bikenibeu Paeniu that New Zealand should spend all its aid in the South Pacific region (Barber 1990:5) are symbolic of a 'claims-mentality' amongst some Pacific leaders. Perceiving aid as an easier revenue-raising mechanism than the tougher alternative of development or management of local resources and industries, some South Pacific governments continue to push for increasing aid levels, as reflected during the recent Barbados conference on small island states and sustainable development. Grynberg's example of the need for better management of regional tuna fisheries (the Pacific accounts for 55 per cent of the world's tuna consumption) is a case in point (Grynberg 1993).

Third, whatever the evidence pointing to an emerging 'aid mentality' in the region, aid dependence has had clear advantages for donor countries, and aid flows have been motivated primarily by their own interests rather than the priorities and needs of recipient countries. Aid is the price that powerful nations have had to pay to maintain their political sphere of influence; a consideration as important in the current era as in the heyday of superpower rivalry. In colonial territories like French Polynesia and the Trust Territories of Micronesia, for example, aid has strengthened the presence of France and the United States as metropolitan powers in the region. Related to this, France has more recently encouraged cooperation between its colonies and independent Pacific states which were previously opposed to French colonialism. This has paved the way for its greater involvement in regional affairs. More importantly, France's aid 'generosity' has helped to silence at least some of the opposition to its nuclear testing policies and continued colonial rule. Development assistance has been used to support France's ascendancy as 'the third superpower' in the region (Chand 1993).

In those independent Pacific Island states which receive high levels of aid (for example, PNG and Fiji)[2], political sovereignty and the prospects for achieving economic independence can also be undermined, with recipient states being continuously vulnerable to political and economic pressures from lending institutions or countries. Sevele (1985) contends that the political, strategic and commercial reasons that determine aid donations ensure that, as Pacific Island economies become increasingly dependent on donor funding, they will continue to serve the strategic and, to a lesser extent, commercial interests of donors. Western countries clearly recognise the strategic and economic value of the region and, in turn, the strategic value of aid as an effective means of maintaining an appropriate political and economic climate. Forum Island countries account for approximately 30 per cent of total New Zealand exports, for example, and are important trading partners for Australia. In addition, Forum member countries hold 13 seats in the United Nations.

The tied nature of most aid in the form of soft loans similarly illustrates economic and political benefits for donors. Only a small fraction of aid inflows is in grant form. As mentioned above, an estimated $US 250 million in ODA is given to the region. But Australia's aid to PNG alone is estimated at over $AUS 300 million (Ministry for Development Cooperation & Pacific Island Affairs 1993:12). The heavy loan component of financial resource flows shows the extent to which aid is tied to commercial returns for donors and the role it plays in promoting indebtedness amongst Pacific Island states.

The responses of aid donors to past Pacific Island fishing agreements with the Soviet Union offer a good illustration of the strategic or political factors that underlie aid 'generosity' in the region. As Doulman (1986) shows, the United States and other Western states increased their aid levels to Kiribati in the 1980s in response to a fishing agreement it signed with the Soviet Union. In Fiji, following the military coups of 1987, offers of substantial aid from non-traditional donors like France and Japan demonstrated overt support for an illegitimate authoritarian regime unacceptable to most other countries (Prasad 1991; AMPO Japan-Asia Quarterly Review 1990). Amongst other objectives, the French and Japanese governments both wished to 'buy' Fiji's silence - the former with respect to continued colonial rule in New Caledonia and a nuclear testing programme in French Polynesia, and the latter over driftnet fishing operations and the dumping of toxic wastes in Pacific waters, both practices having been condemned internationally and by most Pacific Island governments.

In turn, the overtures of Fiji's military-backed government to France and a number of South-East Asian countries had traditional allies like Australia and New Zealand restoring political and economic ties within a relatively short time, for fear of being marginalised (Howard 1991). In spite of its responsibility for extinguishing democracy in 1987, the interim military-installed administration suffered few political losses and, in the long term, few outside-imposed economic costs. Although the country was affected by early suspensions in aid flows and other punitive measures such as trade union-sponsored economic sanctions, foreign aid still continued to flow into the country to assist in the rebuilding of the collapsed economy. This enabled policies favoured by the interim administration to be implemented (Howard 1991; Kasper 1988).

Political and commercial interests continue to influence the aid flows from Japan and France in the 1990s. The $US 70 million Japanese ODA programme announced for the 1990s for South Pacific countries can be perceived as an attempt to continue to 'buy' their acceptance for Japan's nuclear waste dumping plans for the Pacific Ocean (which have not been abandoned), and as a means of winning support for the operations of Japanese companies in the region. Normally quite vocal, Fiji has been non-committal on these issues in recent regional meetings, reflecting not just the aid-based 'divisions' prevalent amongst Forum Island countries competing for scarce aid resources, but also the changing political direction (notably the collapse of democratic structures) in the immediate aftermath of the 1987 military coups. Currently, huge sums of money are paid for Japanese imports; Japan is an export market for the region's valuable natural resources; and Japanese aid is used to promote resource exploitation. Not surprisingly perhaps, fisheries-related aid claims a high percentage of the grant component of Japanese aid, enabling Japan to acquire fishing rights in the Exclusive Economic Zones (EEZs) of regional countries, especially for tuna fishing (AMPO Japan-Asia Quarterly Review 1990; Grynberg 1993). An attempt to clinch bilateral tuna-fishing deals with Pacific Island states could be seen as a related underlying motive of Japan's 'generosity'. Unlike the United States, Japan has to date failed to sign multilateral treaties with the Forum Fisheries Agency (FFA).

Political considerations can also be linked to arguments about the need for donor co-ordination and improved efficiency in the management of aid funds mentioned above. These arguments are part of a broader plan to deregulate and privatise Pacific Island economies. Aid or development 'assistance' is an important political lever that for some donors - especially powerful international financial institutions like the World Bank and the International Monetary Fund (IMF) - is becoming increasingly conditional on the adoption of certain macroeconomic policies which favour a supposedly more efficient private sector. That is, access to assistance (in the form of large loans or development projects) is becoming contingent on meeting certain conditions such as deregulation of the economy, privatisation, export-oriented production and other policies. Adopted by regional governments as part of structural adjustment programmes and in order to promote economic growth, such policies have paved the way for continued donor support from bilateral and multilateral agencies although they do not have the support of the majority of people in the region. The strong opposition to the introduction of value-added tax (VAT) in Fiji (Chand 1991) and a similar goods and service tax in Western Samoa offers two examples of local-level opposition.

Other conditionalities tied to bilateral aid arrangements with the World Bank include substantial cutbacks in the already scarce resources allocated to the social sector, especially health, education and welfare. In Western Samoa, residents are expected to begin feeling the pinch from reduced social services as the government concentrates on merging agencies, cutting jobs and tightening living standards (Aiavao 1993). More generally, current development policies of 'economic growth, export development, privatisation in the sale of natural resources' are already being perceived as detrimental to Pacific development. According to former SPC Secretary-General Atanraoi Baiteke, they are leading to 'worsening malnutrition, over-crowded towns, environmental degradation, worsening crime and broken families' (quoted in *Islands Business* November 1992:12).

The new aid regime: From official aid to NGOs

Non-governmental organisations (NGOs) including churches (which have historically played a key role in education) and other voluntary organisations provide substantial resources to the Pacific Islands (World Bank 1993). There are almost 500 local and foreign NGOs which have based their operations in the South Pacific (Pierce 1991). Both local and foreign NGOs have operated in the region for a long time, with non-governmental aid being administered prior to government aid. Since early colonisation, the churches were the most prominent NGOs active in the Pacific and they continue to dominate (Crocombe 1992). While secular NGOs such as the Red Cross have been in existence prior to World War II, the 1980s have seen a boom of these NGOs in the region. This has been attributed to increasing support for their activities from bilateral and multilateral agencies (World Bank 1993; Pierce 1991).

Compared to other countries in the region, Fiji and the Solomon Islands have the most developed and effective national NGO networks or associations. Fiji also has the highest number of NGOs in the region, followed by the Solomon Islands. But NGOs are active in all countries and are closely involved in health, education, development, environment and women's issues. They have advocated aid for small-scale projects concerned with improving social conditions like health, literacy and law and order which are currently seen as barriers to social progress in certain countries. Although relationships between governments and NGOs have at times had their difficulties or tensions, Pacific governments appear to have generally favoured links with NGOs in order to utilise their well-developed networks and effectiveness in delivering services to grassroots communities (Pierce 1991; World Bank 1993). Official acceptance of NGOs acknowledges the benefits they bring, for example their ability to raise finance and their competence in carrying out successful grassroots projects. Moreover, NGOs are cheap sources of expertise and human resources for struggling Pacific Island states. Not surprisingly, they are increasingly being viewed as 'partners in development' by influential development organisations like the United Nations Development Programme (UNDP).

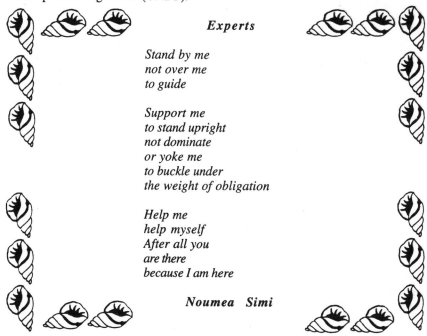

Experts

*Stand by me
not over me
to guide*

*Support me
to stand upright
not dominate
or yoke me
to buckle under
the weight of obligation*

*Help me
help myself
After all you
are there
because I am here*

Noumea Simi

Governments in most countries of the region appear to have become more and more supportive of NGOs over time, although levels of support differ from country to country. The growing prominence of NGOs, their increasing activities, and their closer links with aid agencies are being encouraged by recent moves on the part of international donor agencies like the IMF and World Bank to incorporate them into their programmes. These developments are the result of several factors including World Bank policies of privatisation and deregulation which, as in other parts of the world, aim to further integrate NGOs into government aid policies and projects, and specifically social welfare schemes. The shift towards NGOs as official aid declines (see below) thus does not imply a major change in the objectives of aid, nor a change in the preferred development paradigm. Former aid trends and priorities are basically continuing within the established framework of 'modernisation' and the economic growth model, with the greater role of NGOs being part of cost-cutting measures encouraged for social services by the Bank. By relegating to NGOs certain state responsibilities for development and people's welfare, deregulation policies are in this way enabling governments to reduce their social commitments and to require NGOs to fill the welfare gaps they are creating.

Of more importance perhaps is that once highly acclaimed grassroots organisations appear to be being coopted by donors. The current funding of NGOs by foreign donors raises questions about their ability to remain autonomous, as well as their ability to serve the interests of grassroots communities. Only government-supported and high-profile NGOs are generally provided financial assistance, while smaller community-based organisations are often ignored. The impact of increasing donor expectations and funding of NGOs on their development roles and general effectiveness is a matter of serious concern for the development prospects of the region. So is the extent to which NGO ideologies and independence could be compromised as a result of their increasing co-operation with, and even cooption by, donors.

The intrusion of aid politics into the NGO arena illustrates that the incorporation of NGOs is far from neutral. Of major concern also is that the significant roles of NGOs as development agents, and particularly as independent critics of (or forces of resistance against) current development policies, could be undermined. By diverting NGOs into primarily welfare roles, Pacific Island states may be killing two birds with one stone: the threat of NGOs as an alternative development force is nipped in the bud, while the resources channelled to them are - as far as governments and international financial institutions are concerned - more 'fruitfully' deployed. The dominant neo-classical approach to development and its market policies can in this way continue unchecked, with new-found (and to some extent naive) 'allies'.

Conclusion

The emerging trend in aid flows to the Pacific region is a general decline in official aid (World Bank 1993). New Zealand's aid allocation of $US 5 million to Niue in 1993 is a significant reduction from assistance levels in previous years (it received close to $US 7 million in 1990 or US $3,500 per capita) and is largely due to New Zealand's own economic problems (*Daily Post* 26 May 1993). On the other hand, the closure of a number of offices of the United States Agency for International Development (USAID) in the region, including its office in Fiji, indicates a desire on the part of the US government to adopt a lower regional profile in order to concentrate its resources in Eastern Europe where several aid offices have been established.

This shift does not, however, appear to signal a more widespread trend. Australia, New Zealand, France and Japan have not increased aid levels to the region, but they have maintained past levels. Australia's Minister for Development Co-operation and Pacific Island Affairs, Gordon Bilney, has, moreover, urged the Economic and Social Commission for Asia and the Pacific (ESCAP) to increase funding for Pacific Island states, arguing that they do not receive enough priority or recognition (*Daily Post* 24 April 1993). For New Zealand, an overall decline in aid has in fact seen a cut in Asia-funded projects and a corresponding increase in aid levels to the South Pacific[3], including Fiji, where aid levels are increasing steadily after being drastically cut following the military coups of 1987. New Zealanders have reportedly felt it appropriate that most of the country's aid budget was spent in the South Pacific (Applied Research Consultants 1987).

In spite of economic recession in donor countries and the reconstruction of Eastern Europe - both developments appearing to have drawn aid funds away from the region - Australia and New Zealand continue to recognise the region's importance as a source of trade and resources. Recent trade missions, particularly to Fiji and PNG, confirm this (Tiffany 1993). Despite the growing importance of Asia, the Pacific will almost certainly continue to receive its fair share of attention (and aid funding) and to feature amongst Australian and New Zealand trade and investment priorities. Being the region's largest partner, Australia perceives a need to maintain stability in the region. Australian Minister for Foreign Affairs Gareth Evans has reportedly stated that the region is of the highest foreign policy and security significance and that Australia has 'fundamental, long-standing and unchanging interests' in it (Lakhan 1993:37).

According to the World Bank, a decrease in aid resources will inadvertently have an accentuated negative impact on economic growth (World Bank 1993:xi-xii). But while adjustments to smaller aid volumes may prove difficult for small island states (and particularly their governments) which have come to rely on foreign financial assistance as a crucial source of revenue, reduced aid flows may in the long term in fact enable them to improve their chances of building self-reliant and sustainable development. The high volumes of aid to the region have not, on the Bank's own admission, led to higher economic growth. More importantly, they have failed to improve the quality of life of the ordinary mass of people, including the socially disadvantaged and others who are supposed to benefit from aid. The growing levels of poverty and the widening gaps between the poor and rich in Pacific countries are not being recognised as serious development issues by regional governments. Similarly, the disproportionate and controversial allocations of aid to the military in countries like Fiji and PNG are not being questioned as being contrary to the development interests of people in the region[4]. It is also arguable that aid has undermined efforts to build self-reliance and economic independence by involving trade-offs such as the acceptance of World Bank/IMF prescriptions. The current decline in official development assistance may therefore be opportune. The end of the cold war, and the reduction in aid flows to the Pacific region that has resulted, may yet be a blessing in disguise!

* I gratefully acknowledge the assistance given by 'Atu Emberson-Bain in reworking this paper which was originally drawn from a chapter of my MA thesis 'Collaboration or constraint: NGOs and donor agencies in Fiji' (work in progress).

Notes

1. In 1991, debt servicing claimed 10 per cent of export earnings in Fiji, eight per cent in Western Samoa and less than five per cent for other Pacific members of the World Bank (World Bank 1991:17).

2. Australian aid to PNG is almost three times the amount allocated to the rest of the South Pacific region. For example, in Australia's 1992-93 allocation, PNG received $AUS 334.3 million compared to $118.2 million shared between the other countries of the region (Ministry for Development Cooperation & Pacific Island Affairs 1993:12).

3. Currently 70 per cent of New Zealand's aid, totalling approximately $NZ 100 million, is allocated to the Pacific region, mostly in the form of bilateral aid (which totalled $NZ 60 million for 1991-92) but also through regional organisations, multilateral channels and non-governmental organisations (Crocombe 1992).

4. In Fiji, for example, expenditure has been redirected away from social services and into the military in the years following the military coups of 1987. Between 1986 and 1991, the operating budget of the Fiji Military Forces virtually doubled from $FIJ 16.5 million to $31 million while the social welfare budget fell from $2 million to $1.8 million in 1988, after which it rose modestly to $3 million (Emberson-Bain 1992:149).

References

Aiavao, U. (1993) 'Tough words, tough future: Lutah targets Coleman team' in *Islands Business,* January/February

AMPO Japan-Asia Quarterly Review (1990) 'Japanese aid nets Pacific Islands' vol.21, no.4

Applied Research Consultants (1987) 'Overseas aid and development: New Zealand public attitudes and beliefs', Advisory Committee on External Aid and Development, Wellington, New Zealand

Barber, D. (1990) 'Remember Lange's big promise to boost aid?' in *Pacific Islands Monthly,* October

Canberra Times 7 May 1991, 'The quality of our foreign aid'

Chand, G. (1991) 'Value added tax - Its impact on the working class of Fiji', Discussion Paper, Fiji Trades Union Congress Labour Summit, Suva, Fiji, 21-22 June

--------- (1993) 'France and South Pacific regionalism in the 1980s and 1990s' in *Journal of Pacific Studies,* vol.17, School of Social and Economic Development, University of the South Pacific, Suva, Fiji

Crocombe, R. (1992) *Pacific neighbours: New Zealand's relations with the Pacific Islands,* Christchurch, New Zealand: Centre for Pacific Studies, University of Canterbury & Suva, Fiji: Institute of Pacific Studies, University of the South Pacific

Daily Post 24 April 1993 'Australia urges ESCAP to increase funds'

--------- 26 May 1993 'US 5 million budget agreement'

Doulman, J. (1985) 'Paradise lost? The past performance and future prospects of small island developing countries' in Dommen, E.C. and Hein, P. (eds) *States, microstates and islands,* London: Croom Helm

Emberson-Bain, 'A. (1992) 'Fiji: Women, poverty and post-coup pressure' in Robie, D. *Tu galala: Social change in the Pacific,* Sydney, Australia: Bridget Williams Books/Pluto Press

Fairbairn, T. (1985) *Island economies: Studies from the South Pacific,* Suva, Fiji: Institute of Pacific Studies, University of the South Pacific

----------- (1986) 'Pacific Island economies: Development strategies and options', paper presented to Conference on Island Economies: North-South Relations and the Transfer of Technology, Port-de-France, Martinique, (mimeo), Pacific Island Development Program, Honolulu, Hawaii

Grynberg, R. (1993) 'The tuna dilemma' in *Pacific Islands Monthly,* May

Hoadley, S. (1992) *The South Pacific foreign affairs handbook,* Sydney: Allen & Unwin and New Zealand Institute of International Affairs

Howard, M. (1991) *Fiji: Race and politics in an island state,* Vancouver: Social Sciences and Humanities Research Council of Canada

Islands Business (1992) 'Regional development needs better management, not brakes', November

Jackson Committee (1984) *Report of the Committee to Review the Australian Overseas Aid Program,* Canberra: Australian Government Publishing Service

Kasper, W. et al. (1988) *Fiji: Opportunity from adversity,* GIS Pacific Papers 1, Sydney, Australia: Centre for Independent Studies

Lakhan, A. (1993) 'Regional superpower' in *Pacific Islands Monthly,* January

Ministry for Development Cooperation and Pacific Island Affairs (1993) *Australia's development cooperation program, 1993-94,* Canberra: Australian Government Publishing Service

Pacific Islands Monthly (1984) '"Bloody upset" says Somare', May

Pierce, T. (1991) *Study of non-governmental organisations,* Suva: United Nations Development Programme

Pollard, S. (1988) 'Atoll economies: Issues and strategy options for development', Islands/Australia Working Paper no.88/5

Prasad, S. (1991) 'Fiji: Socio-political dislocation, economic maldevelopment and an increasing role for Japan' in *Research report,* no.16, Institute for Peace Science, Hiroshima University, Japan

Sevele, F. (1985) 'Aid to the Pacific Islands reviewed', paper delivered at the Auckland Conference on Pacific Studies, Auckland, New Zealand, August 19-22

Tiffany, M. (1993) 'More trade expected' in *Pacific Islands Monthly,* May

United Nations Commission for Trade and Development (UNCTAD) (1985) 'Examination of the particular needs and problems of island developing countries' in Dommen, E.C. and Hein, P. (eds) *States, microstates and islands,* Sydney, Australia: Croom Helm

Waqa, V. (1992) 'The new man at top in decision-making must be within the realm of the Pacific Island nations' in *Islands Business,* November

World Bank (1991) *Towards higher growth in Pacific Island economies: Lessons from the 1980s,* vol.1, Regional Overview, and vol.2, Country Surveys

------- (1993) *Pacific Island economies: Toward efficient and sustainable growth,* vol.1, Overview

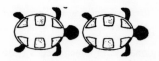

Five

Women, development and population:
A critique of the Port Vila Declaration*

Vanessa Griffen

The Pacific point of view

The Port Vila Declaration on Population and Sustainable Development was formally approved at a meeting of senior government officials and ministers held in Port Vila, Vanuatu, in September 1993. The Vila meeting followed other meetings by Pacific Island leaders at which population and development issues had been raised (for example, the Pacific Island Leaders Conference in Tahiti in June 1993 also came up with a number of statements on population and development). The Port Vila Declaration represented the official Pacific position in preparation for the International Conference on Population and Development (ICPD) scheduled for Cairo in September 1994.

The comments that follow are based on a critical reading of the Declaration and the ideas on population and development that it contains. It needs to be noted that the content of the Declaration is distinct from the ideas expressed in papers and discussions on population and sustainable development at the Vila meeting. Like all declarations, the Port Vila document is couched in official language and it contains statements from representatives present at the meeting, statements drafted in the early stages before the meeting began, and statements that could not be politely, or for political reasons, drafted out. There are, in short, many contributions to the document which arose from this meeting of Pacific Island bureaucrats and politicians (most at ministerial level). The basic draft of the document would also have been prepared by the officiating agency, the Forum Secretariat.

The document is distinguished here then from the papers commissioned for the meeting, many of which raised important and compelling questions on population and sustainable development in the region. Some of the questions raised on development and population, and the need to change present ways of addressing these issues, were not taken up or did not appear to be of interest to the official Pacific Island representatives present. One can perhaps speculate that task-oriented meetings are not the place for such issues to be pursued. The lack of examination of these questions, however, especially those that queried direct correlations between population growth and 'problems of development', surfaces in the Declaration, which has an uneven mix of old and new ideas on population and sustainable development.

The critique that follows will, firstly, be of the Port Vila Declaration as a political text (not that it was intended as such); and secondly, as a document on population (prepared for the Cairo Conference) that has implications for reproductive health and population programmes, which in turn inevitably affect women. The document can be regarded as a political text because of its standing as the region's declaration for ICPD, containing official Pacific ideas and sentiments on population and sustainable development. At face value, it is supposed to represent the collective stand of Pacific governments on population and sustainable development, presented to the world on behalf of the region's people.

The Port Vila Declaration expresses a number of concerns - about sustainable economic growth, about population growth exceeding economic growth, and about the need to 'balance' the two. Recognition of the central role of custom and tradition, and the strong affinity people have with the land (and sea), is paid token attention in statements more directly focused on economic growth and population growth, where the former is the limited concept of development that is to be sustained. The bridging phrase (not just in the Port Vila Declaration but internationally) to obscure the causal connection often implied between population growth and unsustainable development, is the need to maintain people's 'quality of life'. Concern to maintain the quality of life is an argument that has been forcefully put forward, especially at official level, as a reason for maintaining, but with new gender-sensitive additions, population policies that are sometimes narrowly focused on controlling reproduction - i.e. fertility control, which has a direct impact on women.

The Port Vila Declaration contains a number of contradictions while also making statements that express laudable commitments to the environment, people's welfare and the provision of services. Its ultimate commitment, however, is to an uncritically proclaimed goal of economic growth. First on the list of 'key population and sustainable development issues' is 'sustainable economic growth'. In the document there is no Pacific Island definition of development; nor is there any discussion of the type of development desired for Pacific Island people. There is also no effort to spell out the way in which economic growth will produce the desired 'quality of life' or standard of living, or 'development' for the majority of Pacific Island peoples. The ideas about sustainable development for the region are less forcefully presented than the repeated references to sustained economic growth. Indeed, the separation of ideas about 'economic growth' from ideas about 'development' is evident in the document, reflecting the lack of attention given to any broader concept of 'development' in the region.

One major criticism of the document is just how little there is to distinguish it from those of other regions in its general views on, or commitments to, population and sustainable development. One would think that Pacific Island governments could come up with some perspectives on population and development that reflect the unique features of the region. The discussion of population growth accepts conventional demographic definitions of 'high' growth rates and, in the strategy sections, the emphasis on family planning programmes and services is predictable and revealing of fairly narrow fertility control objectives.

The island context or Pacific views of what is considered a good quality of life by and for Pacific Island peoples, are not expressed in the document. The Declaration's 'official' status is reflected in its stated concerns: while there is some reference to island values (custom and tradition), these appear more as essential Pacific rhetorical flourishes rather than sentiments intrinsic to discussions of economic growth, sustainable development and population.

Population and the environment

The Declaration makes commitments to reducing unsustainable patterns of production and consumption and to providing access to safe and effective family planning services. On the environment, concern is expressed about changes brought about by new technology and 'economic activities', but the latter is left as a euphemism which does not differentiate environmentally damaging subsistence activities (which do exist) from damaging commercial activities that are part of the economic growth model supported by most island governments for their countries. The impression is thus given that people (undifferentiated) are having an impact on the environment through their consumption and production activities. Differentiation of the production and consumption activities in the region is not outlined. The extractive economic activities of timber or mining companies usually have a greater and more damaging environmental effect than the indiscriminate or unwise clearing of forests by villagers. The technology and rationale of these 'economic activities' are different. The level of technology involved in logging and mining, for example, has far more impact on the environment in the Pacific, but no recognition of these different impacts is given, even as an indication that population stresses (and people) are not the main, or only, cause of pressure on the environment.

It could be argued that references to the range of impacts on the environment appears elsewhere in Pacific statements on the environment, but what is lacking in the Port Vila Declaration are statements which indicate, strongly enough from the Pacific, an awareness that **some** economic growth activities are in direct contradiction to concepts of sustainable development. The omission of these references in an important regional declaration on population and sustainable development is problematic because it leaves us with the impression that population growth alone is the main factor affecting the environment, development and the quality of life of Pacific Island societies and people.

The document makes references to policies aimed at slowing down population growth and alleviating poverty, and it makes commitments to reducing environmentally dangerous production and consumption patterns. This gives the impression that the problem begins with production and consumption by people at the community level. No reference is made to resource extraction and export activities organised at the level (and intensity) of local, multinational or foreign companies - government-supported economic activities that contribute, in official terms, to economic growth. In some countries, these extractive and export-oriented activities are having far more impact on the environment, and local communities are protesting against the environmental effects (see for example the extreme case of Bougainville, which is by no means simply an environmental issue; and logging activities in the Solomon Islands, Vanuatu and Papua New Guinea).

Development for people

For the Pacific, the emphasis on economic growth is not questioned in the document - it would be surprising if it were. But more than that, the objective of this growth - development for people - is not forwarded anywhere as the rationale for the commitment to economic growth, and this gap is very revealing. Also, there is no attempt to write in sustainable development, Pacific-defined, as a goal in itself. The concern about population is, ultimately, that population growth not unbalance or undermine economic growth, presently pursued quite separately in the Pacific from a commitment to development that is directed towards benefiting people. The view that economic growth (based on unchallenged GDP indicators) will in itself ensure that people have a decent quality of life is an unwritten assumption in the Port Vila Declaration.

The empowerment of women

Recognition is given to the empowerment of women and the need for gender equality. However, in those sections of the Declaration that address the family and reproductive rights, reproductive health and family planning, there is no specific incorporation of these principles in ways that would promote the empowerment of women or greater gender equality. Recognition of women and their central role in development is stated, but the unequal power relations between men and women, particularly in the family, are not addressed. Reference to improving the status of women, without elaborating on the factors that undermine their status, is not peculiar to the Port Vila Declaration. The document has picked up the now obligatory recognition of women's crucial economic and social roles, but there are no strong statements on the need for respect and recognition of women in areas that are far more difficult to address - namely, in the family and in relation to women's position as objects of population policies.

In the section on the family, there is recognition of the central role of the family in safeguarding the well-being of Pacific people. A limitation of this section (and the next section on reproductive rights, reproductive health and family planning), however, is the uncritical and persistent acceptance of the importance of family planning as one of the main strategies for achieving general social well-being and health within the family. The term 'family planning' itself is limiting (see discussion below). A more progressive stance, which would incorporate the empowerment of women, would identify control of women's reproduction by women, as personally empowering and enabling. The document and the ideas expressed do not go this far - although such an argument would be consistent with statements on empowerment and improving women's status mentioned earlier.

Family planning and women

Control of fertility (to be read as women's fertility wherever there is reference to reducing population growth rates) is still the objective of family planning programmes in the region, although emphasis is placed, officially, on the welfare/health aspects of these programmes. Non-coercive programmes have been stressed, and there are important inclusions in the Declaration on the need for improving male responsibility and involvement in family planning programmes. However, the main criticism that can be made of the Port Vila Declaration from a woman's point of view is the apparent lack of change of any significance in the overall philosophy of family planning reflected in it.

Some provisions have been made to include the community: there are welcome concerns for improving services, meeting people's needs, and reducing maternal and child mortality. What may not be strongly enough stated for women, however, is a clearer recognition of their previous/present positions as objects/recipients of family planning programmes and the more difficult questions of the obstacles to women's control over reproductive choice - beginning with their decision-making power or powerlessness within the family, and in relation to men/elders/the community/the church. These sources of control over women and their reproductive choices are not acknowledged. It would be surprising if they were, as that would be getting to the heart of influences on women's reproductive choice. A question that needs to be asked is just how much the Pacific commitment to custom and tradition, and to maintaining the role of the family, overrides any efforts, official or otherwise, to empower women, improve their status and promote their reproductive rights, choice and better health.

Social and economic factors are recognised as contributing to women's limited empowerment and decision-making control over their own fertility. The powerlessness of women at the personal level, imposed by men, social custom and tradition, and the community, is a more severe constraint that will continue to hinder women's reproductive, personal, social and economic well-being and choices. A main criticism of the Declaration is its lack of reference to these factors, including its failure even to acknowledge women's position in the family as child-bearers and mothers, and as economically less powerful (although not necessarily less productive) than men. Some recognition of women's unequal position in the basic unit of the family is essential for any meaningful statements to emerge in the document's later section on reproductive rights, reproductive health and family planning.

References to reproductive rights and reproductive health in conjunction with family planning are limited in many ways because the overall conceptualisation of family planning programmes persists. Such programmes continue to be dominated (and their success measured) by control of women's fertility, with women being the main targets of contraceptive acceptance. The references to reproductive rights and health are barely developed in the Port Vila Declaration: attention is mainly given to promotion of family health and maternal and child health services. Implicitly, women are still the central participants/recipients in these programmes. Empowering women through recognition of their reproductive rights and improvements in their status has not been made a part of family planning objectives or practice, nor does it enter into the Declaration's statements on renewed efforts in family planning programmes.

The document's section on reproductive rights, reproductive health and family planning is too narrowly focused in its location within present family planning activities. Examples of broader reproductive health activities exist in the Pacific, but the Declaration presents some of the more conservative ideas and service practices, while also including some statements clearly indicating new directions (for example, the references to community involvement, and greater involvement of men). Presentations at the Vila meeting, and at least some family planning/STDs/AIDS campaigns in the Pacific have a far broader focus on people's sexual behaviour and reproductive health information and awareness-raising than the maternal and child health (MCH)/family planning outreach programmes on which this section of the Declaration is based.

Points of departure: Women, development and population, and women's reproductive rights and health

What could be recommended, and not just for women, is a broader focus (in health and other programmes) on comprehensive reproductive health information, education and services. A broader-based reproductive health programme would include addressing the roles of men and women, unequal power relations within the family, sexuality, gender violence, reproductive rights and questions of choices. Many debates about what constitutes reproductive choice could usefully be drawn on. At the moment, with the narrow focus of family planning programmes, 'choice' effectively means having a choice of contraceptives and their use. Women's health advocates and others have raised questions about choice - specifically what it means for men and women in particular circumstances, including the increasingly widespread conditions of poverty, illiteracy and powerlessness. For women, health care is also needed not only in relation to their reproductive roles. Women's rights, economic and social equality, self-respect and assertiveness, are also (and should be) part of reproductive health programmes, including those which presently provide 'family planning'.

As they now stand, and particularly when they remain within the framework of family planning and MCH services, reproductive health services leave out men and youth. By not broadly addressing the reproductive rights and health of men and women, the Port Vila Declaration implicitly retains much of the spirit and substance of present MCH and family planning practices which continue to focus on women, by and large, and on contraceptive acceptance. Efforts are being made in population programmes in the Pacific to break through this limited focus and to reach a wider audience. Contraceptive advertisements directed at men and male responsibilities have been launched, for example, by the South Pacific Alliance for Family Health.

The AIDS-awareness newsletter *Pacific AIDS Alert* produced by the South Pacific Commission in Noumea also goes beyond conventional limits by encouraging community awareness and the sharing of information on sexuality, safe sexual practices and respect for individuals. Yet the mainstream family planning approach, directed at women as childbearers, is still very evident in the Port Vila Declaration.

A change in name ('family planning' is too narrow) and a broadening of the conceptualisation and delivery of reproductive health services are needed to include men and youth, and to address the general empowerment and health needs of women. Male influence on women's reproductive choices and health has been ignored. The present conceptualisation of family planning needs to be changed so that it also addresses men's needs for information and promotes awareness-raising not just in terms of contraception, but with regard to safe sexual practices, the better treatment of women, and respect for womens rights - as sexual beings, personally and socially.

Women's labour

Women's Labour includes:
Sacrificing The female body
to the process of procreation of the Species
Homo Sapiens.

The sweat blood and tears subsequent
to the pain agony
and trauma of childbirth

The forced sacrifice
by women of their leisure
to the process
of child-care
and child-rearing

The endless
toil
chore burden of life-long servitude
endured by women
for the maintenance of Family and the Human
Society.

Other than the Biological processes
all other life-sustaining
chores burdens
and processes ought
to be equally
shared by the male and female
of the Species of Humankind

Grace Mera Molisa

Gender violence: An invisible issue

The basic fact that any discussion of violence against women, including sexual violence, is absent from the Port Vila Declaration indicates that a widespread concern of Pacific women and women's organisations has not been heard. Women in the Pacific and elsewhere have launched information campaigns on gender violence and its connection with women's rights and choices, including their control over their own bodies and sexuality. No reference to gender violence, however, appears in the section on the empowerment of women and improving women's status. Yet within the family, we cannot estimate how much such attitudes to women and violence against women, in and outside the home, affect women's status, reproductive/personal rights and choices, and health.

Conclusion

Statements in the Port Vila Declaration on the need for policies 'that will slow population growth' once more convey the emphasis on fertility control, rather than addressing the complex relationships between development and population, resource use and distribution, and the quality of life people enjoy. Family planning programmes and fertility control alone will not necessarily ensure achievement or maintenance of a decent quality of life for all peoples and communities. Other factors have an equally important influence on the quality of life people enjoy: ethnicity, class, gender, democratic participation and unequal social structures. External agencies such as the International Monetary Fund (IMF) and the World Bank also influence the development policies and choices adopted by Pacific governments.

The critique above of 'development', and the lack of analysis of it in the Vila Declaration, are closely connected to the criticisms just made of the narrow focus of the Declaration's statements on reproductive rights and reproductive health and family planning, because population growth, implicitly, is given central place as a problem of development and sustainability - of the environment, livelihoods and quality of life people can or will enjoy. Much less attention is given to the development choices made by governments, under what pressures, and for what purposes. Economic growth features heavily in the Declaration but what does this actually translate into, in terms of social and economic development that affects peoples' lives positively?

In pursuit of an externally derived and directed model of economic growth which 'developing' countries, including those of the Pacific, are under pressure to follow, a particular type of development is occurring in the Pacific that is producing an uneven distribution of resources; investment in economic activities that are guaranteed to provide profitable incomes for a few rather than protection of people's livelihoods; support for export-oriented industries and for business enterprises, foreign or local; and use of physical resources in ways that contribute to environmental losses or degradation. This development, which requires governments to privatise services, cut social spending and control wage incomes, has affected the quality of life of different sections of the population, including women. Population growth rates and women's fertility are not the main threats to the quality of people's lives in the Pacific now or in the future, but 'development' as it is pursued now.

The influence of international agencies on the development strategies being followed by Pacific countries and the impact of externally led development policies are both pertinent to discussions on population, but neither appear in the Port Vila Declaration. A broader framework for analysing population and sustainable development is needed in the Pacific, beginning with a more honest assessment of our development policies and what they are directed at achieving - economic growth (quantifiable according to externally approved criteria) or a form of development that contributes to qualitative improvements in the overall economic and social environment in which most of the region's people live?

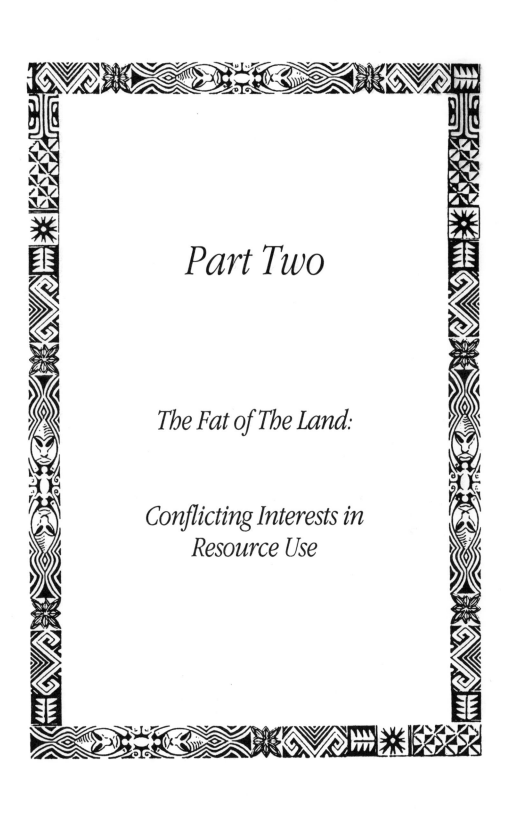

Part Two

The Fat of The Land:

Conflicting Interests in
Resource Use

Six

Mother, farmer, trader, weaver:
Juggling roles in Pacific agriculture*

Peggy Fairbairn-Dunlop

When I came home from field work in rural villages, my husband would ask, 'What do the women need?' The first time I said, 'I'd give every woman a horse'. The women had been carrying heavy loads of coconuts and bundles of *laufala* (pandanus) and thatch down from the plantations. The next time I said, 'I'd set up a small factory of some sort, button making, as in Vanuatu, or a joint venture with an overseas company'. School fees had been due that week, and the women had been working long hours with their families making copra, and the returns from copra were very small. In the evening, they had been weaving mats, some for home use, some *ie toga* (fine mats) for *faalavelave** , and some mats for sale. 'So you're going to set up a sweat shop and exploit the ladies?' was my husband's reply. He asked, 'If it's a question of money, why don't you teach the women management skills, so that they can manage their money better?' I said (very emphatically) 'If you have seen Samoan women scrimping and saving...they don't need to be taught how to handle money or resources. They have long years of experience.' And I thought, what the women really need is to be able to say 'Do we need that much food?' at the next ceremonial presentation.

Rural village, Western Samoa, 1989

---

* *Faalavelave* refers to the times when assistance or recognition should be given, as at weddings and birthdays, or in times of sickness

Introduction

Three general points about Women and Agriculture (WAg) in the Pacific region are discussed in this paper, each of which confirms the pivotal importance of custom or traditional culture in family, community and national decision making. The first is that Pacific women play a major role in the small-holder family units which characterise the semi-subsistence economies of the region. Available data demonstrate their significant contribution to food and cash-cropping, informal trading and community work. The second point is that women's agricultural activities appear to be increasing. The paper explores the reasons for this emerging trend and suggests that the overriding factor is that women are willing to work at any task they believe will benefit the family. This flexible and entrepreneurial spirit has become increasingly crucial in today's changing and depressed economic conditions. A question which must be asked is: Why are women seemingly bearing the brunt of these changes, while at the same time retaining responsibility for their 'family' roles?

Third, Pacific women's access to agricultural training and resources remains limited. However, government agricultural policies which focus on cash-cropping and direct specific programmes to men are totally inappropriate to the social and economic realities of life in Pacific societies today. To some extent, such anomalies reflect the power of custom. While it is true that Women and Agriculture as a concept is largely ignored, rarely supported and sometimes actively discouraged by government measures, it is equally true that the desire of Pacific Island states to preserve traditional cultural practices and values is also helping to perpetuate this state of affairs.

According to early Women in Development (WID) theorists like Boserup (1970) and Rogers (1980), an erosion of women's status commonly occurred in the post-contact period, due to a decline in their traditional roles in production and the introduction of Western concepts of women's inferiority. Women's worsening position, it was argued, could be seen in their increased workload in subsistence farming, cash-cropping and informal trading, and in the diminution of their traditional rights with regard to land, education and decision making in the new national institutions and policy-making bodies. In contrast to this pattern, it is often argued that Pacific women were shielded from the 'worst' effects of development by traditional cultural systems which guaranteed them certain rights, status options and resources.

Yet in these times of rapid social and economic change, it is becoming increasingly difficult to defend the argument that Pacific women have been cushioned by their cultures, thereby having a 'different' development experience. Women increasingly confront the dichotomy between traditional ideals about women's work (values born in an earlier time of family and village self-sufficiency) and the practical reality of surviving in an increasingly monetised and individualistic society, where the traditional base may be losing its meaning[1]. Integration into global economic and ideological networks is influencing Pacific lifestyles in ways which are perhaps not being realised, with aspirations for 'modern' goods and services resulting in the intensification and diversification of women's work in order to meet the cash needs of these desired lifestyles. As new jobs are often undertaken in addition to their customary tasks, many women are finding the extra workload an intolerable burden, particularly as male workloads appear to be decreasing (see discussion below).

In sum, while customary ways provide essential support and a source of status for Pacific women, there are opportunity costs in maintaining them. The dual cash/customary systems present more resource options, but they also create additional demands for cash, custom goods and time. Furthermore, while a dual system strengthens the customary status avenues for women, it obliges them to play the roles which accompany such opportunities. It may well be then that in terms of labour time, the situation of many Pacific women today is approaching that outlined by Boserup and Rogers. Whether the rewards women are reaping in terms of rights and status are sufficient to offset the greater workload is a question for further research.

I begin with an overview of Pacific agriculture, which highlights the powerful influence of tradition and custom.

Pacific agriculture

Agriculture is the principal sector in all Pacific economies. Some countries such as Papua New Guinea (PNG), New Caledonia and Vanuatu have rich mineral wealth, and commercial centres and factory zones are beginning to emerge in other parts of the region, supplementing the government-dominated wage sectors. But apart from this, the land and sea are the region's major resources, and most development plans focus on the primary sector. An estimated 80 per cent of the Pacific population rely on agriculture for food security and cash needs[2], and for the goods used in cultural exchanges and community activities[3]. Families are the main production units, and women's agricultural work is performed within these units. Families practise semi-subsistence mixed cropping on small scattered parcels of customary land, with access being acquired through lineage ties[4]. Cultural systems influence what and how crops are grown, who does the growing, and how crops are used. But the attitude that agriculture is a low-status option is pervasive: agriculture is the job for untitled (lower status) men, the last scholarship taken, the option for those who fail at school.

A point of increasing concern is that in spite of its cultural and economic importance, agricultural production has been declining steadily in all countries for some years. Reasons for this include the insecurity of global markets, crop vulnerability to adverse physical conditions, (reported) shortages of labour and certain customary practices. Be that as it may, decreases in agricultural exports, the neglect and degeneration of the traditional subsistence sector, and an alarming increase in food imports are occurring. This situation has implications for national food security, and has been disturbingly linked to the rising incidence of malnutrition and nutrition-related diseases through the region. And this is not just an urban phenomenon, as in the past: malnutrition amongst children is also becoming a rural problem. Poor nutrition has been treated as an educational rather than a production issue; but if people are selling the foods they should have eaten, and eating cheaper (and nutritionally inferior) substitutes, then it is obvious that poverty is also a problem.

The deterioration in food security presents a challenge to Pacific nations that have long claimed that traditional social systems ensure that all Pacific Islanders have a roof over their heads and food in their stomachs. It is also a challenge to planners who continue to work on the assumption that 'food security will take care of itself'. The urgent need to address food security and nutrition issues within national agricultural policies has been recommended by many regional and national workshops, including a regional Women and Agriculture meeting in 1994[5]. (see discussion below)

Women's agricultural work

The failure of national data collection methods in the Pacific to account for women's work has often been discussed, a major difficulty being that the adopted formula do not allow for the mixed cash and subsistence agriculture in which many Pacific women are involved. National statistics do not include informal sector activity, nor the range of other traditional exchange systems (such as reciprocity, customary presentations or exchanges incorporating cash and 'in-kind' goods and services) which characterise daily life in the region's typically small semi-subsistence economies[6].

Available regional data (Table 1) show that women's agricultural work has increased in most countries, despite the fact that there has been an overall decline in the relative numbers of people working in agriculture. For example, while male participation decreased by seven per cent in Fiji between the 1966-1986 inter-censal years, women's participation tripled (from 8% to 24%). A similar trend is evident in Kiribati and Palau, with an even greater surge in women's agricultural activity in Kiribati. How much of the agricultural work recorded in Table 1 is in subsistence, cash or other agricultural activities cannot, unfortunately, be determined (Booth 1993). However, case study materials reveal the extent and variety of women's agricultural work, and in so doing, emphasise the urgent need to revise government agricultural policies and training provisions which focus on cash-cropping, and which are generally directed towards men. While three distinct categories of agricultural activity are described in the following discussion, it is important to note that women may be engaged in all three activities at any one time.

Table 1: Percentage of labour force engaged in agriculture by gender, 1970, 1980, 1990 census (rounded)

Country	Year	% of labour force engaged in agriculture			Total economically active			Economically active in agriculture		
		Both Sexes	Male	Female	Both Sexes	Male	Female	Both Sexes	Male	Female
American Samoa	1970	2	2	1	5413	3450	1963	82	70	12
	1980	1	2	0	8308	5043	3265	101	90	11
	1990	6	7	4	14741	8648	6093	871	661	270
Cook Islands	1971	23	31	2	6269	4506	1763	1421	1384	37
	1981	29	35	15	5801	4051	1757	1697	1429	268
	1986	18	22	9	6722	4444	2278	1189	984	205
Fiji	1966	54	57	8	125809	116433	9376	67501	66785	716
	1976	44	48	23	175785	146315	29470	76886	70037	6849
	1986	44	50	24	241160	189929	51231	106305	94133	12172
French Polynesia	1983	13	15	8	62445	42481	19964	8014	6400	1614
	1988	10	13	5	75393	47434	27959	7555	6024	1531
Guam	1970	0	1	0	32473	25274	7219	157	139	18
	1980	1	1	0	31807	19446	12361	269	224	45
	1990	1	1	1	66534	41632	24902	909	607	302
Kiribati	1968	68	71	3	11068	10541	527	7532	7516	16
	1978	71	60	86	23990	13592	10398	17110	8188	8922
	1990	71	64	79	32610	17475	15135	23150	11254	11896
Marshall Islands	1970	8	8	4	4991	4108	883	382	348	34
	-	-	-	-	-	-	-	-	-	-
	1988	19	25	2	11488	8353	3135	2150	2080	70
Micronesia	1970	8	9	4	5030	3784	1246	394	343	51
	-	-	-	-	-	-	-	-	-	-
	1990 (LFS)	48	47	49	-	-	-	-	-	-
Nauru	1966	0	0	0	2504	2284	220	2	2	0
	1983	0	0	0	3444	2405	1039	0	0	0
New Caledonia	1969	34	27	49	39185	26722	12463	13357	7277	6080
	1976	17	22	6	43058	30748	12310	7462	6671	791
	1989	12	12	12	65945	41211	24734	7763	4849	2914
North Mariana Islands	1970	6	7	4	2236	1635	601	141	116	25
	1980	4	6	1	6229	4114	2115	259	230	29
	1990	3	5	1	26774	15191	11583	806	697	109
Palau	1970	15	19	6	2006	1418	588	308	272	36
	-	-	-	-	-	-	-	-	-	-
	1990	14	15	11	6520	4062	2458	881	617	264
Papua New Guinea	1971	85	79	94	1080346	661928	418418	915978	54133	391815
	1980	80	70	91	1339203	723176	616027	1065904	506295	559669
Samoa	1971	67	73	33	37901	32551	5350	25403	23616	1787
	1981	60	68	16	41506	35262	6244	25059	24070	989
	1986	64	73	25	45634	37054	8580	29023	26874	2149
Solomon Islands	1976	45	43	53	22659	18856	3803	10133	8129	2004
	1986	84	77	92	134705	70609	64096	113526	54315	59211

Source: H. Booth, data compiled for UNSTAT (1993).

Women and cash-cropping

   A picture of women's cash-cropping work is emerging from studies such as that on cocoa growing in Vanuatu (see Table 2). Preliminary studies of the Fiji ginger industry (Case 1 below) show women to be similarly engaged at each stage of the enterprise, from planting through to post-harvest. The data also reveal the variations which can occur in women's household work and point to the growing polarisation of economic livelihoods and quality of life which is emerging in Pacific countries. The vanilla and squash growing industries in Tonga are amongst other examples of cash crop activity which depend heavily on women's labour. In a slightly different example, women and children undertake many of the routine control measures for the eradication of taro blight in Western Samoa, including the daily inspection of leaves for spore development, the removal and destruction of infected leaves, the monitoring of a rigorous spraying regime, and the observation of strict hygiene standards.

Table 2:   Percentage of households planting cocoa reporting use of labour by gender and activity, Vanuatu

	Clearing bush %			Marking hole %			Digging holes %			Planting cocoa %			Cleaning cocoa %		
	M	F	C	M	F	C	M	F	C	M	F	C	M	F	C
Banks/Torres	100	64	25	100	38	51	100	38	58	100	84	81	100	38	75
Santo/Malo	97	79	62	97	60	11	97	88	11	97	77	11	97	80	68
Arbao/Waawo	100	44	22	100	8	19	100	8	38	74	6	38	100	8	16
Pentecost	100	100	19	100	100	19	100	79	38	100	79	38	100	100	38
Malekula	98	80	39	98	38	35	98	88	37	98	69	38	98	38	42
Ambryn	83	60	62	98	35	82	96	24	82	90	82	82	90	35	82
Pabra															
Epi	100	100	100	100		100	100		100	100	100	100	100		100
Shepherds	100	100	100	100	100	100	100	100	100	100	100	100	100	100	100
Efato	100	47	47	100	47	47	100	47	47	100	47	47	100	47	47
Tafea															
Vanuatu	98	74	44	98	38	40	98	57	43	98	85	43	98	38	49

Source: Vanuatu Country Paper presented to Women and Agriculture Regional Workshop, Vanuatu, 1993, USP/CTA, Report of KAP Survey of Vanuatu Cocoa Development Project. Vanuatu Govt/AIDAB/FSP.

79

Case 1 Ginger growing, Fiji

Ginger is a highly labour-intensive crop, especially during planting and harvesting, and the demand for women's labour is high. In planting and maintenance periods, the main job for women is to weed the crop. During harvesting, women uproot the ginger, and clean, trim and grade the plants before these are sent to the factory or the exporter. These activities usually take up to seven hours a day, two to three days a week during peak periods. Ginger farmers also hire women from neighbouring farms to pack ginger: a family can pack 50 cases a day using household labour.

Distinctions between ethnic Chinese and Indian ginger farmers are emerging. Indian-owned farms are usually hilly, with no electricity or piped water system. These families rely on the river, creeks or wells for their water supply, which means walking for long distances; and women collect firewood for use on the open-fire cooking facilities. Chinese farmers, on the other hand, have bigger farm holdings and better housing and kitchen facilities. Their homes have water tanks and some have water piped into their homes which makes work easier. They use kerosene or gas stoves for their cooking. It is also apparent that most Chinese ginger farmers have well-stocked backyard gardens and poultry (Naikatini 1993).

Women as informal traders

Not only are women's cash-cropping activities diversifying in these and other ways. Women are also the major informal traders throughout the region, and are highly visible as market and street vendors, as well as sellers to commercial outlets. If the 'self-employed' category is used as an indicator of informal sector activity, then almost one-quarter of Pacific women are engaged in informal trade (see Table 3). The Marshall Islands and Tuvalu report a very high proportion of employers 'own account', while Fiji, with its more developed formal sector, has a lower figure of 10 per cent.

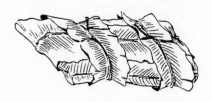

Table 3: Distribution of the female economically active population by status in employment, and % female in each status

Country/Year	% distribution of female econ. active population by status in employment			All econ. active	Percentage female		
	Employers own-acct.	Employees	Unpaid fam. fam. wkr		Employers own-acct.	Employees	Unpaid fam. wrkr
American Samoa							
1970	-	-	-	36[5]	23[4]	37[4]	65[4]
1990	1	90	0	41	22	42	68
Cook Islands							
1971	5	67	18	28	7	29	64
1986	6	78	8	34	26	36	39
Fiji							
1966	-	-	-	7	-	-	-
1986	16	52	16	21	10	26	20
French Polynesia							
1988	10	49	5	37	28	33	48
Guam							
1970	2	93	0	22	30	31	65
1980	2	92	0	39	30	39	70
1990	3	86	0	37	41	42	55
Kiribati							
1973[2]	0	16	0	38	26	21	64
1985	1	17	0	36	24	25	50
Marshall Islands							
1970	0	87	2	18	11	18	19
1988	23	56	7	27	29	26	28
Micronesia Fed States							
1970	4	81	5	25	22	24	43
1989	-	-	-	30	-	-	-
Nauru							
1966	1	96	1	9	43	9	100
1983	1	70	-	30	40	25	-
New Caledonia							
1969	16	44	38	32	23	24	68
1989	13	68	3	38	31	39	75
Northern Mariana Islands							
1970	3	91	0	27	32	26	50
1990	1	96	0	43	25	43	54
Palau							
1970	4	79	4	29	19	28	81
1990	1	82	0	38	23	37	50
Papua New Guinea							
1966	21	33	46	19	17	10	68
1980	1[9]	3[10]	-	46	42[11]	13[11]	68
Samoa							
1971	10	70	19	14	3	27	12
1981	7	86	7	15	5	30	3
1986	13	69	17	19	9	37	8
Solomon Islands							
1986	7	8	-	40	39	20	-
Tonga							
1963	-	-	-	-	6	-	-
1986	4	68	6	21	7	31	4
Tuvalu							
1973[3]	0	5	0	52	50	16	100
1991[7]	98	65		33	54[8]	38	-
Vanuatu							
1967	-	-	-	45	-	-	-

Source: H . Booth data compiled for UNSTAT July 1993.

1. The distribution may not add up to 100 because of workers not classified by status.
2. Indigenous population Gilbert Islands.
3. Indigenous population Ellice Islands.
4. Persons aged 13+ in non-agricultural industries.
5. Persons aged 14+ excludes subsistence.
6. Chuuk State only.
7. Resident indigenous population.
8. Work for sale.
9. Includes unpaid helper excludes rural village sector.
10. Excludes rural village sector employers.
11. Excludes rural village sector.

The significant increase in women traders relates directly to the present adverse economic conditions, and also to the increase in female-headed households in the Pacific. The following Solomon Islands data (Case 2) give some idea of the extent and diversity of women's activities in informal trading despite low literacy levels, limited resources and traditional family responsibilities. It also confirms the importance of agricultural production to the informal sector. The limited (financial and other) resources available to women traders emphasises the need to develop appropriate support services in the informal sector. The fact that many of today's successful Pacific businesswomen had their beginnings in small-scale trading[7], also stresses the economic logic of establishing the infrastructure that will foster the transition from small-scale informal trading activities to fully-fledged 'development' ventures.

Case 2   Informal sector, Solomon Islands

From a sample of 323 women, more than two-thirds were self-employed at the time of the interviews. A total of 75 per cent said that they spent 16 hours or more on their income-generating venture during the week. The types of activities were: farm gardening (38%), food catering (21%), crafts (15%), and textiles (11%). The women sold their products directly to consumers at the market (40%), out of home (34%), or in shops (16%).

More than 75 per cent of the women interviewed were married (average five children) and 25 per cent lived in households with more than seven persons. More than one-third of the self-employed women were sole income providers. Over 75 per cent had not received any assistance, whether from relatives, banks or other sources to run their businesses. More than 50 per cent had received only a few years of primary school education, and almost one-fifth no formal education at all; 25 per cent were not able to write in any language, and almost one-third could not do any calculations.

Source: International Labour Organisation/United Nations Development Programme (1993)

Subsistence, culture and community

The crucial importance of household subsistence and community activities to economic survival and welfare at the family, community and national levels in semi-subsistence economies has never been fully appreciated by planners. The assumption has been that food security is 'natural'; and that village meetings, family reciprocal exchanges and customary ceremonies are 'nice', but not really necessary and/or a hindrance to 'real' production and development. The importance of these activities is slowly being recognised in official documents, with particular acknowledgement of the ways communal networks have helped to soften the harsh effects of economic restructuring measures. The implications of the 1993 United Nations Development Programme (UNDP) Human Development Report, for example, are that a high level of subsistence effectively absorbs external shocks, and that the stable social fabric of Pacific societies created by village and extended family systems provides the essential stability in these small nation states.

Women's contribution to both subsistence and community activities is substantial. Census estimates of their subsistence activities show expected 'highs' in countries where women customarily engaged in agriculture. For example, in PNG in 1990, over 50 per cent of women were engaged solely in subsistence agriculture, compared to only 33 per cent of men. Similarly, Vanuatu's 1989 national census recorded that as much as 84 per cent of women were engaged in agriculture. In countries where women's traditional involvement in agriculture has been less extensive, significant increases in their agricultural work appear to be emerging. For example, data for the Cook Islands show that 10.2 per cent of women are self-employed in the subsistence sector, and 15.2 per cent engaged in agriculture and fisheries, compared to 17 per cent and 35.2 per cent respectively for men. In Tuvalu in 1985, approximately two-thirds of all women, and about three-quarters of all males, in outer island villages were engaged in home duties, village work and subsistence agriculture (Siwatibau 1993).

Every country in the region has its own community activities which operate through village, church, extended family and other networks. At the formal level, such activities may be legitimised by the exchange of customary status goods, for example by using 'male goods' of livestock and staple crops, and 'female goods' like fine mats and *tapa* (beaten bark cloth). The nature and quantity of goods exchanged have been well documented, as has the enhancement of women's status that is an integral part of these ceremonies. Case 3 draws attention to some of the many informal and unrecorded uses of agricultural goods occurring on a daily basis in the semi-subsistence societies of the Pacific.

Another example typifies the practice of Pacific Island groups travelling overseas who usually take customary goods in recognition of the hospitality they receive. When the Apia Rowing Team of 48 members went to Auckland in 1991, they took 100 sleeping mats, 300 fine mats and 100 bags of taro to distribute amongst their hosts. Table 4 gives some idea of the amount of time women can spend producing such custom goods. It also shows how tasks may be age-related.

Case 3　Use of agricultural goods

When Faapusa's family began building a new house, members of his extended family and friends helped. Each day a gang of between 10 and 20 men worked at the site, while women and children carried sand and rocks from the beach for the house foundations. Family members brought bags of taro, fruit, chicken and fish to feed the workers, and they prepared and served this food. The young wives' group of the village each weaved six *pola* (blinds) as their contribution, and when the building was completed, families contributed *ie toga* (fine mats) to make up the number to be given to the builder in recognition of his skills (Fairbairn-Dunlop 1991).

Table 4　Average time (hours) spent weaving by women from three Samoan villages, 1989

Age	Rural	Peri-urban	Urban village
25-34 years	4.93 (n=8)	3.81 (n=11)	0 (n=0)
35-44	6.92 (n=7)	9.75 (n=2)	4.33 (n=6)
45-54	11.50 (n=8)	11.0 (n=6)	1.00 (n=3)
55+	7.62 (n=8)	14.56 (n=6)	12.00 (n=1)

Note: Number of women in each age category is noted in brackets

The fact that custom goods which would never have been sold in the past are now being marketed is an obvious response to growing family needs for cash. A common sight at the Apia Market today is the impressive array of mats for sale, ranging in price from $200 to $700 (tala[*]) per mat. Women say that on a good day they can sell up to seven to 10 mats, but that sometimes they can go for weeks without making a single sale, so that 'in desperation, we have sold some mats for as little as $5 or $6 each'. The reasons given for selling mats include the fact that school fees are due but no family member is in waged work; and that families have to supplement incomes because the taro leaf blight has

---

[*]　One US dollar is equivalent to about 2.5 Samoan *tala.*

destroyed their taro plantations. The women report that after spending all day selling, they often spend the evenings weaving (*Samoa Observer* March 24 1994).

This brief discussion of women's agricultural work through food production, cash-earning activities and production for cultural and community activities highlights the overall importance of women's work within small-holder units. Furthermore, it demonstrates the extremely narrow definitions of 'economic' and 'agriculture' that prevail in national development planning and data collection; and which continue to focus on cash-cropping and to assume that men are primarily responsible for agricultural work. For example, none of the non-cash goods exchanged in Case 3 - the food, value-added goods (blinds and fine mats) or the timber used to build the house - are included in agricultural planning. Educational and research resources are therefore not allocated to such activities, although non-governmental organisation (NGO) programmes do endeavour to address these needs.

Factors influencing women and agriculture

It may be that women's agricultural work has not actually increased in nominal terms but that the work they did in the past was not acknowledged. For example, each Pacific country has its own norms about which tasks should be performed by which gender; and the extent to which these are observed differs between and within countries. Although descriptions of the division of labour often imply a rigid and precise demarcation of gender roles, it is probable that multiple (and to some extent gender-blind) occupations were undertaken in the past, as they are today. That is, family work was allocated according to needs, priorities and available resources rather than strict observance of a gender division of labour, and the labour specialisation this implies. The sharing of essential work is at the core of semi-subsistence life. Simply put, subsistence households cannot afford the luxury of some members not working, as is seen in the following case study.

Case 4   Allocation of family labour

When Evelina's husband managed to get a job in Apia, Evelina and their four children stayed with her parents in the rural village, while her husband commuted to the village at the weekends. Evelina assumed the role which her husband might have played within the extended family unit. She went to the plantation daily with her father and did an assortment of jobs including weeding, checking the cattle and gathering coconuts for copra making. While she was at the plantation, her mother and younger sisters cared for her children. Usually her mother weaved at the same time. When Evelina returned in the early afternoon, she assumed the role of 'daughter' again, taking over the household tasks from her mother (Fairbairn-Dunlop 1991).

Despite the significant exchange of roles shown in Case 4, the work of women and children continues to be seen as 'helping out' (hence it is not recorded, acknowledged, or provided for in planning processes). The view that men do the agricultural work thus persists. But in today's rapidly changing times, family security is even more dependent on the examination of options and the rearrangement of roles (as in Case 4), the major difference being that new options such as migration, waged-work and informal trade have been incorporated into the balancing process, as have new 'needs'. A major question is that while aspirations for 'modern' goods oblige families to work harder, why is it that women's agricultural work appears to be increasing relative to that of men?

Some reasons for the increase in women's agricultural work are the changes in family composition, such as the nuclearisation of the family and growing numbers of female-headed households. The family labour force may be further depleted by out-migration and school attendance, while the new wage-earning opportunities such as joint-venture garment factories (Fiji), fish canning operations (Solomon Islands) and the Yazaki car wiring assembly factories (Western Samoa) also draw people away from the land, and in the process increase the labour burdens of those who remain behind.

The greater diversification of Pacific agriculture is another factor influencing women's work. The drastic fall in world prices for traditional exports has brought an urgent search for 'niche' crops, such as ginger, passionfruit, vanilla and spices. These crops require different skills and labour inputs to those used in growing traditional staples. Not surprisingly, women figure prominently in each of these ventures because the work is relatively light and routine, and it can be performed around the homestead while they are minding the children. Furthermore, there are no traditional gender norms associated with these new crops which might otherwise prevent women's participation. For example, while Tongan women still do not as a general rule work with yams, the male status crop, they do work with vanilla and squash.

The rise of the 'part-time' farmer in Pacific countries also influences women's workload. Farming has become an expensive and risky business, and returns are variable, unpredictable and irregular. Many families are no longer relying on agriculture as their main source of income. More often, it is the male of the household who gets a (supplementary) waged-job, leaving the women and children to carry the weight of the farm work.

A final factor influencing the greater role of Pacific women in agriculture today is that many projects now deliberately target them as a group who will 'make up' for the poor state of agricultural production. Women and Agriculture issues now appear on national and regional agendas[8], and are incorporated into debates about sustainable development/population growth/human resource development/poverty alleviation and national food security. A less positive point is that while the rhetoric of these programmes often gives the impression that, at donor level at least, a more holistic view of agriculture has replaced the conventional cash-oriented emphasis, this is not always the case. And somewhat paradoxically, these people-centred ideas of 'development with a human face' are being promoted at the very time when economic restructuring measures are seriously straining the limited resources of families.

Conclusion

Pacific communities are extremely vulnerable today as prices for traditional agricultural products fall, aid funding declines, and migration restrictions bring huge drops in the remittances on which families have come to rely. The pursuit of all cash-earning possibilities has become crucial. Pacific women are adjusting to the changing social and economic circumstances while shouldering many of the new burdens these have brought. They are continuing to perform their traditional family roles, but at the same time are taking on an increasingly important role in agriculture, both in the informal and formal sectors, in cash-earning, food-producing and community work. They are weighing up and balancing the options, and they remain the backbone of family livelihoods.

Despite the indispensable nature of their agricultural work, Pacific women continue to face a range of problems whose origins are structural as well as attitudinal. In 1993, delegates to a regional workshop on Women and Agriculture noted that women did not have automatic and regular access to agricultural information; and that development focused on cash-cropping at the expense of food-cropping, and often did not take sufficient account of possible long-term effects on the environment. They also argued that women experienced difficulty getting access to land for projects; that 'good' land was taken for commercial projects, leaving them to walk further to plant their food crops; and that family food security and cash-earning options were adversely affected by mining and logging operations. The lands cleared by these industries were areas where women had customarily collected foods and medicinal plants. The growing individualisation of landholdings, as seen in the planting of long-term tree crops and the erection of permanent concrete dwellings, were additional causes for concern, foreshadowing the possibility that land ownership could be a major issue for women in the not too distant future.

At the beginning of this paper I described Samoan women's work in one village in 1989. What is the situation for these same women in 1994? As in 1989, women are still balancing their needs against their resources, but the options are different today. First, the women aren't making copra: the coconut mill has closed due to a shortage of coconuts following the recent cyclone, and the fall in world market prices for copra. Second, some women are working at the Yazaki factory, a joint-venture firm, and others are on the waiting list for a job there. The Yazaki women work for long hours, in poor conditions, but 'it's clean work, and it's money in the hand'[9]. Mat-making is still a central task lasting all day, and some women who haven't made a mat for years have begun cultivating their *laufala* (pandanus) patches. Many families have planted extensive food gardens around their houses, and some are also planting staple crops as well[10].

The questions that we perhaps need to ask are: Who are these crops feeding? Are they for family use, or will they be sold? Any further shifts away from consumption-oriented agriculture could raise some disturbing implications for the future livelihoods of Pacific Islanders.

Notes

1. Why traditional cultural norms and practices endure in the Pacific will not be discussed in this paper, except to say that these are integral to personal and community identity, and that the network of relationships and roles which come under the rubric of culture effectively ensure family and community security. This is particularly crucial in the absence of government provision of essential village services and in the present times of rapid change.

2. For example, agriculture, forestry and fisheries provide around 50 per cent of Western Samoa's GDP, 50 per cent of the workforce, and up to 80 per cent of export earnings (World Bank 1991:213).

3. A 1991 Western Samoa study showed that 23 per cent of goods were used in exchanges which did not involve the exchange of money (Fairbairn-Dunlop 1991). The amount, type and direction of these goods warrant further research.

4. For example, almost 80 per cent of land in Western Samoa is held in customary tenure and 83 per cent in Fiji, while in Papua New Guinea (PNG) the figure stands at 97 per cent.

5. This regional workshop was held at the University of the South Pacific Centre in Vanuatu and delegates from all member countries of the university region attended.

6. The disaggregation of available data, and small household studies, would be first steps in the lengthy process of unravelling the extent and type of women's agricultural activities.

7. For example, Aggie Grey's international hotel complex (Western Samoa) had its beginnings in vegetable and handicraft sales, while trucking operator Maria Kunjib of Mount Hagen (PNG) used profits from coffee and vegetable sales to meet the deposit needed for her first truck. Papiloa Foliaki, the owner of one of the largest tourist hotels in the Kingdom of Tonga, reportedly raised money to renovate her first bus 'by producing gifts and produce'.

8. Women and Agriculture is a primary focus of the Pacific Regional Programme for Action for Beijing.

9. Apart from any exploitation of labour in these new areas of employment, the social problems associated with the dislocation of women from villages and their concentration in urban areas need researching.

10. Staple crops are usually grown on land allocated for food gardens away from the home.

References

Booth, H. (1993) Statistics prepared for United Nations Statistical Office (UNSTAT)

Boserup, E. (1970) *Women's role in economic development,* New York: St Martins Press

Fairbairn-Dunlop, P. (1991) 'E au le inailau a tamaitai: Women, education and development, Western Samoa', unpublished Ph.D thesis, Macquarie University, Sydney

------------ (1993) *Women's status in the South Pacific,* Bangkok, Thailand: Economic and Social Commission for Asia and the Pacific (ESCAP)

Government of Vanuatu (1993) 'Vanuatu country paper' prepared for the Women and Agriculture Workshop, University of the South Pacific/Technical Centre for Agriculture and Rural Co-operation (CTA), Vanuatu

International Labour Organisation/United Nations Development Programme (1993) *Employment for women in the Solomon Islands,* Solomon Islands: Women's Development Division, Ministry of Health and Medical services and ILO (EMPLA Project)

Naikatini, U. (1993) 'Fiji country paper' prepared for the Women and Agriculture Workshop, University of the South Pacific/CTA, Vanuatu

Rogers, B. (1980) *The domestication of women,* London: Tavistock

Samoa Observer March 24 1994

Siwatibau, S. (1993) 'Mainstreaming women and agriculture', paper prepared for the Women and Agriculture Workshop, University of the South Pacific/CTA, Vanuatu

World Bank (1991) Towards higher growth in Pacific Island economies: Lessons from the 1980s, vol.2, Country Surveys

Seven

De-romancing the stones:
Gender, environment and mining in the Pacific*

'Atu Emberson-Bain

When people saw the effects of the mine, when they saw it with their own eyes, it was something that they never expected ... Many Bougainvilleans would regard land as a fragile thing. I mean it's something that is so valuable to them. Why is it that valuable? Because if there was no land, there was no water, there was no bush, what have you, there is no island. You know, it means that there is no life.

Bougainville mother/health worker, March 1993

Introduction

Discoveries of rich mineral wealth in the Pacific region have generally been welcomed as a panacea for island states increasingly confronted with their vulnerability within the global economy. Pounded by problems ranging from large trade deficits, rising national debts, and heavy aid dependence (in some cases amongst the highest per capita by international standards) to escalating unemployment and sluggish economic growth rates[1], this reaction is perhaps not surprising. In the debilitating clutches of international development and financial institutions with their conditions for debt relief and preferred free market economic policies, Pacific Island governments are placing a premium on development strategies conducive to boosting economic growth. Large-scale mineral exploitation is regarded as one means to this end.

Mining development has characteristically created an important source of export revenue for independent Pacific states, helping to diversify narrow, primary commodity-based economies inherited from the colonial period. It is regarded as a

91

valuable source of employment and even infrastructural development. In some countries like Papua New Guinea (PNG), Nauru and New Caledonia, the industry has claimed such pre-eminence within the cash economy, that it has effectively become **the** earner. For Nauru, the prosperity generated since local control was established over the phosphate industry in 1968 has become the source of massive overseas investments and trust funds. In PNG, the mining sector outshines the performance of other sectors like manufacturing or agriculture. By 1987, the rich Panguna mine on Bougainville and the Ok Tedi mine in the Star Mountains of the Western Province were together responsible for as much as 60 per cent of total export earnings (Jackson 1991:19), dwarfing the relative contribution (around 15%) of PNG's second export, coffee. In mid-1989, at the time of the Panguna mine's closure, Bougainville Copper Ltd (a joint Australian-PNG venture) contributed 10 per cent of GDP and 36 per cent of export earnings on its own. In 1991, PNG's mining sector (principally the Ok Tedi, Porgera and Misima mines) were responsible for around seven per cent of PNG's impressive nine per cent growth (Mannur 1933:B2.1-2.2).

Nickel mining in New Caledonia is a potent example not only of the economic importance of mineral resource development (and in this instance the benefits extend to the metropolitan as well as the colonial economy), but also of the political economy of resource extraction within the contemporary Pacific. Both characteristics foreshadow intensified state protection of the industry in the approach to a crucial referendum on independence in 1997. As one of the strategic remnants of the French empire, New Caledonia's nickel industry boasts 40 per cent of the world's nickel deposits and produces over one-third of its nickel output, as well as comprising 90 per cent of the territory's own exports. It is dominated by one of the world's largest nickel-producing companies, the state-owned Société Métallurgique Le Nickel (SLN), which owns as much as two-thirds of the territory's richest concessions and the only operating smelter (Connell 1992:69). The mining of this strategic metal services both the French and Japanese nuclear industries as a source of nuclear-based energy, supplying as much as 80 per cent of France's electricity. As an important ingredient in the manufacture of nuclear arsenal, nickel is also critical to the military-offensive capability of metropolitan France (Newborn 1992:2), directly supporting its nuclear test programme in its other major Pacific territory, French Polynesia.

In spite of (or perhaps because of) its apparent benefits, mining is increasingly steeped in controversy and conflict, in particular bitter opposition from local communities who have been affected most directly and adversely by it. The tensions and opposition created by the industry have varied in scale and intensity, and in a number of instances - Nauru, Bougainville, and New Caledonia - their origins go far back into history, linking localised protests against mining operations to broader political (anti-colonial, post-colonial and secessionist) struggles. In Nauru, opposition has ranged from local discontent over government mining policy and management of phosphate revenues amongst landowners and elements of the landless middle class (Howard 1991:3) to public demonstrations organised by Nauruan women, and high profile government-sponsored litigation at the International Court of Justice in support of rehabilitation claims. In New Caledonia, calls for nationalisation of the mining industry have their origins in the aftermath of World War II. Since then, there have been calls for the 'territorialisation' of the SLN and sporadic attacks on mining property and operations linked to a militant nationalist struggle during the 1980s (Henningham n.d.: 11-12).

Nickel

(translated from the French original Nickel)

The yellow waters of the rivers of your land
are the soiled tears of your loved one
crying for the mountain ridges ripped apart, the
shredded slopes
of the sacred hills of your life
destroyed by the tentacles, the fetters
of the industrial machinery
of capitalism

...The noise of the trucks carrying the ore,
the crushing mill which grinds the piles of raw material,
the machines which extract the nickel
rooting out the natural wealth
your green capital,
these are the last words of your loved one.

... New Caledonia means Nickel
Third largest producer in the world
Overseas territory of French colonialism
Nickel boom of the last few years
A 20th century Eldorado
Nickel rush
Uncontrolled establishment of those giant companies
Mining concessions of every kind
Relentless expropriation
of Kanak land
Money and 5.5*
Monopoly of SLN

New Caledonia means the paradise of easy business
where at the smelter at Doniambo
the furnaces sometimes explode
and workers die
where at the mines of
Thio, Poro, Nepoui and other places
a truck sometimes races down the clay slopes
and someone slowly dies in a ravine
under the watchful eye of the guardian spirits of
our freedom fighters
Because the paths that climp up to the plateau are slippery
workers die
But the company doesn't give a damn
and its owners give even less of a damn

You hear a gasping breath in the ravine
you see a carbonised body in the furnace
you hear the sobbing, see a tremor of life as the body takes
its last breath ...

Déwé Gorode

* One French franc = 5.5 CFP (New Caledonian currency)

In Fiji, the mining industry - which is focused on gold operations in the company town of Vatukoula - has been plagued by industrial disputes including an historic three-year strike offensive launched in 1991, a court challenge by the landowners of Nasomo, and allegations against an Australian company of political activities linked to the 1987 military overthrow of the Labour-led Bavadra government[2]. In PNG (Bougainville, Mt Kare, Porgera and Ok Tedi), people's protests over mining-induced destruction of the environment and their marginalisation from mining benefits have in one instance - Bougainville - pushed the conflict into the bloody domain of civil war and a brutal military invasion. As the recent military/paramilitary offensives against Bougainville landowners and Fiji mine strikers demonstrate, state protection of foreign mining operations in the Pacific does not appear to stop short of violent suppression of their detractors.

While it is not possible here to explore the details of populist resistance to mining in the Pacific, it provides an important reminder of the urgent priority that should be given to evaluating the impact of mining development on the indigenous peoples of the region. All too often, grassroots implications and perceptions are a postscript to development analyses, if indeed they are accommodated at all. The elitist, and in many respects patriarchal, biases of development thinking have significant policy implications. The marginalisation of women from the process of formulating development policy is one obvious outcome. The dominance of a growth-led, export-oriented model of development is another.

The sustainable development debate - including criticisms of its limitations - highlights the desirability of focussing on the local-level impact of development policies. It emphasises the need to redefine development (and so shape policy) according to its ability to guarantee minimum standards in the quality of life for the majority of ordinary people and to promote a more equitable distribution of resources. Sustainable development should translate into sustainable livelihoods, putting people's welfare first (Sen & Grown 1985). It is not enough, indeed it is contradictory, to merely inject existing development strategies (based on economic growth) with a dose of environmental sensitivity. The root of the problem would appear to lie with the growth model itself. As Trainer (1990:78-79) succinctly puts it, the basic problem for the third world is 'not lack of development...it is *inappropriate* development' because 'a development strategy making growth the top priority *creates* poverty'.

As a general rule, mining in the Pacific has probably proved to be one of most destructive and unsustainable forms of foreign-initiated development. The living human scars of this rapacious industry are starkly visible in the suffering endured by the people of Bougainville during the course of a protracted military offensive which has inflicted over 3,000 deaths through a medical blockade, wiped out over 6,000 village homes, and killed, injured and tortured hundreds of innocent people (Forster 1992:20-21). But while Bougainville might be singular in so far as its human 'time-bomb' (as Colin Filer has termed it) has already exploded, it is by no means alone as a victim of mining development. In most other areas of the region, the history of Pacific mining weaves a woeful tale of expropriation and exploitation, social and cultural isolation, and environmental damage.

Mining, a boon for the Pacific - but who benefits?

The perceived macroeconomic benefits of mining mask less savoury 'realities'. Indeed, it is one of its paradoxes that the industry has tended to consolidate, rather than reduce, conditions of economic dependence for Pacific countries; and that in the process, it has caused a decline, rather than an improvement, in the quality of life for many of its supposed beneficiaries. The implications of dependence are especially serious because the industry (in some instances like Nauru, the entire economy) is founded on a wasting, non-renewable resource. At the macro-level, this dependence is represented in the foreign orientation and control of the industry. Mining has drawn the Pacific more decisively within the orbit of the global capitalist economy - as a cheap source of raw materials - and under the control of its powerful brokers, the International Monetary Fund (IMF) and the World Bank. Foreign ownership and control have encouraged the expatriation of mining revenue including the outflow of dividends to foreign shareholders and (expatriate) employee remittances. The reliance on foreign technology, expensive machinery and material imports has been another drain on mine earnings and is aggravated by practices like transfer pricing.

The drawing on domestic capital reserves for mine infrastructure and development, and the further surrender of economic returns through government tax concessions, have also been a feature of the mining history of Fiji, PNG and New Caledonia. In PNG, the military offensives against the Island of Bougainville have deprived more productive and needy areas of the economy of resources. They have exacerbated the country's debt burden and increased its dependence on Australian (military and economic) aid. The trend looks likely to continue as further (financial and human) resources are diverted to mounting military defences of mining operations around the country, including a further $US 29 million budget in 1992 alone for the re-establishment of control over Bougainville.

Agriculture is the mainstay of most Pacific economies and the means of livelihood for the bulk of their populations, contributing 30 per cent of gross domestic product (GDP) in the region (Shaw 1992:17). The tendency of mining to siphon off resources from such a key sector would seem to be an important indicator of its unsustainability. In New Caledonia, mining has, along with cattle ranching, made large claims on land and financial resources. Howard (1991) argues that there has been a conspicuous neglect of agriculture and fisheries. Indeed, the territory has the dubious distinction of having one of the smallest (20%) agricultural workforces in the Pacific. The situation is made worse by the steady outflow of labour to the industrial urban economy (Connell 1992:69-70). In general, other macro-level effects of mining include the dependence on food imports that is encouraged by the loss of food grounds, and, of course, the problem of landlessness itself. Nauru is a case in point in both instances, 'boasting' one of the highest population densities (457 persons/sq.km) in the region and a high food import bill (around 30% of total imports) in spite of consistent trade surpluses (South Pacific Commission 1993). Trade data on nickel-rich New Caledonia similarly reveals that in 1991 food imports amounted to around $AUS 180 million, representing 17 per cent of total imports and 33 per cent of export earnings (ibid). In Papua New Guinea, per capita food and agricultural production dropped by eight per cent between 1975 and 1986. Import dependency in lieu of self-sufficiency is especially ironic given the abundance and richness of its land-based resources (Mannur 1993: B.2.5 & B 2.10).

It is at the micro-level of the household that the effects of this pattern are felt most harshly. The land demands for mine infrastructure and housing settlements, for example, have subjected some indigenous communities to permanent exile or resettlement. The peoples of Banaba (Ocean Island), Indonesian-occupied West Papua, and Bougainville have suffered such a fate. Environmental degradation has undermined the self-reliance of traditional Pacific economies, encouraging household dependence on less nutritious imported store foods. In places like Bougainville, expropriation has deprived people of planting land for food gardens and cash crops (Oliver 1973:164). In both Bougainville and Ok Tedi, there has been contamination of local river systems and destruction of forest by the daily dumping of hundreds of thousands of tons of toxic tailings. This 'poison' has killed huge quantities of fish and other marine life - important features of traditional diets. It has destroyed water and timber supplies (Connell 1989 & 1991; Hyndman 1991; Moody 1991). New Caledonia is another environmental disaster (Bird et al. 1984).

But it is probably Nauru that encapsulates the full irony (and heavy price tag) of the dependent development promoted by mining. As the most prosperous Pacific Island economy (enjoying the highest per capita GDP at over $AUS 22,000), it is one of the worst victims of environmental damage. There have been 80 years of plunder of Nauru's phosphate resources with virtually the entire island being 'surrendered' to the production of cheap fertiliser for the farms of the economic North. What remains is a barren landscape of tall limestone pinnacles resembling 'freshly dug graves with white headstones' (Weeramentry et al. 1988:1032). The destruction of coconut, tomano and pandanus trees has eradicated an important part of the traditional diet, as well as a source of craft (house- and boat-building) materials and cash crops like copra. The losses of food land have imposed a diet regime almost entirely based on nutritionally-deficient imported food. They have also paved the way for a relatively sedentary lifestyle for the island's 10,000-odd people who are now confined to just 465 hectares of their 2130 hectare home. It is these trappings of an 'affluent' lifestyle, or the so-called benefits of phosphate development, that have sentenced Nauruan men and women to one of the highest rates of diabetes in the world. In sum, mining has directly affected the nutritional and health status of the island's people - ultimately reducing their life chances[3] (Weeramentry et al. 1988:184-185; Howard 1988:126-168).

There is a special significance to the land losses and degradation resulting from mining that have intensified the sense of deprivation experienced by local communities and fuelled the flames of discontent, resentment and conflict. Traditional Pacific values have no parallel in Western capitalist notions of land as an alienable and disposable material commodity. Land is crucial to physical survival; it is central to the reproduction of traditional social relations; and it has a spiritual value that enshrines a sacred link between the dead (ancestors) and the living. Communal rather than private tenure predominates in customary land systems; and there is no tradition of proprietorial rights being vested exclusively in individual males. The claim of the state to ownership of minerals has no traditional legitimacy. Nor has the distinction between surface and subterranean components of land, a device historically used to legitimise this claim. For the Bougainville villager,

Land is our life. Land is our physical life - food and sustenance. Land is our social life; it is marriage; it is status; it is security; it is politics; in fact, it is our only world. When you [the Administration] take our land, you cut away the very heart of our existence. We have little or no experience of social survival detached from the land. For us to be completely landless is a nightmare which no dollar in the pocket or dollar in the bank will allay; we are a threatened people (Connell 1989:24).

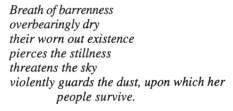

Pinnacles

Ruggedly tall and imposing
staring menacingly
vibrating eeriness
intimidating the stranger
with its unwelcome ugliness.

Breath of barrenness
overbearingly dry
their worn out existence
pierces the stillness
threatens the sky
violently guards the dust, upon which her
people survive.

Makerita Vaai

97

Available evidence suggests that mining has proved an iniquitous form of development, generating social inequalities that have become sources of community tension and conflict. Within the distribution system (covering royalties, compensation, wages and other monetary gains), the benefits have largely been the privilege of local and foreign shareholders, national governments and local elites. Paradoxically, those who lay claim to the mineral-rich land and those responsible for digging it out are amongst the most economically marginalised. With the probable exception of Nauru, the 'trickle down' of high earnings from mining has been just that: a trickle. Neither Fiji nor New Caledonia concedes a royalty to landowners; and while their counterparts in PNG and Nauru have been the beneficiaries of royalties and/or compensation payments, the returns have represented a small proportion of the value of extracted minerals and corporate profits. In addition, their unequal distribution (a product of many factors including disregard of customary land rights) has undermined the redistributive mechanisms that were a feature of customary life before mining. On Bougainville, individual cash payments for occupation fees and compensation have varied widely (O'Fairchaillaigh 1980:480; Connell 1992 & 1989:18).

Another perceived benefit of mining - employment - does not offer much more support for the 'trickle down' theory. Outside the construction phase, mining shows a smaller capacity for employment (and in turn income) generation than some other sectors of the economy. In New Caledonia and Nauru, employment opportunities for the indigenous people have been negligible as a result of a heavy reliance on immigrant labour. In PNG, the local benefits have in cases like Bougainville and Ok Tedi been limited by the preference for non-local Papua New Guineans (Oliver 1973:42; Kreye & Castell 1991:32). In Fiji, although ethnic Fijians have dominated the mine workforce, employment in the mining sector averages only between one and two per cent of total employment. Moreover, in both Fiji and PNG, the industry has, in spite of national commitments to localisation, continued to display features of a colonial division of labour. It has typically maintained a highly paid senior expatriate (white) elite within management, a discriminatory wage system, and a ceiling on the upward mobility of indigenous workers (Emberson-Bain 1994; Wesley-Smith & Ogan 1991:21; Moody 1991:66). In colonial New Caledonia, the situation is probably worse, with Kanak nickel workers concentrated in unskilled mine jobs and enjoying few opportunities to move into higher-paid skilled work (Henningham n.d.:9; Connell 1991:69).

The failure of mining to deliver sustainable livelihoods can similarly be seen from wages and other returns to labour as well as living conditions in the mine settlements. This has unfortunately been a relatively neglected area of mining studies. From labour research undertaken on Fiji's mining sector, it is apparent that mine wages have persistently lagged behind other sectors of the economy with few exceptions, notably agriculture. For large numbers of mineworkers who live off company (supermarket) credit and wage advances, day-to-day survival does not come easy. Housing for most Fijian families provides outdoor and communal washing, bathing, cooking and toilet facilities that are substandard (Emberson-Bain 1992 video & 1994). On Bougainville too, before the closure of the Panguna mine in 1989, impoverished squatter settlements had sprung up; and relocation had created overcrowding, dilapidated housing and poor facilities (Thompson 1990:12-13; Connell 1989). Health problems including respiratory ailments (e.g. bronchial/chest infections and asthma), gastro-enteritis, skin problems and child malnutrition appear to be linked to sulphur pollution,

98

poor living conditions and poverty in the mining community of Vatukoula (Emberson-Bain 1994). New Caledonia's problem may be even more serious given its high rates of lung cancer and childhood leukaemia and 'the world's record for asthma-related mortalities' (Newborn 1992:3).

The impact of mining on women

One aspect of the social impact of mining which has received less attention than it deserves is women. While there has been some interest in how mining has affected women's lives, research has mainly been confined to PNG; there are no separate studies; and accounts of the Bougainville crisis, in so far as they do show an interest in women, focus on the traditional, stereotypical preoccupations with women as passive victims, women as mothers and wives. There is an urgent need for more comprehensive, critical studies on the changes in women's social, economic and health status resulting from mining. Equally important is the need to examine the ways in which women have (actively and creatively) responded to the changes, including the role they have played in community-based struggles against mining development.

The importance of integrating gender analysis into studies on mining rests in part in its ability to enhance our understanding of the social impact of mining. Existing evidence suggests that while women have reaped fewer of the rewards/benefits of mining, they have borne the brunt of the most dislocating and alienating aspects of it. The negative effects that mining has had on living standards in the Pacific, including the poverty it has generated, are especially problematic for women given their traditional responsibilities as caretakers of the family. The channelling of village male labour into the industry - a feature of Fiji in the past and PNG still today, for example at the Porgera mine - has increased women's workload by leaving them responsible for subsistence farming and food production. Family recruitment in lieu of migrant labour systems has generated its own form of dislocation. The breaking up of the extended family system has reduced the physical and emotional support available to women within the newly located nuclear households.

Other factors also highlight the burdens that mining has imposed on women. Environmental damage, in particular the depletion and contamination of sources of water and firewood, and the damage to land and fishing grounds, have all undermined women's capacity to provide food and take care of their families. They have also increased their work loads (e.g. the distances that have to be travelled on foot to collect firewood, tend to food gardens or fish). The inadequacy of household cash earnings and poor living conditions in some Pacific mining towns, for example Vatukoula, constitute additional pressures. Congested, sometimes impoverished and culturally alienating settlements outside the realm of traditional mechanisms of social control, have brought the novel (or greater) problems of domestic violence, alcoholism, extra-marital sexual relations, and teenage pregnancies.

Employment

Barriers to women's employment in mining exclude them from one of the few material benefits that local Pacific communities can potentially derive from large mining projects. Male dominance of mining-generated business/cooperative ventures such as the significant Bougainville Development Corporation (Wesley-Smith & Ogan 1991: 22-23, 18) also emphasises women's greater economic marginalisation relative to men. In small mining towns like Vatukoula where opportunities for non-mine work seldom exist, the overwhelming preference in favour of males has implications for women's educational/literacy status (and in turn economic independence) by reducing the perceived 'need' to educate girls, particularly when money is short. Women comprise a very small proportion of the mine workforce in PNG and Fiji, and possibly none at all in Nauru and New Caledonia. Of the 20,000 women classified as wage or salaried employees in PNG, there are a total of only 243 women in the mining/quarrying sector: four per cent of the total 6,326 employees. In 1987, women claimed just three per cent (2,524,000 *kina*) of the total wages and salaries bill paid in the mining sector (81,570,000 *kina*) (Government of PNG 1987).

The gender bias of the mine labour market reflects the general dominance of patriarchal values as well as the industry's own economic rationale, both of which prescribe an essentially domestic and reproductive (or prostitution) role for women. In Fiji, prohibitions exist on underground mine work for women, and restrictions on night work are also laid down in law. Women are therefore largely confined to certain types of lower-status, lower-paid surface jobs deemed suitable for them. In the past, work opportunities for ethnic Fijian women did not extend beyond very low-paid domestic work in the houses of European management or a short-lived prostitution trade (Emberson-Bain 1994). Today, women are still employed as cheap domestic servants but they are also found in the research, geology, administration and stores sections on the surface, as well as in the mill as rocksorters. In fact, traditional stereotypes about women's 'unsuitability' for mine and night work and the supposedly protectionist values underlying them appear to be quite flexible on the production floor. Women at Vatukoula perform fairly strenuous manual work in the mill (shovelling soil and rocks) and they work the night shifts. Women rocksorters, paid at the minimum unskilled rate of $FIJ 1.55 an hour, work in a dusty, hot and poorly lit environment, spending many hours of the day standing bent over a conveyor belt.

Conflict, violence and other controls

The extent to which mining has weakened or reinforced traditional controls over Pacific women, and improved or lowered their economic/social status, including their vulnerability to male violence, urgently needs researching. The fragmentary information that exists suggests that the changes in women's status are probably considerable and that (female-directed) violence may well be an endemic feature of Pacific mining communities. Heavy alcohol consumption (noted as long as 20 years ago on Bougainville), sexual and domestic violence, and prostitution (with its attendant health risks) typify some of the most problematic features of mining development for women, but it is difficult to generalise about the scale and intensity of their impact. At the Ok Tedi mine, the establishment of exclusive and competitive male (beer) drinking gatherings at night has led to a high incidence of violent drunken behaviour amongst men, including rape and other serious assaults on women (Hyndman 1991:84). Heavy consumption of beer by male mineworkers on the island of Misima has also resulted in an escalating incidence of domestic and other violence (Gerritsen & McIntyre 1991:47-48).

In terms of women's general status, the Ok Tedi case suggests that Wopkaimin women have lost important aspects of their former economic and social independence. Traditionally, women engaged in independent food collection and consumption and lived in separate housing. As a result of mining, they have become dependent on their husbands for food and housing. Further, as cash has increasingly displaced the traditional valuables used to pay bride price, women have become prey to a competitive, entrepreneurial marriage market: a form of male-controlled 'business development' that has permitted men to exploit and generally increase their control over women's sexuality (Hyndman 1991:83-85). These indicators of a general lowering of status for Wopkaimin women within the family almost certainly have implications for their health (as well as the welfare of their children), particularly since wages to buy food are eroded by (male) alcohol consumption and because of the rising violence associated with this.

In general, it is likely that women bear the major burden of mining-linked social conflict and violence whether this occurs at the level of the household (in respect of marital and kin relations) or the wider community, where coercive measures by the state or mine employers probably encapsulate the violence of the industry in its crudest form. The PNG military offensives and economic and medical blockade against Bougainville are unprecedented in the post-colonial history of the Pacific. So is the use of riot police squads (to quash the three-year mineworkers' strike) in the post-colonial industrial history of Fiji. On Bougainville, women have not made war but they have paid dearly for it. And they have not only endured the pain of losing husbands and children. As their homes have become part of a war zone that has delivered heavy casualties, cut off medical and educational services, destroyed homes and food gardens, the demands on their labour have risen. Worse, amongst the human rights atrocities inflicted on Bougainvilleans during the crisis, women have had to deal with the additional menace of rape and the trauma of rape-induced teenage pregnancies (Emberson-Bain 1993a & b). The violence of the war has even reverberated on women within PNG itself. In at least two provinces, East Sepik and Wewak for example, women have complained about the increase in domestic violence committed by husbands returning from military service on the island (*PNG Times* 11 February 1993).

Women's land rights

The erosion of women's land rights (along with the status these conferred on them within traditional society) also appears to be an outcome of mining development, more especially in the matrilineal societies of Bougainville, Lihir and Nauru where women have had more to lose. Matrilineal descent systems which transferred land rights through women did not necessarily confer significant levels of autonomy, power and authority on them. In Nauru, for example, women's matrilineal status was circumscribed by their limited access to positions of traditional political leadership and authority (Pollock 1991:92-94) and by controls over their sexuality. It is nevertheless notable that on Bougainville, the matrilineal principles of land inheritance accorded women a position of some importance within traditional society, and gender relations tended to be marked more by 'complementarity' than the 'hierarchy' typical of PNG's highland societies (Wesley-Smith & Ogan 1991:11). On Nauru, the matrilineal land system provided the vehicle through which women 'indirectly controlled much of the subsistence economy' (Pollock 1991: 97).

Mining development on Bougainville has brought about an increasing contradiction between the traditionally dominant matrilineal system of the Naisioi-speaking people and the patrilineal values associated with the cash economy and private property (Filer 1990:92-93). The high money stakes of mining compensation and royalty incomes have strengthened intruding patrilineal claims. While the extent to which women's status has been affected by the changes is unknown, the failure of the compensation system to account for the custom of matrilineal inheritance (Okole 1990:16-24) suggests that it has almost certainly deteriorated. A decline in women's position relative to men has also resulted from mining because the compensation system has boosted (male) cash-crop farming, and employment and business opportunities have favoured men (Wesley-Smith & Ogan 1991:23).

On Nauru, it has been argued that 'women's control' within the phosphate economy 'has continued' unaffected; that women have, along with men, become the recipients of an independent source of cash income from mining; and that the distribution of mining royalties to landholders has been based on matrilineal principles (Pollock 1991:98, 104). Yet against this, it needs to be noted that, in spite of their traditional status, women do not appear to have exercised much, if any, influence over negotiations for compensation, or to have had a say in the management of phosphate resources. Furthermore, the destruction of the subsistence economy appears likely to have undermined an important basis of women's status within the traditional division of labour. It has reduced their economic and social independence by preventing their cultivation of pandanus, a crop which was regarded as more valuable than coconuts (which men usually tended) and which required them to live away from their husbands for a few months of every year (Weeramentry et al. 1988: 182-184). The loss of the central plateau known as the Topside has disrupted women's role as food providers and craft-makers, eroded the prestige they enjoyed as transmitters of cultural knowledge (through the production of craft valuables), and forged a more dependent, domesticated lifestyle which has led to a decline in their health.

Writing women in

The scant attention that has been paid to the impact of mining on women reflects the perception of it as a 'male' industry. Such a view is also probably responsible for the marginal role women have been permitted to play in the public domain of community debate and decision making about this form of 'development'. Yet the male-centric definition of mining is misleading, and fails to account for the central role that women have played in the industry, as well as the numerous ways in which their economic and social status has been dramatically affected by it. To my knowledge, the contribution of human labour power to the process of profitable mineral exploitation has nowhere in the world consisted simply of male mineworkers. In the mining economies of the Pacific, no less than their counterparts of Southern Africa, the unpaid labour of women has been a crucial factor in maintaining low-cost labour systems. Women's labour has taken various forms outside direct employment including unpaid household management, food production and social security support to dependants in village economies stripped of their young able-bodied males; their paid sexual labour services (prostitution) in bachelor mining outposts; and their unpaid social and biological reproductive labour in mining centres that have opted for family settlement. Every mine labour process has in one way or another been dependent on, and subsidised by, women's productive, sexual and reproductive labour. To depict the industry as a male enclave is, for all these reasons, therefore, to misrepresent the real situation. It is important that any study seeking to understand the social impact of mining in all its complexity, including the dynamics of exploitation and power within the labour process, should account for its gender component.

The case for writing women into the social history of mining in the Pacific also rests on the important, yet inadequately documented, role they have played in community-based responses to mining. The cases of Bougainville and New Caledonia probably stand out as the most obvious beacons in the history of women's involvement in community struggles. On Bougainville, the protests of the Rorovana women - who in 1969 fearlessly resisted the attempt by 100 armed riot police to seize their land on behalf of the Australian-owned Conzinc Rio Tinto Ltd (CRA) (Moody 1991:70-71) - are but one instance of the courage and inspiring example they have shown. In Fiji, the ongoing mineworkers' strike at Vatukoula has drawn more recent attention to the increasingly public and militant role women are assuming in struggles against mining companies (Emberson-Bain 1992b & 1993a).

Mining development - how sustainable? [4]

Mining is proving a problematic and controversial form of development in the Pacific region. It has brought certain national benefits such as foreign exchange, and it has generated domestic earnings and employment. However, the limited, unequal and discriminatory nature of the distribution of these benefits at the local level (with respect to workers, landowners and women) is a conspicuous anomaly. Other negative outcomes underscore the unsustainable features of this form of development. Indeed, like other extractive industries, mining would appear to exemplify some of the least desirable features of growth-led development, including irreversible damage to the environment. While more research is needed, available evidence would already seem to stress the need to look long and hard at the opportunity cost of this industry. Certainly, the destructive legacy of mining on Bougainville, as in Vatukoula and Nauru - the environmental damage, the human suffering and dislocation - is enough to demand some serious rethinking.

The Vatukoula example provides evidence of the unsustainable livelihoods that can result from mining development. As a woman born and raised in the town describes, an ironic fate has befallen many who have left their villages in search of a better material life as mineworkers:

Life in the village is the same in some ways as here because there we also struggle to make ends meet, fishing and planting. But because of the low wages, we are worse off at Vatukoula. My uncle came back to the village when he retired after 55 years of working as a miner. He found that we had a better house than him because he couldn't make enough money to build his house out of his wages here. The people in the village are just planting but they can raise enough to get their roofing iron and buy other things. But when my uncle came back from Vatukoula, he was poorer than the people in the village.

You know, our old people, our fathers who were here before us, they really struggled ... they had to work so hard but they earned only just enough to buy their bread and butter. When they packed up to go back to the village, they just packed a suitcase, that was it. Today, it's just the same, maybe worse (Vatukoula mother 1993, Vatukoula, pers. comm.).

Amongst Bougainvilleans, there seem to be some strong feelings that it is desirable and possible, given the island's abundant natural resources, to abandon large-scale mining projects with a view to exploring other forms of land-based development such as cash crops like cocoa and copra. These views obviously conflict with those of the PNG state which is keen to reopen the besieged Panguna mine. At Vatukoula, where industrial disputes have been more explosive than the landowners' struggle, the situation is rather different. Worker demands focus on improving conditions of employment, including rights to collective bargaining, and they extend to a worker stake in mine ownership and management. The call of local landowners, on the other hand, has been for compensation and a fairer share in the benefits of goldmining (including more job opportunities). In neither case has there been any serious suggestion to close the mining operation down. One of the reasons that might be suggested for this more accommodating position is that unlike Bougainville, Vatukoula is a town that exists solely because of the mine. However difficult life is, however great the hardship, there is a dependence on the mine for employment, an attachment to the town because it is home, and the realisation that the mine's closure would mean having to build a new life elsewhere.

Reforming the (mining) development process

The idea of scrapping large-scale mining projects may be politically unacceptable for Pacific governments, and, in cases like Vatukoula, such a solution may in any event not be perceived as desirable by the local community. But there is still much that can be done to avert the social and environmental problems that have been inflicted on Pacific Islanders. Recent trends show an increasing acceptance by regional governments of the relevance and importance of environmental impact assessments (EIA). Yet the lack of resources and technical knowledge, as well as the political forces that influence negotiations between foreign mining companies and governments/local elites, have hampered the development (and implementation) of EIA that are really independent, frank and comprehensive. In Fiji, for example, despite the long history of mining exploration and development by foreign companies, government assessment of the environmental implications of new ventures (such as the massive copper development proposed for the Namosi area) has progressed no further than evaluations of company-sponsored EIA. The lack of independent assessments is a serious disadvantage that could, and should, be rectified.

The failure to take EIA beyond narrowly defined environmental questions is another shortcoming. An assessment of the likely social effects (including their gender dimension) of mining projects under review would seem to be crucial if we are to deepen our understanding of the benefits and problems associated with mining development, and if the process is not going to end up being a continuous replay of Bougainville or Vatukoula. In the long term, social impact assessments should help, in a very practical way, to minimise the adverse effects of the industry on the human and physical environment. They would also help promote more sustainable development policies in those Pacific countries where mineral or natural resource exploitation is already, or is likely to get, under way.

The Bougainville crisis demonstrates very starkly other undesirable features of the development process in the Pacific. In particular, it exemplifies how development continues to be imposed from above by (often ill-informed) political elites rather than shaped by (local-level) community concerns, knowledge and cultural values. The significance of community (including women's) opposition to mining on the island would surely seem to lie in the fact that disaffection has been deep enough to sponsor a populist armed uprising. Although resistance is closely linked to (and complicated by) a struggle for independence against PNG, it needs to be remembered that it has a long history of its own. The eruption of a fully-fledged guerilla war by a tiny islander community against a powerful nation-state says as much about the authoritarian nature of the development process as it does about the strength of feeling and tenacity of ordinary villagers. The lessons must surely be learnt.

Undoubtedly, there are different and conflicting views of the Bougainville crisis just as there are of Pacific development. At the very least, however, it would seem fair to conclude that whatever the perceived economic benefits of mineral resource exploitation by regional governments, the upsurge of community protests sends out clear distress signals. Whether these can be responded to adequately by throwing out the bath water but not the (mining) baby - or whether in this instance the 'baby' should go as well - is the crucial question! For the NGO community, the challenge would seem to be to understand and respond to these community signals - ultimately to find constructive ways of acting on them. The limited development choices available to Pacific countries, and the political and economic realities of the region, may make it unrealistic for island states to withdraw completely from mineral resource extraction as a development option. If this is in fact the case (and it is surely for local communities themselves to determine), negotiating a less destructive form of exploitation may be the most that can be hoped for. But the marginalisation of Pacific communities, including women, from policy planning and decision making is testimony to their powerlessness. Equally telling is the heavy hand with which local opponents of mining development have been treated. An important challenge facing Pacific peoples, as well as the regional NGO community, must therefore be to find ways of pushing for this political space and development agenda; and to empower local communities so that they are better equipped to prevent the most harmful and destructive features of mining, to have a greater influence over mining policy, and ultimately, to help shape a more socially equitable and sustainable form of development. Otherwise, the bleak prospect of further conflict, violence and bloodshed may be the only alternative.

*   This is a revised and expanded version of a paper originally prepared for a Pacific regional meeting of the Canadian University Students Organization (CUSO), Suva, November 1992 (and published by *Tok blong SPPF,* Canada, in February 1993). I would like to express special thanks to Wendy Poussard (formerly of CUSO Pacific, Suva) for her original interest in, and support for, this research; and to Tarcissius Kabutaulaka and Roman Grynberg of the University of the South Pacific for kindly sharing data and documentation on mining in Papua New Guinea.

Notes

1.   According to the 1993 World Bank Report, growth rates averaged 2.2 per cent between 1990 and 1992 for the seven World Bank Pacific regional member countries. This excludes Papua New Guinea.

2.   For a discussion of labour issues, industrial conflict and the Nasomo land dispute, see Emberson-Bain (1994 & 1992 video).

3.   Heart and kidney disease, and blindness, are amongst the serious health problems of Nauruans. Research in the late 1970s revealed that as many as 64 per cent of men and 60 per cent of women aged 20 years and over had hyperuraemia, the highest rates ever recorded. (Weeramentry et al. 1988:23, 193-195).

4.   These last two sections of the paper are drawn from Emberson-Bain (1993a).

References

Bird, E.C.F., Dubois, J-P and Iltis, J.A. (1984) *The impacts of opencast mining on the rivers and coasts of New Caledonia,* Tokyo: The United Nations University

Connell, J. (1989) Statement of John Connell, Supreme Court, Victoria

-------- (1991) 'Compensation and conflict: The Bougainville copper mine, Papua New Guinea' in Connell, J. and Howitt, R. (eds) *Mining and Indigenous Peoples in Australasia,* Sydney: Sydney University Press and Oxford University Press

-------- (1992) 'Logic is a capitalist cover-up': Compensation and crisis in Bougainville, Papua New Guinea', in Henningham, S. and May, R.J. (eds) *Resources, development and politics in the Pacific Islands,* Sydney: Sydney University Press and Oxford University Press

Emberson-Bain, 'A. (1992a) 'Perilous pursuits: The environmental and social impact of the mining and nuclear industries in the Pacific', paper presented to Social Science Research Council (New York)/DAWN Workshop on Population and the Environment, Mexico, January-February

-------- (1992b) 'Fiji: Women, poverty and post-coup pressure' in Robie, D. (ed.) *Tu Galala: Social change in the Pacific,* Australia: Bridget Williams Books Ltd/Pluto Press

-------- (1992 video) *Na Ma'e! Na Ma'e!* (We stand until we die!) 58-minute documentary

-------- (1993a) 'Catching a common vision? Mining, development and the perspectives of Pacific women', research paper for the International Women's Development Agency (IWDA), Melbourne, Australia

-------- (1993b) 'Bougainville: Women's voices from a Pacific war zone' 30-minute radio documentary

-------- (1994) *Labour and gold in Fiji,* Cambridge, United Kingdom: Cambridge University Press

Filer, C. (1990) 'The Bougainville rebellion, the mining industry and the process of social disintegration in Papua New Guinea' in May, R.J. and Spriggs, M. (eds) *The Bougainville crisis,* Bathurst, New South Wales, Australia: Crawford House Press

Forster, M. (1992) 'Bougainville: Background to the Republic of Bougainville', unpub. paper, Interim Government, Bougainville

Gerritsen, R. and McIntyre, M. (1991) 'Dilemmas of distribution: The Misima mine, Papua New Guinea' in Connell, J. and Howitt, R. (eds) *Mining and indigenous peoples in Australasia,* Sydney: Sydney University Press

Henningham, S. (n.d.) 'Mining and politics in New Caledonia', unpublished draft paper, Canberra, Australia

Howard, M.C. (1988) *The impact of the international mining industry on native peoples,* Sydney: University of Sydney, Transnational Corporations Research Project

---------- (1991) *Mining, politics and development in the South Pacific,* Westview Press

Hyndman, D. (1991) 'Zipping down the fly on the Ok Tedi project' in Connell, J. and Howitt, R. (eds) *Mining and indigenous peoples in Australasia,* Sydney: Sydney University Press

Jackson, R. (1991) 'Not without influence: Villages, mining companies, and government in Papua New Guinea', in Connell, J. and Howitt, R. (eds) *Mining and indigenous peoples in Australasia,* Sydney: Sydney University Press

Kreye, O. and Castell, L.F.P. (1991) 'Development and the environment in PNG' in **Catalyst,** vol.21, no.3

Mannur, H.G. (1993) 'Development frustrations of a small country: A case of Papua New Guinea' in Crosbie Walsh, A. (ed.) (1993) *Development that works! Lessons from Asia-Pacific,* Palmerston North, New Zealand: Massey University Development Studies, Monograph no.3

Moody, R. (1991) *Plunder! The rise and future fall of the world's most powerful mining conglomerate,* London and Christchurch, New Zealand: Partizans/CAFCA Publications

Newborn, S. (1992) 'The mining and smelting of garnierite in New Caledonia: Blood money for the French and Japanese nuclear industries', unpublished paper, Auckland, New Zealand

O'Fairchaillaigh, C. (1980) 'The role of foreign investment in mineral development: A comparative analysis', unpublished Ph.D. thesis, Australian National University, Canberra

Okole, H. (1990) 'The politics of the Panguna Landowners' Organization' in May, R.J. and Spriggs, M. (eds) *The Bougainville crisis,* Bathurst, New South Wales, Australia: Crawford House Press

Oliver, D. (1973) *Bougainville: A personal history,* Melbourne: Melbourne University Press

Government of PNG (1987) *Census of employment,* Port Moresby, Papua New Guinea: National Statistics Office, Government of Papua New Guinea

PNG Times 11 February 1993

Pollock, N. (1991) 'The status of women in Nauru' in Hill, H. (ed.) *On the status of women in Pacific Island countries',* draft background papers for the South Pacific Regional Seminar on the United Nations Convention on the Elimination of All Forms of Discrimination against Women (CEDAW), Rarotonga, Cook Islands, 18-21 March

Sen, G. and Grown, C. (1985) *Development, crisis and alternative visions: Third world women's perspectives,* New Delhi: DAWN

Shaw, B. (1992) 'Pacific agriculture: A retrospective of the 1980s and prospects for the 1990s' in *Pacific Economic Bulletin,* vol.7, no.1, June

South Pacific Commission (1993) *South Pacific economies statistical summary,* Noumea, SPESS, no.13

Thompson, H. (1990) 'Mining and the environment in Papua New Guinea', working paper no.39, Murdoch University, Australia

Trainer, T. (1990) 'A rejection of the Brundtland report' in *Ifda Dossier,* May/June, 71-84

Weeramentry, C.G., Challen, R.H., and Degidoa, G. (1988) 'Republic of Nauru Report: Commission of Inquiry into the Rehabilitation of the Worked-out Phosphate Lands of Nauru', unpublished document, Australia

Wesley-Smith, T. and Ogan, E. (1991) 'Changing relations of production in Bougainville' draft paper for *The Contemporary Pacific,* 4 (2)

Eight

Development distortions: The case of Bougainville*

Ruby Mirinka

Introduction

Being a Bougainvillean who has recently come out of the war-torn island, I regard this as a privilege and a welcome opportunity to be invited to speak at this first Global Conference on the Sustainable Development of Small Island Developing States.

The concern of the various island leaders for sustainable development in their respective states has also been shared by the Bougainvilleans for many years. And therefore, given this opportunity, I shall speak of the concerns for sustainable development on Bougainville by attempting to answer questions such as: Is there potential for sustainable development on Bougainville? How and why is there a war on Bougainville? How has the war affected the environment, health and lives of the people of Bougainville? When and how could Bougainville begin the process of and progress towards its social, physical, economic and political development?

But before these questions can be answered, I will briefly mention the history of Bougainville, for the sake of those who do not know about it. Bougainville is an island located six kilometres north of the Solomon Islands and about 1,000 kilometres east of Port Moresby, the national capital of Papua New Guinea. Bougainville covers an area of some 8,000 square kilometres, with a population of 160,000 at the beginning of the crisis in 1989. The island was named by the French explorer Louis de Bougainville who sighted it in 1768. It was later annexed by the German New Guinea Company as part of territories which included the north-eastern section of the big island of New Guinea, New Britain, New Ireland and all the Solomon Islands.

In 1899, an agreement was signed between Germany and Great Britain, as noted in conventions and declarations between the two countries, for the settlement of Samoa and other questions. The agreement was signed in London on 14 November 1899 and ratifications were exchanged in London and Berlin on 16

February 1900. The Solomon Islands were then given to Great Britain and Bougainville remained under German control. However, after the defeat of Germany in World War I, the German territories, collectively termed New Guinea, became part of a League of Nations mandate. After World War II, Bougainville became a United Nations Trust Territory under the Australian Administration.

Ever since the 1899 agreement to separate Bougainville from the Solomon Islands, Bougainville has objected to being held as a separate entity from its traditional brothers, sisters and relatives, who for 10,000 years had traded and intermarried with people from the Shortland and Choiseul Islands of the western part of the Solomon Islands. Due to the close relationship and family ties with the people of the Western Solomons, Bougainvilleans have had similarities in culture, beliefs and practices; and they have the same black skin as people from the Western Solomons.

Cultural values about land

Bougainvilleans are normally peace-loving people. Their disapproval and anger, however, began developing when they realised that their land would be totally destroyed with the commencement of mining. As far back as 1962, when the Australian-owned mining company, Conzinc Rio Tinto Australia Ltd (CRA), first negotiated plans to open the Panguna copper mine, Bougainvilleans expressed their disapproval.

The disapproval was more evident amongst the women as they were the chiefs of the land in our matrilineal society. Although culturally they never spoke out openly and it was usually the uncles who were the spokespersons in the settling of land disputes, power and support were always given to the men by the women, and women retained a strong influence over their men in negotiations between tribal groups over the settlement of land disputes and land ownership.

The women in our culture are regarded as chiefs of the land in the areas where they live. As such they have maintained the right to be heard and to be involved at all decision-making levels on matters of social, physical, economic and political development. However, these fundamental rights of our women, and the cultural values, beliefs and practices of Bougainvilleans have been continuously ignored by the political administration, resulting in major political unrest. This unrest has been most violently expressed in the Bougainville crisis, now entering its sixth year.

Land is highly valued among the women of Bougainville. To see how much value is placed on land, I would like to mention one of the cultures of the Naisioi area of Central Bougainville. In Naisioi tradition, women have always forced their teenage daughters from the age of 11 years and upwards to marry after they have completed grade six level of their education. This is for fear that when a girl leaves home to further her education in another place, she might marry a man from another area or province and lose her entitlement to ownership of the land. This custom is still practised today. The importance of the land is also one of the main reasons why one cannot see women from Kieta employed in the private sector and/or even in government. The Bougainville women you will find in those jobs are mostly from other districts, such as Buka, Siwai and Buin.

Culturally women are actually chiefs. Although we have men who are usually put as the spokespersons, the women are always chiefs. The men speak on their behalf. They speak with the knowledge that has been given to them by the women. This means that especially in terms of land rights, women are the ones who make the final decisions. So in this sense, with the Bougainville mine, I feel that the people who started the mine overlooked that kind of status for the women. And I think that's where the whole problem is.

Bougainville health worker/educator
(Emberson-Bain 1993)

Both these examples show how much cultural value is placed on land by the women of Bougainville, unlike Western culture which allows for land to be easily traded and abused. Westerners will mine and extract all the wealth from land, not caring about the indigenous people whose life is centred around the land they inhabit.

Environmental damage from mining

Bougainville has rich resources for the development of the island. For example, the Panguna mine was extracting copper and other minerals such as gold. Also, since the establishment of the mine, the surveyors have discovered lime in the Manetai area, and other minerals throughout Bougainville. There are documents which clearly indicate that there are mining plans for Buka Island, the Tinputz area, the Panguna mine in Central Bougainville, and the Buin area in the south.

In other words, if the foreign mining companies are not controlled, they could open mines in all these areas. The fear of the people is that they would be forced out of their villages and their land destroyed if these mines opened. They remember what the Panguna copper mining company did to the villagers in and surrounding the mine site.

At Panguna, people were forced out from their land, and their homes and gardens were destroyed, as the operating area of the mine expanded without consideration for their culture, beliefs and practices of family life. The rivers and streams surrounding the mine site were polluted and all the fish killed. Today, the Java River, which received waste direct from the mine, does not have life in it anymore. Soil in and around the river was poisoned, killing vegetation. Birds were killed by the pollution from the mine. Flying foxes have all disappeared. Food crops and fruit trees were affected and did not yield well, either in quantity or quality.

I personally feel that the mine should be closed indefinitely. If it does have to open, sure enough it will create another problem. We have seen the effects of the mine which caused more damages - not only to the earth, but even to the human beings. There is a chaotic situation here, and even though I am speaking for myself, I believe there are many women with the same feelings on the island. They just feel that mining is not the only way you can generate revenue for the island.

Bougainville health worker/educator
(Emberson-Bain 1993)

Also, shellfish from as far as Siwai, in South Bougainville, were destroyed by the mining chemicals and the people of that area reported the abnormal appearance of shellfish. Due to the continuous washing down of tailings from the mine site into the Java River, a large land mass developed along its bank, which caused the sea level to rise to the extent that it almost sank the smaller islands. These have been the tragic environmental effects of the Panguna copper mine.

It is clear then that there are resources and the potential for sustainable development on Bougainville. But how and why is there a war on the island? As mentioned earlier, land is highly valued among the people of Bougainville. As our women put it:

> The land is a mother, it is wealth, it is life, food and health. It
> is where we will be born and die. When the land is taken away,
> we are nothing.

It is this strong cultural value placed on the right to ownership and development of their land that was clearly demonstrated in 1962, when Bougainvillean women led a demonstration march objecting to the opening of the Panguna mine. In 1964, another protest march was led by the women opposing the building of Loloho Port after the mine was opened. During that time, women were harshly dealt with by police attempting to stop the demonstration.

Although these marches were organised by women mainly from Central Bougainville, the feeling of being deprived of the right to ownership and protection of the land was felt by women throughout the island. In 1975, Bougainville women were joined by their menfolk in their non-violent protest march requesting respect and freedom for their right to ownership and protection of their land.

By 1989, frustration had escalated when Bougainvilleans realised that out of approximately 20 per cent of the mining revenue given to the Papua New Guinea (PNG) government from the Panguna mine, only 0.1 per cent was re-injected into Bougainville for the island's development. So Bougainvilleans demanded that the mining agreement be reviewed. In fact, the agreement was supposed to have been reviewed every seven years, but this had been ignored, and it was then the 11th year and no review had been made. The landowners were also frustrated over their compensation claim for the environmental damage caused by the operations of the Panguna copper mine.

When negotiations over the above claims deadlocked in 1989, the Panguna mine was forcibly shut down by the Bougainvilleans the same year. Police and government authorities were sent to Bougainville to settle the grievances but the situation got worse and the national government then deployed 1,000 members of the security forces in an attempt to control the situation. But the involvement of the security forces has only worsened the situation. Since 1989, there has been a political and military war raging on the island. It is now entering its sixth year, and it has affected the environment, health and lives of the people in many terrible ways.

By 1991, according to reports by the International Red Cross, this war had caused the death of 5,000 people. By 1994, the death toll had probably reached between 7,000 and 8,000. I have lived and worked in Bougainville during the last five years of the crisis, and as a nurse educator I have witnessed more deaths recently than in the early part of the crisis. They have largely resulted from preventable diseases. In addition, young Bougainvilleans are today being used as frontliners by the PNG military, which means that Bougainvilleans are killing each other. I have witnessed this happening.

Within the corners of the rectangle

(translated from the French original,
Dans les pans du rectangle)

*For the people of Koindé**

Dogs howl at death
within the corners of the blue white and red rectangle
draping the violence 'made in France'
The aggression against our people up
there in the hills of the legendary Atai~
The hunting down of women and children
of that tribe
by the mobile forces
A pursuit to protect the vested interests of this sawmill
which pollutes our rivers our fields
all that is shielded from the howling
And yet amongst us some lackeys
who cry crocodile tears
Tell them my sister
Tell them comrade
'Do not come to cry
at my death
you who never stand
alongside us
Do not come to pray
you pious creatures
and all the other swine
flooding the churches of hypocrisy and racism
where the dogs howl at death'.

Déwé Gorode

* Koindé is a tribe in La Foa, New Caledonia, where in early January 1983 the indigenous Kanaks faced a massive military offensive by the colonial French mobile forces. The Kanaks fought back, killing two gendarmes. The violent repression of the Koindé people was aimed at protecting the interests of the owners of a sawmill whose operations were polluting their source of water.

~ Atai was the Kanak chief who led the great insurrection of 1878 against the French colonial state.

Conclusion

In considering the Bougainville conflict, what is evident is: firstly, the failure by the Australian mining company and the national government to play a more consultative role with the landowners and local community prior to the opening of the mine; and secondly, the inconsistent reviews of the mining agreement. It is also clear that there cannot be sustainable development on Bougainville when the island is in a state of war and the people are opposed to the mine. As Rodda states in her book *Women and the Environment,* for sustainable development to evolve, the culture of a society (and by this she means the economic base, social organisation, knowledge, norms, regulations and political authority) must first be understood. In addition, safety is a crucial factor in the planning of sustainable development; and the community needs to participate in, and have control over, development programmes or projects.

As a result of the war on Bougainville, many people are suffering and dying in the jungle. Even as I speak to you now, this is happening, particularly amongst the civilian population of more than 70,000 who are still in areas affected by the government blockade which was imposed in March 1990. The war is killing and destroying both people and the environment. Under no circumstances can sustainable development be achieved in the state of war Bougainville is undergoing at present.

For the sake of the women and children, and the future of Bougainville, I want to appeal to the women of the world through this conference to raise their voices to strongly condemn the genocidal and inhumane war on Bougainville; to protest to the government of Papua New Guinea that it stop the war on the island and allow Bougainvillean leaders time to sort out differences amongst themselves so that they can come up with a common voice; and further, that Papua New Guinea be persuaded to begin dialogue for peace negotiations that will restore lasting peace on Bougainville.

*   This is an abridged version of a paper presented to the First Global Conference on the Sustainable Development of Small Island Developing States, Barbados, Caribbean, in May 1994

Reference

Emberson-Bain, 'A. (1993) *Bougainville: Women's voices from a Pacific war zone,* 30 minute radio documentary

Nine

Logging our heritage*

Nahau Rooney

... There is a widely held assumption that forestry projects in Papua New Guinea are going to open up new land for agriculture and even food production ... This has not happened in the past and with forestry projects penetrating even deeper into our remote, sparsely populated areas, it is even less likely to happen in the future. In fact, it is interesting to note that in New Ireland where huge areas of remote mountainsides are being denuded by forestry operations, little if anything at all is being done with these newly cleared areas, while at the same time thousands of hectares of new agricultural development of cocoa and oil palm are being developed on traditional gardening and old coconut plantations, all associated with the major population locations along the established Buluminski Highway. Thus, the assumption that there will be increased agricultural activity following logging has to be treated very sceptically.

... it could be argued that the land is not valuable for anything, and profits may as well be extracted now from exploitation of the forest as well as carrying on a more intensive utilisation of the land traditionally used for gardening and, in recent times, cash agriculture' .... However, this is very dangerous because the traditional lifestyle of our people is very much dependent on the forest areas for purposes other than agriculture ... The forest abounds with a wealth of game that is hunted for protein. There are also edible vines, roots and fruits which provide a valuable reserve of food especially in times of drought or famine. As far as food production goes, the destruction of the forest and the inevitable pollution of streams has a profound downstream effect. With streams being clogged by excessive sediments and tree debris, fishery resources in the river deltas are under threat and, in some cases, sago has been destroyed by excessive sediment and drying of the environment. Sediment loads also pose an immediate threat to the offshore reef resources which are an important foundation of life for our island and coastal communities.

As well as being dominated by the problems of food production and agriculture, a woman's life is profoundly affected by the quality of the family house, the provision of drinking water and freedom from disease. It is from the edges of the forest that most of the building materials come ... the saplings for house framing, vines for basket-making and handicrafts, and the durable timbers for the house posts. It is from the edges of the uninhabited forest that the unpolluted water springs are found. It is also the edges of the forest which are the first areas to be exploited by the loggers, making the distance over which building materials have to be carried simply uneconomic, so that there is a trend towards relying on purchased sawn timber and materials.

With the inevitable pollution of drinking water sources, cash must also be expended for iron water-catchment roofs and galvanised water tanks. Such a trend towards the purchasing of these cash-oriented materials is, of course, made possible by the increased cash circulating in the community from the royalty payments, but it need not necessarily be seen as 'development'. A corrugated iron-roofed tin box is definitely not, and is uncomfortable compared to traditional thatched houses. An unpolluted hillside spring undisturbed by heavy machinery and the removal of trees, does not become filled with unhealthy sediment and rust out within five years, as does an iron water tank.

Questions of agriculture, building materials, water supplies, loss of plants useful for traditional medicine and customary practices, loss of canoe logs, and the trauma of suddenly losing an environment which for generations has been looked upon as being the natural, permanent, ancestral way things should be, are

120

the immediate, direct impacts of logging activity. It is, however, the indirect effects which could be the most disturbing for women and family life. In the past, survival and subsistence have revolved around the family as a whole, with women playing a major role, working together to produce gardens for the maintenance of an adequate food supply to meet daily needs and customary obligations.

With the arrival of logging camps in close proximity to the village, there is a tendency for the breakdown of customary methods of subsistence. The men, who usually have a major role in the initial clearing of the garden, find employment for very low wages with the loggers. The young girls are easily enticed by the lure of easy money to the all-male camps. With an increase in the amount of mosquito breeding sites caused by water in wheel tracks and road pot-holes, malaria usually breaks out on an epidemic scale once logging starts in a new area. With the sudden input of money into the community from wages and royalties, alcohol begins to have its usual unpleasant effects. Diet quickly becomes degraded from a variety of home-grown staples and vegetables and fruits, and hunted protein and fish, to limited white rice and tinned fish. With the excitement of strange machinery in the area and the logging boats anchored close by, school attendance suffers.

None of these social disruptions need be considered disastrous and incapable of being overcome. After all, we have seen it all before ... What makes the logging scene different, however, is that all these disruptions are caused by what is really a very insignificant sum of money injected in an unplanned and uncoordinated way into communities totally unprepared for the impact. Despite all the claims of sustained yield and alternative land use, this disruption occurs over a relative short period of time, say 20 or 25 years, and is, to all intents and purposes, permanent.

The forests will take at least 250 years to recover to the stage that they were at before, if in fact they ever recover at all. Societies will never be as they were before and it will take some time for them to work out how to make lifestyles better rather than worse. All of this could, of course, be reduced to the simple question of whether the benefits are worth the environmental and social costs that are being paid.

---

*   This paper is an extract from a presentation given to an Asia-Pacific Development Centre (APDC) Pacific workshop, October 1989.

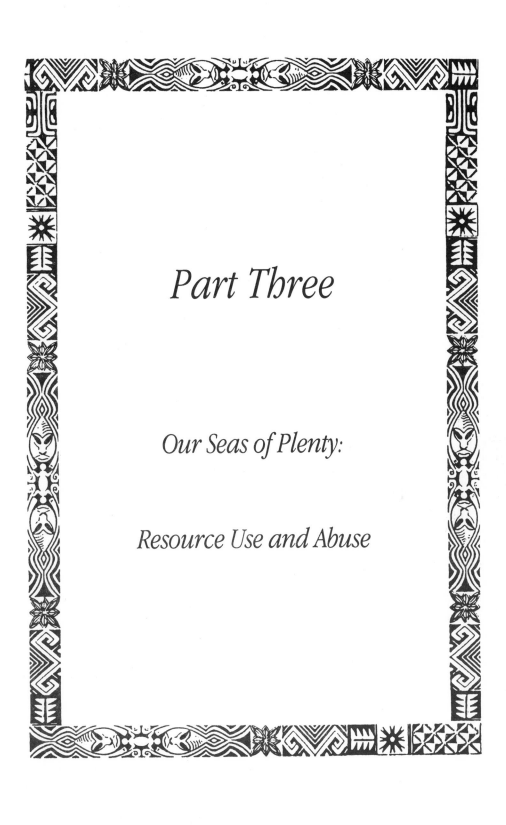

Part Three

Our Seas of Plenty:

Resource Use and Abuse

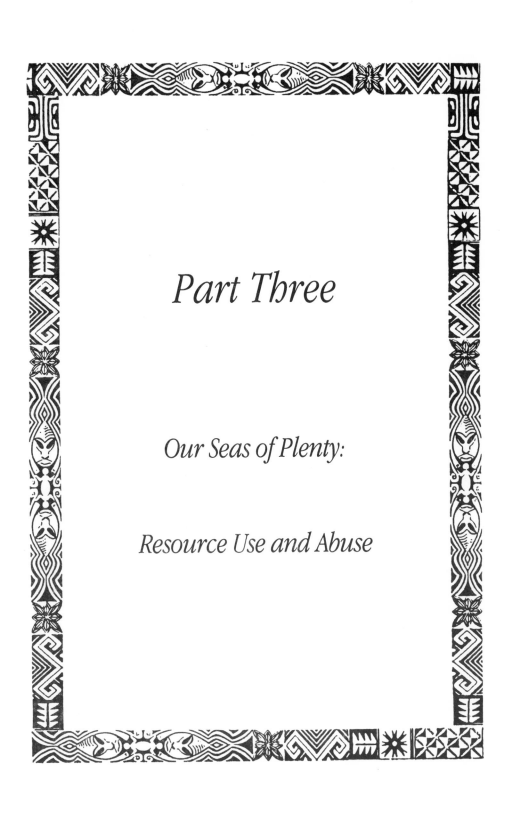

Part Three

Our Seas of Plenty:

Resource Use and Abuse

The subsistence and semi-subsistence activities of women involve simple (and less costly) technology such as hand lines, hand nets, digging sticks, goggles and traps; and their fishing trips are usually of short duration and regulated according to immediate needs for food and income. By contrast, the fishing activities of men usually require more sophisticated technology such as boats, larger nets, trolling lines, etc. and they are less oriented towards immediate household consumption. Furthermore, the actual use of such equipment or gear is dependent on the availability of other necessary inputs like bait, fuel and ice. If there is an engine breakdown or a need to repair fishing gear, there can be periods when no fishing is possible.

With the increasing dominance of the cash economy in the region, there is growing pressure on the subsistence sector to exchange surplus produce for cash (as opposed to sustaining customary redistributive practices for example) in order to meet basic needs such as school fees, transport expenses, clothing and other food items. As family needs change with the heavier demands for cash, more and more women are supplying a variety of marine products (such as prawns, crabs, clams, octopus, bêche-de-mer, seaweed, seashells and some species of fish) to the markets. In fact, the (commercial) supply of aquatic, non-fish products is now largely carried out by semi-subsistence women fishers.

The subsistence fishery in the Pacific, including its changing pattern, has been inadequately documented in official fisheries reports. Quantitative research data is limited with the result that there is a continuing failure to assess in a comprehensive way women's socio-economic role. Another problem resulting from the lack of research is that the impact on the environment and fisheries resources by women (as a major group of resource users) has been overlooked. Estimates of subsistence production are usually based on fairly crude assessments and the potential for variance is considerable. Another problem is that very limited extension (i.e. technical, infrastructural and financial) support is given to this important category of producers. For example, in Fiji, Vanuatu and the Solomon Islands, more than 90 per cent of extension officers are male, and most of their support is oriented towards male-dominated fisheries.

ii.   *Artisanal-commercial activities*

This category of fisheries generally represents operations which employ more advanced technology, require permits or licences to operate, and involve the sale of all or part of the catch to the market as a means of generating income. Artisanal-commercial fisheries are primarily focussed on domestic fin-fish found inside the reef and in the outer-reef and deep-sea areas, artisanal aquaculture and shellcraft.

Women in the Pacific generally carry out their fisheries activities within limits imposed by their domestic responsibilities, cultural expectations, and access to the means of production. Consequently, their involvement in artisanal-commercial fisheries is essentially confined to activities within the coastal and inshore areas where they support or facilitate fishing by their husbands or the household. Women's work includes mending and repairing nets, gear and equipment; processing and preserving the catch; marketing and distributing the catch; and, in some cases, managing the finance. As a result of this division of labour, the processing of (fish or non-fish) marine products in the region has come to be performed almost exclusively by women who undertake traditional processing through labour-intensive activities like salting, drying, and smoking.

Sometimes, when ice is not available, highly perishable commodities, for example trochus and octopus, have to be cooked (boiled) to prevent deterioration and wastage.

Women vendors also dominate the domestic markets in some Pacific Islands. In Kiribati, for example, Taniera and Mitchell (1992) have shown that women are responsible for the handling and marketing of fish for domestic consumption. A similar situation can be found in Western Samoa and Tonga where many women vendors sell the catch brought in by their husbands who tend to be engaged in full-time fishing. In the area of artisanal-aquaculture, which includes the culture of tilapia in Fiji, pearl oysters in the Cook Islands, seaweed and milkfish in Kiribati, and giant clam trials in Tonga and the Solomon Islands, women are actively involved in the day-to-day operations as well as maintenance work. Their tasks include the preparation of ponds, cages and planting materials; harvesting; and feeding. Another area of artisanal-commercial fisheries in which women are to be found is shellcraft and the use of coral to manufacture jewellery and ornaments. In those islands frequented by tourists, these activities provide an important source of income for women, and, in turn, for their households.

In light of current regional development priorities and policies which are keen to promote artisanal-commercial fisheries, a large proportion of government assistance, projects, extension services and other support is directed towards modernising the fisheries sector. The target group is usually men. For example, in the case of aquaculture, although women are directly involved in daily operations including the maintenance of farms, ponds and cages, they have not been integrated into the 'development' aspects of these projects. They have accordingly been excluded from training opportunities, extension or development assistance, and decision making. As in the case of subsistence fisheries, the use of sea-shells and coral for craft manufacture has also not been assessed in terms of its impact on the marine environment. Nor are there any practical guidelines for women in resource harvesting or training in craftwork skills.

The emphasis given by artisanal-commercial fisheries programmes to increasing production levels and, to this end, improving efficiency, not only excludes women but has had limited success, especially in view of the large amounts of government resources invested in such projects. Two good examples of this problem are the Rural Fishermen's Training Scheme in Fiji and the Fisheries Development Project in Vanuatu. These programmes were introduced to commercialise the rural subsistence fisheries sectors by training fishermen and giving them better equipped and larger vessels that were expected to improve production yields. However, many boats were subsequently confiscated because of defaults on loan repayments. Production increases have also been marginal and, in the case of Vanuatu, a research study undertaken in 1992 revealed that protein levels generated through commercial village fishing constituted only between three and five per cent of total protein supply. By contrast, small-scale subsistence and semi-subsistence village fisheries accounted for 61-65 per cent of protein supply (David and Cillaureen 1992).

It is evident that fisheries projects focus on increasing production through the use of improved catching techniques and technology (such as better vessels and equipment). However, the handling and marketing of produce should also be taken into account at the same time in order to raise real consumption levels of fish and fisheries products. In a more general way, the post-harvest handling of fisheries catches in the Pacific is poor because of the limited use of ice, the lack of storage facilities, and the insufficient attention paid to the importance of quality control. Because these activities are given low priority in fisheries programmes, women (who are the key players) receive inadequate attention. They must also endure poor marketing conditions and limited infrastructure, often having no shelter, selling their produce in overcrowded conditions, and lacking access to an adequate water supply.

In addition, fisheries extension services and training are generally targeted at men on the assumption that they are the heads of households. This gender-bias reinforces the subordinate position of women within the household: because women are given no direct access to training, their only 'training' is acquired indirectly and informally through their husbands. Aside from the implications of this process for women's social and economic status, extension experience has shown that this method is often ineffective. What the fisheries officers and planners do not usually realise is that all fishing activities of the household are complementary tasks aimed at achieving certain production and, in turn, consumption objectives. Studies have demonstrated that there is a clear division of labour within households. Therefore, target groups for extension training and assistance, for example in post-harvest technology, aquaculture production and marketing, should include women since they perform many of the key jobs. As a consequence of the low priority given to these areas of regional fisheries, women have been further marginalised from the benefits of training programmes and development assistance.

iii.   *Industrial fisheries*

This area of regional fisheries is capital-intensive, requiring skilled labour, high technology and investment in the catching, processing and marketing of fish catches. It is characterised by joint-venture operations and foreign investment, and it is dominated by tuna and, to a lesser extent, deep-sea snapper fisheries. In the tuna canneries, women provide the bulk of the labour force at the operational level. Their jobs include cleaning, packing, labelling and quality control.

Export-oriented tuna fisheries continue to be given high priority in terms of capital investment in order to increase exports, employment and revenue. However, large-scale specialised industrial operations such as tuna may not be sustainable in the long term unless some investment is redirected to alternative fisheries activities. The experiences of Atlantic Cod, the Peruvian Anchoveta and the herring fisheries of the North Sea offer good examples of the dangers of over-capitalisation, over-exploitation and eventual collapse of pelagic fisheries ventures. The focus on tuna also means that insufficient attention is being given to strategies for coastal-based and self-reliant development, such as the subsistence activities of women.

Women working in industrial fisheries, for example in the canneries and shell-button factories, are engaged in unskilled tasks and endure poor working terms and conditions. As a result, they do not usually benefit from training opportunities which restricts their opportunities for promotion or advancement. Additionally, the nature of industrial fisheries limits women's participation to a few activities within the production and distribution process. Women do not participate in the catching of fish and export marketing and, overall, most of the jobs are carried out by men. As industrial fisheries develop in the region, women may become further marginalised unless adequate and specialised training and educational opportunities are made available to them.

Other issues which influence women's involvement in fisheries

A number of other factors influence the status of women in regional fisheries development. In most Pacific Island states, deep-rooted social and cultural attitudes continue to insist that women's economic and social roles should be confined to a subordinate position within the household. These values result in restricted opportunities for women's education and training (including fisheries training) and in their lower literacy levels (Booth 1993). They also sustain the conventional belief that women's traditional roles in regional fisheries are informal and of little, or no, economic importance. The lack of specific data and statistical information on the informal sector prevents proper assessments of the economic value and potential of women's fisheries. It also undermines planning and development of the fisheries sector at national and regional levels.

Another important factor is the deteriorating quality of the region's coastal areas due to overfishing, pollution and destructive fishing practices. Such practices are seriously threatening the future survival of crucial sources of protein and food for coastal communities as well as the resource-base for women fishers. Women are never consulted on such matters. Women's fisheries is also handicapped by the fact that most large fisheries projects are funded under foreign aid. Projects are therefore often prioritised according to the specifications and goals of the external funding agencies. Because accountability for the use of funds is important to donors, they tend to support development projects in the formal sector, thereby neglecting women's projects. A few projects for women have been introduced, for example rural women's training in Fiji under the Food and Agriculture Organization/United Nations Development Programme in 1986 and 1987; but they have usually not been followed through because of a lack of funding and the low priority attached to them.

Implications for sustainable development of fisheries

In view of the need for sustainable fisheries in the Pacific Islands, it is important that small-scale coastal fisheries be given high priority. This is not only because this area of regional fisheries supports a large number of people, but also because most fish for household consumption will continue to come from coastal resources in the future. In addition, coastal resources contain the greatest diversity of fisheries resources and the most complex ecosystems. Strategies for sustainable fisheries development in the Pacific should include increasing post-harvest technology, development of aquaculture techniques, promotion of subsistence fisheries, and use of community-based strategies for resource use and management, including traditional knowledge and customary marine tenure systems. In practical terms, women are as directly involved as men in all these areas. Such alternative strategies continue to be inadequately addressed in the fisheries development plans and policies of most Pacific Island states.

For example, there is a general belief that men in coastal communities possess a vast store of traditional knowledge on resource use and management. However, studies have indicated that women also possess and apply traditional knowledge and skills, in this way fulfilling their obligations to satisfy household needs for food and income (see for example Matthews 1991). Coastal fisheries development and management must take into account the role of 'the other half' of its human resources and production agents. Inclusion of women's activities is essential for the long-term development and management of fisheries and for the well-being of the region's coastal communities.

Women and Fisheries Network

From the above overview, it is evident that women play a significant role in the fisheries sector. However, their activities have largely gone unnoticed by fisheries planners and policy makers. Development policies that ignore or undermine the crucial role of women without offering any alternative strategy for community-level development can have a drastic impact on the status of women, the well-being of local communities, and the status of the fisheries resources and production.

The work of the Suva-based Women in Fisheries Network is aimed at ensuring that issues which affect women in fisheries are adequately addressed by regional governments, funding agencies and the people of the region. The network is therefore involved in creating public awareness; lobbying for development support for women involved in the fisheries sector; and exchanging scientific and research information on development and fisheries issues, with particular focus on improving the socio-economic status of women in fisheries (Women and Fisheries Network Brochure 1993).

---

* This paper was given to the Annual General Meeting of the Women and Fisheries Network Suva, Fiji, in June 1994

References

Bibi, H. (1990) 'The women's catch - kai fishery in Fiji' in Asia and Pacific Women's Resource Collection Network (1992) *Asian and Pacific Women's Resource and Action Series: Environment,* Kuala Lumpur, Malaysia: Asian and Pacific Development Centre

Booth, H. (1993) Data compiled for United Nations Statistical Office (UNSTAT)

Chapman, M. (1987) 'Women's fishing in Oceania' in *Human Ecology,* vol.15, no.3

David, G. and Cillaurren, E. (1992) 'Traditional village fishing: Security and development of fisheries in Vanuatu', Noumea, New Caledonia: ORSTOM

Lal, P. and Slatter, S. (1982) 'The integration of women in fisheries development in Fiji', Report of an Economic and Social Commission of Asia and the Pacific (ESCAP)/Food and Agriculture Organization (FAO) initiated project on improving the socio-economic conditions of women in fisherfolk communities, Suva, Fiji: Ministry of Agriculture and the University of the South Pacific

Lamour, G. W. (1992) 'Roviana women in traditional fishing', paper presented at the Science of Pacific Island Peoples Conference, Suva, Fiji, 5-12 July

Matthews, E. (1991) 'Women and fishing in traditional Pacific Island cultures', paper for South Pacific Commission 23rd Regional Technical Meeting on Fisheries, Noumea, New Caledonia, 5-9 August

Ram, V. (1993) 'Women in commercial fisheries in the South Pacific: A focus on the situation in Fiji' in South, G.R. (ed.) *Marine resources and development,* Ray Parkinson Memorial Lecture Series, Suva, Fiji: Pacific Island Marine Information System (PIMRIS)

Schoeffel, P. and Talagi, S. (1989) 'The role of women in small-scale fisheries in the South Pacific: Report of case studies in the Cook Islands, Papua New Guinea, Solomon Islands, Tonga, Vanuatu and Western Samoa', London: Commonwealth Secretariat

South Pacific Commission (1994) 'The present status of coastal fisheries production in the South Pacific Islands', Paper for South Pacific Commission 25th Regional Technical Meeting on Fisheries, Noumea, New Caledonia, 14-18 March

Taniera, T. and Mitchell, J. (1992) 'Women and fishing: Notes from Kiribati', paper presented to CUSO Meeting, Suva, Fiji, August

Women and Fisheries Network Brochure (1993) Suva, Fiji

Eleven

For food or foreign exchange?

Regional interests versus global imperatives in Pacific fisheries development*

Claire Slatter

Introduction

Although small in land mass terms, Pacific Island countries have vast, and resource-rich, territorial extensions in their 200-mile Exclusive Economic Zones (EEZs), recognised by international law since 1982 as integral parts of their national jurisdictions. For individual island states, sovereignty over the seas within a 200-mile radius of their shores means economic control over, and exclusive access to, the resources that lie within their 200-mile zone, including those that might lie beneath the ocean floor.

EEZs have greatly expanded the prospects of Pacific Island nations for increased foreign earnings. Indeed, the economic exploitation of pelagic fishery resources, specifically tuna, has mainly been geared to external demand. The Pacific has become a significant exporter of fish to Distant Water Fishing Nations (DWFNs) whose large, high-tech fishing fleets have for several years been harvesting the South-West Pacific Ocean at a feverish pace under extremely generous licensing agreements with individual island states or, as in the case of the United States, under a multilateral agreement.

While unequivocally a source of much-coveted foreign earnings, especially for those states with few (or no) other known natural resources, the living resources of the sea represent an invaluable form of wealth or natural capital to island communities in an even more vital respect. They provide a readily available source of precious protein food to a region whose people are primarily dependent on semi-subsistence livelihoods. With the subsistence economy supporting at least two-thirds of the region's entire population, the

131

importance of subsistence fisheries for domestic food supply, specifically for protein staples, is undeniable.

The future sustainability of the Pacific's fisheries resources cannot, however, be taken for granted. The frantic search for increased foreign earnings through expanded export production, combined with an emphasis on private sector initiatives (both of which are part of World Bank-prescribed economic growth strategies), are indeed encouraging Pacific Island states to more intensively exploit their natural resources, including fisheries. Furthermore, the changing direction of development assistance toward private sector initiatives, in line with free market thinking, is encouraging large-scale, export-oriented fisheries projects, often with a considerable degree of foreign control or management. All of these developments, together with explicit designs on the part of the global tuna industry to substantially expand tuna catches in the South-West Pacific waters in the next few years, do not augur well for the sustainability of fisheries resources in this region. This is especially so in light of the current crisis in world fisheries: 50 major world fish stocks are already overfished and the remaining fisheries are under severe threat from the insatiable demands of the profit-driven fisheries industry (Greenpeace International 1993a & b). This paper argues that emphasising export-oriented fisheries production at the expense of subsistence fisheries could have critical implications for the future food security, health and very survival of Pacific Island communities. Protecting the semi-subsistence livelihoods of Pacific Island peoples, which have long insured them against poverty and want, and particularly protecting their interests in fisheries, the principal source of their protein food requirements, are absolutely vital to the future well-being of these communities.

As the more regular subsistence fishers - traditionally women harvested aquatic resources more frequently and more regularly than men (Schoeffel 1992) and currently they are the more regular harvesters of inshore fishery resources to meet family food needs - women are not only primary stakeholders in the sustainable utilisation of the inshore fishery resource. They are also well-placed to perform a central role in the management of inshore fisheries resources. Such a role could only be played, however, if there is acknowledgment of the extent and value of their fisheries activities and knowledge; an appropriate allocation of development resources is made to support and strengthen the subsistence fishery where women predominate; and structures and mechanisms are created to empower them at the local level to assume a leading role as resource managers.

Resource extraction in our seas of plenty: Short-term gain, long-term loss?

The Pacific Ocean is perhaps the most resource-rich ocean in the world. Aside from the enormous potential wealth that still lies buried beneath the ocean floor in the form of deep sea mineral resources[1], in biodiversity terms, the Pacific Ocean is teeming with literally thousands of different marine species. It is estimated that some 1,850 species of fish inhabit Papua New Guinea's 200-mile zone alone (Callick 1994). Certainly, as far as the international fisheries industry (dominated by Asian, and to a lesser extent, American companies) is concerned, the Pacific Ocean is a marine goldmine. The South-Western Pacific region is currently the source of 60 per cent of the tuna processed globally in canneries around the world, and the industry's large tuna fleets hope to substantially augment their catch from this corner of the Pacific Ocean to over one million tons (Hagler 1993). In the mind of the industry, the region's fisheries resources are there for the taking, subject to access agreements with island states.

Although most island states have long had ambitions of establishing national (state-run) fisheries industries (Sutherland & Tsamenyi 1992:21), only four of the independent states (Fiji, the Solomon Islands, Kiribati and the Federated States of Micronesia) have done so (albeit with limited success), with Fiji and the Solomon Islands also engaged in the production of canned and/or frozen or chilled tuna, primarily for export. Without the technology, capital and industry or marketing know-how necessary to exploit the tuna fishery independently under national jurisdiction, most Pacific states have been content to simply trade access to their EEZs for foreign exchange paid as licence fees or 'fishing rent' by DWFNs. Papua New Guinea (PNG), the Solomon Islands, Tonga, French Polynesia, Tuvalu, Kiribati, Niue, Palau, Nauru, Cook Islands, the Marshall Islands and the Federated States of Micronesia have all leased rights to exploit fishery resources within their 200-mile zones to foreign commercial interests.

With the exception of PNG, the Solomon Islands, Tonga and French Polynesia, fishing rents in all countries mentioned above constitute an important source of foreign exchange. Yet, compared with the market value of the resource, the income derived from these rents has generally been paltry - around four per cent of the value of the reported catch - as indicated in figures for 1988. In that year, $US 1.1 billion worth of tuna caught in the Pacific region by Japan, Taiwan, South Korea and the United States realised, by way of access fees, a mere $US 30 million for the island states of the Forum Fisheries Agency (FFA) (Sutherland & Tsamenyi 1992:4, 6). At the 1994 meeting of the South Pacific Forum, Pacific Island leaders agreed to negotiate multilaterally in future on licensing agreements with Japan, Taiwan and Korea, along the lines of the multilateral licensing agreement concluded some five years ago between the United States and the Forum Fisheries Agency (FFA). Under the agreement, the United States paid $US 12 million per annum between 1988 and 1993, and will pay $180 million for a 10-year period of access from 1994 (Kunatuba 1992)[2]. At a yearly rental of only $18 million, the American tuna industry is clearly laughing all the way to the bank! At the end of ten years, the cost to the Pacific region of oceanic pillaging by American and Asian fishing fleets may well be incalculable.

Assessing the costs and benefits of renting our EEZs entails much more than trying to estimate exactly how much tuna is being caught and ensuring that what is received in licensing fees or fisheries rent is a fair price. Yet, to some extent, these seem to be the principal concerns of Pacific governments. FFA's first 10 years of work have been primarily taken up with assisting access negotiations between Pacific Island countries and DWFNs. This is perhaps not surprising given that one of the main purposes underlying the establishment of the Agency was 'to generate the maximum financial benefits from the fisheries resources' (Forum Fisheries Agency n.d.). At the 1994 South Pacific Forum meeting in Brisbane, island leaders appeared to be single-mindedly focused on the economic value of tuna and the need to secure more than 'sub-economic rates of return' through multilateral negotiations[3]. Plans to improve the monitoring and surveillance of fish stocks (through satellite tracking of foreign fisheries vessels) appear to be instrumental to protecting the region's economic interests in fisheries. As far as deep sea fisheries resources are concerned then, the paramount interest of island states is to use the economic leverage they (theoretically) possess through their 'control' of the world's largest tuna fishery to obtain the best possible price for their resource. As FFA's outgoing director, Sir Peter Kenilorea, has put it:

> This region accounts for 50 per cent of the world's tuna, this is
> a very strong stick that Pacific countries have, the world cannot
> do without our resource (sic) (Aiavao 1994:22).

It may be true enough that small Pacific Island states have a 'strong stick' to wield in their negotiations with economically powerful DWFNs, especially if they adopt a regional approach to managing the tuna fishery by insisting on multilateral access agreements. However, it is also a fact that pursuing short-term gains such as licensing fees from the fisheries industry could - if we are not careful - cost us dearly in the long term. Recognising this is as important as actually minimising risk-taking with the tuna resource. As Greenpeace points out

> Attempts by governments to manage fisheries exploitation ...
> are a big part of the problem. Permissive management has
> brought global fisheries to the brink of collapse and nations
> responsible for the calamity continue to behave as if there were
> no tomorrow. Governments are offering little in the way of
> hope or vision to act upon (Greenpeace International 1993b:2).

Aside from fishing rent receipts, the only other economic gains for host countries from foreign fishing fleets are: (since 1993) port-servicing receipts (which should net $US 10 million in 1994) from foreign fisheries vessels which are now required to come to port to carry out transhipment of their catch and be serviced; the limited employment of Islanders as crew on foreign fleets; and the marketing opportunities provided to local commercial fishers who supply tuna or baitfish under regular contract. The last-mentioned of these is a somewhat dubious benefit. This is because the regular supply of baitfish for pole-and-line tuna fisheries up until the 1980s (when pole-and-line fishing became effectively eclipsed by purse-seining[4]), has negatively impacted on the inshore fisheries on which semi-subsistence island communities depend for their protein foods.

The operation of domestic tuna industries based on the production of either canned or frozen/chilled tuna solely or mainly for export in three Pacific Island countries - American Samoa (which has two of the largest canneries in the world), Fiji and the Solomon Islands - has likewise entailed some questionable 'benefits'. Ownership of these industries has been substantially foreign, with the exception of Fiji where the cannery is fully state-owned; there is large-scale exploitation of female labour (with tuna processing being the only aspect of the tuna industry or of deep sea fisheries which involves women); and extremely generous tax and other operational conditions (tax-free concessions in the case of Fiji) prevail. In short, the tuna industry appears to be principally benefiting (i.e. enriching) not Pacific Island states and their peoples, but private foreign fisheries interests.

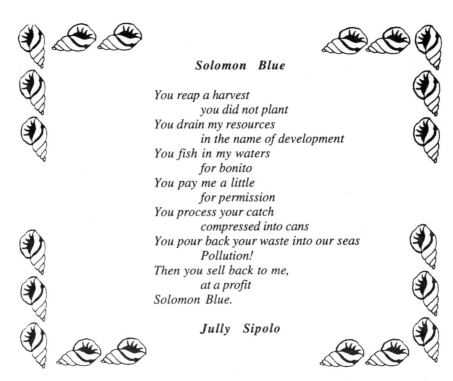

Solomon Blue

You reap a harvest
you did not plant
You drain my resources
in the name of development
You fish in my waters
for bonito
You pay me a little
for permission
You process your catch
compressed into cans
You pour back your waste into our seas
Pollution!
Then you sell back to me,
at a profit
Solomon Blue.

Jully Sipolo

Stocktaking Pacific tuna: how reliable the accounts?

The Pacific Ocean currently sustains the world's largest tuna fishery but it is being intensively exploited. The licensing of foreign fleets, which began some 15 years ago as an 'interim measure pending the development of domestic fishing industries' (FFA 1994:8), has resulted in a rapid escalation of tuna harvesting. In just 11 years (1980-1991), total catches of the Pacific's major commercial species - yellowfin, skipjack, bigeye and albacore - have increased by more than 100 per cent, largely as a consequence of the expanded fisheries activities of DWFNs. In 1993, a staggering 1300 foreign fishing vessels were engaged in fisheries activities in the waters of Pacific Island states. Their numbers greatly overshadow the 85-odd domestic vessels whose 1993 catch represented a mere five per cent of the total value of reported tuna landings (FFA 1994:8). With the value of the domestic vessels' catch assessed at $US 66 million (ibid), the combined value of the Pacific catch for the DWFNs would have been of the magnitude of $US 1.25 billion.

Assessing the extent to which such expanded levels of exploitation may pose a threat to the Pacific tuna fishery appears, to some degree, to be a matter of conjecture. This is in spite of the fact that such assessments are prepared by technical experts in the Oceanic Fisheries Programme of the South Pacific Commission (SPC) and are based on elaborate analyses of various fishery indicators, including tagging data. A 1993 Commission paper on the status of tuna stocks in the SPC area, for instance, indicated that the region's two main tuna species were only being moderately exploited. It set 'maximum safe' harvest levels for both yellowfin and skipjack tuna at double the present level of exploitation - up to 800,000 metric tons for yellowfin and two million metric tons for skipjack (Hampton 1993:5-12)[5]. A year later, however, using 'a more conservative biological reference point (an exploitation rate of 0.4)', a 1994 update on the status of tuna stocks has revised these maximum safe harvest levels downwards - to 600,000 metric tons and 1.3 million metric tons for yellowfin and skipjack respectively (SPC 1994:3). The 1994 report also cautions against 'continued fishing [of albacore tuna] at the current or increased levels' as indications of 'declining catchability' and 'declining population biomass' suggest that the species is being overfished (op.cit.:5-6).

The difficulties of accurately monitoring tuna stocks in the region and of being able to reliably determine maximum safe harvest levels are immense. Much of the data on which assessments are based is dependent on the accuracy (or honesty) of daily catch records maintained by fishing fleets. The SPC's elaborate regional tuna tagging project is concerned with estimating the natural and fishing mortality rates of the main (commercial) tuna species. It relies on regular reporting by both commercial fleets operating in Pacific waters and Pacific Rim countries in whose waters tagged tuna may eventually be caught. The proportion of the stock which is tagged is far too small to enable reliable assessments to be made, and data analysis appears necessarily to entail a fair bit of extrapolation. As such, conclusions reached should, judiciously, be treated with caution. The SPC's own revision (within the space of a year) of 'maximum safe' harvest levels for just two fish species, and its cautioning on further commercial exploitation of a third (evidently based on new information or indices and a more conservative reckoning), underline the impossibility of establishing, with absolute precision and certainty, maximum safe harvest parameters where the tuna resource is concerned.

Monitoring and assessment programmes aimed at establishing maximum safe harvest levels had tragic consequences for the Atlantic Cod. This precedent alone should compel us to question the wisdom of relying on science as a guide to establishing sustainable levels of commercial exploitation of the tuna fishery. The general paucity of scientific knowledge about the deep sea fishery and marine life in general makes such caution especially desirable. Similarly, while it is known that skipjack tuna is a highly migratory species 'capable of unrestricted movement throughout the Pacific Ocean', and that spawning mainly occurs in the Western Pacific where most of the catch is taken (Hampton 1993:7), it should also be noted that, as a highly migratory species, tuna stocks are immensely susceptible to 'crashes' (Robin South 1994, Suva, pers. comm.). Korean crew of a fishing vessel operating in Fiji waters recently observed that their purse seine tuna catch had begun to include a large number of young tuna (Ronni Alexander 1994, Suva, pers. comm.). This could suggest early signs of an impending 'crash'.

Although Pacific Island nations have successfully secured undertakings from DWFNs not to use destructive fishing technology, such as 'wall-of-death' driftnets, their incapacity to adequately police their 200-mile zones[6] leaves them vulnerable to plundering by unscrupulous companies. And, while it may be validly argued that present levels of exploitation of pelagic species such as yellowfin and skipjack tuna pose little threat as yet to these resource stocks, the explicit intentions of the global fisheries industry to intensify its harvesting of tuna resources in the South West Pacific Ocean could, with the unwitting complicity of Pacific states, potentially result in the depletion of the region's tuna fishery. This has already happened to certain commercial species in other fisheries around the world (Hagler 1993).

Rapacious harvesting of the seas by a profit-driven and foreign-controlled industry has already laid waste other formerly abundant oceans, and the industry continues to use sophisticated and potentially destructive and wasteful fishing

136

technologies to maximise its catch. For these reasons, large-scale commercial fisheries could be even more ecologically and socially damaging in the long run than other forms of profit-driven natural resource extraction in the Pacific region. Indeed, the interests of Pacific Island states (and especially people) are diametrically opposed to those of the foreign-dominated fisheries industry. For the industry, which is bent on simply maximising catches and fishery profits without any concern for the depletion of stocks, a tuna in the net is certainly worth two in the ocean. For Pacific Island peoples, on the other hand, the living and non-living resources of the oceans are their heritage. Preservation of the tuna fishery and of other living marine resources, is a long-term interest, fundamental both to sustaining the semi-subsistence livelihoods of thousands of Islanders and to protecting the rich biodiversity of the Pacific Ocean.

The profit-driven global fish drive and the crisis in world fisheries

Contrary to conventional wisdom (and thinking in the industry), fisheries resources are not infinitely renewable. As the April 1992 issue of the *New Scientist* puts it:

> Fish is a finite resource. You can run out of them. The world is doing just that. And this will be serious for the large number of people who rely heavily on fish for protein (cited in Greenpeace International 1993b).

Data supplied by the Food and Agriculture Organization (FAO), which until recently was itself a major proponent of large-scale fisheries exploitation, indicate that four of the world's 17 major fishing regions have been seriously depleted of their fish stocks, while catches in nine others are declining (Greenpeace International 1993b). The industry's targeting of specific fish species may drive some species to commercial extinction. As Greenpeace points out, the phenomenal 33 per cent increase in world landings between 1980 and 1989 was largely the result of increases in catches of only five fish species. In addition, the use of destructive and wasteful fishing technology, namely the mammoth trawl nets used for 'vacuuming up mountains of fish' of all species, may spell biological extinction for many species and ecological disaster generally (Greenpeace International 1993b).

According to Greenpeace, the threat to coastal communities dependent on fish as a staple food comes from the combined impacts of

> fisheries development schemes, large-scale factory ships, many of them foreign fleets fishing ever closer to shore, and the export-driven economic development policies of indebted national governments [which] have meant that even though more fish are being taken from their waters, these coastal communities are eating less fish (Hagler 1993:1).

As the crisis in the world's fisheries deepens, the implications for the Pacific region of what Greenpeace International terms the 'global grab for declining fish stocks' are severe. Despite (or perhaps because of) the crisis, an 'industry race' has begun 'to expand and intensify fishing - to "optimise" the utilisation of already heavily exploited stocks, and to develop under-utilised species wherever they can be found' (Hagler 1993:2).

A recent disclosure in Japan that the highly prized, bluefin tuna available to consumers on the Japanese market for 'sashimi' (raw fish) was sometimes up to five-years old[7], while reflecting in part the traditional practice of freezing this temperate zone species, certainly suggests massive-scale overfishing and stockpiling of high-grade species by an industry propelled into competitive overdrive by the expectation of eventual, if not imminent, depletion of the resource. As a result of intensified exploitation, bluefin did crash and is consequently now subject to strict international controls. While industry behaviour may, to some extent, be influenced by deteriorating market conditions - for instance, a current oversupply of imported fresh (chilled) yellowfin tuna on the Japanese market has had the effect of pushing prices down - other considerations, such as the fact that freezing tuna at minus 60 degrees centigrade ensures the destruction of up to 80 per cent of any bacteria in the fish, effectively guarantee a market for stockpiled (and frozen) high-grade species. According to Greenpeace, the pressure of a supply-side crisis, caused by the depletion or decline in many traditional commercial fisheries, is pushing the industry into a 'global grab' for declining fish stocks. If present trends continue, the FAO predicts there will be a 'supply shortfall of up to 25 million tons of food fish by the year 2000' (Hagler 1993:1).

Aid, fisheries development and the export imperative in the Pacific

The serious depletion of four of the world's largest fisheries regions is a sober reminder of how vulnerable the Pacific's fisheries resources are, especially in the face of enormous pressure on island states to increase their foreign exchange earnings and achieve economic growth. It is evident that the resource bases which sustain semi-subsistence livelihoods - the land and the sea - are today being increasingly used to satisfy demands for economic growth and expanded foreign earnings rather than developed to meet the present and future needs of those who are (and/or will be) primarily dependent on them, and whose inheritance they are. As a recent article in *Pacific Islands Monthly* put it:

> With donor countries showing signs of aid fatigue, and aid flows slowing in real terms, trying to get more money from the exploitation of local fish resources is increasingly important (Aiavao 1994:22).

Although there are still a lot of aid funds channelled into fisheries development - with multi-million dollar projects being planned and implemented in the region by big donors - most of the funding is now going into export-oriented commercial fisheries. The fisheries programme of the United States Agency for International Development (USAID), for instance, recently concluded its South Pacific Fisheries Development Project which provided development assistance (worth $US 5.5 million) to fisheries divisions in 10 Pacific countries over a six-year period. The project was replaced by another entitled Pacific Islands Marine Resources Project which will provide more than double the aid funds ($US 13.7 million), but it is specifically directed to private sector fisheries in six countries. The project activities include the development of black pearl culture in the Cook Islands; a small-scale longline tuna fishery in Tonga; small-scale bottom fishing in Tuvalu; resource assessment and management of the Tarawa lagoon in Kiribati; small-scale export, private sector fisheries in PNG; and extensions to the Lami Jetty in Suva, Fiji (SPC 1992a).

Projects funded under USAID's new programme are put up for tender within the United States as well as regionally. In the case of black pearl culture on Penrhyn Island in the Cook Islands, the tender was awarded to an American consultancy firm (Anna Tiraa Passfield 1994, Suva, pers. comm.). The changing direction of fisheries aid towards export-oriented, private sector initiatives means comparative neglect of the subsistence fisheries. Only a few aid projects, such as the $AUS 2.5 million project of the Australian International Development Assistance Bureau (AIDAB) in Western Samoa on sustainable management of nearshore resources, invest in subsistence fisheries in the Pacific (Hugh Walton 1994, Suva, pers. comm.). Japanese grant-in-aid fisheries projects (in Tuvalu, Vanuatu, Fiji and the Federated States of Micronesia) would appear to have been principally motivated by the economic-strategic interest of securing access agreements with Pacific Island states.

Primarily because of the considerable revenue it earns, the tuna fishery tends to command a disproportionate share of official attention and development resources at both regional and national levels, to the evident detriment of artisanal and subsistence fisheries which are given lower priority. Although both the SPC (Fisheries Programme) and the FFA have research and technical advisory programmes whose aims include supporting artisanal and subsistence fisheries within Pacific Island countries, preventing over-exploitation of fish stocks and protecting the marine environment, both agencies have been mainly preoccupied with offshore fisheries, mirroring the priorities of national fisheries divisions[8].

The development of small-scale commercial (artisanal) fisheries has been actively encouraged by national fisheries divisions, which have typically offered training and development assistance (boats, gear and credit) to prospective commercial fishermen. But despite the considerable outlay of resources, artisanal fisheries remain largely undeveloped outside Fiji. In Fiji, a well-developed commercial fishery, supplying both the domestic and export markets, has diversified considerably in recent years. Up to 40 vessels (longline and bottom fishing enterprises) are engaged in the production for export of chilled (bigeye and yellowfin) tuna and snapper, although a single company has managed to acquire a virtual monopoly over the highly lucrative chilled tuna export business. The company is expected to have a turnover in 1994 of around $FIJ 40 million[9]. In addition to receiving fishing rent at the usual rate of around four per cent of the value of the catch, Papua New Guinea (whose domestic deep sea fisheries collapsed in the 1980s) has a well-developed export-oriented commercial prawn fishery established under a joint venture arrangement.

Generally the indications are that attention and resources will increasingly be channelled towards supporting private sector initiatives in exporting 'niche market' products. Already, a number of such products, including chilled tuna, bêche-de-mer, trochus, mother-of-pearl and, more recently, Eucheuma seaweed are being promoted and developed within the commercial fisheries sectors of several Pacific Island countries. In many instances, the success of these export industries (notably bêche-de-mer) may be said to hinge on the patient, if unacknowledged, labour of women[10]. As with agricultural exports, most marine products (with the exception of canned tuna) are exported in their raw (unprocessed) state, although there is now considerable interest in identifying feasible value-added industries for marine products, trochus shell button factories (in Fiji) being one such example.

The promotion of export fisheries is likely to mean a contraction in the national development funds allocated to rural (subsistence and semi-subsistence) fisheries. The Fiji Fisheries Division, faced with a declining operating budget allocation in 1991, confessed that 'the division will have to think very hard about the type of service it provides to the public' (SPC 1992b). Attention to subsistence and semi-subsistence fisheries in the future is, in fact, likely to be motivated primarily by the concerns of preventing the over-exploitation of inshore resources and protecting the marine environment, since semi-subsistence fishers are commonly (sometimes erroneously) held responsible for the former while being considered absolutely vital to achieving the latter.

Pacific status quo

quietly open the shadows
of my mind
to find the thwarted confusion
within.

portfolios of progress
line each shore,
fallout effects reflected in
common waves.

pacific solidarity
suggests a unification of heads
and outstretched palms,
synchronized hand movements
to the drum's beat.

the slow dissolution
of night into day
goes unheeded
as concrete dollars
block the sun.

a pot of pacific
culture's boil
in a deserted cauldron,
and the bones of pacific gods
fumigated
in DDT discovery.

and while our brothers
guard our EEZ
our sisters lose their virginity
to Tom Dick Harry and Sam.

Vaine Rasmussen

141

The subsistence fishery and women: neglected worlds?

Traditional resource-use systems have long served island communities in the Pacific region well, enabling them to survive over many centuries, even in times of inclement weather and following natural disasters, to which the region is prone. Although not always abundant, the natural resources of the land and sea generally met the basic needs of island populations; and access to these resources within the traditional subsistence economy, while determined by different socio-political arrangements, were generally sufficiently equitable to provide everyone with a means of subsistence. Social practices of wealth-sharing, and the ethic of providing for, and sharing with, one's kin - common to most Pacific cultures - acted as social levellers and extended social security to weaker members of society. Customary conservation practices and traditional food-processing techniques insured against over-use and waste and provided sustenance during natural disasters.

Today, subsistence fisheries provide the main source of protein foods for coastal communities and account for the largest segment of total fisheries production in the Pacific. Statistics provided by the SPC show that the subsistence catch represents 59.5 per cent (51,851 metric tons) of the total nominal fish landings (87,063 metric tons) reported for 22 countries in the region, although nominal fish landings do not include industrial fisheries production, which either outstrips (as in the case of Kiribati) or equals (as in the case of Fiji) the total subsistence fishery production (SPC 1992c). However, since much of the subsistence catch remains unrecorded, the total catch is probably considerably underestimated. The estimated per capita consumption of fish in the Pacific is said to be high by world standards, ranging from 20 to 76.5 kg per annum (South & Veitayaki 1993:7), reflecting the region's protein-rich status.

Despite the abundant natural protein existing in the region's rich fisheries resources, protein malnutrition has emerged as a problem in some island countries. In others, inshore over-fishing (made possible with new technology such as outboard motors and nets) together with a host of malpractices including the use of destructive fishing 'technologies' (e.g. dynamite and poisons), water pollution from the discharge of industrial and household wastes, and mangrove reclamation for urban development, already pose serious threats to coastal fisheries, endangering the main sources of natural protein for semi-subsistence communities. In almost every country, coastal communities report that they are not catching the fish they once used to catch. In some countries, commercial over-exploitation of particular species is threatening stock in specific locations.

While commercial exploitation of deep sea fisheries resources may not directly affect inshore fisheries, the impact of baitfishing to supply the pole-and-line tuna fisheries, as already mentioned, has certainly been destructive to the inshore fisheries. Moreover, it is argued by some that knowledge of the complex marine ecosystems of the Pacific region, particularly of the life cycles of, and inter-relationships between, different species of marine life, is still much too elementary to provide an understanding of the relationship between the deep sea and inshore fisheries. Citing Johannes (1981) and Grandperrin (1978), Chapman, for instance, emphasises that the fry of commercial fish species often 'move inshore after a period spent as members of the pelagic plankton community', or, as adults, 'depend on coastal species of fish for food, as some tuna... have been found to do' (Chapman 1987:282). This certainly suggests the importance of the inshore marine environment and its living resources to pelagic species. How dependent the inshore fishery is on the deep sea marine environment and its biodiverse life forms may not, however, be as well understood.

In their discussion of the various obstacles to sustaining the coastal fishery, South and Veitayaki mention the limited knowledge we have about the complexities of the inshore fishery and the biology of the most sought-after species. They argue that a fair degree of 'guesswork' is involved in the regulation of the inshore fishery (South & Veitayaki 1993:1-2) and contend that it is now 'over-fished'; that present catches are unsustainable; that in urban centres the customary marine tenure systems (through which coastal fisheries are principally managed) are 'under great strain or close to collapse'; and that commercial exploitation of the inshore resource has often entailed selective capture of preferred species, some of which are 'at the top of the food chain', thereby creating 'serious imbalances in the complex multi-species ecosystems of the reefs and lagoons which ultimately may have a long-term detrimental effect on the biodiversity' (op.cit.:1-2, 9).

South and Veitayaki rightly question the contribution that state-supported fisheries development programmes, which emphasise increased production and greater employment and entail the provision of new technology (boats and gear), have made to the problem of inshore overfishing (op.cit.:10). It may be said that the over-emphasis of Pacific governments on exploiting their deep sea tuna fisheries for foreign exchange is matched by an equally strong preoccupation with maximising economic returns from the inshore fishery through expanded production for sale. Thus, instead of supporting or shoring up the inshore fishery, thereby protecting this vital resource base which is sustaining countless thousands of Pacific people who are primarily dependent on semi-subsistence livelihoods, governments have been unwittingly encouraging intensified exploitation of existing inshore commercial species. Through its coastal (i.e. artisanal-subsistence) fisheries management programme, SPC is making efforts to encourage diversification into 'new resources' or underexploited fisheries (e.g. demersal and reef slope species, flying fish, squid and near-shore tuna fishing around fish aggregating devices [FADS]). These efforts need strengthening in the interests of sustaining the inshore fishery.

The centrality of women's subsistence fisheries to protein provision in Pacific Island communities has been highlighted by numerous researchers[11]. The regularity and dietary significance of women's fishing activities in semi-subsistence communities and the considerable knowledge that women have about the inshore marine environment are both becoming more widely acknowledged by researchers[12]. However, this has not resulted in either official recognition or support for women's fisheries activities. Less positively, women's semi-subsistence fisheries activities have begun to claim the attention of those concerned with over-exploitation of the inshore fisheries. As the most frequent and regular harvesters of the inshore fishery for domestic food needs, and with the primary responsibility for family health and welfare, Pacific women certainly have a vital stake in sustaining these resources and should be included in fishery resource decision making and management.

It could be argued that state neglect of the subsistence fishery, in which women predominate, reflects both the usual non-recognition of women's work (gender bias) as well as the general undervaluing of non-cash production (market bias). National fisheries development programmes and training have tended to either exclude women altogether or to engage them only in marginal and poorly-resourced projects. The neglect of subsistence fisheries has its parallel in the neglect of subsistence agriculture. Without their inclusion in fisheries (like land) resource decision making and management, women's present role as food and protein providers is undermined, and their potential role as resource managers is denied. Acknowledging the critical role that women play in the provision of basic needs in semi-subsistence communities is a necessary first step in any effort to shore up the subsistence economy.

Conclusion: Health for all or wealth for a few?

For most Pacific Island countries, the living resources of the sea are their greatest natural resource. These resources represent an invaluable form of wealth since they provide an easily obtainable natural source of protein food. The renewability of these resources cannot, however, be taken for granted. Profit-driven resource extraction is rampant and intensified exploitation of both offshore and inshore fisheries for export dollars poses a grave threat to these precious natural resources. The unmitigated exploitation of the region's fishery resources, both deep sea and inshore, may augment national foreign exchange earnings and enrich a small number of private investors in the fisheries industry, but in the long term it could sorely impoverish the region's peoples.

It should be recognised that threatening the semi-subsistence sector means threatening the livelihoods - and therefore the capacity to survive - of entire Pacific communities. Conversely, sustaining and supporting this sector mean insuring rural communities against the very real risks and dangers not only of serious dietary-related diseases and debilitating ill-health, but also of poverty and want, and their likely social/political effects. The critical role that women play within semi-subsistence communities in Pacific Island states, especially in the provision of basic needs, should give them a vital stake in fisheries resource management and decision making. Indeed, with customary conservation practices becoming increasingly ineffective in regulating the use of inshore fisheries resources, the challenge for effective fisheries resource management in the present decade and beyond is to find a way of reconciling the principles and practices of customary resource management with the various demands currently being placed on the resource. Involving women and drawing on their considerable knowledge base in the management of the inshore fishery could well be a key to meeting this challenge. Furthermore, empowering women to enable them to assume leadership in inshore fisheries management may well be an absolute necessity if the resource is to be protected for future generations to enjoy. Indeed, it may offer our only salvation.

*   I would like to record my sincere thanks to Hugh Walton of the South Pacific Commission's Fisheries Programme for offering critical comments and suggestions on an earlier draft and for kindly providing recent data. I am also grateful to Mike Hagler of Greenpeace International for providing materials on the global fisheries crisis.

Notes

1. For example, see Jones (1986:14), and Sutherland (1987) who argues that poly-metallic nodules existing within New Caledonia's 200-mile EEZ are potentially important sources of manganese, nickel, copper and cobalt, and that France has the most developed technology for vacuuming these nodules off the ocean floor.

2. While Asian DWFNs like South Korea, Taiwan and Japan prefer to negotiate bilateral access agreements with individual Pacific Island states, regional pressure applied through the Forum Fisheries Agency (FFA) is likely to result in all DWFNs signing multilateral access or licensing agreements. Under the terms of such multilateral agreements - which aim to increase the overall rent paid for fishing in the EEZs of FFA-member countries - even those island states whose waters are not currently being fished stand to benefit from fishing rent (Aiavao 1994:22).

3. Forum spokesman and Australian Prime Minister Paul Keating was quoted as saying that wealthy nations such as Japan and South Korea should understand that they could 'not secure valuable resources at sub-economic rates of return' (Aiavao 1994:22).

4. Pole-and-line vessels operating in the region have declined from around 500 vessels to some 40 vessels since 1980, while purse seiners have increased from around five to close to 150 during the same period (Hugh Walton 1994, Suva, pers. comm.).

5. The 1993 assessment of the region's tuna fisheries by the SPC's Tuna and Billfish Assessment Programme was based on various fisheries indicators and analyses of tagging data. It indicated that yellowfin catches, which have doubled in the past decade and are presently in the order of 370,000 metric tons annually, can be safely harvested at up to double the present level (i.e. up to 800,000 metric tons) without threat to stocks (Hampton 1993:5). The assessment programme also revealed that total skipjack catches - which have more than trebled since 1980, largely as a result of increased purse seine fishing, with the 1991 catch being in the order of one million metric tons -can likewise be safely harvested without threat to stock up to the level of two million metric tons (op.cit.:7). In addition, current levels of bigeye catch - currently between 150,000 and 200,000 metric tons per year Pacific-wide - are considered to be sustainable (op.cit.:12).

6. Monitoring and surveillance of the fisheries activities of foreign fishing fleets operating in EEZs will be improved with the implementation of a multi-million dollar European Commission-funded programme which will put transponders on licensed fisheries vessels so that they can be tracked by satellite (Aiavao 1994:22).

7. This information was revealed in a personal communication (August 1994, Suva) by Professor Ronni Alexander of Kobe University, Japan.

8. FFA's mandate is, however, considered to be primarily in offshore fisheries management, while that of SPC is both in oceanic fisheries and coastal (ie artisanal-subsistence) fisheries.

9. The company is, by its own account, already netting 0.5 million Fiji dollars a week (Ronni Alexander 1994, Suva, pers. comm.).

10. Other projects in which women have come to play a central role, albeit often by default, include the SPC's export-oriented tuna jerkey project in Tokelau which primarily draws on women's labour in the marinading process (one day's labour per woman a month); export-oriented Eucheuma (seaweed) farming in Kiribati in which women are reportedly extensively involved; and the experimental giant clam cultivation research project in the Solomon Islands which involves women in the harvesting and marketing of clams and in providing data to the research organisation running the project. In many instances, it appears that women were given responsibility for projects, having been initially excluded from involvement and training.

11. These include Botkin (1980); Schoeffel & Kikau 1980; Narsey Lal & Slatter (1982); Schoeffel (1985); Chapman (1987); Schoeffel & Talagi (1989); Mathews & Oiterong (1991); Taniera & Mitchell (1992); and Gina-Whewell (1992).

12. On the last point, Chapman argues that Pacific women's 'considerable knowledge about the marine environment', specifically their 'knowledge of the daily and seasonal cycles which affect marine organisms' could valuably expand biological understanding of the region's complex marine ecosystems since 'life on the reef where women fish is intimately bound up with life in pelagic areas where many of the commercial fish species ... are found' (Chapman 1987:282).

References

Aiavao, U. (1994) 'Fishing for more money: Divided the islands will fall' in *Pacific Islands Monthly,* September

Botkin, S. (1980) 'An anthropological study of subsistence fishing in Fulaga, Lau: A progress report', Suva, Fiji: Fisheries Division, Ministry of Agriculture and Fisheries

Callick, R. (1994) 'Fishing for a break from Moresby' in *Islands Business,* February

Chapman, M. (1987) 'Women's fishing in Oceania' in *Human Ecology,* vol.15, no.3:266-288

Forum Fisheries Agency (n.d.) *Ten Years,* Honiara, Solomon Islands: Forum Fisheries Agency

---------- (1994) Director's Annual Report, Forum Fisheries Committee 24th Meeting, Honiara, Solomon Islands

Gina-Whewell, L. (1992) 'Roviana women in traditional fishing', paper presented to the Science of Pacific Island Peoples Conference, School of Pure and Applied Sciences, University of the South Pacific, Suva, Fiji

Grandperrin, R. (1978) 'Importance of reefs to ocean production', Noumea, New Caledonia: South Pacific Commission Fisheries Newsletter, 16:11-13

Greenpeace International (1993a) *Global Fisheries - Amazing Facts,* paper circulated at the United Nations Conference on Straddling Fish Stocks and Highly Migratory Fish Stocks, New York, July

---------- (1993b) *It can't go on forever - The implications of the global grab for declining fish stocks,* Amsterdam, Holland

Hagler, M. (1993) 'Implications of the global fisheries crisis', background paper prepared for the Women and Fisheries Network, Suva, Fiji: Greenpeace

Hampton, J. (1993) 'Status of tuna stocks in the South Pacific Commission area: A summary report for 1993', working paper 3, Sixth Standing Committee on Tuna and Billfish, Pohnpei, Federated States of Micronesia, 16-18 June, Tuna and Billfish Assessment Programme, South Pacific Commission, Noumea, New Caledonia

Johannes, R.E. (1981) *Worlds of the lagoon,* Berkeley: University of California Press

Jones, P. (1986) 'The militarisation of the Pacific', paper presented to the United Nations University Conference on Peace and Security in Oceania, Auckland, New Zealand, 2-6 April

Kunatuba, P. (1992) 'Aquaculture development, customary fishing rights and fisheries access agreements', paper presented at a panel discussion, Ray Parkinson Memorial Lecture Series, University of the South Pacific, Suva, Fiji

Mathews, E. and Oiterong, E. (1991) *The role of women in the fisheries of Palau,* Koror: University of Oregan Micronesia Programme, FAO Regional Fishery Support Programme and Palau Job Training Partnership Act

Narsey Lal, P. and Slatter, C. (1982) 'The integration of women in fisheries development in Fiji', Suva, Fiji: Fisheries Division, Ministry of Agriculture and Fisheries and University of the South Pacific

Schoeffel, P. (1985) 'Women in the fisheries of the South Pacific' in *Women in development in the South Pacific: Barriers and opportunities,* Canberra: Development Studies Centre, Australian National University

Schoeffel, P. and Kikau, E. (1980) 'Women's work in Fiji: An historical perspective' in *Review,* 11, vol.1, no.2:20-28, School of Social and Economic Development, University of the South Pacific

Schoeffel, P. and Talagi, S. (1989) *The role of women in small-scale fisheries in the South Pacific,* Report of Proceedings, Preparatory Meeting of Development Agencies, London: Commonwealth Secretariat

South, R. and Veitayaki, J. (1993) 'Coastal fisheries in the tropical South Pacific - A question of sustainability?', paper presented to International Conference on Fisheries and the Environment: Beyond 2000, Faculty of Fisheries and Marine Science, Universiti Pertanian, Malaysia, 6-9 December

South Pacific Commission (1992a) 'Information Paper 17', SPC 24th Regional Technical Meeting on Fisheries, Noumea, New Caledonia, 3-7 August

---------- (1992b) 'Fiji Country Paper', SPC 24th Regional Technical Meeting on Fisheries, South Pacific Commission, Noumea, New Caledonia, 3-7 August

---------- (1992c) 'Coastal Fisheries Statistics in the South Pacific', SPC 24th Regional Technical Meeting on Fisheries, South Pacific Commission, Noumea, New Caledonia, 3-7 August

---------- (1994) 'Status of stocks in the SPC area: 1994 update', working paper 3, Seventh Standing Committee on Tuna and Billfish, Koror, Republic of Palau, 5-8 August, Oceanic Fisheries Programme, South Pacific Commission, Noumea, New Caledonia

Sutherland, W. M. (1987) 'Struggle for sovereignty: Self determination and vulnerability in the Pacific Islands' in Gauhar, R. (ed.) *Third World Affairs,* London: Third World Foundation

Sutherland W.M. and Tsamenyi, M. (1992) *Law and politics in regional cooperation: A case study of fisheries cooperation in the South Pacific,* Hobart, Australia: Pacific Law Press

Taniera, T. and Mitchell, J. (1992) 'Women and fishing: Notes from Kiribati', paper presented to CUSO Meeting, Suva, Fiji, August

Twelve

Backbone of growth:
Export manufacturing and Fiji's tuna fish wives*

'Atu Emberson-Bain

Introduction

During the last decade or two, the Pacific region has been swept up in the net of export processing, the significant manufacturing arm of export-driven economic development which has expanded in leaps and bounds around the third world since the 1960s. The establishment of export processing zones (EPZs) in South-East Asia, the Indian Ocean and Latin America has emerged as the institutionalised expression of this economic strategy. It has produced a 'development' prototype that is now being enthusiastically promoted by several Pacific Island states, albeit in economic and political circumstances that are very different, and arguably much more austere, to those that faced the first trailblazing industrialising states (NICs) of the 1960s[1]. The labour process that has evolved globally in export-oriented industrialisation has had singular implications for women, and the Pacific pattern shows every sign of emulating its long-established blueprint. Industrial workers are overwhelmingly female, whether we look to the garment factories of Fiji, Tonga and Micronesia, the tuna fish canneries of American Samoa, the Solomon Islands and Fiji, or the Japanese automotive wire assembly plants of Western Samoa. While data on the gender distribution of employment in export manufacturing around the region is minimal, it is safe to say that close to 20,000 Pacific Island women are habitually engaged in this important growth area of production.

This paper offers a critical assessment of aspects of the labour process, especially its effects on women workers, at Fiji's 'showcase' export tuna factory at Levuka, on the island of Ovalau. The profitability crisis hitting the cannery in 1994 - attributed to shortages of fish stocks, and an industrial dispute and hurricane damage in late 1993, as well as the perennial problems of a highly competitive global market - is demanding cost-effective operations, improved

149

output levels and higher productivity. These pressures appear to be exacerbating already poor labour standards and they directly impinge on the welfare and livelihoods of women workers. Preliminary research findings point to the extreme vulnerability of those who represent the productive backbone of export processing, and they stress the importance of questioning regional development strategies that do not adequately take account of their social or labour impact.

Indeed, in recent years, mounting pressure from regional and international NGOs has placed concerns about the environmental impact of large-scale commercial fisheries in the public domain. Resource depletion from overfishing and the impact of environment-unfriendly technology (e.g. driftnet fishing methods) have sounded persistent alarm bells. The environmental lobby has emphasised the need for more environmentally sensitive fisheries 'development' and its success can be measured by achievements such as the banning of driftnet fishing in the region. In the case of Fiji's tuna cannery, the significant input of tuna caught by pole-and-line fishing, which incurs the smallest by-catch (the catching of non-targeted species) of the large-scale commercial fishing methods, has at least partly derived from environmental considerations. It is against this backdrop of incipient responsiveness to environmental concerns that the seeming indifference of Pacific Island states to the interests and needs of fish cannery workers (and even the absence of a parallel NGO lobby for 'worker-friendly' development) emerges as a curious irony.

The political economy of Fiji's manufacturing sector

The manufacturing sector has proved to be Fiji's own little economic miracle or success story. It is a miracle that has been built on the foundations of an export-driven development ideology, and which has been made possible by access to the relatively cheap and tractable labour of thousands of Fiji's women. Manufacturing contributes an estimated 12 per cent of gross domestic product (GDP) and it is one of the largest sector employers of women. Through their employment in garment-making alone, women make up over half the estimated 22,000-strong manufacturing workforce (World Bank 1993:32). Moreover, in individual industries like garment-making and food (including fish) processing, the numerical significance of women workers relative to men is much greater, with distribution tipping the scales at between 85 per cent and 90 per cent in their favour.

Following a period of economic stagnation and poor (less than 1%) growth in Fiji during the first half of the 1980s (the result of a downturn in tourism, high oil prices and low primary commodity prices amongst other factors), the encouragement of export manufacturing, notably the garment trade, became one of the hallmarks of a new and invigorated development phase. Under the direction of the World Bank and the International Monetary Fund (IMF), private sector investment, 'market-friendly' policy initiatives that included deregulation of trade and the labour market, and optimising production for the export market all spoke the convincing language of the dominant free market growth ideology. State support and resources were redirected away from public sector enterprise, interventionist central planning, public expenditure, and import-substitution (aimed at promoting local industry and reducing dependence on imports). Since 1989, an export processing policy first nurtured during the 1970s has crystallised into a full-fledged tax-free factory/zone scheme bountifully adorned

150

with 13-year tax holidays for exporting companies and other benefits to foreign and local investors. The concessions have been the backbone of a policy aimed at increasing competitive export-oriented industrialisation although it has, on the Bank's own admission, had limited success in encouraging higher levels of private sector investment and economic growth, especially since 1990.

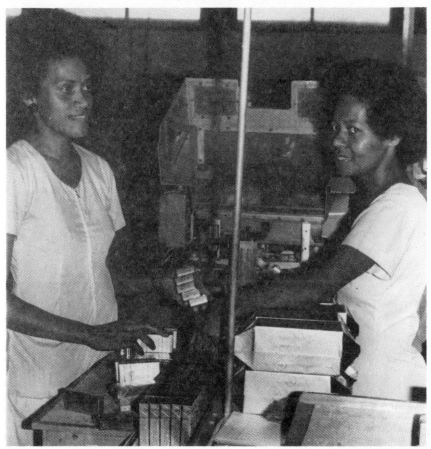

Peddling the basic principle of 'earn more and spend less', structural adjustment has been a critical catalyst of this new development phase, consolidating the reliance on market forces and preoccupation with national macroeconomic returns. Structural adjustment programmes (SAPS) have been promoted by the World Bank in circumstances of Fiji's ostensibly 'sluggish' economic growth (7.7% in 1986 but reduced to minus 6.6% in 1987) and its rising though, by world standards, relatively modest national debt ($FIJ 701 million or 49% of GDP in 1987). According to the World Tables published by the Bank, Fiji's external debt alone (i.e. excluding local borrowing) rose from $US 281 million to $409 million between 1980 and 1990. The adoption of the Bank's package of market policies reflects the overwhelming dominance of the market system within the world economy and the severely weakened position of traditional commodity producers like Fiji, especially in the recent wake of major global trade deregulation initiatives. Since the 1987 military coups and the economic crisis they triggered, the World Bank's vision has assumed even greater

151

importance. Adjustment policies have flourished with the frenzied responses to dislocation in the country's sugar and tourism industries, the virtual halt in foreign investment, the plummeting of GDP (by 8% for 1987), the draining of capital and skills, including high losses of professionals and those with trade skills (from which the country has yet to recover)[2], and the sharp rise in unemployment due to widespread retrenchments.

Corporatisation and privatisation of public enterprises have been accompanied by a range of austerity measures that have had quite critical implications for Fiji's workers and, conversely, created a more congenial business environment for the private sector. They have included wage deregulation and labour controls; cuts in health and education expenditure; tax reforms including the introduction of a new goods and service tax (VAT); and devaluations of the Fiji dollar aimed at stopping the outflow of capital and facilitating the opening-up of the economy to competitive export production. Labour deregulation has been one of the more prominent features of the adjustment package, punctuated by a multi-pronged assault on the trade union movement in the form of a series of labour decrees that carry the misleading tag of 'reforms'.

The boom in manufacturing (particularly garment-making), and women's contribution to this, are especially significant then in view of their vital contribution to national economic recovery since the 1987 coups. Overall, manufacturing has witnessed its most rapid growth in the post-1988 period. Largely due to the garment industry's impressive expansion, it was responsible for more than 50 per cent of the estimated 13 per cent increase in national employment between 1988 and 1989. Sectoral employment rose by a dramatic 40 per cent in 1989 from 14,040 to 19,666. By 1991, garment exports were valued at $US 91 million, contributing 24 per cent of domestic exports (World Bank 1993:58).

The other side of the miracle

While the take-off in the manufacturing sector has been the cause for official celebration (and relief), and has appeared to vindicate the faith of Fiji's 'growth' disciples, certain factors stress the desirability of more cautionary responses to the boom, in particular the need for a critical look at the employment opportunities it has created. In 1989 (there have unfortunately been no official wage data published since then) manufacturing had the lowest mean daily wage rate of $FIJ 11.36 compared to $11.92 for agriculture, $15.60 for electricity/gas and water, $13.92 for construction, and the industrial average of $12.64. The manufacturing sector was also noticeable for the high (36.4%) proportion of wage earners who earned less than $1 per hour. As a general rule, the sector has tended to lag well behind all other sectors in annual wage adjustments. Taking the years 1987-1992, total improvement in the mean daily manufacturing wage was a mere four per cent, compared to 49 per cent for agriculture, 30 per cent for construction and 23 per cent for services.

Moreover, wage trends through the 1980s show that the hourly (mean) wage in 1989 ($1.42) was 7 cents lower than it was six years earlier in 1983 ($1.49), resulting in an even bigger fall in real wages in view of the 35 per cent increase in consumer prices (including a 47% rise in the cost of food) over more or less the same period (1984-1989) (Annual Employment Survey 1989; Bureau of Statistics unpublished data 1994; World Bank Fiji 1993:73). Sectoral wage movements in the 1990s confirm that in a period of more intensive deregulation and continuing inflation (5-8% annually until 1993), manufacturing remains a significant casualty. Wage rates have languished in the lower rungs of the sectoral wage table, with only agricultural workers marginally worse off. In 1992 and 1993, construction, electricity and transport workers earned a daily wage that was between $FIJ 4 and $8 higher than manufacturing workers (between $20 and $40 if weekly wage comparisons are made) (Bureau of Statistics unpublished data 1994; 1991 & 1992 estimates; and 1993 projected figures).

Since its introduction in 1991, wage 'liberalisation' has been integral to the presently favoured policies of labour market deregulation. It has included the relinquishing of indexation (or the linking of wages to movements in the cost of living) and thus the effective withdrawal of workers' rights to maintain the real value of their wages. An equally important move has been the removal (in 1991) of national wage guidelines and the substitution of wage/labour consultations within the (government/union/employer) Tripartite Forum by market-based negotiations. Pressure to abandon minimum wage protection and other traditional forms of state protection like arbitration machinery is also a feature of the current wages/labour policy. The underlying aims of the deregulatory initiatives are: to reduce labour costs, particularly unskilled and public sector wages; to return workers to the supposedly neutral and just workings of the free market; and to enshrine productivity, 'affordability' and direct employer/worker (or enterprise) bargaining (as opposed to collective bargaining by trade unions on behalf of workers) as the pre-eminent wage-determining principles.

The new labour policies have disturbing implications for worker rights and livelihoods, especially in those areas of the economy which rely on unskilled or lesser skilled and unorganised workers. (Under 40% of wage and salary earners are unionised). It should also be noted from Fiji's 1993 World Bank Report that the policies are being applied at a time when per capita incomes (for 1991) have scarcely risen above what they were 10 years ago (1981), despite a steady inflation rate averaging an annual seven per cent. The post-coup recovery strategy of tax-free factories - with its guarantees of compliant and low-wage workers - lends additional bite to the stranglehold of deregulation. Overall, the market is simply not neutral, nor is it necessarily just; and state policies would appear to be sanctioning (and reinforcing) its iniquitous tendencies.

The employment conditions endured by women workers within the manufacturing sector give additional grounds for a more circumspect approach to the manufacturing development miracle. Women face wage discrimination on the labour market, and specifically within the manufacturing sector. Gender-based differentials operate even with respect to minimum wage legislation and they fly in the face of skill components in women's work. Perhaps the best example of this is Fiji's garment workers, whose sweatshop conditions have long been a matter for public debate and controversy, and for whom base rates (72 cents an hour for learners and 94 cents for skilled workers) fall between 52 and 38 per cent short of the statutory minimum wage for manufacturing of $FIJ 1.50[3]. Rates in the garment trade also lag well behind those awarded in other, mainly male-dominated, manufacturing trades. The 1993 Building and Civil and Electrical Engineering Trades Order, for example, permits a juvenile (under 18 years) unskilled worker to earn 26 per cent more (at $1.27) than an experienced and skilled (adult) garment worker. The gap is wider under the terms of the 1993 Wholesale and Retail Trades Order which gives an unskilled worker on the $1.57 base rate a lead of over 60 per cent. Gender differentials are also evident in allowances. Under the 'protective' umbrella of minimum wage legislation, Fiji's women garment workers enjoy an annual sick leave entitlement of just five days on completion of three months employment. Other manufacturing workers are guaranteed 10 days leave, and without a qualifying period of employment[4].

Labour market deregulation especially threatens the interests of women workers because of their weak bargaining position and generally disadvantaged status on the labour market, including their higher unemployment rates (15% as opposed to 5% according to 1989 Social Indicators published by Fiji's Bureau of Statistics)[5]. Left to the wayward workings of the free market, and the position of relative strength enjoyed by employers, women workers have less prospect of improving either their occupational status in relation to men, or their conditions of employment and standard of living generally. They will even have difficulty safeguarding the conditions they enjoy now. The removal of minimum wage legislation would strip those working in the garment and other unorganised manufacturing trades of very basic protection. So would any attempt to de-unionise any of the export industries that employ women, a strategy mooted in the 1993 World Bank report.

More growth, more women: Processing Pacific tuna

Fish processing has emerged as a new growth export following the 1987 military coups. Exports of prepared, preserved and canned fish rose from 4.8 million kg in 1987 to 7 million kg in 1988 (World Bank 1993:59). Production is dominated by the (98%) government-owned tuna cannery operations at Levuka known as the Pacific Fishing Company Ltd (PAFCO) which enjoys a monopoly in the export of canned tuna. Although recently beset by financial and production problems including shortages in fish supply (net losses of $FIJ 81,301 and $2,331,560 were reported for 1992 and 1993), tuna exports from PAFCO have earned Fiji over $176 million dollars since 1987, with annual sales revenue for even the unprofitable years of 1992-1993 holding out at close to $40 million (PAFCO 1993). Exports of fish products have been responsible for an average nine per cent of total domestic exports between 1987 and 1992 (World Bank 1993:58), with the contribution of canned fish ranging from 5.3 per cent of exports in 1992 to nearly nine per cent in 1988 (Fiji Current Economic Statistics 1993)[6]. Significantly, the bulk of canned fish exports is the product of a single tuna cannery, whose workforce is only around 1,000 at its peak.

Fiji's commercial fisheries are dominated by the private sector and joint-venture or foreign interests, with PAFCO being an interesting exception as a fully localised and largely government-owned operation. PAFCO was initially a joint venture between (two) Japanese companies and the Fiji government, whose operations were focussed on the running of a tuna transhipment port to service Japanese, Korean and Taiwanese vessels fishing in the Western Pacific. Since the mid-1970s, a sizeable cannery has been in operation at Levuka, enabling corporate activities to expand into the processing of Pacific tuna. Today, following recent expansion of its cold storage facilities along with other infrastructural improvements funded under a $FIJ 17 million Australian aid package, the cannery has a maximum daily capacity of 100 metric tons. It is supplied by Taiwanese and local fishing vessels, notably the government-owned Ika Corporation, and it produces between 5,000 and 8,000 metric tons of canned skipjack, yellowfin and albacore tuna for export every year (Fiji Fisheries Division 1992).

The Levuka tuna canning factory is a labour-intensive operation with regular employment figures fluctuating between 500 and 700, and boosted to around 1,000 by the engagement of temporary and short-term casual workers when fish stocks increase significantly. Total employment (staff, workers and management) for 1993 was over 1,000 with the overwhelming majority being hourly-paid female production workers. PAFCO is the single most important source of employment for people on the small island of Ovalau and the neighbouring islands of the Lomaiviti group, the majority (close to 90%) of workers being ethnic Fijian women drawn from villages beyond Levuka town. Outside PAFCO, the employment opportunities are negligible, particularly for unskilled or lesser skilled workers. To this extent, Levuka (like other cannery 'homes' in the Pacific such as Noro in the Solomon Islands) shows features of the captive labour market (and even perhaps the company town), with workers feeling the full weight of economic dependence, vulnerability and a weak bargaining position in relation to their employer. The discussion that follows on wage trends, employment conditions and other peculiarities of PAFCO's labour system (including the heavy reliance on non-permanent workers and rotation of labour quotas amongst different villages) would appear to offer evidence to justify the 'captive' market tag. At the very least, labour conditions at the cannery testify to a position of advantage for PAFCO in the local labour market[7].

The gender preferential employment policy of PAFCO has had some unusual social consequences for Ovalau, although in the absence of more research it is uncertain just how critical these have been. In many households, women are the sole or primary breadwinners with their dependants including husbands as well as parents, in-laws and children. Many men, either unemployed or engaged in irregular casual jobs, remain in the villages during the day as caretakers of the children. In practice, this somewhat unconventional arrangement does not appear to have led to a radical adjustment in the traditional division of labour, or even to a reduced domestic workload for women. Daytime childcare is, in fact, often left to other women (typically grandmothers or aunties), while much of the domestic work, including cooking the evening meal, getting school-age children fed and ready for school, and subsistence inshore fisheries (to feed the family), is still undertaken by PAFCO's 'working wives'.

There is also evidence to suggest that the childcare role of husbands, in so far as this is performed, has interfered with their (traditional) food gardening responsibilities. These would normally be expected to supplement the wages earned by the women. This has adversely affected family livelihoods, especially in view of the low wage system that prevails at PAFCO (see below). Other negative social outcomes include male-inflicted domestic violence (a contributing factor being men's frustrations about their economic dependence on their wives), and child malnutrition and behavioural or discipline problems (truancy amongst school children for example). All of these problems are sources of preoccupation and concern amongst local community workers, government officials and (Fijian) chiefs (Levuka 1994, pers. comms.; also see Malani 1991).

The ideology and implications of a preferential labour policy

The preference for women workers at PAFCO is a policy inherited from the company's former Japanese management. It conforms to the long-established trend set by world market factories in regions like Asia and Central and South

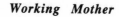

Working Mother

My children don't know
me:
They call me Jully
not Mummy.
They see me,
Two hours before
bedtime,
An hour in the mornings.
No time for a cuddle,
or play;
No time to feed, bathe
or clothe them -
Just a peck on the cheek
and,
'Bye bye, be good!
See you at four.'
I'm never home
during the week -
Too busy making money.
The only times I see them
They are asleep in bed.
I spend the nights alone
With the house-girl.
My children don't know
me.

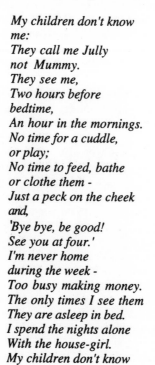

Jully   Sipolo

America, and it replicates the practice on the emerging production or assembly lines of the Pacific, including the fish canneries of the Solomon Islands[8] and American Samoa. The policy has its roots firmly planted in the economic benefits that derive from the so-called 'traditional' gender division of labour which encapsulates discriminatory values about 'women's work' and well-worn arguments about their 'natural' dexterity and precision (or 'nimble fingers'), patience, speed and efficiency, and thus their suitability for assembly line work.

Both stereotypes are used to legitimise lower earnings, the 'natural skills' argument being an especially effective mechanism of labour cost control because it denies the skills that women bring to or acquire in the workplace. All women employees with the exception of staff are classified as unskilled, and the standardisation of wages reflects this form of deskilling. With the exception of temporary workers who are paid at the slightly lower hourly rate of $FIJ 1.50 for a period of six months, and the 11 cent per hour loading paid to all workers employed before 1990 (in accordance with a 7% government wage guideline in that year), the minimum rate of $1.53 applies across the board to women production workers, irrespective of job, skill level, experience or productivity (PAFCO/NUCFW 1989-1993).

Unskilled job classifications (and accordingly unskilled wages) for women cannery workers sit uncomfortably alongside company promotional materials which acknowledge their skills with pride. They also contrast with the skill differentials applied to men's work, ('semi-skilled' and 'skilled' classifications are ascribed to male fitters, turners, mechanics and carpenters) and the slightly higher value placed on all men's work, irrespective of whether it is undertaken in the skilled trades or in production jobs like pushing fish-laden baskets, carrying boxes, or moving fish in and out of the cooking furnaces.

A related feature of the labour system is the engagement of large numbers of 'casual' or 'temporary' workers. Paid on a weekly basis, and without the guarantee of continuous employment and income, casual workers enjoy limited job security although many are in reality 'regular' hands who have accumulated years of experience. A shift system commonly employs groups of women on a week-on-week-off basis, rotating the job opportunities amongst different villages. As mentioned above, temporary workers (who enjoy greater security than casual workers but nevertheless tend to be retrenched during spells of maintenance work) are paid at a lower rate than permanent employees over a period of six months. After this time has elapsed, they qualify for the basic minimum rate, but not for reclassification as permanent workers. Moreover, although they are eligible for paid annual holidays and sick leave, these benefits are not guaranteed because they are contingent upon there being no breaks in employment. (Three months and twelve months continuous employment are mandatory for sick leave and annual leave respectively.)

Dependent on the supply of a raw material, PAFCO operations are constrained by the seasonal variations of tuna (the skipjack season in Fiji, for example, runs only for six months) and related problems of erratic or inadequate stock. Through its employment policy, the company has passed some of these disadvantages on to its workforce, thereby rendering casual (and to a lesser extent temporary) workers especially vulnerable to regular spells of retrenchment. A provision in the company's collective agreement with the National Union of Commercial and Factory Workers (NUCFW) gives the company 'the right, after consultation with the Union, to stand down employees due to lack of or no fish to pack or over-stocking through decrease or less of sales'. During the past year, there have been at least two mass retrenchments, one of which (in late 1993) involved a complete shut-down of the cannery for eight weeks.

At the other end of the employment spectrum, the company's many long-service production workers receive little material recognition of their accumulated experience and skills. Apart from the provision of special leave benefits (21 days and 42 days for 15 years and 25 years service respectively), there is no service-related wage adjustment or bonus in operation (annual increments are given only to salaried staff); nor is there any system of promotion outside the handful of jobs as production supervisor, for whom a $FIJ 15 weekly bonus applies. This means that a worker who might have given the best part of her productive life (say 15 to 20 years) to PAFCO is currently paid 14 cents more an hour (at $FIJ 1.64) than a woman who joined the company yesterday (at $1.50) as a temporary employee. Even the special leave benefits are not guaranteed for 'old hands' on account of their stringent conditions, notably a minimum 10-year period of unbroken or continuous employment, and lay-offs that do not aggregate

157

more than three months in the following five years (for 15-year employees) or ten years (for 25-year employees).

The PAFCO regime: Women on the production line

Behind the 'romance' of foreign exchange earnings and other economic benefits scored by Fiji's tuna exports is another story: the workplace realities that face the hundreds of women whose daily labour takes tons of huge albacore, yellowfin and skipjack along the smelly, messy and monotonous journey from pre-cooking through to the final stages of packaging for shipment. On the processing or production line of PAFCO, work begins with the decapitation of thawed and pre-cooked tuna, after which the fish is moved by conveyor belt down to the 300-odd workers in the cleaning section of the cannery. In six lines of 50, 25 back to back on either side of the belts, the women divide the fish and cut, clean and remove the bones, skin and red meat (which are used for pet food and fish meal). They separate the flakes from loin and prepare the fish for canning as solid meat, chunks or flakes.

Between 50 and 75 metric tons of tuna pass through the production plant every day. Each woman on the cleaning line would therefore prepare between 373 lb and 560 lb of fish a day for canning. Because of the limited labour capacity of the cleaning area, increases in the supply of fish have important implications for women's workload and productivity levels. The processing line continues until the cans are filled; vegetable oil, water or brine is added; weights are checked; and can ends are sealed. Workers responsible for controlling weight range are required to adjust incorrectly filled cans. After the cans have completed re-cooking and cooling, other women check machine labelling under approximately 30 different brand names, handsticking defective faulty labels with glue. Another group of women is involved in packing and stock-taking in the warehouse.

Women employees of PAFCO contend with a long, disciplined and tiring working day. Work begins promptly at 7.30 am and ends at 5 pm, although overtime until 8 pm (the statutory limit for women industrial workers under Fiji's Employment Act) appears to be a fairly regular occurrence. Notwithstanding the hour-long lunch break, and two short tea breaks of 15 minutes each, the working day accordingly ranges from 9.5 hours to 12.5 hours. Unpaid travel time to and from work (including waiting time for transport) further lengthens the day. In a town which does not enjoy the 'luxury' of a public transport system, this can amount to an additional three hours a day.

Worker ethics and the work environment: Double standards?

The workplace at PAFCO is fairly regimented. Management's attempts to iron out lax habits (like absenteeism and late arrivals) and to improve worker efficiency and productivity have resulted in an austerity package of rules and regulations. One of these is the ban on talking on the production line, especially in the cleaning area which is closely supervised. For many workers, the opportunity to talk during the working day is more or less confined to the 15 minute tea breaks in the canteen and lunchtime. Another unwritten rule which appears to have sporadic bursts of flexibility is the time allowed for going to the toilet. At present, there are pressures to minimise the time spent away which include a supervisor's instruction to 'hurry up' if a worker takes 'too long'.

I remember in 1991, the company chose one girl to watch all the girls going to the toilet and to write down the time and their names. If you go to the toilet at 3 o'clock, they write down your name and 3 o'clock. You come back after 15 minutes, they write down 15 minutes. How many times you go to the toilet, they write down your name for that. We were fighting all the way from that point. We told the company 'there's no use writing down the names, you are going to finish one big foolscap, then another one, and another one. And then where does it all go? It finish in the rubbish.

PAFCO woman worker discussing company rules, Levuka, Fiji, 1994

A draconian rule that carries stiff penalties of dubious legality relates to poor time-keeping. Arrival to work between one minute and 15 minutes late (7.31 am - 7.45 am) is penalised by the deduction of one-half-hour's pay; arrival between 16 minutes and 30 minutes late (7.46 am - 8 am) results in a one-hour wage deduction; and anyone turning up at 8.01 am or later is sent home, thus forfeiting a whole day's wages. Other new rules introduced by PAFCO in recent months reflect a curious mixture of commercial 'ethics' and fundamentalist Methodism. Daily morning prayer sessions for section representatives, and less frequent but regular church meetings on the job site, instil the virtues of non-confrontation, love and unity. They are the product of an official company ideology of 'family togetherness', designed to pacify union militants and placate other disaffected elements within the workforce, in the wake of a bitter industrial dispute last year. The imposition of (Christian) familial values is also mediated through the company prohibition on adultery, an 'offence' which brings instant dismissal according to former Acting General Manager and incumbent Director of Fisheries, Peniasi Kunatuba (1994, Levuka, pers. comm.). It is difficult to reconcile this extraordinary intrusion into the private lives of workers with their rights under Fiji's (controversial).1990 Constitution. All told, PAFCO's 'familial' ideology conveniently obfuscates (and even legitimises) the less-than-philanthropic intent of its battery of rules and regulations.

In contrast to the strict regime governing workplace behaviour, the area of occupational health and safety reveals a largely unregulated environment for PAFCO's women workers. Health problems include the excessive heat and overcrowding on the production line; the long hours of continuous standing (which causes joint pains and is a problem especially for pregnant and older women); and the deafening sound levels in sections of the factory floor. Without provision for sitting during working hours, workers stand a minimum of eight hours every day and, whenever overtime is worked, up to 11 hours. The heat is the result of a number of factors including the archaic structural features of the 20-year old cannery, the general congestion around the conveyor belts (there is little space between individual workers), and the fact that the lines are flanked on both

Sereima's story

Sereima is the mother of five children and is 49 years old. When she shared her story at an evening meeting, most of her fellow workers were hearing it for the first time. Many were moved to tears. The following is a translation.

In 1992, I was working at the machine that suction packs the white tuna flakes, when the can hammer caught my left hand. There were no supervisors around at the time. I somehow managed to reach the switch to turn the machine off, while hanging on to the can to protect my hand which was caught under it. Then with the help of a male worker, who saw me in trouble, I was able to lever the hammer up and free my hand. My clothes were covered in blood, but I got myself across town to the government hospital.

I received no pay for two weeks while off work. In the third week, I received $35. I don't know what this money was for. I was off work for three months. My hand was bad, I couldn't do anything at home. And I hadn't got one cent from the company apart from the $35. I went back to them and asked them why they were doing this to me. They sent me to the doctor to get a medical certificate. I went to the doctor but he said that I was fit to go back to work. I went back to the company and pleaded with them. I said, 'there is no way I can go back to work', and I asked for another two months. The company said: 'the time for you to rest is over'.

So I returned to work. On the second day, I fainted. I fell where I was standing because my hand was still really weak. Up to the fourth month, I couldn't do any work with my hand. After six months, I hurt the same hand again. I went back to the company and explained that my fingers were bent and I couldn't work. The company said 'it's better for you to resign and go and rest.' I went to the Labour Department [in Suva] and they sent me back to Personnel [PAFCO] to get a letter from them to prove that I had got injured in the factory. When I asked the Personnel Officer for the doctor's report, he wouldn't give it to me. He said I should go back to the doctor.

After one year, the arthritis in my hand affected my whole body. I can't do the things I used to do with my hand anymore. The only thing I can see is that the Labour Department and those who work in the office at PAFCO are working together doing this terrible unforgivable thing. And there have been other cases. I know they were hiding the doctor's reports. I went back to them but all I could say was, 'Thank you for hiding all the information.

Levuka, Fiji, April 1994

sides by several huge, high-temperature cooking furnaces. The thick fabric used for the women's uniforms and the heavy boots they are obliged to wear increase the discomfort. Airconditioning, a facility which is provided in the tuna canneries of both the Solomon Islands and American Samoa, is enjoyed by PAFCO's office workers courtesy of Australian aid. It has been ruled out for production workers on the grounds of cost (PAFCO Acting General Manager 1994, Levuka, pers. comm.).

In the huge freezing works, a protective rule (maximum 30 minutes exposure) is applied to male workers, as well as a special allowance of 22 cents an hour. But the company conducts no monitoring of heat in the main production area where women predominate. Moreover, a general government factory inspection to monitor noise, heat and ventilation levels, and other conditions covered by Fiji's factories legislation, such as overcrowding and sanitation, has never once been conducted, according to the Labour Department. Nor have there been any checks of labelling (and other potentially hazardous) machinery to which women are exposed (see Sereima's story). Mandatory inspections are only undertaken for steam boilers, pressure vessels and lifting gear (Labour Department 1994, Suva, pers.comm.).

Staff shortages are the reason given by government labour officials for the shortcomings of the inspection process. According to Fiji's Senior Inspector of Factories, 'the inspectorate is obliged to make some 80,000 inspections in 1994. There are just 12 inspectors and we have one landrover which is 10 years old. This means that a total of nearly 7,000 inspections have to be undertaken by each inspector during the year, which is impossible to achieve.' (1994, Suva, pers. comm.). Even if individual officers are conscientious and committed, the chances of a tougher inspection regime emerging to safeguard the interests of workers look decidedly slim in the current climate of deregulation and public expenditure cuts.

Discriminatory wages and worker indebtedness: Double trouble

Perhaps the most serious problem affecting PAFCO's women workers is wages. The company's total wages and salaries bill since its takeover by the Fiji government in 1987 until October 1993 was $FIJ 23,162,459, representing just under eight per cent of its aggregate sales revenue over the same period of $300,112,069. Compared to other areas of women's employment like the garment trade or domestic work, PAFCO wages are relatively high, a situation that may partly result from their having been organised into a union since the 1970s. The majority of women earn marginally more than the statutory minimum wage for the manufacturing sector and they are paid nearly double the wage of a qualified garment worker. Their rates are also slightly better than those paid to women employed in Fiji's only other fish cannery, Vo-Ko, a smaller joint venture between Korean and local business interests based in Suva which pays a minimum wage of $1.52. However, there has been little improvement in PAFCO's wages since the late 1980s during a time of continuing inflation (17%-18% between 1990 and 1993) and the payment of more competitive wages by other employers in the manufacturing sector (NUFCW 1993). Outside Fiji, PAFCO wages contrast with a much higher base rate of $US 3.00 an hour in the American Samoan canneries and a lower hourly rate of around 70 cents in Thailand (Ronni Alexander 1994, Suva, pers. comm.).

Given the long tradition of union membership and collective bargaining at PAFCO, the gender-discriminatory structure of earnings is one of the more disturbing (and perhaps surprising) features of the company's labour system. Women cannery workers earn less than men through the female-gendering of jobs on the production line, as well as because of the unequal value ascribed to comparable or the same work. The base (unskilled) hourly rates for adult women on the production line, adult men (who work in the freezers, cook the fish, or move and stack cartons on forklift trucks) and 14- or 15-year-old boy novices are $1.53, $1.65 and $1.54 respectively. Allowances paid over and above base rates (e.g. for work in the freezer, the fish meal plant, on Sundays, or in the engine and control room) apply almost exclusively to male workers. A special loading of five cents an hour is even paid to male 'butcher hands' responsible for cleaning (i.e. gutting and gilling) fish before the pre-cooking stage. Women who clean and process the same fish by hand after pre-cooking receive no allowance.

Gender differentials in respect of office work at PAFCO are more overtly discriminatory because they involve men and women engaged in the same work. There are currently over 20 office work categories at PAFCO where a gender wage gap of between 11-12 cents an hour amounts to a difference in ordinary (i.e. excluding overtime) weekly earnings of about $FIJ 5.00. They include jobs like Assistant Clerk (male/female rates: $1.65/$1.53); Accounts Clerk ($1.85/$1.73); Computer Operator ($1.90/$1.78); and Senior Clerk ($1.95/$1.83) (PAFCO/NUCFW 1993).

Yet the problem of wages runs deeper than the issue of gender discrimination. Low disposable incomes resulting from a yawning gulf between gross and net earnings arguably present a more serious predicament for women workers. Weekly earnings of between $FIJ 65 and $70 for a 42.5 hour week are whittled away by a range of deductions. A typical pay slip shows deductions for income tax, superannuation, insurance, and union dues. What are not shown, but which are also deducted at source, are obligatory weekly repayments of between $20 and $30 on personal bank loans that usually amount to between $FIJ 2,000 and $3,000. The loans have proved a necessary supplement to wages, helping workers meet the costs of basic necessities like school fees, electricity bills, lay-by payments and housing needs, as well as traditional and church obligations. However, they carry high interest rates and weekly repayments claim between one-third and 50 per cent of gross earnings. After all deductions, a typical cannery worker can be left with as little as $10 to cover the costs of food, transport and other basic needs for the week. Entering another round of the debt cycle and/or working longer (overtime) hours are the common options in the face of such hardship.

The easy accessibility of unsecured personal loans for PAFCO workers raises some disturbing questions, not least of which are the underlying aims of the loan system and its implications for worker (in)dependence. The loans are a 'service' that were arranged by PAFCO in 1988 with the Australian-owned Westpac Banking Corporation, which until recently enjoyed a monopoly in Levuka. The service currently ensnares a minimum 400-500 PAFCO employees in debts of up to $FIJ 3,000, with some women running two or more debts concurrently. An exorbitant 16 per cent interest - at present reduced to 15.25 per cent - is unusually punitive, particularly in view of the low earnings of cannery workers, not all of whom have 'permanent' status. While under normal circumstances, the risks involved in providing unsecured personal loans might justify high interest rates, the PAFCO loan system shows little evidence of being a high-risk operation for Westpac. For one thing, the role it plays as banker and paymaster for PAFCO gives it control over the disbursement of worker earnings. In such circumstances, prolonged repayments and serial loans arguably pose few handicaps for the bank. On the contrary, it could be said that the worker debt-trap has offered opportunities for long-term profiteering.

Veniana's story

*My husband asked me to get a loan to help him get an outboard
engine so that he could help me with the expenses for our
household. I have been repaying the loan for the last four years and
I'm still repaying it. I did get my husband the engine which cost us
$FIJ 2,000. I was only allowed $2,000 because I was just a
temporary worker for the company.*

*The outboard motor needs to be maintained to keep running. Due to
strong winds and bad weather, the boat went underwater and this
damaged the engine badly. My husband asked me to go for another
loan. Right now I'm still paying off that loan too. Last year I still
owed $1,800 to the bank.*

*Then my mother passed away last year and I didn't have a single
cent to my name. The wages I got from the factory did not meet my
needs because I had seven children, a husband, mother and a niece to
look after. Since I didn't have any money, the only place I could go
to was the bank again. I already owed $1,800, and on top of that I
had to borrow another $500. This extended my loan to $2,300.*

*Then we had the company lay off for two months. I didn't think that
the interest would be charged on my loan, but after the two months
were up and we went back to work, I found that the loan had gathered
enough interest to bring the total amount to nearly $3,000. I nearly
died! One thing that really oppresses us women who work for
PAFCO is the bank loans. They have imprisoned us, we are slaves
to our work.*

Levuka, Fiji, April 1994

Yet, despite the advantages, Westpac recognises that neither 'overlending'
nor the 'excessive commitments' of PAFCO workers is desirable. Recent months
have accordingly seen moves to reduce the level of personal loans and to tighten
up the lending criteria, although loans are confined to what effectively remains a
subsistence check-list: 'essential purposes like education, living expenses and
housing' and 'cutting down on loans for traditional and church obligations'
(Westpac Levuka General Manager Abele Matai 1994, Levuka, pers. comm.).
Loan reductions are in line with head office policy that is itself a response to
spiralling bad debts around the country. But the adjustments in Levuka may have
less to do with toeing the company line than with persisting industrial tensions at
PAFCO (especially in the wake of the 1993 'illegal strike') and the uncertain
future of the cannery in the face of national deregulation initiatives. Whatever the
bank's reasons, it is difficult to be sure of the effect that the new 'austerity'
measures will have on workers. Some positive benefits may result in the long
term, such as a loosening of the debt 'noose'. But in the short term, at least,

greater hardship could well result, particularly in the absence of more realistic wages. However cynically the loan system might be viewed, it has acted as a much-needed buffer to workers and their families, shielding them from destitution.

Marica's story

Marica comes from the village of Nauouou, several miles out of Levuka. She is a single parent and a solo earner, having been deserted by her husband some years ago. She began work for PAFCO in 1976 making pet food out of rejected fish parts. Today, she is classified as a permanent worker and is assigned to the cleaning area of the main processing line. She has done three different jobs since she began but has always been paid at the same rate.

Marica's day begins between 4 am and 4.30 am when she prepares breakfast and cooks lunch for herself and her two school-age children (8 and 12 years). She cleans the house and sometimes does some washing before leaving the house with her children by carrier (truck) at 6.30 am. Because she now has a relative staying with her, she is fortunate to have dinner cooked by the time she returns home at the end of the day. Her evenings are usually spent ironing and doing other domestic chores. She must also attend evening village functions, including meetings every Monday night. Usually she goes to bed between 12 pm and 1 am.

Marica earns the hourly rate of $1.64 which gives her a gross income of around $FIJ 269. She used to get credit from a money lender but now has an unsecured personal bank loan of $FIJ 3,000 which is paying for the construction of her kitchen and her children's school fees. She pays $20 a week in loan repayments. After further deductions for the Fiji National Provident Fund (FNPF), income tax, and her credit union, which claims loan repayments for funeral expenses and *soli* (village fundraising contributions), her weekly take home pay is $FIJ 28. With this she must buy food, pay for transport, and cover other family needs.

Marica has had continuous lower back ache for several years, requiring treatment three times in Suva. She also complains of pains in her knees. Because of these health problems, she uses her tea breaks to sit down. She has spent one pregnancy at PAFCO, during which time she stood the full 8.5 hours every day. She recalls receiving a total $FIJ 85 for the duration of her maternity leave period.

Levuka, Fiji, April 1994

The new political order and the PAFCO paradox

A number of factors, including the tenuous future of the sugar industry, are likely to keep manufacturing amongst the forerunners of Fiji's economy, as well as a sector where there will be pressure to expand. This has implications for the status and welfare of women workers, especially in view of their 'preferential' employment status in the sector and the central role that their cheap labour plays in promoting export-competitiveness. Under influence from the World Bank, government priority will increasingly be given to private sector growth (and thus to reducing private sector costs) and to opening up the economy to further foreign investment and trade. In such circumstances, labour and wage controls will almost certainly continue to be crucial pillars of the system. The latest recommendations of the World Bank are a decisive pointer in this direction. In its 1993 report on Fiji, it proposes 'rationalizing labor legislation and wage-setting procedures' as one way of 'reduc[ing] the costs of doing business in Fiji'. It advocates measures to boost investor confidence which include 'exemption from unionization for selected export oriented firms', 'the vigorous implementation of labor laws in the case of illegal strikes'[9] and, somewhat ambiguously, 'strengthening the arbitration functions of the Ministry of Labor to ensure that alternative institutional arrangements exist for fair resolution of disputes'. The Bank takes the firm stand that Fiji 'can ill afford disruptive labor behaviour if it is to build a substantial manufacturing base and attract foreign investment' (World Bank 1993:vi, 27).

Fiji's latest (1994) budget echoes these sentiments and gives every indication that the government will remain a faithful disciple of Bank policies. Committed to the process of deregulation, the budget places a premium on the market; hails the private sector as 'the engine of development'; and sends out clear signals that the powers of Fiji's unions will be further curtailed if they don't play ball in a deregulated labour market. According to former Minister of Finance Paul Manueli, 'sensible labour market policies' conducive to economic growth call for 'establishment or workplace-based' (i.e. enterprise) bargaining (Fiji Budget Speech 1994:26-27). More recently, in a rather extraordinary public statement, Manueli's successor, Berenado Vunibobo, has also pressed the World Bank line on labour policy, hinting that the days of Fiji's longstanding industrial relations machinery may be numbered. Commenting on a public sector wage claim before arbitration, the Minister has said:

> I do not wish to unduly influence the arbitrator in his deliberations on the dispute. But I cannot help thinking that it is not right to give the arbitrator the responsibility to determine our tax levels or our debt burden, or our degree of competitiveness. I have to agree with the former Minister of Finance's statement in his 1994 budget address that these considerations are the responsibility of government. They are not the responsibility of an administrator or an arbitrator (Vunibobo 1994).

But while global financial giants like the World Bank have placed an indelible stamp on development thinking and policy in Fiji, the country's post-coup political environment has been shaped (and sharpened) by other forces as well, notably a strident ideology of ethnic-Fijian nationalism and paramountcy. Economic and social policies, including the post-coup Constitution, reveal the persistent attempts of the Fijian state to promote and institutionalise ethnic separateness and inequality. Such policies have been consistently justified as a legitimate defence of indigenous Fijian interests, even as obligatory 'affirmative action'. It requires little reflection to grasp the contradictions that PAFCO exposes in the new political order. A Fijian, state-owned operation with an overwhelmingly ethnic Fijian workforce; a largely ethnic Fijian management; and

166

a board of directors with traditional Fijian chiefly representation (one of whom is a woman) combine to make the company a unique phenomenon in the current political economy of Fiji. But where the uniqueness ends, the PAFCO paradox begins, encapsulated in the exploitative conditions endured by Fijian women cannery workers who have received few, if any, benefits from the so-called defence of indigenous rights.

In a sense, the colonial and post-colonial histories of Fiji would suggest that it is not really a paradox we are looking at, at all, but merely one of the more imaginative 'outfits' of the global market economy wardrobe: a reality that appears paradoxical only because the politics of ethnicity and the rhetoric of indigenous rights conveniently obscure the fundamentals of class contradiction and exploitation. Yet the irony needs to be noted, and there is still more to be discovered if we reflect on the cultural values of reciprocity and redistribution that have for so long formed the ethical (and sustainable!) backbone of Fijian society and which so obviously have no place in the scheme of labour exploitation at the Levuka cannery. Curiously, tradition has not been totally discarded by those hurtling down the fast lane of 'development'. Some features of the traditional Fijian way evidently have an instrumental value and are being exploited at PAFCO. The company philosophy of 'family togetherness' which can usefully manufacture loyalty to the company (rather than the union) is a case in point.

Towards worker-friendly development

As the winds of deregulation gain momentum in Fiji, along with the pressures of competing in a tough global market (against low-cost countries like Taiwan and Thailand), the privatisation of PAFCO and a relocation of its operations from Levuka to Suva are emerging as possible options for the future[10]. The relocation option underscores the vulnerability (indeed expendability) of women cannery workers and their families who, in spite of the hardship they face in company employment, are nevertheless dependent on it for their livelihoods. The problem is shared by workers in other Pacific tuna canneries (for example American Samoan cannery workers in the wake of the North American free trade agreement); and it is symptomatic of the structural insecurities that have faced workers in export manufacturing zones and countries around the third world since the global market economy took its industrialising turn in the 1960s. Capital relocation to greener pastures (or lower-cost female labour havens) has been a typical response to uncongenial political or economic conditions in 'host' countries. In the Pacific, the loss of the American Samoan tuna canneries (to a cheap labour haven like Mexico, say) would have wide ramifications. Not only are canned tuna exports the mainstay of the territory's economy; they are also a crucial source of employment and remittances for other Pacific Islanders (notably Western Samoans and Tongans) who have been the backbone of a migrant workforce for the canneries.

The vulnerability of women manufacturing workers, such as those at PAFCO, emphasises the urgent need to assess the labour implications of regional development trends. Growth-driven and export-oriented development is being undertaken at considerable social cost and there is evidence of increasing hostility to the interests and rights of workers - the very people whose labour sustains the growth currently enjoyed by Pacific Island states. Part of the explanation for the worker-unfriendly climate that prevails would appear to lie in the narrow macroeconomic concerns that are defining regional 'development'. The priority attached to being competitive in the international market, for example, has become a tacit instrument of labour exploitation. It has demanded that workers pay the price of export competitiveness. Similarly, arguments about employment generation, for example in the manufacturing sector, are typically reduced to a numbers (or quantity) game. Rarely, if ever, is employment discussed (at the official level) in terms of its quality. In this way, employment policies have become instruments of carrot-and-stick blackmail, offering workers low-paid jobs (employment) or no jobs at all (unemployment). Small wonder that cheap labour systems are beginning to flourish around the region.

Noro

Noro, a pearl
slowly sinking in the pigsty of development

Noro, a diamond
twinkling in the midst of
rotten fish guts and blue flies

Noro, an opal
glistening between bug-infested copra

Noro, an emerald isle
floating in a sea of suspicion
land disputes and greed.

Jully   Sipolo

Pacific development (including our participation in the global economy) should not have to resort to selling off our workers at bargain basement prices, however strapped for cash Pacific Island economies might be. If people are what development is all about, as a timely reminder from the United Nations Development Programme spells out, then there are obvious contradictions inherent in economic policies that are based on exploitative and unhealthy labour practices. The clash with traditional Pacific values is no less conspicuous. Certainly, the PAFCO experience underscores our need to create more 'worker-friendly' development so that workers (both men and women) do not have to continue to subsidise and otherwise bear the cost of the 'chosen' development path. A good place to start might be to craft a more holistic definition of the 'environment' as the basis for regional development policy and planning - i.e. a definition that goes beyond concerns about the physical environment to embrace social, including labour, issues. The dignity of work and the right of workers to sustainable livelihoods can, and should be, fundamental tenets of Pacific development.

* This paper represents research-in-progress on women workers in Fiji's manufacturing sector which is being undertaken for the Fiji Women's Rights Movement. I gratefully acknowledge the assistance, data and information provided by women workers at PAFCO; Director of Fisheries, Fiji and former Acting General Manager PAFCO, Peniasi Kunatuba; Labour Department officers Abdul Khan (Principal Labour Officer Industrial Relations) and Atekini A. Duaibe (Senior Inspector of Factories); Inoke Cavuetaki, Nauouou village, Ovalau; National Union of Factory and Commercial Workers, Suva; Audrey Stratton, Levuka YWCA; and Hugh Walton, South Pacific Commission, Noumea. I would also like to thank Claire Slatter for her helpful critical comments on an earlier draft of the paper.

Notes

1. As development writer and critic Susan George has argued, a less competitive global market and a development ideology that sanctioned, indeed demanded, an interventionist role by the state in the 1960s are circumstances that stand in marked contrast to the highly competitive market facing more recently recruited disciples of export manufacturing such as those found in the Pacific. Export manufacturing Pacific Island countries are, in addition, handicapped by the fact that they are endeavouring to pursue such a strategy as deregulation policies simultaneously demand that the state withdraw from an active role within their national economies.

2. According to World Bank estimates, approximately 16,000 skilled people migrated between 1987 and 1990, representing a significant eight per cent of the total workforce of 200,000. Amongst the categories of professionals recording high rates of out-migration were doctors (50%), lawyers (70%) and accountants (40%) (World Bank 1991 & 1993).

3. Wages Regulation (Garment Industry) Order 1993 effective from 1 December 1993 and Wages Regulation (Manufacturing Industry) Order 1993 effective from 27 July 1993. For more detailed discussions of working conditions in the garment industry, see Slatter (1987 & 1991) and Emberson-Bain (1992).

4. These different conditions are specified under the Wages Regulation (Garment Industry) Order 1993 and Wages Regulation (Manufacturing Industry) Order 1993. Further discussion of gender-discrimination in Fiji's employment laws can be found in Emberson-Bain (1994).

5. It is not known how accurately these figures reflect the situation today. Fiji's Household Economic Activity Survey for 1989-90 (Fiji Bureau of Statistics 1989-90) records a fall in unemployment levels to eight per cent for women and four per cent for men. According to Heather Booth, the declining rate for women may be due to improved reporting of their work in the subsistence economy for the 1989-90 year, as well as to the greater employment opportunities available in the manufacturing sector (Booth 1994:27).

6. Note that after 1988, data provided in Fiji's Current Economic Statistics are provisional only.

7. The view of PAFCO's management is, by contrast, that company operations are seriously handicapped by location on a small island at some distance from Suva. The isolation, the company argues, means that it is reliant on a limited pool of largely unskilled and poorly educated labour (Peniasi Kunatuba, Acting General Manager PAFCO 1994, Levuka, pers. comm.) However, the view of the 'captive employer' would seem hard to justify. Certainly, the labour surplus that exists on Ovalau and the limited need of the cannery for formal trade skills and higher education amongst the bulk of production workers (especially women on the processing line) lend little credence to this argument.

8. For an overview of the Taiyo export tuna cannery at Noro, New Georgia Island in the Solomon Islands, including the conditions facing women workers, see Sasabe (1993).

9. Coincidentally, an industrial dispute at the cannery in late 1993 was branded an illegal strike by the Ministry of Labour with charges laid against a number of (men and women) union officials and strike supporters. Court proceedings are currently under way.

10. The perceived advantages of relocation for the company include access to an unlimited labour market and a higher level of skills, and the elimination of hefty (Suva-Levuka) freight costs which currently run to around $FIJ 1.5 million a year (Peniasi Kunatuba 1994, Levuka, pers. comm.).

References

Booth, H. (1994) *Women of Fiji: A statistical gender profile,* Suva, Fiji: Department of Women and Culture

Emberson-Bain, 'A. (1992) 'Fiji: Women, poverty and post-coup pressure' in Robie, D. *Tu galala: Social change in the Pacific,* Sydney, Australia: Bridget Williams Books/Pluto Press

---------- (1994) 'A mixed bag of tricks: Legal structures and their impact on women's employment in Fiji', in Maybin, J.A. *Women and Work,* Proceedings of the Fourth Conference of the Fiji Association of Women Graduates, 29-30 January, Suva: Fiji Association of Women Graduates

Fiji Budget Speech (1994) delivered by Hon. Paul F. Manueli, Minister of Finance and Public Enterprises, Suva, Fiji, 6 April

Fiji Bureau of Statistics (1989) *Social Indicators for Fiji,* issue no.5, April

Fiji Bureau of Statistics (1989-90) *Household Economic Activity Survey*

Fiji Current Economic Statistics (1993) Suva, Fiji, October

Fiji Fisheries Division (1992) Annual Report

Malani, L. (1991) 'The health status of PAFCO employees', unpublished paper prepared for the South Pacific Alliance for Family Health, Nuku'alofa, Tonga

NUFCW (1993) 'Reply by the National Union of Factory and Commercial Workers to arbitration submissions by the Pacific Fishing Company Ltd', Suva, Fiji, December

PAFCO (1993) 'Arbitration tribunal hearing. A dispute between the Pacific Fishing Company Limited and the National Union of Factory and Commercial Workers', PAFCO submission, Suva, Fiji, December

PAFCO/NUCFW (1989-1993) Collective agreements between Pacific Fishing Company Ltd and National Union of Commercial and Factory Workers

Sasabe, M. (1993) 'Current situation surrounding the female workers of Taiyo cannery in the Solomon Islands' unpublished paper, Suva, Fiji

Slatter, C. (1987) 'Women factory workers in Fiji: The half a loaf syndrome' in *Journal of Pacific Studies,* vol.13

---------- (1991) 'Economic recovery on the backs of women workers: Women and tax-free enterprises in Fiji' in *Review* vol.12, no.19, May

Vunibobo, B. (1994) 'Address by Minister of Finance to the Annual Convention of the Fiji Chamber of Commerce and Industry', Lautoka, Fiji, 10 September

World Bank (1991) *Towards higher growth in Pacific Island economies: Lessons from the 1980s,* vol.1, Regional Overview

--------- (1993) *Pacific Island economies: Toward efficient and sustainable growth,* vol.2, Fiji: Country Economic Memorandum

--------- (1993) *World Tables,* Baltimore, Maryland: John Hopkins University Press

Thirteen

Marama*

Vanessa Griffen

The Fijian woman spat generously on the small piece of bait on her hook, then she straightened up from her half-crouching position on the sea wall. She turned slightly sideways, and spun her line, making a wide hissing circle as the nylon cut through the air. Then, with a swift movement of her arms, she flung it far out into the still sea. She stood for a minute, watching the ripple where it had fallen, then she crouched down again, tucking her skirt about her, to wait.

There was in her pose an air of tireless, endless patience. The woman held the line lightly between her smooth hard·fingers, and the slightest twitch brought her fingers firmly down on it. Sometimes she felt a harder tug at her bait, then she jerked the line quickly so that her hook would tear at the fish's mouth. With unhurried swiftness she then pulled in her line. There was nothing on it. Again, patiently, she spat on the bait, rubbed her hands together, and cast her line into the water. She sat down to wait.

This Fijian woman, any Fijian woman, was a common sight on the sea wall, sitting crouched, with faded cotton skirt billowing in the wind, or standing tall against the sky. Beside her, in a basket plaited out of green coconut leaf, she kept her bait.

A long interval of waiting passed and she scratched her head often and frowned against the glare of the sun. She watched the inter-island cutter chug past in the distance, and all the time her fingers were ready at her line.

Gulls appeared out of the sky to perch on the black beacon, and behind them the borders of the reef curled white and brilliant. The Fijian woman sat on, with these things about her so familiar that she hardly noticed them. At last her patience was rewarded. When she pulled in her line, there was a small fish flipping at the end of it. Still holding the line, she thumped the fish on the rough sea wall, until it lay still, silver and dead. She held it in her brown hand, and reaching in, took out the hook, and placed the fish in her basket.

The woman added fresh bait, spat, spun her line and cast it into the

173

water. Again, she crouched down to wait. The sun, getting lower in the sky, shone indirectly, the sky deepened and the breeze grew cool.

She was interrupted by a dog sniffing around her basket. She was about to cuff it, when, looking up, she saw that it belonged to a European couple who were hurrying up. Instantly, a wide, shy, good-natured grin spread across her face. The man got hold of the dog and smiled briefly at the Fijian woman.

'It's all right, he won't bite you', he said.

But the Fijian woman had been more worried that it might take her fish. Though they walked on, her peace was in a way broken. Though the dog had not got her fish, there now seemed to be more flies than usual hovering over it.

By sunset the Fijian woman had only two fish in her basket. The reef, gulls and sea had become indistinct in the greyness of the oncoming night. Behind her the cars went past on the road. A streetlight flashed on and she knew it was time to go. She stood up, and her hand went to her aching back, stiff from crouching. To the cars that went past then, she was the dark bent shape of a Fijian woman tired after an afternoon's fishing. To the woman, her back ached because she did not fish often now, and when she did, the fish were slow in coming. But there were no cars to see the Fijian woman straighten up, and stand strong and with a strange stolid dignity, looking out to sea.

She turned and set off for home, holding her basket. She came to the single room which she shared with her married son and his two children. The two children were waiting for her. They both had running noses and were fighting each other and whimpering for food. She said a few words to them and pushed them out of her way. Then she sat down to prepare her fish. In the pot on the primus she found one last piece of taro; and her two fish were not enough. She went to the unlit corner, and took a 50 cent note from a tobacco tin.

'Come,' she said to the older child, 'go to the store and get one tin of corned beef, and one bread'.

The child ran off with the note in his hand, and the Fijian woman sat down to wait.

*   This story was first published in 1972.

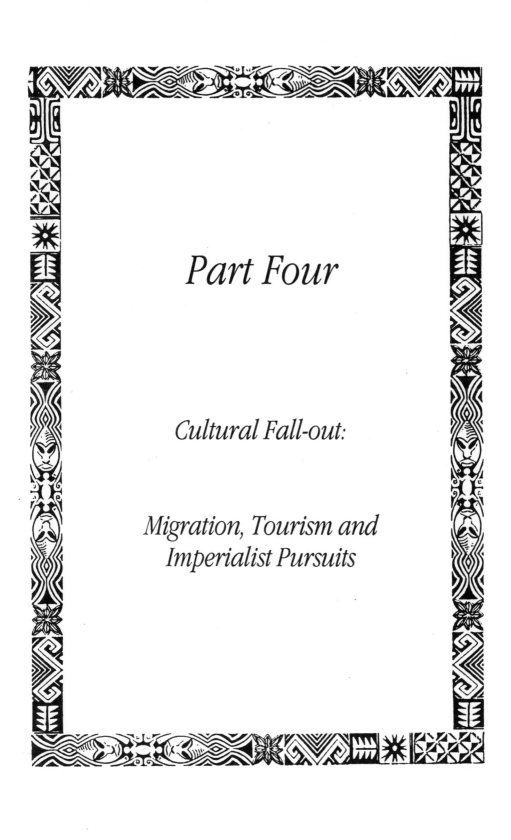

Part Four

Cultural Fall-out:

Migration, Tourism and Imperialist Pursuits

Fourteen

If I plant a tree, will my children be here to see it grow?

Peggy Fairbairn-Dunlop

Herstory

“In 10 years we have gone from being a family of eight children, me and my husband, to a family of me, my three daughters - one a widow with four children who has just remarried - and a father in the States, who may come back. He doesn't make enough money to send. In fact often he asks me to send him money. I can't really say that migration has been good for us from the point of view of money, or for us as a family.

In 1983, we stayed with our eight children on the family plantation, about 10 miles from Apia. Me and my husband ran the plantation as all of his other eight brothers and sisters had migrated. Six were in New Zealand, one in the States, and one in Australia. My husband was the *taulelea* (untitled son) whose job was to stay in Samoa and mind the *maumaga* (land) and care for his widowed mother too. The others in New Zealand asked his mother to go there, but she didn't want to.

Lots of the old people in our village are going to New Zealand and might come back when it gets cold. Their children like to shower them with presents, 'let them see the good life', and give them a bit of luxury. There's a big group of Samoans in New Zealand so that they don't feel homesick anymore. There's churches, bingo groups, TV and Kentucky Fried Chicken. After a hard life, they're entitled to it. Also they go to mind the grandchildren, some of them, while the young people go out to work. That's a hard job, sitting in houses while children sneak outside, get into all sorts of mischief while Granny's not watching.

Anyway, we were lucky. The family plantation was very big. His mother and father had cleared this land high in the hills and almost anything could grow. As I said, our job was to plant the land and grow enough food for the family to eat, and for the *faalavelave*[1], and to sell at the local market. We also exported taro. We kept cattle too. It was always our beasts that were used when there was a *faalavelave*. We had no truck in the early days, and so all the produce had to be carried by bus.

Life was okay. We stayed up at the plantation all week, and usually at the weekend we would come down to the town house in Apia, where his mother stayed. We sort of lived between the two houses. Sometimes the children came and stayed down in Apia with his mother and went to school there. I will be honest and say that we didn't always send the children to school. We often didn't even get the children to visit the health nurse. Up on our farm we were far from everyone. It was too far, we had too much to do, and the children had to work on the farm too. And sometimes we didn't have the money for school fees and uniforms. My husband's brothers and sisters kept telling us to send our kids to them so that they would get a good schooling. So in about 1985, we sent one of our sons to America, and then one to New Zealand. Those two are still there today. Both have finished school now and are working. They don't send us money, and I don't want them to. They've got their own lives to lead. Late in 1985, one of our daughters was adopted by a sister and went to New Zealand for schooling. She didn't stay long though. She was a teenager and couldn't fit in well and was getting into trouble. Maybe if she'd been a bit older. That was a pity, as that was her chance. Now she's come back here to Samoa and probably won't get away, ever.

We had to work harder when the boys left. I slaved as hard as him and so did the children. We planted bananas, passion fruit, any new crops we tried. Most of the agricultural bonus schemes we joined. I usually sold at the market on Thursdays and Fridays. He wouldn't sell at the market. He said 'that's women's work'. He was useless anyway because he always liked to give the goods away. He didn't like to sell. But he didn't mind doing the exports. We all had our stands at the market. There weren't many women selling taro and bananas at that time. In those days, women mainly sold vegetables, mats and things like that. I was the only one selling taro and bananas. That's all changed. Almost half the people selling taro now are women.

Then in 1986 he got a development bank loan to buy a truck. I thought 'this will make things easier'. But do you know, we worked harder than ever because he wanted to pay the truck off in the shortest time. My older daughter had got married by that time and had two children. She and her husband farmed next to us. We were selling a lot of goods and making good profits. We started building our own town house in the village. My husband wanted it to be the best - a huge two storey house. There's the foundations and half the walls over there just standing, half finished. It'll never be finished now. There's lots of half-finished places like that around Samoa.

In 1987, he decided we should go to America - life on the land was too hard. That was to be our new life. Also, that was the way to get quick money to finish our house. His brother sponsored him, so he went. The idea was that he would get started and then send for us. Actually there's three other women in this village with the same plan. Really that was the beginning of what I call our 'bad times', or maybe they just seemed bad because it was just me and the kids. My husband used to write, and telephone quite regularly. But it was hard. The boys

---

1   *Faalavelave* refers to the times when assistance or recognition should be given, as at weddings and birthdays, or in times of sickness

were getting older too. They wouldn't listen to me when I asked them to work. They started going out. Then my husband started writing to me for money too as he was out of work in the States. We sold the truck to get the money to send to him. We didn't make much of a profit. Then we started spending more time in town.

It was about that time my daughter's husband died in an accident. So she moved back with me along with her two kids. That worked okay as she became the mother of the house and I left the young kids with her and went up to the plantation all the time with the boys. Then one of my sons had an accident. They were diving at the waterhole and he hurt his neck. We had to fly him to the States for medical treatment. Luckily the church helped with that, but then he couldn't work anymore on the plantation. My last boy got married and came to live down in the village because his wife was a town girl and didn't really want to live in the bush. So he wasn't working on the plantation much, and now he and his wife have gone to Auckland.

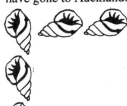

Shadows off the flames

Shadows off the flames
make their faces look lost
in a mixed colour of orangish brown
while they dance to a music they call
their own yet,
foreign to their fore-fathers.

They don't know who they are,
their identity is a worn out
jig-saw puzzle with missing parts
nobody cares about, so
they pretend not to care
and willingly fill the empty spaces
with dreams and idealisms
made by others
Still they are lost
and still the sad but,
Hopeful spirits of the ancestors
look upon them with tears
in their eyes -
Hoping for their Return.

Saili Paulo

For the past three years, it's been me, my two younger daughters and my daughter who now has four children. She's got a new husband now. We tried to keep the farm up by moving her there with her new husband. They do the farm jobs but they've come back to live in the village. It's too hard up there, no electricity, no truck. So there's no-one at the plantation now. The brothers in New Zealand keep telling us to go back and mind the plantation. They're scared that if we don't, someone else will go there and plant and then we'll lose the land.

177

If my husband was here, I would. But my children are all strung out all around the world now. So is my husband.

    We've settled here in town and my last daughter and my grandkids go to school and church. I sometimes get a job in town helping out in the hotels, and my other daughter sometimes gets a job in the new factory. We aren't selling anything from the farm. In fact, we're lucky to get enough to eat. I've got a good garden around our house here growing cabbages, beans and other small things that we can sell in the village if we have to. But mainly I use the garden to make food for the children.

    We still do the family things, take the *ie toga* (fine mats) and things like that to the *faalavelave* and mind the mother. It's a problem now without the farm. What makes it worse is that everyone thinks that because we've got someone 'outside', we have plenty of money. That's another hard thing. We hardly get money from outside. Yet we pretend we do so that people will think things are okay. I donate to the *faalavelave* under his name. I don't want people to think that he can't provide for us.

    You know, we don't really have a place in the village now that the father has gone - in fact his family could chase us out whenever they liked. I think I'll try to get the last children out of here. To New Zealand or something like that. I don't think we're going to get to the States. I think he is telling the truth when he says things are hard in the States so there's no money. I don't think he's got another wife there.

    I just wish he had come back. We could still go back and work the land. But I'm getting older now. I've been watching the trees I've planted just getting overgrown. In fact, if we go up to the old house, we can look out and see all the patches of the different things we've started: passionfruit, pumpkin, taro, everything we grew. I really don't feel like planting. What's the use? If I plant a tree, will my children be here to see it grow? I can't see us making a good life in Samoa. I used to. I'm trying to get my youngest girl to New Zealand to a good school. She's very clever. If I go, I'll leave my other two daughters to mind this place. But I think I'd like to get all the girls to New Zealand. That's the only way.**"**

Apia village, Western Samoa, 1991

****

    Regional migration data yields a picture of the numbers of people migrating, but it cannot reveal the effects on families, whole communities or countries in the region of the continuing exodus of workers, mothers and fathers, those with skills, elders (the guardians and transmitters of cultural beliefs, practices and values), or potential village leaders. Nor have migration studies analysed the impact of remittances on local communities apart from noting their officially recorded volume, and the fact that they appear to be spent on consumer goods rather than invested in development enterprises (Ahlburg 1991:2). It is apparent that the varying and unequal distribution of migration opportunities and remittances is contributing to the emergence of groups of 'haves' and 'have-nots' in every village. As elsewhere, it is often those with access to resources who set the standards and expectations of 'giving' in Samoan society. Another missing link is the lack of studies on the supportive outflow of money and goods from Pacific Island countries to overseas migrant communities.

178

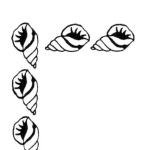
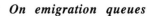

On emigration queues

Why are they standing in the rain
knocking on unopened doors
locked by chains of frozen smiles
and bland insensitivities
Why is it that the warmth of island life
has failed to allure our people to stay
and build a future in a land of their own
Some say they prefer
to grovel in the grime
of sleazy freezing works
for the hard earned dollar to pay
for their children's education
or someone's funeral
The youth are deluded
by the flashing neon lights
illusions of hollow promises of a
        slick life
and remittances
Don't they understand that they remain
nameless in a passionless society
known only by the colour of their skin
and their misdemeanours
Don't they know that they will only add
to the ghettoes of Auckland
and second rate services of zoning systems
O people come out of the rain
your country raises its blinds
and welcomes you to shelter
It offers you money in the soil
and kindred sharing and a place
of belonging

Noumea   Simi

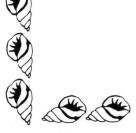

Current estimates show 76,200 Western Samoa-born individuals to be residing overseas, representing roughly 48 per cent of the 1989 home population (Ahlburg 1991). It is no wonder that Samoa and Tonga have been labelled 'labour export economies', and migration, their 'demographic and social safety valve'. So extensive is out-migration in both countries that over-population is not a priority issue and neither country has been forced to pursue a national family planning programme in a serious way. Nor have gerontocratic traditions been forced to change as much as they might have if there had not been such large-scale migration of educated and skilled young people (Ahlburg 1991). A less positive factor, however, is that migration quotas are determined by the economic conditions prevailing in host or destination countries. This makes the Samoan community, like other migrating Pacific Island communities, extremely vulnerable. Curiously, however, this vulnerability appears to act more as a catalyst than as a deterrent for further migration. It reinforces the desire to 'try to get overseas while we still can'.

Migration has been 'Samoanised' in a number of ways. For example, it is not undertaken as a matter of personal or individual choice. Its major purpose is to maintain and enhance the status of families, both socially and economically, both at home and abroad. In effect, there is always a 'looking ahead, and a looking back'. As a family 'enterprise', it is the family that decides who will go and who will stay in Samoa to look after the family resources. Notably, an equal number of females and males migrate because 'a daughter's *alofa* (love) to her family lasts much longer and she is likely to send more remittances'. At the same time, the prospective migrant understands very clearly the obligations which underlie his/her opportunity. The duty to 'look back' - to work towards enhancing the status and reputation of the family back home - reinforces the perception of migration as a short-term measure. Migrants fully intend to return home, someday.

The huge volume of remittances received annually is another characteristic of Samoan migration, and testifies to the continuing importance of the family as an institution to Samoans. General estimates put remittances through official channels at 40 per cent of Gross Domestic Product (GDP) with money entering the country by unofficial channels believed to represent an additional 33 per cent. In 1989, remittances were equivalent to 50 per cent of the cost of imports (see Table 1). Western Samoa's dependence on remittances ranks amongst the highest in the world. That the sheer amount of remittances is resulting in actual hardship for migrant families is evident in the advice given to New Zealand migrants in the April 1991 New Zealand edition of the *Samoa Observer:*

> You (Samoans) have families here to feed and clothe, and children to give a proper education to. And each year you send millions of dollars to Samoa to keep that country going. It is time now to think of priorities.

Table 1 Remittances and their size relative to other economic aggregates, Western Samoa 1970-90

| Year | Remittances | | Remittances as % of | | |
	Nominal (million **tala**)	Real	Exports	Imports	Trade Deficit
1970	1.5	-	42.6	14.8	22.6
1975	5.2	-	115.2	25.2	32.2
1980	17.2	17.2	112.6	30.3	41.1
1985	53.1	26.2	146.6	46.1	67.2
1989	86.6	33.5	296.6	49.6	59.6

Source: Ahlburg (1991:18), calculated from data of Central Bank of Samoa.

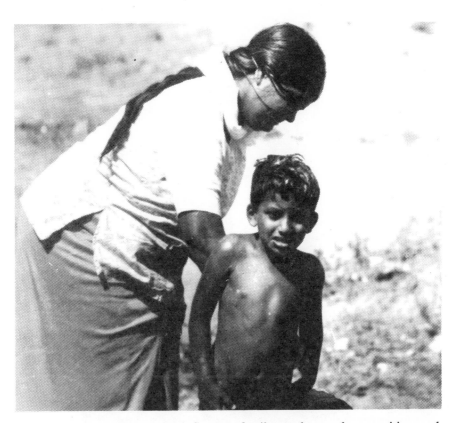

Lastly, migration also influences family numbers and composition, and the quality of family life. But perhaps more important, its uncertain nature undermines the family will to plan ahead and follow a course of action through. The case study presented above illustrates this as well as other problems associated with Samoan migration. In circumstances of changing aspirations, and economic uncertainties and pressures, many Pacific Islanders are looking to other countries to provide a 'better' future for their children, albeit aware of the personal, social and cultural costs that may be entailed. The title words of 'Herstory' capture the uncertainty of what the future holds for some families: 'If I plant a tree, will my children be here to see it grow?'

References

Ahlburg, D. (1991) *Remittances and their impact,* Canberra: National Centre for Development Studies, Australian National University

Fairbairn-Dunlop, P. (1991) 'E au le inailau a tamaitai: Women, education and development, Western Samoa', unpublished Ph.D thesis, Macquarie University, Sydney

------- (1993) 'A positive response to migration constraints: Western Samoa' in Mc Call, G. and Connell, J. (eds) *A world perspective on Pacific Islander migration,* Sydney: Centre for Pacific Studies, University of New South Wales

Fifteen

Environment-friendly or the new sell?

One woman's view of ecotourism in Pacific Island countries*

Konai Helu Thaman

Introduction

The editor of the Tongan magazine *Matangi Tonga* ends an editorial on the privatisation of government services with a warning. He says, 'Democracy, yes; free enterprise, yes; but at the same time we should not allow the process of change to alienate Tongans within their own country' (Fonua 1994:9). I'm afraid that if tourism development (or any kind of development for that matter) in Tonga and most of her Pacific Island neighbours continues in its current direction, we may find more Pacific Islanders feeling alienated in their own lands (if they do not already feel so).

> *the old man in the boathouse*
> *is growing weary*
> *he told me that he knew*
> *the origin of the sea and sky*
> *the moon and even the sun*
> *but he did not know*
> *why men deceive*
> *and women keep on*
> *loving them*
>
> *it was at halaliku*
> *that i met him*
> *he only had the rain and the surf*

the land he gave away
they are building runways
hotels and warehouses on it
it was a stormy day
when he paddled away
in a borrowed canoe

During the 1960s, Tonga, the country of my birth, opened up to tourism (with a small t). Overseas visitors came for a day at a time on cruise ships which called in at the capital, Nuku'alofa, once every two months. My high school classmates and I would act as tourist guides aboard specially decorated buses, which took our guests around our small island, stopping at various 'tourist spots' to buy hastily put-together souvenirs. At the end of each tour, the tourists went back to their ship, having had a taste of Tonga (we thought) and we went home 50 *seniti* (cents) richer and having had another opportunity to practise our English.

Tourism development in Tonga has been rather different from that in neighbouring Fiji where it mirrored a model typical of neocolonial economies. Although a major foreign exchange earner, tourism in Fiji has continued to serve the interests of mainly foreigners and non-indigenous locals who dominate the island nation's commercial activities. Although on a much smaller scale, Tongan tourism is only now beginning to develop linkages with metropolitan markets and companies. Having not been directly colonised, Tonga had no external authorities to exploit air-traffic rights and no large local non-indigenous communities to lobby for tourism development (Britton 1987).

A government-owned hotel was established in Tonga in 1966, partly aimed at housing guests attending the King's coronation that year. An increase in the number of cruise ships visiting the Kingdom in the 1960s and 1970s led to the development of the handicraft industry which is totally controlled by Tongans. Local entrepreneurs have since established more tourism accomodation and tours, and there has been a gradual but cautious growth of tourism over the years, coinciding with the expansion of air transport facilities and the establishment of a national airline. However, during the past five years, there has been some aggressive lobbying from local and well as foreign business interests to speed up tourism development in Tonga, often under the guise of the now popularised concept of 'ecotourism'.

Post-independence Pacific Island leaders constantly implore their citizens, particularly before general elections, to try to hang on to their cultural heritages while at the same time developing 'modern' skills and practices. Some elements of indigenous cultures, such as those relating to performing arts and certain crafts, have been perceived as necessary for economic success and survival. In these areas, locals receive assistance from foreign aid donors and businesses whose interests are, in many ways, just that - foreign. Now, ecotourism is being encouraged because it is not only environment-friendly but also culture-friendly, and as such will protect the Pacific Islands and Islanders from the 'evils' of mass tourism experienced elsewhere in the world.

However, there seems to be an inherent contradiction between cultural conservation and the ecotourism business, or any business for that matter, because years of modernisation have taught us that all 'modern' activities have cultural costs. We know, for example, how difficult it is to fight the impact of the new (transnational) culture, even with the promise of an eco-armour. Like a

184

fire, this culture is spreading throughout our islands with renewed vigour and intensity, fanned by advertising and the mass media. There are signs that many people have been burnt and are suffering.

> patches politely parched
> with no water flowing
> from the mountain top
> scars burn on my soft skin
> you've cut a piece of me away
> leaving my bandaged heart
> to endure the pain
> of your tying me
> to yourself

This transnational culture, symbolised by automobiles, supermarkets, shopping malls, fast foods, hotel chains, television, night clubs, credit cards, value-added tax, consultancy firms, etc., is dominating the thinking of many Pacific Islanders, especially urban dwellers, many of whom regard cultural conservation, and those who talk about it, with disdain. They point to the inevitability of social change and the need to accept that nowadays money (with a little influence added) is the all-important vehicle which will enable us to achieve the 'good life' (read *palangi*-style)[1].

However, there are those of us who, while enjoying certain elements of the new culture, feel that there are important cultural skills, knowledge and values which ought to be maintained. This is firstly because our indigenous cultures are important in themselves; and, secondly, because they often provide important solutions to some modern-day problems (Schulte-Westrumy 1982; Thaman R.R. 1988; Thaman K.H. 1993).

The rationale for cultural conservation is also relevant to the current and widespread concern about Pacific Island environments. Pre-industrial cultures have been shown to be ecologically conservative and relatively compatible with the laws of ecology. Our ancestors were more environmentally aware than we are today. Through their gentler use of scarce resources, they were able to provide for large populations for hundreds of years. They lived close to the land and the sea, and they had the ability to read the diurnal, monthly and seasonal cycles of their environments. Plants and animals were integral parts of island ecocultures (Thaman R.R. 1988).

Today, many Pacific Island people, especially the young, have lost the knowledge and awareness of their island environments, partly because of the forces of modernity, not the least of which is formal education. What has happened to many Pacific Islands during the past 40 years, in my view, has largely been the result of our embracing a development model which has treated culture as a variable rather than as the basis of our development. This model has not only given rise to the cultural alienation of most of our young people. It has also caused the slow haemorrhaging of traditional, environment-related knowledge, skills and values - the blood of the land which kept the heart of our cultures alive.

---

1   *Palangi* is the Tongan word for European, literally meaning 'touching the sky'.

The ecotourism promise

So what has ecotourism to offer us? It is being sold as development that is environment-friendly and sensitive to the issues of conservation and sustainability. But tourism, any kind of tourism, creates conflict because it implies both creative and destructive processes: compromising cultural values and relationships for the sake of generating revenue, which is seen as necessary to raising our standards of living.

Ecotourism in the Pacific Islands has become the modern marketing manager's source of inspiration for the new sell. It has got a lot going for it. It makes great pictures; it offers pretty much what people want when they wish to escape the pressures of metropolitan lifestyles and polluted urban environments; and it offers an expiation of guilt for our contribution to the degradation of our own planet. For tour operators and investors in tourism projects, both in the region and overseas, ecotourism is another bandwagon to join on the journey to greater riches. For some of them, the argument in favour of ecotourism is that natural and cultural assets need protection, but only for as long as they yield a competitive return on their investment. Indeed, the very concept of 'ecotourism' suggests a 'culture' which places concern for profitability before that of conservation. Questions need to be asked. For example, whose culture and development are to be rendered sustainable? Who will decide? And who are the ecotourists? Are they concerned about the peoples whose unspoiled lands and 'wilderness' they have come to view before these 'treasures' disappear (often as a result of the viewing)?

186

For some of us who are educators, there is the added issue of how to deal with the mass media, politicians and others who have used the term 'ecotourism' as propaganda, continuing a trend set for other 'in-words' like 'development', 'growth' and 'sustainability', and making them synonymous with 'good' and 'desirable'. Furthermore, many people sometimes overlook the fact that so-called development in general, and tourism development in particular, are manifestations of a particular political system - the capitalist system. Whether it is state- or private-run is beside the point. Such development has a linear vision of change, with the creation of a modern consumer society being its ultimate goal. Is this the kind of society most Pacific Island peoples wish for their children and grandchildren?

Cultural integrity

One often hears people in the tourism industry talk about its cultural integrity. They commonly refer to the authenticity of cultural presentations, for example in dancing, costumes, food preparation or rituals. In my view, cultural integrity ought to be integral to the total process of development, and not just applied to one aspect of it. This would mean that we would experience development that adapts to Pacific cultures, rather than the other way around. If this were to happen, then we would witness what I have on a previous occasion called 'ecocultural tourism development' - tourism development based on the culture of the host community and NOT on the culture of the tourists, developers or aid donors (Thaman K.H. 1992). This approach, in my view, would be more appropriate for the semi-subsistence societies of the Pacific, where people are inextricably part of their ecosystems and have a more holistic view of their environments. A people's culture, I would suggest, is logically the most appropriate basis and framework for development. It should not be a mere variable of development.

What I am suggesting requires a change of paradigm; a change in the way most people perceive the development process. A different, culturally grounded perspective of development would ensure more people participating in the process, as well as sharing the benefits that result from turning their islands into a marine park or a forest park. The whole community, and not just urban-based civil servants, politicians or business enterprises, would be part of the decision-making process. Women, for example, who use the reefs and the forests to gather foods, medicines, ornaments and other necessities of life for the whole community, would have an input.

Finally, by having to work within this alternative development paradigm, development agencies and foreign aid donors might come to recognise the constraints which the Western development discourse and model impose on Pacific Islanders: the foreign languages, ideologies and cultures. There is a need for a commitment by all who are involved in 'development assistance' in our region to respect the cultures and world views of those they purport to assist.

187

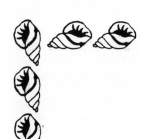

Togi Falls

The banyan tree in virginal stance
guards the rhythmical splendours
of silvery crescendo
echoing the past
in the enclaves of Togi Falls
The banyan tree has not yet seen
the wrath of ages rape
splitting the membranes
of momentous idyll
It is but a dream
that the banyan tree
will not shred itself dry
to wrinkles of spoils
of tourism mania
and fallacies of development
But for now let me drift
in the misty sprays of Togi Falls
and let me feel the heart throb
of this cavernous mystery
Let me feel the dew of maiden springs
for soon the gushing life of Togi Falls
will cease to drip
like the metered taps
of urban water supplies
development they say

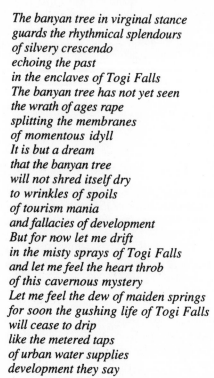

Noumea Simi

Ecotourism is also regarded as less destructive and exploitative of scarce island resources compared to, say, mining. In Western industrial societies, where large amounts of land are privately or state-owned, and where legislation can be enacted to promote conservation and wildlife protection, and prohibit resource degradation, tourism and conservation verge on the symbiotic. This (idealised) view of ecotourism becomes problematic in the context of Pacific Island societies, where economic livelihoods (20%-80% of real incomes) and cultural integrity depend on the continued use of ecosystems on a sustainable basis, be they forests, the sea, rivers, beaches, reefs, or agricultural and village lands.

With its emphasis on the wilderness and unique and/or endangered species, ecotourism will create conflict in societies where there is no notion of 'wilderness' (it simply does not exist as such in the Pacific Islands) and the priority for people is the sustainable utilisation of their resources. Furthermore, the concept of 'parks' and other related notions of the wilderness are part of the cultural baggage of the Western world, that has been imposed or imported with varying degrees of local understanding and approval. In many developing countries, parks are planned by foreign advisers, mainly from the U.S.A., staffed partly by foreigners, developed with hotels, signs, brochures and personnel

188

uniforms based on foreign examples, and used by foreigners (Marsh 1987:35). In the context of the Pacific Islands, this is hardly ecotourism but cultural imperialism at its worst!

For example, an entire group of islands known as Ha'apai in central Tonga has been declared a World Heritage Park. It apparently encompasses some of the world's remaining 'undisturbed' reefs. The area has been 'billed' as the next big deal in tourism development in Tonga and a potential target for ecotourism investment. Besides the development of a Marine Tourism Centre, there are plans to develop resorts as well (*Matangi Tonga* 1992:5). Obviously many of the decisions relating to such a development are being made by Tongan authorities (government planners) and entrepreneurs who would usually wish to respond positively to foreign investors and donors who offer conservation aid money, conferences, or trips overseas to view similar areas, such as the Great Barrier Reef Marine Park in Australia. Foremost in the planners' minds would undoubtedly be commercial profitability, without which there would be no returns or prestige guaranteed for the investors and/or donors.

I doubt that most of the people of Ha'apai, whose livelihoods depend on the surrounding reefs, know what is being planned on their behalf. One would hope that the interests and needs of the local communities, including their land use and conservation patterns, will be integrated into the planning of this ecotourism feat. This is important because there is a need to consider the opportunity costs of locking up land/or fishing grounds and other places traditionally accessible as sources of livelihood. The extent to which such considerations will be taken into account will of course depend both on the Tongan leadership and the foreign donors/investors who are going to be involved. My guess is that the important decisions will have already been made, and not in Lifuka (the capital of Ha'apai), but most probably in Nuku'alofa, or more likely London, or Washington, or San Francisco, or Taipei or Tokyo.

Because ecotourism is fairly capital-intensive, it will attract profit-oriented individuals and/or groups (both foreign and local) whose priority is to maximise returns in the short term. Although conservation-oriented, many would not be concerned about the social and cultural implications of this, regarding the environmental aspects of development as 'external entities' (separate from people) to be viewed, preserved and enjoyed because of their aesthetic, scientific, humanitarian, recreational or 'wilderness' value.

It is unfortunate that many Pacific Islanders themselves regard their own cultures as constraining their efforts to modernise and compete in a commercially oriented world. Paradoxically, however, they see Culture (with a capital C) as something to be exploited in order to further their own commercial endeavours. Where tourism is concerned, profitability often takes precedence over cultural conservation. Many of these more entrepreneurial-minded people belong to a category of Islanders who increasingly identify with what Hau'ofa (1987) calls a 'regional' culture, one based not on ethnicity, but on a common (material) lifestyle and language, assimilated into the metropolitan cultures of past colonial masters. Many of those in this group are extremely influential in decision making regarding tourism and other development projects in our island nations. Some have reaped huge benefits from these projects. Hopefully some of them will come around to seeing that the economic benefits which they seek are causing their ecological and cultural blindness; and that these can only be short-lived and unsustainable.

many of my friends are civil servants
with uncivil thoughts
they smile at my weaknesses
and thrive on my poverty
their bodies though weakening
from muscular indifference

but they cannot erase my existence
for my plight chimes with the hour
and my blood they drink at cocktail parties...

Sustainability

An alternative concept of 'ecocultural tourism' would ensure some measure of sustainability because it involves everyone in the community. Communities would be targeted for development because of the way they are, not because of the special features they possess. It would represent development based on a holistic understanding of a community and its living, functioning culture (or cultures). Overseas visitors, as well as people from neighbouring areas, who are interested in learning about a particular community, would visit and learn in ways that are culturally acceptable to their hosts.

In ecocultural tourism development, the 'conservation' aspects (be they forests, reefs, traditional art or craft) are seen as integral parts of a total cultural process and not as an outcome of some external global concern. All participants in a given culture would have a say in how they were going to be part of, and affected by, an ecotourism project. This process would undoubtedly have to include women who often bear the heaviest burdens of cultural preservation while being left out in development planning and ignored in development literature because of the dominance of men and their views.

Conclusion

Ecocultural tourism is about living, rather than making a living. It can satisfy many people's limited cash needs without necessarily destroying both the material and non-material bases of a way of life which are perceived as unique and worthy of conserving. To this end education, both for ecocultural tourists as well as host communities, will be important. Education will ensure that both host communities and visitors are made aware of 'culture-environment' as a total entity, not as bits and pieces to be isolated and manipulated for a few people's personal profits. Ecocultural tourism might lead us a little closer to achieving a more sustainable use of the gifts bequeathed by our ancestors as well as nature.

*   An earlier version of this paper was presented as a Keynote Address to the Ecotourism Business in the Pacific Conference, Auckland University, New Zealand, in October 1992.

References

Britton, S. (1987) 'Tourism in Pacific Island states: Constraints and opportunities' in Britton, S. and Clark, W.C. (eds) *Ambiguous alternative: Tourism in small developing countries,* Suva, Fiji: University of the South Pacific

Fonua, P. (1994) *Matangi Tonga,* Nuku'alofa, Tonga: Vava'u Press

Hau'ofa, E. (1987) 'The new South Pacific society: Integration and independence' in Hooper, A. et al. *Class and culture in the South Pacific,* Suva, Fiji: Institute of Pacific Studies, University of the South Pacific

Marsh, J.S. (1987) 'National parks and tourism in small developing islands' in Britton, S. and Clark, W.C. (eds) *Ambiguous alternative: Tourism in small developing countries,* Suva, Fiji: University of the South Pacific

Matangi Tonga (1992) July-August, p.5

Thaman, K.H. (1993) 'Looking towards the source: A consideration of cultural context in teacher education' in *Access* 2:(2):44-50

Thaman, K.H. (1992) 'Ecocultural tourism: A view for maintaining cultural integrity in ecotourism development', Keynote Address delivered to the Ecotourism Business in the Pacific Conference, Auckland University, New Zealand, 12-14 October

Thaman, R.R. (1988) 'Environmental issues in the Pacific Islands: Constraints to sustainable development' in *Pacific Issues* 1:3-10

Schulte-Westrumy, T. (1982) 'Ecoculture - a strategy for survival', unpublished manuscript, London: Ecoculture

Sixteen

Psyche under siege:
Uncle Sam, look what you've done to us*

Laura M. Torres Souder

Drenched by heavy rains, up to their ankles in mud, heads bowed low, spirits sagging, the Chamorros at Manengon, Maimai, Tai, Talofofo, and Inarajan were desperately clinging to a last ray of hope. In the silence of the night, Pete Rosario began to sing several lines of a song he had composed - 'Sam, Sam, my dear Uncle Sam, won't you please come back to Guam'. It was 1944, and Japanese Imperial Forces had occupied Guam for nearly three years. The brutalities and atrocities of a cruel war on an innocent people had taken their toll. Japanese losses in the Pacific were mounting. Guam was being readied for battle. The Japanese herded Chamorros in long arduous marches into concentration camps. Many died. Exhausted, vulnerable, weakened by malnourishment and disease, the Chamorros waited like sheep.

Prayers were answered in that rain-soaked month of July with the second coming of dear old Uncle Sam. Sam came back with thousands of troops to reclaim 'our land' for democracy. The joys of 'liberation' were sweet. Chamorro survivors of World War II embraced all that was American with overwhelming gratitude and profound respect. Uncle Sam and his men were worshipped as heroes, and rightfully so. No-one who lived through the tyranny of Japanese occupation went unscathed. Survival became synonymous with American Military Forces.

In deeply felt acts of Chamorro reciprocity, our people extended the most valuable of their possessions, albeit the only possessions they had to give - land and their very spirits - to Uncle Sam. Why? Uncle Sam brought freedom from the Japanese. Yes, he brought food to the hungry: K-rations like spam, corned beef, cheese, pork and beans, bacon, powdered eggs, and powdered milk - some of which have become island staples. Yes, he brought medicines to the sick and rebuilt the hospitals and clinics to minister to the health needs of the people. Yes, he brought clothes to the needy through the American Red Cross, a welcome relief to most whose only wardrobe consisted of the clothing on their backs. Yes, he provided shelter to the homeless, first pup tents and quonset housing, and then wooden houses with tin roofs. Yes, he built schools and provided jobs.

The war-torn island community of Guam underwent a total facelift and reconstruction in the years following the war, as Uncle Sam got on with the business of establishing a well-fortified American outpost. Yes, Uncle Sam helped an injured people in many ways. His coming set the foundations for the kind of American community that Guam has become. Many of us in this room, are living products of Uncle Sam's presence in more ways than one!

This is why Chamorros, particularly those who suffered during the war, feel obligated to Uncle Sam. The Chamorro proverb, *Maulek-na man gagao ya ti manae ki manae ya ti un chuli* ('It is better to ask and not be given than to be given and not to accept'), gives us some insight into the Chamorro way of thinking. Reciprocity continues to lie at the heart of the social world of Chamorros. Generosity, such as Uncle Sam's, is understood and responded to within the framework of Chamorro exchange and obligation. The responsibility to reciprocate, as individuals and as a collective community, to the benefits brought by Uncle Sam obligated Chamorros to give the best that they had. And so our people gave precious land, and continue to offer their sons and daughters to show their appreciation to Uncle Sam. Obligation being a sacred duty, Chamorros have since been caught in a never-ending cycle of paying back.

Never mind that Agana, the capital city for centuries, had been razed to the ground by an American bombardment that, according to military information later declassified, was not essential to the takeover of Guam in 1944. Never mind that because of the bombing of Agana and the subsequent rebuilding of Guam, the material culture of thousands of years of island heritage was swiftly levelled by bulldozers, making way for military installations. Never mind that island residents were arbitrarily relocated away from their traditional homesteads, repeating a policy of relocation dating back to the late 1600s. Never mind that the choicest lands - extending from Tarague in the North to Orote in the South - were taken without just compensation for the 11 military bases that now grace our tiny homeland of 212 square miles. Never mind that these lands were the site of the most productive farms, rice fields, and coffee plantations which contributed to the self-sufficiency of Chamorros before the war. Never mind that Chamorros today must suffer the reputation of being a lazy, shiftless lot who have become totally dependent on handouts without due consideration to the causes of dependency. Never mind that Chamorros today must suffer the humiliation of being fenced out of ancestral lands - I have personally witnessed and experienced the pain of having been turned back at the gate to the Naval Air Station (NAS), and told that 'this is US government property, Mam', while my mother in the car was trying to explain to deaf ears that my grandfather owned a big chunk of NAS. Never mind that we are a generation whose environment has included barbed-wire fences erected to keep the natives in their 'rightful place'. Never mind that the postwar generations on Guam cannot conceive of life on Guam without the military. Never mind that English-only policies have threatened our ancestral language and way of life.

One wonders how Chamorros are able to deal with such mixed feelings. Another Chamorro proverb gives us a clue to Chamorro coping strategies: na mesngon hao sa i mesngon mangana ('be tolerant and courageous for it is the tolerant and courageous who win in the end'). This attitude helps explain the propensity of Chamorros not only to turn the other cheek, but to offer their left sides and their right sides and everything in between.

The value placed on tolerance, courage and reciprocity has helped Chamorros deal with the increasingly apparent reality that Uncle Sam didn't come back in July of 1944 to save the Chamorros but to 'save face' and to secure a bastion of defence of what I have recently come to learn is called the 'Pacific theatre'. Chamorros have long known that Uncle Sam needs us. Masterful survivors of colonisation, Chamorros are skillful at making it seem as if the need is ours. Perhaps our biggest fault is that we have guarded this secret too well.

We are nearing our 100th year as an American colony, and we are still talking about promises unfulfilled. To most Chamorros, the very thought of scrutinising Uncle Sam's motives in our homeland is tantamount to calling down the wrath of God. As our leaders speak out for an improved political status and removal of economic constraints, as a growing number of Chamorros are pressing for self-determination, as we have begun to confront power with truth, we are accused of being un-American. The media and the military chastise us for being ungrateful, of all things! 'Naughty, naughty, you should not bite the hand that feeds you. Remember, life boils down to this, he who holds the purse strings rules the roost'.

Guam's story in the 20th century is inextricably linked with the American experiment of colonial empire-building overseas, which began with Hawaii in 1893. To understand the present struggles and circumstances of Guam and the other American flag territories in the Pacific, we need to take a critical look at this colonial legacy and how it has impacted on the psyche of the indigenous people of the so-called 'American Pacific'.

Uncle Sam is typically viewed as a great benefactor, a white-bearded Santa Claus whose generosity is unparalleled, and from whose hands have come American citizenship for Chamorros, federal dollars by the millions, rehabilitation funds during disasters, food stamps and other assistance programmes, modern health and sanitation facilities, access to American education and the media, unrestricted travel to and from the States, a language passport to the world via English, and perhaps most significantly - to peoples in search of freedom and justice - the ideals of democracy and democratic government.

This overwhelming picture of generosity is often depicted as a one-way flow of 'goodies' from Uncle Sam to his misbegotten Pacific wards, whose lives would have remained impoverished and culturally destitute save for 'Westward Ho! and Manifest Destiny and Mission'. We who have paid the price exacted from this costly relationship with Uncle Sam know better. We have been slow to realise that, for us, the war has not ended. Our whole relationship with Uncle Sam has been continuously defined in the context of war. It was the Spanish-American War that first brought Uncle Sam to our shores. It was World War II that brought him back. Uncle Sam brought Guam into the Korean and Vietnam conflicts. Today, we are the unwitting hosts to over 365 nuclear warheads. All this in the name of defence?! Is being a sure target in the event of another war, an act of protection? I have a really difficult time making sense of this line of reasoning. And yet, we are expected to believe that 'all of this' somehow serves our best interest.

A search suspended

Distant memories
speak again
Another attempt
squashed and crumbled
The search for
self-respect
dignity and equality
remains located
on a distant horizon
somewhere far - far away

Momentarily elated
after a century of waiting
With hope - less
but often despair
The pride of an ego
artificially inflated
At a drawn trigger ·
A search suspended
apparently, forever

But haste brings no good
and perhaps I speak too soon
Could it be that self-respect
is not located
on a distant horizon
But on our own
Isn't the journey
across the `dark waters'
to be crossed but once
in the lifetime of a people

Isn't self-respect
self-respect
Here and there
everywhere and nowhere
Hasn't a century of waiting
brought not a day of liberation
Wouldn't a day of struggle
bring a lifetime of freedom.

Kushma Ram

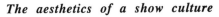

The aesthetics of a show culture

The important qualities:
Look holistically at the contestants -
Sort out the essentials for celluloid acceptance -
A secondhand fostering of stereotypic measure
*   labelled 'traditional'*
There is a marketplace commonality about it all -
Another reflection of a brainwashed sense of style.
If its not Kamehameha dripping from their fingers
Its conch shells tripping their aped walks.
The aesthetics of a culture are on show here ...
It could be like trawling inside a fish bowl hoping for
*   a conversation piece*
And all you come across is a bald headed **asiasi**[*]
Deemed diseased from swimming too long in polluted waters;
Or a multicoloured hereford of mixed pedigree.
Lets see,
Lipsticked legs, tree trunked and bullet proofed
Mostly scar salted and conveniently hidden inside
*   synthetic lengths*
Lushly lined in coconut shells
Off the shoulder creations
Reminiscent of etiolated colonials of a past age.
One feels the modesty of quasi-mutated genes
That will never feel the heat of international spotlights
Or walk the length of a foreign runway.
Perhaps a point is missed here, but there seems to be
A longing for past perfections when the glitter
Was genuine and the glitz class touched.
Todays crowns are plastic buckets
Yesterdays-real jasmined tiaras.

Momoe Malietoa von-Reiche

We have become the worst kind of mistress to Uncle Sam. Much like women throughout the world who are 'kept' by possessive, oppressive husbands or lovers, whose silence is interpreted as docile acceptance of benevolent patriarchy, the island people of the 'American Pacific' have been whopped into docile submission, so to speak. There is no greater testimony to Uncle Sam's success in the Pacific than this mindless dependency. Our psyches are under siege! Our spirits as indigenous people are held under lock and key. We are typically afraid to speak out for fear of reprisal. Our creativity and self-sufficiency have been stymied. We long for justice!

Fortunately, like women throughout the world who refuse to be silent any longer, who would rather struggle and suffer through a less glittery but

---

[*]   *Asiasi* is the Samoan name for yellowfin tuna.

197

wholesome self-initiated plan for survival with or without their 'keepers', we who have been rendered inarticulate by colonisation are garnering the courage and commitment to reclaim our destiny.

We must confront power with truth. We must put an end to this war! We must examine and understand the devastating effects that American colonisation has had on our psyche as colonised people, and on our ability as island people to remain connected with our island cultures and to self-direct future alternatives as we move into the 21st century. We must have the courage to say no and to demand justice. We can no longer afford to be inhibited by the fear of reprisal. The price for such silence is too great to pay.

As community service providers, I am sure that social workers can share countless stories of courage. We must take inspiration and learn from the wisdom offered by a four-year-old girl who garnered the courage to say to her sexually abusive father, 'Daddy, I'm not going to let you hurt me with your stick anymore'.

We must put Uncle Sam into focus and recognise him for what he is and for what he represents. He has filled our mouths with candy; we must not let him get away with claiming no responsibility for our rotten teeth. We must recognise and admit that Uncle Sam is here because of Guam's strategic importance to American defence and not for reasons of love. In our enthusiasm to welcome Uncle Sam we have given him the status of mother's brother. We must tactfully put Uncle Sam in his rightful place, and remind him that he is after all a visitor, one who has received the royal carpet treatment, but a visitor nonetheless. This is an important psychological distinction because Chamorros could never charge an uncle rent for example, but a visitor - well, maybe. We must recognise that Uncle Sam is the bearer of colonisation and that colonisation can never be equated with liberation or freedom. War is not justice. Dependency is un-American. Benevolent dictatorship is not democracy. We must be courageous enough to rewrite the song, 'Sam, Sam, do listen and be kind, look what you've done to us'.

*   This paper was originally presented at the Ninth Annual Social Work Conference, Guam, in March 1989. It was published with conference proceedings in 1991 (Rubinstein & Dames eds 1991)

Reference

Rubinstein, D.H. and Dames, V.L. (1991) *Uncle Sam in Micronesia: Social Benefits, Social Costs,* Papers from the Ninth Annual Social Work Conference, 1989, Guam: Micronesian Area Research Center, University of Guam

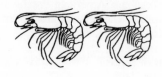

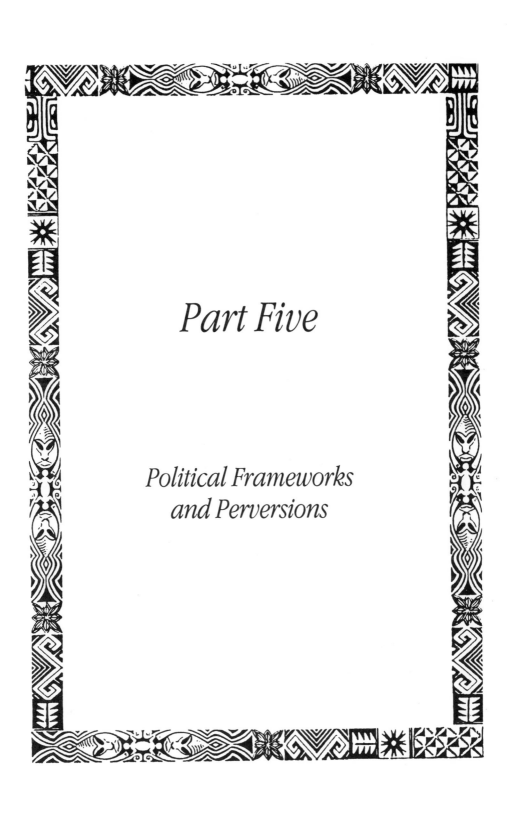

Part Five

Political Frameworks and Perversions

Seventeen

The 'peace' signed with our blood*

Susanna Ounei-Small

Introduction

I have been labelled an 'extremist' all my political life, so I am among those Kanaks whom the Matignon Accords were designed to shut out of the political process in my homeland, Kanaky/New Caledonia. In August 1988, when French Prime Minister Michel Rocard concluded the accords with the presidents of the pro-independence FLNKS[1], Jean-Marie Tjibaou, and the anti-independence RPCR[2], Jacques Lafleur, a clear if unwritten part of the agreement was to isolate the so-called extremists on both sides. Now I am writing from Aotearoa/New Zealand, where, despite this 'peace plan', I have been effectively forced into exile.

In this essay I want to explain how it is that our independence movement can have some elements acceptable to France and others that must be excluded. The history of the Kanak liberation struggle shows that many of the political aims and strategies that earned myself and others the extremist label have since gained wide support among our people. By relating some of our experiences in the struggle, I want to explain what ideas we represent and why the French government and its allies in Kanaky want to neutralise us.

I also argue that the Matignon Accords have never been accepted by the Kanak people. They were designed to create division within the independence movement. The accords might be isolating the so-called extremists from the French government, but they are also beginning to isolate the people who support the accords from the mass of the Kanak population, especially the youth.

... Neo-colonialism and the women's struggle

... Formal independence with a flag and a national anthem was not enough for us. We had seen the sort of independence of other former colonies in the Pacific and around the world, and we wanted something better. We were certainly not interested in encouraging the Kanak people to struggle, suffer and make sacrifices, only to end up with neo-colonialism - formal independence with all the political and economic power being controlled by foreign capital and a small Kanak élite of well-paid politicians, civil servants and junior business partners. Kanak Socialist Independence is total self-determination - political, economic and cultural.

Another essential element in our analysis of neo-colonialism is the role of women during the struggle and after independence. There are many things that are not ideal within Kanak society, and the treatment of women is one of the worst. Because of the influence of religion, no-one talks about contraception. Yet when young women get pregnant, they are regarded badly. Domestic violence against women is common, and so is rape - even gang rape, known as *la chaîne*. Within the movement too, women are expected to be secretaries, cooks, cleaners and mistresses, while the men make all the important decisions.

Neo-Colonialism

Neo-Colonialism
a parasite
accommodated
by hosts
open
and susceptible to
external
influences
usually
certain
well-trained
Colonial
civil-servants
and weak politicians;
our bunch
of dissidents
a classic case.

Neo-Colonialism
witlessly
playing
into the hands
of Foreign sharks
ready

to swallow up
unsuspecting prey.

The real game
discreetly
played
in the seclusion
of closed doors
and secrecy.

The cat and mouse
comedy
choreographed
by journalists
skilled psychologists
dishing out
diatribes
for the consumption
of the undiscerning
who legitimise
political
manouvres
by their
simple vote.

Grace Mera Molisa

Déwé Gorodey and I first began to analyse the women's struggle when we were in jail together in 1974. When we raised it in the movement, almost everyone - men and women - was hostile. We were accused of copying 'women's libbers' in France and 'dividing couples' and 'dividing the movement'. We were told it was against custom to talk about contraception and to try to take the place of a man. When Gina Monawa (now married to Paul Neaoutyine) returned from France, she joined us too. In 1976, when Déwé was given responsibility for PALIKA's[3] international relations and Gina and I were elected to the co-ordinating bureau, we were the first women to hold leadership positions within a Kanak political party.

We were the extremists among the extremists. Only a few men listened to us and supported our ideas, and no political party seriously addressed the issue. Instead, they tried to undermine us and protect their own power by creating low-status and non-threatening 'feminine sections' to make cakes and sew dresses to raise money for the party. The French government is now doing the same thing: trying to undermine the growing consciousness of Kanak women by sending the Secretary of Women's Affairs, Michele Andrée, from France to offer encouragement to the polite Kanak women's groups who talk about everything except the struggle against French imperialism.

We were accused of being divisive elements. We are supposed to avoid these important issues for the sake of unity. Although we agree that we must fight for independence alongside our brothers, we want to be clear about what sort of society we are fighting for.

Many young people feel this way too, because the movement relies on them but often excludes them from important decisions. At times of mobilisation, for example, the leaders make radical declarations that encourage the young people to take great personal risks. But then when they come to negotiate, they make political compromises without consulting the people.

One of the leaders who refused to compromise was Éloi Machoro. When the French presidential envoy, Edgard Pisani, demanded the barricades be dropped before talks could begin in January 1985, Jean-Marie Tjibaou agreed but Éloi refused. It was Éloi's determination to defy Pisani and continue the mobilisation that led him to being isolated by other FLNKS leaders and murdered by French troops. There were no foreign dignitaries at Éloi's funeral because he died an 'extremist'. France erected no monument in his honour, but he will live forever in the hearts of the Kanak people.

Éloi Machoro was the sort of person the Matignon Accords were designed to exclude from the political process. Like Alphonse Dianou and Djubelly Wea, he knew that France would never give away its power in Kanaky and he decided that his people's liberation was more important than his own life.

After Éloi's death and the FLNKS acceptance of the Fabius Plan[4], there was a general feeling of disillusionment among the young activists whose courage had forced France to abandon the Lemoine Statute it had been trying to impose. To have risked their lives on the barricades did not count as a qualification when it came to applying for jobs in the regions. The young people in Pierre Lenquette (the Kanak ghetto I was living in), for example, had organised round-the-clock security for the area so that people could sleep at night during the mobilisation. Within a few months, some people within the movement were referring to these same people as 'delinquents' who had to be 'kept under control' by the leaders. It is no wonder so many of them went back to smoking cannabis, getting drunk or joining fundamentalist sects. They felt like they had been used and discarded.

In order to avoid the seduction of our elected representatives in the regions by the high salaries France was paying them, the FLNKS decided they should give 20 per cent of their income back to the movement that placed them there. Out of 16 councillors, only a few 'extremists' (including Djubelly Wea) were committed enough to follow this policy. In general, the ones considered extremist at this stage were those of us who were committed to the FLNKS strategy of using the resources provided by France in the Fabius Plan to develop independent political and economic structures. These included our own media (Radio Djiido and the newspaper, *Bwenando*), Kanak Popular Schools (EPK - Écoles Populaires Kanak) and co-operative stores, as well as a local decision-making structure based on autonomous struggle committees. These structures belonged to the people and provided the only real channel for the energies of the grassroots activists.

The EPK education experience

Of all the revolutionary structures, the EPK was seen as the most extremist by the colonial authorities. What made it so threatening was not just that it used Kanak languages for teaching, but that it was based on a rejection of the colonial idea that all knowledge comes from France. This is a very important point - the French administration has always tried to convince us that we should not be independent straight away because we are not capable of running the country. It was this kind of logic that some people - the so-called 'reasonable' or 'moderate' ones - accepted when the FLNKS agreed to go along with the Fabius Plan in 1985 and the Matignon Accords in 1988. The EPK demonstrated that Kanak people were able to take control of their own schooling - both the content and the pedagogy.

The *animateurs* (teaching facilitators) included different sorts of people; young activists with qualifications but no job; people who resigned from teaching jobs in the colonial schools to work without wages in the EPK; and some, such as those who were expelled at the age of 14 or 15 during the school boycotts in 1979, who were talented but unqualified.

Right from the start the EPK were under siege - from both the French authorities and a number of FLNKS leaders. The administration did not recognise them as legitimate and cut the meagre social security benefits of the people who sent their children there, and the military sometimes raided the schools in their hunt for young people refusing to do their military service. They were starved of resources, receiving virtually nothing from the three FLNKS regions, which were dominated by the UC (Union Calédonienne), or from foreign NGOs. The only support from the anglophone world came from the New Zealand development aid agency CORSO, which had to hand its grant in cash to the FLNKS Education Minister, Simon Naaoutchoue, after the Banque de l'Indosuez in Noumea refused to handle a bank draft destined for the schools.

Isolation of this tendency in the movement applied not just to money, but to physical contact as well. A large broad-based delegation we organised from Aotearoa/New Zealand in January 1987 was denied entry, almost certainly because the French knew it would meet these so-called 'extremists'. Similar groups from Australia and elsewhere were not barred entry and were able to send money into the country.

The New Zealand and Australian governments also support the policy of isolating the people and groups who want more than a neo-colonial independence. The New Zealand Labour government twice took the unusual step of refusing to ratify its advisory committees' decisions to subsidise CORSO grants to the

EPK[5]. And both New Zealand and Australia have lobbied hard to encourage the South Pacific Forum to give the French authorities the benefit of the doubt and refuse requests from the independence movement. It was only the aggressive arrogance of the Chirac/Pons administration from 1986 to 1988 that left the Forum no choice but to take the Kanak cause to the United Nations.

French war crimes on Ouvéa

Aggressive violence from that French administration forced us to unite in resistance in Kanaky. In April 1988, despite the demobilisation of the previous three years, Kanak people stood up to the French military. The strongest resistance came from Canala and Ouvéa. In Canala, the military lost control of everything except a few key buildings. On Ouvéa, too, they were afraid to venture off the main roads. But, as Ouvéa is a very small island, it was possible for the military to completely isolate it and concentrate a massive force there.

On 22 April 1988, a group of activists from throughout Ouvéa led by Alphonse Dianou and Vince Lavelua tried to occupy the *gendarmerie* at Fayaoué. The officer in charge called on his gendarmes not to resist, but some did. Although the Kanaks had just a few guns between them, the gunfight that followed left four gendarmes dead. Alphonse and the others decided to take 27 other gendarmes hostage and head for the bush. An early report that the four dead gendarmes had been hacked to death with axes and machetes - they actually died of gunshot wounds - was sent around the world by racist Western wire services. After this, the military cut off all communications and transport to and from the island as they tried to find the hostages. With Ouvéa totally isolated, the military declared war on the people and broke all international war conventions.

In the EPK building in Gossanah, the French military set up headquarters to co-ordinate their terror campaign: locking up civilians in inhuman conditions, tying civilian prisoners to posts, beating them and torturing them with electric shocks. They also tried to break the spirit of the Kanak prisoners by humiliating them, stripping them naked in front of their brothers and sisters. The civilian populations of Gossanah and Teouta were locked in a small hut for two days and nights. One of the women, Manaky Wea (the wife, now widow of Djubelly), had her period. All the men in the tribe saw her blood, which is taboo in our custom. It is a humiliation even to write about this, but Manaky told me that it was important for people to know what the French military did to them.

When it came to those holding the hostages, France had to use more underhand tactics, which were based on pretending to negotiate. Alphonse Dianou and the others had engaged in the negotiations in good faith and agreed on a date (just after the French presidential elections) for releasing the hostages. But France had only used the 'negotiations' - like its control of the news media - as a means of preparing for its real goal of treating our people with such barbarity that no-one would dare challenge the French again. Their assault on the cave on 5 May 1988 was designed to inflict the maximum casualties.

The first attack came in the early morning, when a helicopter gunship that people had been told would bring a television crew to film the release of a sick hostage opened fire on the outer guard posts, and hundreds of ground troops rushed them at the same time. Vincent Daoumé, known everywhere as *l'As* ('Ace') and with a reputation in Noumea of always being in the front lines in dangerous situations, was in charge of these posts and had organised the capture of a second army group that had approached the cave. He and about eight others were killed in this first attack.

Eventually it became clear to the others that they would have to give themselves up. But releasing the hostages and forcing a surrender was not enough to satisfy the military's thirst for blood. After the fighting was over, two people were executed in front of witnesses. One of those executed, Vince Lavelua, had been identified as they key to the Kanaks winning the gunfight at the *gendarmerie*. An autopsy later revealed that Vince died from a single bullet wound through the middle of his forehead. The other, Ammossa Waina, was a young EPK *animateur* who was only there to bring food for the activists and the hostages. Alphonse Dianou was wounded in the knee and left to bleed to death. Samuel Wamo and Martin Haiwé (who would be the chief of Gossanah if he were still alive) were seen only slightly injured after the hostages had been freed - but their mutilated bodies were later found in the bush near the cave.

After the killing, people saw the army helicopters flying overhead with nets hanging underneath and thought that they were moving their equipment to another part of the island. In fact, the bodies of our 19 martyrs were swinging above them, nourishing our land with their blood. They were dumped in a tin shed at the airport and left for three days. There was a total confusion about who was dead. The name of my old cousin, Ignace Nine, was on and off the list about three times. In fact, he was alive and, when the bodies were finally released, had to identify his own two sons, Philippo and Nicola, and his daughter's husband, Athanase Dao.

All the bodies, except Alphonse's, were bloated and badly infested with maggots. Most were burnt and/or mutilated almost beyond recognition. They were buried in a mass grave in Hwadrilla, but their stench clung to the people's clothes and hung in the air for weeks afterwards.

When Saddam Hussein put his prisoners of war on television, France joined the chorus calling for him to be tried for war crimes. Where was the international outrage about French war crimes on Ouvéa? It was covered over by the Matignon Accords. The blood of our brothers killed by the French military had barely dried. And, without even visiting Ouvéa or consulting the movement, a few 'leaders' made a deal with France.

The violence of the Matignon Accords

The Matignon Accords were signed in blood - the blood of my brothers and cousins and nephews from Ouvéa. Beneath the appearance of a peaceful agreement lies extreme state violence. President Mitterrand was in power before, during and after the Ouvéa massacre and the Matignon Accords. Bernard Pons and Jacques Chirac are still in Parliament and the military is still commanded by the same generals. Prime Minister Michel Rocard was not directly responsible for the torture and executions himself, but the implicit threat that such acts could happen again helps his government to maintain authority over my people and our land. The Matignon Accords are simply a more subtle way for France to achieve this aim.

The accords put off a referendum on independence until 1998. At that time, people who arrived in the country as recently as 1984 will be allowed to vote on the future of Kanaky. In the 10 years leading up to this vote, the French government promised to give extra money for development in the Kanak areas as well as specialised training in France for 400 cadres. It also indicated that, if the Kanak people co-operated in the plan, dozens of political prisoners jailed in France and New Caledonia would be released.

A massive news media campaign urged voters to back the accords in the November 1988 referendum. The campaign was endorsed by the FLNKS leadership, who pushed the line that Kanaks should vote 'yes' to free the prisoners. The results showed that very large numbers of Kanaks ignored the party leaders and did not vote[6]. The overall rate of abstention in the territory was 37 per cent, but in Kanak areas the rate was much higher. The highest of all was Ouvéa (97% Kanak), where more than 54 per cent of registered voters did not vote and a further six per cent voted 'no'. Even some of the prisoners' wives told me that they had boycotted the vote. And some of the prisoners themselves told me that they opposed the accords and were angry at being used to push people to vote.

Despite the accords, the people of Ouvéa (particularly in the northern tribes of Gossanah and Teouta) maintained their call for an international inquiry into the war crimes committed during the military occupation of our island. They became a symbol for activists throughout Kanaky but an embarrassment to the FLNKS leadership. Their resistance worried the French authorities, who denied the island any financial aid and kept a heavy military presence there.

Disturbing alliances and a sacrificial act

Since the Matignon Accords, there has been growing concern within the independence movement - including many who are prepared to work within the accords - about the close relationship between elements in the UC and right-wing settler groups. These concerns came to a head in the municipal council elections in March 1989.

The UC decided to stand on its own and not in partnership with the other parties in the FLNKS. If no party wins a clear majority, an alliance is needed to determine the mayoralty. In six communes, the UC joined with the RPCR. In Yaté, the FLNKS list (headed by Raphael Mapou - another so-called extremist) won seven out of fifteen seats and was only a dozen votes short of winning an absolute majority. But the UC (with four seats) won the mayoralty through an alliance with the RPCR (three seats) and LKS[7] (one seat). In Ponérihouen, the UC candidate defeated the FLNKS by gaining the support of the neo-fascist National Front. But he was forced to resign a few weeks later by outraged members of his own party.

While there are very real splits within the independence movement, the colonial authorities are also actively seeking to divide us even further. One of the most important state agencies involved in this psychological warfare is the Bureau d'Études et Liaison (BEL), which was set up during the Algerian war of independence with the aim of 'contaminating' the liberation movement. It spread misinformation among Algerian activists and even used to intercept and alter passages in the movement's newspaper between Rabat, where it was typeset, and Tunis, where it was printed. BEL was so successful at generating suspicion and division that it led to the liquidation of some agents of the French Centre de Co-ordination Interarmées (CCI) and to a complaint by the CCI chief, Colonel Simoneau, that it was becoming too hard to infiltrate the movement.

The BEL office in Noumea, headed until recently by Colonel Bordahandy, is considered by the governments of New Zealand, Australia and other countries - and even some people within the independence movement - to be a reliable source of information. One of its most effective campaigns was to convince people that Djubelly Wea's assassination of Jean-Marie Tjibaou and Yeiwene Yeiwene on 4 May 1989 was the result of a complex conspiracy involving a wide group of people in Kanaky and abroad. As organiser of a customary ceremony in Hwadrilla (his maternal tribe and the site of the graves of the army's victims) held to mark the first anniversary of the Ouvéa massacre, Djubelly shot Jean-Marie and Yeiwene at point-blank range, crying, 'Rocard's friend is dead. Down with the Matignon Accords. Long live Kanaky'. He was himself shot by Jean-Marie's bodyguards. The conspiracy rumour sparked off a destructive witch-hunt within the movement. I was very close to Djubelly Wea politically and personally - he was my uncle and was married to my cousin, but no-one, not even his wife or brothers, knew what he was planning to do. The gun Djubelly used was not smuggled in from abroad but was brought to Ouvéa by the French military. Rumours about money and air tickets - probably spawned by BEL - are ridiculous since it was so obviously a suicide act carried out in front of hundreds of people, including Jean-Marie's bodyguards.

History will decide how the Kanak people will judge Djubelly. What French officials and foreign commentators think of him is of no importance. The Kanak people *know* that Djubelly was not a nobody and he was not a hired hit-man. Even those who disagree with his action cannot deny that he was a sincere and committed political leader who sacrificed his own life for what he believed in. Increasingly, Kanak people are recognising the real dangers in the Matignon Accords and are coming to understand what pushed Djubelly Wea to his last sacrificial act.

Djubelly could have got someone else to do what he did, or he could have sneaked up at night and then tried to escape. Who he was, the fact that he carried out the act himself and the way that he did it: all this points to Djubelly assuming total responsibility for his own action.

The real motive of those who generated the rumours of a complex conspiracy was to isolate the opponents of the accords. The focus has been not so much on political parties but more on particular people within a range of parties and some who are members of no party. The people targeted by these rumours have had a hard time, especially in the first few months after the assassinations. Many were forced to keep a low profile and did not even communicate with each other for fear of adding further 'evidence' of conspiracy for the witch-hunters to use against them.

I felt this pressure, but my personal circumstances make me vulnerable in other ways too. For the second time since my marriage to a New Zealander in 1986, our plans to live in Kanaky were blocked by the French authorities refusing my husband, David Small, a visa. Today, anyone from Europe or from any French colony around the world can move to Kanaky and stay there as long as they want. But, I am forbidden to bring my husband home to live in the land of my ancestors. French colonialism dictates that the only way I can go home is to leave my husband. What power do the Matignon Accords give us if we cannot even decide who is allowed to live in our land? All the Matignon Accords allow us to do is administer the laws France dictates to us.

Development for whom?

The French government likes to talk about all the money it is giving to aid 'development' in Kanaky. But it assumes that development in Kanaky means making our country more like France. One of the weaknesses of our movement is that it has never resolved this issue of what kind of development we want, what kind of future society we want to build. The people who want to have these issues addressed are told by the French and by some leaders of the movement that we are being 'too theoretical' or 'unrealistic'. But the Kanak people are now paying the price for these issues being ignored. The money from the Matignon Accords is not meeting the real needs of the Kanak people; it is going on big contracts for French multinationals like Buink and Dumez.

The Matignon Accords are good business for the big companies, providing them with political stability and financial subsidies. The businessmen are sure of themselves. The huge new shopping malls that have been built in Noumea since 1988 are as modern as anything in New Zealand - and even the big tourist companies are starting to invest in overseas promotions again. Plans are also proceeding for the establishment of a new Club Med complex on my ancestral land on Ouvéa, the first foreign-controlled tourist hotel on the island since the Relais d'Ouvéa was reduced to ashes in 1983 within months of it being rebuilt after an earlier arson attack.

If the development of Kanaky is designed to make our country the same as France, Kanak people know what roles are reserved for us - beggars and servants! Our hope for the future comes from what we do for ourselves, not what France decides it will give us.

To Djubelly

Unlike Jean-Marie
Whom they say you shot and killed with your
        assassin's bullet,
Your death
At the hands of a French élite-corps bodyguard
Is an ignominious one.
Many will remember you now
Only as a rabid extremist,
A villain-assassin
While Jean-Marie, thanks to you,
Will be consecrated
As a moderate, nationalist hero,
A peace-loving martyr,
A Saint.

Rocard has lost a friend, he says,
Unashamedly shedding tears
For the one he found willing to enter
Into a peace accord without a mandate
And, as you considered, over the dead bodies
Of Ouvéa's brave martyrs.
That peace accord has cost Jean-Marie,
And Kanaky, dearly.

The mourners for Jean-Marie are many.
Both camps - French and Kanak -
Lament his passing.

I weep for you Djubelly, long time friend,
And one-time pacifist,
And for all of us who have come to
Lose faith in the wisdom or integrity
Of those who assume leadership of our struggles.
I weep for the loss of one of Kanaky's
Most passionate and committed sons;
For the loss of the seasoned,
Unwavering Pacific activist,
I wonder at the analytical course your mind took,
At the agony of arriving,
With single-minded clarity,
At the decision to carry out
That last desperate political act -
And to carry it out yourself
Knowing you would probably lose your own life
And consign yourself to infamy.

Djubelly, history may yet be kinder in her
Judgement of you.
Who knows yet the consequences of your own
Self-inflicted martyrdom?
Your tragic death, and that of Jean-Marie
And every other Kanak
Who has fallen victim to the real slayer -
French colonialism -
Should not be in vain.

Claire   Slatter

As long as there is no blood in the streets, the international news media will ignore Kanaky. But this does not mean that our struggle has ended. Several groups are doing effective grassroots work, and their work is the only guarantee we have for the future of Kanaky. This is because they belong to **us**, the Kanaks. They do not depend on French money and they respond to the real needs of the people.

At the union level, the USTKE (Kanak and Exploited Workers Union) has been growing rapidly as a result of the many successful actions it has organised in Noumea, and exploited agricultural workers are gaining strength through a new union of coffee producers on the east coast. In the area of public works, STTCH 2000[8] has been tendering for contracts from municipal councils and helping to provide training and wages for the many skilled unemployed Kanaks. A people's health network, ADSPPK, has also been established. One of its main activities has been educating young people about the dangers of sexually transmitted diseases and AIDS, which are rapidly increasing in Kanaky.

In the field of education, the remaining EPK - at Ouvéa, Yaté, Pouebo, Canala and Lifou - are working well in spite of the hardships faced. Within the colonial school system, there is a resistance to racism and elitism in education through the actions of pupils such as the hunger strike by Doxucas Naisseline and Marcel Wenewa (sons of two long-time activists) at Collège Baudoux at the end of 1990.

Youth will decide the future

Kanak youth are highly politicised - too politically aware to allow a few Kanak leaders to set up a neo-colonial state in collaboration with the French government and local businessmen like Jacques Lafleur and Jean Lecques. In the independence movement today, party membership actually means very little; if all you know about Kanaks is their party membership, you actually know very little about their politics. When the young people move, many things will become more clear. We will see which groups or individual leaders support them and who tries to control them or stop them.

There are hardly any people of my generation who are respected by the youth. The young ones took all the risks and have gained none of the rewards. Even with the famous '400 cadres' - this figure includes non-Kanaks and among the Kanaks receiving training there are many older people who have already got jobs and have never done anything for the struggle. When I was in Noumea recently, a long-time activist and well-known leader told me how the elected officials and the people with the good jobs are viewed: 'Remember, Susanna, in the 1970s when we were laughing about all our elders who were so ridiculous when they were in the institutions? Today young people everywhere are laughing about us'.

The Matignon Accords have alienated and excluded more than just a handful of so-called 'extremists'. Among the Kanak people, few ever embraced the accords enthusiastically, a few more went along with them because they had already been signed, and others voted for them out of a concern for the political prisoners. The most cynical of all are the young people, and they are the majority - they are the force of our movement and they are the future.

The FLNKS is due to evaluate its position on the accords in 1992, but young people are already making their assessment. As one of the 1979 generation of grassroots activists told me: 'Every time the young people die, it is a few leaders who fill their pockets. We are sick of being used. But we're getting close to 1992, and when they come back to see us for barricades we will tell them it's their turn to build the barricades and stand in front - but we will not go to die for them'.

---

*   This paper was published in Robie, D. (ed.) (1992) *Tu galala: Social change in the Pacific,* Sydney: Bridget Williams Books/Pluto Press

Notes

1.   The pro-independence FLNKS (Front de Libération Nationale Kanak et Socialiste - Kanak Socialist National Liberation Front) was founded in 1984.

2.   The RPCR (*Rassemblement pour la Calédonie dans la République* - Caledonian Republican Rally Party) is an anti-independence party.

3.   PALIKA was one of the founding parties of the FLNKS in 1984.

4.   The FLNKS rejected the Lemoine Statute for two reasons: it did not accept the Front's call for a vote on independence to be restricted to only those with at least one parent born in Kanaky (needed to counter French immigration policies of the 1960s and 1970s); and it put off the vote on independence until after the 1986 elections in France. Éloi Machoro said at the time: 'As soon as [Jacques] Chirac comes to power in France in 1986, we are done for'. The Fabius Plan divided Kanaky into four regions and proposed a vote on 'independence in association with France' for September 1987.

5.   These committees (for the Voluntary Agencies Support Scheme [VASS] and the Development Education Programme [DEP]) have a majority of NGO members and agreed to the subsidies, but cabinet ministers accepted the advice of the Ministry of Foreign Affairs and declined to ratify the funding recommendations.

6.   In metropolitan France and its overseas territories overall, the 1988 referendum vote was 81 per cent in favour of the Matignon Accords - but only 37 per cent of the electorate cast a vote.

7. The LKS stands for *Libération Kanak et Socialiste* - Kanak Socialist Liberation party

8. STTCH 2000 (Société Tous Travaux et Constructions Horizon 2000 - Horizon 2000 Building and. Works Company); ADSPPK (Association pour le Dévéloppement d'une Santé pour le Peuple en Kanaky - Kanaky People's Health Development Association).

Eighteen

The down-side of Matignon:
Squatting in Kanaky*

'Atu Emberson-Bain

'I have been waiting to get a house for over a year and now my landlord has evicted me from the flat I was renting. I had no where else to go but here'. André carries his three-year old daughter on his hip and shrugs his shoulders in despair as he points down to his half-built *cabane* (shack) nestled in a valley on the suburban fringes of New Caledonia's capital Noumea.

André is a Kanak who comes from New Caledonia's Northern Province, but he has been living in Noumea for over 10 years, supporting his family on earnings as a dockworker. He is now an illegal squatter on state land. And he is not alone. He joins another 30-odd families in just one of the many squatter settlements that have mushroomed in and around Noumea in recent years. The families lead a precarious existence. They have no access to electricity or running water. They are visited frequently by the police intelligence service, and they live in fear of eviction or demolition of their houses, both of which have been regular occurrences to make way for real estate development.

Adèle, a Kanak woman also originally from the North, lowers a bucket into a deep well of dirty green water oozing with disease potential. Her three semi-clad children stand silently by, watching her work. There are six eight-gallon containers waiting to be filled. 'This is the water I use to bathe my children and to do our washing. It's no good as drinking or cooking water. We have to make trips into Noumea for that'.

New Caledonia's squatter problem has claimed public attention over the past year or so. In April 1993, a public meeting organised by the Committee for the Defence and Support of Squatters was attended by several hundred squatters and their supporters in downtown Noumea. Emotionally charged speeches highlighted the plight of the increasing number of families who live on the lonely fringes of this affluent and very French Pacific capital. Colourful banners screamed out: 'Decent housing for everyone'; 'Solidarity and unity with the squatters'; 'No to property speculation'; and 'No to the uncontrolled rise in rents'.

The Squatters Committee estimates that the squatter population in Noumea alone - which has a population of about 75,000 - is close to 1,600. According to active committee member Sosefo Polelei, the *cabane* dwellers are essentially confined to the Southern Province and, contrary to popular belief, the overwhelming majority are wage and salary earners who have been working in the area of Greater Noumea for up to 20 years. Moreover, while Kanaks and Wallisians (migrants from the Wallis Islands, another of France's colonial possessions in the Pacific) feature prominently, the problem knows no ethnic or racial boundaries, including even some *caldoches* (descendants of white settlers).

To a large extent, the squatter problem is a product of the territory's high cost of living, in particular the phenomenal cost of rent in Noumea. New Caledonia has one of the highest costs of living in the region, surpassed only by French Polynesia, France's other strategically important Pacific territory. In Polelei's view, the property and financial speculation promoted by the Southern Provincial Government, which includes Noumea, has been a major contributor to escalating rents and the predicament facing *cabane* dwellers.

Louis Uregei, President of the Kanak and Exploited Workers Union (USTKE), New Caledonia's largest union with a membership of around 6,000, confirms that

> the squatter phenomenon has resulted from the lack of accessible rent and insufficient housing. What is available is very expensive. The vast majority of squatters are workers whose wages are too low to enable them to pay rent at market prices. They are left with no alternative but to build a *cabane* in the bush without electricity, water, or sanitary toilet facilities (1993, Noumea, pers. comm.).

A quick comparison of rent and wage data in the territory bears out this depressing testimony. In Noumea, it is difficult to find a modest two-bedroom flat on the open market for less than 100,000 francs (CFP) a month, and house rents can be as much as 300,000 CFP[1]. Even in the overcrowded poor Kanak neighbourhoods known as the *quartiers populaires*, subsidised rent can still tip the scales at 50,000 CFP a month. By contrast, the minimum wage in the territory is 70,000 CFP with the average monthly household income around 255,000 CFP.

It is against the political backdrop of the Matignon Accords that New Caledonia's squatter problem throws up some interesting questions. A controversial agreement endorsed in 1988 by the pro-independence Kanak Socialist National Liberation Front (FLNKS), notably its assassinated leader Jean-Marie Tjibaou, and the anti-independence right-wing party, the RPCR, headed by Jacques Lafleur, the Accords have provided the blueprint for boosted economic development in the lead-up to the scheduled referendum on independence in 1998. They have triggered a proliferation of development projects, especially visible in the tourism sector. The purchase of one of Lafleur's nickel mines and shares in the Club Med tourist resort at Hiènghène have given the Kanak-controlled Northern Province a stake in two key sectors of the economy.

But to what extent has there been a trickle down of the territory's growing prosperity? Is it a mere coincidence that the Southern Province, controlled by the RPCR, should simultaneously be the thriving commercial centre and expanding squatter capital of the territory? Have some people simply had to pay the price of New Caledonia's development and be literally moved aside?

Development

Big word
Lotsa meanings
Staka dollar
Magnetic circle
Entices me
Urban drift
Empty villages
Customs forgotten
Loose living
Lost identity
Rat race
Dollar talks
Values change
Wantoks ignored
Every man for himself
I want to develop too!

Jully   Sipolo

There may be no definitive answers to these questions. But what is evident is that the squatter problem cannot really be understood in isolation from the broader political economy of this French colonial territory. For some of the more cynical observers, the Matignon Accords have essentially failed to deliver sustainable livelihoods for most Kanaks. In the sharp-shooting rhetoric of one member of the Squatters Commmittee

> We hear all this talk of the Matignon Accords but for Kanaks, after 140 years of colonisation, they continue to live in poverty and misery. Our young people have to live on the streets because there is no housing for them. Those in power simply don't care.

Uregei offers a more sober assessment. However, he agrees that the development boom has not delivered to everyone and that the squatters are amongst its more prominent casualties.

> The Matignon Accords have generated a prosperity in the country which has driven the cost of living up and led to skyrocketing rentals. Wages, on the other hand, have not increased at the same rate. While the Accords have brought an immense amount of money into the territory, the problem is that it is used to do things like run the institutions and it does not reach everyone. Many people do not benefit from this money at all while there are others who have done very well by it. The squatters are amongst those who have not benefited in any way (1994, Noumea, pers. comm.).

Perhaps one of the more telling features of the squatter problem is that it stands little chance of being addressed and resolved as a social issue. This is because it is intimately bound up with local politics in the territory. For the leadership of the Squatters Committee, including Polelei, the dominant position of the right-wing parties, including the National Front, in the municipal council, is a major reason for the failure of the French administration to show more constructive concern. Other critical observers, including USTKE, argue that even if a lot more money were to be earmarked for government-subsidised housing, the existing system of political favouritism would still hold sway.

Uregei explains further that a political decision was taken five years ago to build subsidised housing for people living in the *cabanes*:

> Unfortunately, once the houses were built, they were handed over to RPCR cronies instead. It is for this reason that USTKE denounces the politics of low-income government housing which are unjust because they are based on political favouritism. We believe that priority must be given firstly to those who are genuinely in need, that is those living in the *cabanes* and those living in the council estate at Doniambo[2]. Unfortunately for the squatters, instead of the housing issue being treated simply as a social problem, it is governed by political considerations.

Even if the political odds are against them, Noumea's squatters have displayed an intrepid determination to press their claims for a better deal as well as an impressive capacity to organise. The Squatters Committee has won support from the trade unions, a number of political parties, the customary Kanak chiefs of the Southern Province, and the churches. It has made numerous representations to the French authorities. Polelei pushes a strong case for more realistic rents for workers, ideally between 10,000 and 15,000 CFP, and for a housing programme that will meet the needs of the squatters and the poor. He insists that the Committee will 'continue to struggle for the dignity of the *cabane* dwellers' and that because of continuing official negligence 'the problem is now no longer just a priority but a matter of extreme urgency'.

But there have been some successes. One of the earliest was the establishment of a squatter settlement next to the territory's prison at Nouville, 'home' to many Kanak activists and leaders at various times during the history of political struggle against French colonial rule. It is a scenic location overlooking Noumea's extensive harbour. There are no facilities, the sea provides the only place to bathe, and drinking water has to be collected regularly from Noumea. In defiance of the authorities, the families have managed to remain in their *cabanes*, cultivating food gardens on land openly classified as 'military property'. The sweetness of this particular victory, small though it may be, is not lost on Polelei.

The higher moral ground might also be claimed by the squatters. According to Polelei, who is of Wallisian ancestry, the word 'squatter' (the English word curiously being used in French as well) is a politically loaded term that is inappropriate to describe Kanaks living in the *cabanes*. He speaks with a simple but disarming logic, criticising the impression the word gives of the uninvited occupier or intruder. 'How can you describe the Kanaks as squatters? It is their land, their country. They own it and it is impossible to be a squatter on your own land. It is the French, through their colonisation of Kanaky, who have squatted on Kanak land'.

* This article was originally published in *Pacific Islands Monthly* in July 1993.

Notes

1. 1,000 CFP is equivalent to about $US 10.

2. Doniambo is the site of New Caledonia's nickel smelter in Noumea. It is operated by the state-owned Société Métallurgique Le Nickel (SLN) which dominates the territory's mining industry.

Pacifico, Timan
Malago Ham, Na
Bai Infan Matai
Ginen I Binenon
I Atamic.

Nineteen

In defence of our nuclear-free Constitution

Cita Morei

On 9 July 1993, we, the people of Belau (officially called Palau), celebrated the 13th anniversary of our nuclear-free Constitution. Four months later, under economic duress, we went to the polls for the eighth time in 10 years to amend the nuclear-free provision in our Constitution. This amendment was designed to allow the United States government to have military access to Belauan lands and water as provided under the Compact of Free Association (COFA). Since the inception of our Constitution, we have been told by the United States that its nuclear-free clause conflicts with the political status defined for Belau under the Compact by Washington D.C. We were told to take it or leave it: either drop our anti-nuclear Constitution or there would be no deal on Belau's independence.

The terms of the Compact of Free Association provide for an aid package to Belau of $US 428 million and a possible continuation of some US federal programmes for a period of 50 years (these may be negotiated from time to time). In exchange for this, Belau would be obliged to give military options to the United States, that is, to grant it full authority to use any Belauan land for nuclear-propelled and nuclear-capable ships and aircrafts, and for warfare training and manoeuvres (COFA Subsidiary Agreements, Annex A). Belau would have to give these lands to the US military within 60 days of a request.

A grassroots movement of concerned Belauan citizens, mostly women, has consistently opposed this exchange of Belau's nuclear-free Constitution and lands for a pseudo-independence, as the negotiated end to our colonial status. We feel we are being coerced into choosing between 'independence' for our country and the integrity of our Constitution. It is our belief that Belau's Constitution is an act of self-determination, and that it represents a political status that was defined by an overwhelming 92 per cent of Belauan voters in 1979.

Our struggle continues as memories of World War II still linger in the minds and hearts of our people. We were made victims of a war we did not create. Families and individuals were forced to relocate and to live in the jungles. Food was scarce, and starvation and malnutrition were the daily menu for both Belauans and the Japanese civilians left behind before the outbreak of war. (Civilian Japanese were evacuated before war broke out in Belau). We feel that as long as there is a military presence, whether on the part of the United States or otherwise, this will remain a symbol of aggression and domination of our environment. We believe that the presence of a military base in Belau could ruin our unspoiled natural environment. Elsewhere in the world, massive destruction has already been caused by nuclear weapons, nuclear tests, nuclear fall-out, oil spills and other pollutants.

Behind the walls

(translated from the French original, Derrière les murs)

Behind the walls
the seconds stretch out
where the pulse of oppressed peoples
and its quickened rhythm
stir our prison solitude,
guiding handwriting that trembles
from anger, tenderness, rebellion, love,
And its throbbing tempo
shocks the repressed words of
generations crushed, brutalised, humiliated
in the icy silence of colonial vaults
And slowly
imperceptibly
takes hold
Of the body, the fingers which long
to resist
behind the walls.

Déwé Gorode,
Camp-Est*, October 1974

*   *The tight security French colonial*
   prison located at Nouville, which
   overlooks the main harbour of
   Noumea, the New Caledonian capital.

We are fearful for the future of our island if we let ourselves be victims of insensitive acts of government and individuals who are concerned only with their self-interest. As women, we feel that it is our duty, our obligation, to take care of our land, our children, and our future by being active in policy making, and exercising a good influence on our government. The pains of labour do not end in the delivery room. They are part of a life-long process that our organisation believes must be felt at the decision-making table. Our strong stand against the nuclearisation and militarisation of our land has been a painful process.

We have been accused of being communists. We have been intimidated. Our houses have been bombed. We have even been the victims of murder. We believe that we have to make a difference. Policies were made by men, and so they can be changed to reflect the common good and the integrity of Creation.

Our struggle will continue as long as the injustice remains; as long as inequality lingers; as long as colonialism sits on the throne of our government. The lawsuits we have filed at different times are an act of faith in our democratic system. It is a system that we believe should ensure protection of the minority as well as recognising the will of the majority. The defence of our Constitution will continue as long as each generation of Belauans believes that the land and the water surrounding us are our lifeblood.

Belau Be Brave ...

Belau be brave ...
thy nobleman's creed is in the grave,
decaying by greed,
their loyal deeds once engraved,
at Ulong in Wilson's log,
are gone, lost in history books,
dusty, buried in Leeboo's grave.

Why do people rave? why do I feel rage?

221

We were never wanderers; we've been Adventurers.
We were never drifters; We are Navigators.
We were never beggars; We are Providers.
We were never without a Home.
We never lived without Hope.

Disasters, diseases and deaths,
come and gone; we were not alone,
Family and friends bound us as one.
We survived.

Beachcombers, traders and foreigners
came and claimed ...
They exclaimed, 'What beautiful real-estate,
best they be barriers for our disasters,
maybe, forward bases for carriers ...'

For goodness sake, is not Bikini enough?
Mururoa, Hiroshima? Nagasaki?
Is Three Mile Island still without life?

Belau be brave, our lives at stake.
Never sell your seas, your soul
For everlasting food stamps.

Belau be brave ...
your dignity, your pride
will take in its stride
with your sons and daughters yet to come.
We must survive.

Cita Morei

Twenty

The Pentagon's 'chosen' people*

Isabella Sumang

My name is Isabella Sumang. I speak not only on my own behalf, but also for the numerous Palau women's organisations which have joined together to try to prevent the loss of our lands and waters to United States military or nuclear development. Thank you for listening.

Since World War II, the records of this Council have been filled with the repeated accounts of dislocation and destruction resulting from American military use of and experimentation in Micronesia. It has recorded the devastation of the atolls of Bikini and Eniwetok in the Marshall Islands. The Council has heard the extensive documentation of nuclear damage to virtually all of the Northern Marshall Islands. And, of course, there have been repeated accounts of the failures of any government, whether American or indigenous, to resolve the problems of poverty and dislocation resulting from American military research and development at Kwajalein Atoll.

Each time Palauans read or heard of the damage in the Marshall Islands coming from US military activity, or read or heard of the 40-year-long struggle of the people of Guam to obtain compensation for their lands and waters taken by the US military, we realised that - but for the grace of God - it could have been Palau.

If the whim of some far-off Pentagon planner had chosen Babeldaop instead of Guam, Peleliu instead of Bikini, Angaur instead of Eniwetok, then we would have been before you many years ago, recounting our damage from radiation and dislocation. But, in reality, the far-off Pentagon planners **have** chosen Palau. They have just not put the radiation into our land and waters - yet.

White ashes

there are men who are making
a big white cloud
bigger than they had ever had before

they are bringing the big white powder puff
right down here
because there's more clear open space in the sky
and what's below doesn't count

and puff!
it goes up and up and out
filtering and floating and dusting
the clear wide space of the sky

and then
the airy white ashes fall and fall
out across the blue innocent ocean
sprinkling so gently the secret coral worlds
as it passes over the reef's foam
down it falls
into long slow rivers
which curve and move
with its deadly message
rivers rushing and tumbling into
our gaping defenceless mouths

where shall I store it
my little piece of ash
perhaps in my bones

the wicked white thing
the secretive sick thing
coursing through my blood

cementing in my bones
stayed buried, buried!

a swimming wriggling fish
joyfully enters the deep warm whirlpool
and forms, slowly and painfully
cell by cell
over nine long nourishing months
my beautiful new thing
my soft pink bud
how I shelter it for its birth

ah yes!
what a birth that shall be
the grey forgotten ghost

224

the ash will come, come
screaming forth evil godmother
running riot amongst the tenderness
tearing at the petals
of my poor pink bud
and when the bud opens
liquidly and through pain
petals will be missing
disease will gnaw at its soft centre

oh mother, mother
hold me
oh mother, mother
keep me
oh mother, mother
help me
what am I?

and with what pain shall I look
into the pale, weak eyes
of my soft dying bud
and with what agony shall I touch
the limp drooping petals

and then
from the core of my being
warm, pulsing, red
where buds were meant to grow
and open
in crying pink beauty
from these depths will shudder forth
the shrill, piercing wail
echoing helplessly
my body's plan denied
my bud's life betrayed.

Vanessa Griffen

In our Palau culture, it is women who have responsibility for preserving the land for generations still to come. So when the women of Palau realised that our overwhelmingly male-elected leadership was not going to stand up to US military ambitions, we took it upon ourselves to take action. It is we, the women of Palau, who have organised ourselves and sought help from beyond Palau to fight the plans in the Compact of Free Association to use Palau for foreign military purposes. It is we who know that the risks of nuclear or toxic waste disposal in our beautiful islands are too real to ignore.

We are sure that the US government representatives will say that the United States has no plans to dispose of nuclear or toxic waste in Palau and no present plans to actually build military installations in Palau. If that is the case,

225

we call on them to write that into the Compact, to write it into law. If they truly do not intend to use Palau for any such purposes, it would be easy for the US Congress to amend the Compact to include provisions that make US environmental law applicable to Palau and so ensure that Palau will never be used for US nuclear or toxic waste disposal.

If the US government really does not mean to make Palau its future nuclear waste dump, it can start by giving us the information we have asked for under the US Freedom of Information Act regarding its environmental studies relating to Palau.

I want to tell you about our environmental litigation in Honolulu. On 18 February 1994, Mrs Nancy Wong and I, together with two other Palauan women, Toyomi James, who lives in Hawaii, and Isebong Isimang, who lives in Palau, filed suit in the United States District Court in Honolulu under the United States National Environmental Policy Act (NEPA). We are asking the Court to stop implementation of the Compact until the United States has complied with its own environmental law and prepared complete studies of the prospective environmental impact of the military and nuclear clauses of the Compact. We have also sued the Palau government for the economic losses it has caused for all Palau landowners by signing up, without our consent, for unlimited American military land acquisition. In the Honolulu NEPA case, we have asked that the Federal Court also declare the November 1993 Referendum to be invalid, due to the failure of the United States to have complied with its own environmental laws in relation to the Compact.

How has the United States reacted to our case? I regret to tell you it has essentially ignored it. Under American law, it was required to answer our requests under the Freedom of Information Act by 13 May 1994. It did not do so and the Court Clerk has entered a default against the US government for its failure to file any response to our requests for information.

When we met with the Federal Court in Honolulu on 16 May 1994, neither the Justice Department in Washington D.C. nor even the United States Attorney's Office in Honolulu sent anyone to the scheduling conference being held by the Court. The Justice Department had sent the Court a three-page memorandum, telling it that it should not schedule a trial date for our case because the government planned to file a motion to dismiss the case. Only after the Court telephoned the US Attorney's Office did anyone representing the US government show up. The lawyer who came had never heard of our case and knew nothing of the paper filed by the Justice Department asking that no trial be scheduled.

Notwithstanding the US government's position that the case should not be scheduled for trial, the Court has set a trial date of 14 February 1995. And recent American precedents are highly favourable to us. Only last year, the Federal Appeals Court in Washington D.C. extended the reach of NEPA to government activities in Antarctica. We do not think it is too much to ask that Palauans be given the same environmental protection now afforded to penguins.

We ask the Trusteeship Council to take particular note of the implications of our claim under the US National Environment Policy Act. This law requires any US government agency that intends to take any action that may have a significant impact on the environment to produce a formal study of the potential impact of the action or project. This is information that US law mandates must be made available before important government decisions are made.

As you know, Mr President and Members of the Council, for many years Palauans have been reporting to you at these meetings and to members of visiting missions who have come to Palau, that we have not had enough information about the Compact and its consequences to make an educated, free choice about it. Palauans have repeatedly stressed that the lack of informed, relevant, fair, and open discussion about the Compact raises doubts about the legitimacy of the many attempts to have it ratified in Palau.

Now, our lawsuit alleges that the Administering Authority has failed to carry out a very particular obligation under US law. By failing to follow its own laws requiring disclosure of environmental information about the Compact, the Administering Authority has made a large and negative contribution to our problem of having no accurate information about the Compact and its consequences for the land, waters and people of Palau.

While the women of Palau will fight the potential in the Compact for a military or nuclear land grab as long as we can, we are asking this Council to tell the American government, privately if not publicly, that its ambitions for Palau are entirely and totally inappropriate; that if it wants to dispose of nuclear waste or build military bases, it should do those things on American soil.

We view the undertaking under Section 162 of the Compact for consultation between our government and the United States to be a joke, particularly given the unbridled right of the United States to unilaterally opt out of any compliance under Section 163. We call upon this Council to help us stop the advance of unchecked and unconscionable environmental irresponsibility before it gets to Palau.

We want to acknowledge assistance from conscientious people around the world in our fight against US military or nuclear expansion into Palau. The Right Livelihood Foundation and its founder, Jakob von Uexkull, have been steadfast supporters of our efforts. We would like to thank our attorney, George Allen, for his help in our cases in Palau and Honolulu. We regret that our elected leaders have felt they had no choice but to yield to American military and nuclear prerogatives.

We know we have right on our side. We pledge ourselves to carry on our struggle to keep military and nuclear facilities out of our country. This is the only right thing to do. We ask the help of this Council in holding the United States to its responsibilities.

We therefore respectfully ask the Trusteeship Council:

1. To request that the United Nations Environment Programme prepare an independent evaluation of the potential environmental impact on Palau of the implementation of the Compact of Free Association, particularly its military provisions, and present copies of that report to the Trusteeship Council, the Government of Palau, the Administering Authority, and each Palauan citizen who has presented a petition before the Trusteeship Council in the past 15 years.

2. To request that the Administering Authority make monthly reports to the Members of the Council on the status of all litigation about the Compact pending in Palau or the United States.

3. To refrain from making any recommendation that the Trusteeship be terminated or taking any steps towards termination as long as any litigation about the Compact is pending in either Palau or the United States.

3. To urge the Administering Authority and the government of Palau not to take any further steps towards implementation of the Compact until all litigation pending in either Palau or the United States has been resolved.

* A submission to the United Nations Trusteeship Council on behalf of the Coalition of Women's Organizations of Palau to Keep Palau Nuclear-Free, New York, in May 1994.

228

Twenty-One

'Our mothers and children are dying':
Military offensives against the Island of Bougainville*

Ruby Mirinka

Introduction

It is the purpose of this report to reveal to the world, including Papua New Guinea (PNG) itself, the truth about the cruel physical, environmental and psychological torture inflicted on Bougainvilleans by the government blockade. It is the belief of the mothers and children of Bougainville, whom I represent here, that the United Nations should develop a workable strategy that will open dialogue between all Bougainvillean leaders and PNG, and find a lasting solution to end the crisis.

I would like to begin by presenting an overview of the type of health services and living conditions Bougainvilleans enjoyed before the outbreak of the crisis. This will provide you with a better understanding of why and how the blockade has affected the health of the people.

Before the war, our health system consisted of one major hospital which was located in Arawa, the capital of Bougainville, in the central region of the island. This hospital provided for both primary and secondary health care and, in addition, offered some specialist medical care in areas like surgery, paediatrics and gynaecology. To receive specialist medical care, therefore, patients came to the Arawa General Hospital from all over Bougainville.

In the rural areas, where most of the population lives, primary health care services were previously provided by health centres, which catered for local populations totalling between 10,000 and 20,000; health sub-centres, which serviced populations of between 5,000 and 10,000; and aide posts, which served rural populations of between 2,000 and 5,000. To obtain services from these health institutions, people travelled by road vehicle, boat or even aeroplane, particularly to visit the major hospital. But most rural people went on foot, with a walk of about 15-30 minutes being enough to get them to medical treatment.

The health impact of the blockade

The health system I have described is no longer in existence. All the health personnel and the services were withdrawn by the PNG government, forcing all institutions to close down in March 1990. When the blockade was imposed on the island, it left the people without medical services. Today, they are walking for days and weeks before they can find medical help.

In Central Bougainville, a few remaining staff struggled to continue providing basic health care until October 1992 when the PNG Defence Forces landed in Arawa. The October landing forced the closure of the Arawa General Hospital on 12 February 1993. Since then, there has not been a health clinic operating in Central and some parts of South Bougainville. A few health workers have remained on the island but have been unable to operate the small health clinics simply because of a lack of drugs.

The medicines donated by other countries since the blockade have either not been received, or have arrived only in very small quantities. Most drugs destined for Bougainville are either stranded in the Solomon Islands because of very tight security by the PNG Defence Forces at the Solomon Islands/Bougainville border, aimed at preventing border crossings; or they are 'held up' at the government-controlled 'care centres' where they are used by only a minority of Bougainvilleans. The shortage of drugs is more severe in the areas that are not occupied by the military.

But the lack of drugs and medical services is not the only reason why people are dying in their hundreds. The blockade has also deprived Bougainvilleans of their basic human rights and needs. People once had good houses, safe water supplies, good lighting, clothes, soap, toothpaste, love, security and education. But these rights have been taken away from them, leaving them as prisoners of war in their own land.

In addition, people fleeing into the jungles and caves around March 1993 have faced even greater difficulties. The environment has become a continuous threat to their health. Mothers have provided drinks for their babies from contaminated water because they have had no matches to light fires in order to boil water. Our babies are dying in the cold and windy jungle environment because of the lack of clothes and sunlight. The dirty, unhygienic environment under the shade of big trees and in caves, together with the use of unsterilised instruments by untrained village midwives, also explain why there is a high neo-natal death toll.

As an example, I would like to share with you an experience I had in November 1993. A mother who had attended my ante-natal clinic gave birth to her baby before a health worker could arrive at her bush camp. To reach her camp, the health worker had to walk for four hours up a steep mountain. Awaiting the arrival of the health worker, attending village midwives used an unsterilised instrument to cut the umbilical cord. The infant died two weeks later, I suspect of neo-natal sepsis.

Mothers have also been repeated victims of the blockade. Due to the lack of hospital facilities, drugs and clean environments, the lives of many mothers have been lost after contracting problems like puerperal sepsis, post-partum haemorrhage, anaemia and infections such as malaria. One of my more recent experiences of this took place on 18 December 1993. An 18-year-old mother died of severe malaria and anaemia while she was still being carried to the nearest clinic to get medical help. It was a five-hour walk to the clinic. We had only walked the first two hours when she passed away. In March 1993, the same mother had given birth to a dead foetus which had died two days earlier in her uterus. Due to the lack of antibiotics, she was never treated for any possible infection. So she died young, when her death could have been prevented. This is just one example. There are many young mothers who are dying from similar problems because they have no access to medical care.

Where we were in Arawa, when the army landed at Tunuru mission, we women were facing a very hard time, carrying children on our backs, and our luggage, running, moving further up into the mountains. So we were having to carry our belongings and move from Arawa town because they were just throwing mortars from helicopters, they were spraying cars or any object moving around in town ... yes it really happened there. I tell you, my tears came out then when we were running. It was really hard for me carrying our child and my things. It was really frightening for us.

PNG, if they withdraw from the island, life would be back to normal. Not normal, but things would be quietened down and they will sit and talk and find a solution for this crisis. That's one of the main things that the women impressed, that the army should withdraw from Bougainville Island because we've already seen a lot of lives on Bougainville lost -thousands, children and women - and we don't want to go back to Papua New Guinea, how they mistreated us. We are fighting for our own land, we've got all the right because this is our mother land. There are a lot of women and children who have died since this crisis started. Because women and children, we are all innocent uh?

Bougainvillean women, March 1993, (Emberson-Bain 1993)

But there is yet another major threat to the lives of many new born babies. Not one baby born since late 1989, particularly in the PNG-occupied areas of Bougainville, has been vaccinated in protection against childhood illnesses. It is not known if babies in the occupied areas have been vaccinated. We suspect they have not.

It is therefore obvious that children in both occupied and non-occupied areas are suffering and dying from various health problems. One example was confirmed by a media report on 8 January 1994, which revealed that 11 children had died from gastro-enteritis in Siwai in the southern part of Bougainville, which is under PNG government control. Another eyewitness account has confirmed why children in the PNG 'care centres' are dying of diarrhoea. Unhygienic conditions were reported in one centre, with flies and rubbish in living and eating areas. The food people are eating in the centres is mainly rice, canned fish, biscuits and cordial. Such a diet does not help to maintain the health of the people but lowers their resistance to all forms of infection.

All Bougainvilleans, irrespective of where they are - PNG 'care centres' or bush camps controlled by the Bougainville Revolutionary Army (BRA) - are undergoing physical, environmental and psychological torture. Physically, the people are being shot at or bombed, and are being killed as a result. Environmental factors have also cost many people their lives. The drinking of contaminated water by those in hiding and the unhygienic conditions that exist in the bush camps have brought diseases which could have been prevented.

People have also been affected psychologically. I have witnessed a patient who was suffering from hypertension collapsing and (a few hours later) dying, simply out of fear. This took place after she was told of the arrival of the PNG troops in Arawa. I have also struggled to treat a female patient with asthma, and saved her life, when a severe attack was brought on by fear, anxiety and stress. In fact, I can safely say that 100 per cent of Bougainvilleans are today living in a state of fear and anxiety, not knowing what tomorrow will bring. This is itself a health problem. People can no longer continue to endure such conditions.

The diseases and health problems whose incidence has risen since the war, and which have killed many Bougainvilleans, are the following:

- pneumonia - many older people and new born babies have died from this disease

- urinary tract infections - these have affected all age groups, male and female, but are very common amongst teenagers and women, particularly after menstruation

- malaria - this has affected all age groups

- gastro-enteritis - this has mainly affected babies and children

- malnutrition - this has affected mainly children, nursing mothers and older people

- worm infestation - all age groups are affected, particularly from age two years upward

- leprosy - this is affecting all age groups except new born infants

- tuberculosis - all age groups are affected except new born infants

- asthma

- hepatitis

- abdominal pain (PID) - this is very common amongst females of child-bearing age following abortion, still births and deliveries

- enlarged spleen - this affects any age group but is very common amongst children

- arthritis - this has mainly affected adults, both male and female

- skin diseases (tinea, fungus, scabies, boils, eczema, general itchiness) - all age groups are affected

- dental problems - these are affecting men, women and children.

Agenda Item No 12 - Bougainville

My name is Ruby Mirinka. I am a nurse educator and have recently escaped from behind the Papua New Guinea (PNG) blockade of my island, Bougainville. I was accompanying 12 patients who were seeking urgent medical treatment in the Solomon Islands. I am standing in this Assembly as a mother, health worker and educator, and one who has been witness to the tragic effects of the blockade on Bougainville for the last five years. This blockade is genocidal and must be condemned by this Commission.

For five years our people, particularly mothers and children, have gravely suffered. They have died tragically behind 'closed doors'. It is the strong wish of the mothers and children of Bougainville, whom I represent today, that I convey to this Commission the need for a workable strategy to end the sufferings of our people. These sufferings continue as I speak to you.

Since 1991, as a result of the blockade, more than 5,000 people have died from normal preventable diseases like malaria, pneumonia, gastro-enteritis, tuberculosis and urinary tract infections. In addition, babies are born under very tragic situations. They are born on leaves under trees, or in caves, delivered without clothes and hospital facilities, as a result of the blockade. Mothers are delivering their babies and are bleeding to death because there are no hospital facilities to give them the transfusions they need to save their lives.

Mothers and babies are carried on stretchers to be rushed to the nearest clinic but often die on the road. Because we are living in the jungle, when it rains we must cut the leaves from banana trees to cover our children from the rain. And to keep our children alive in the jungle, we carry food on our backs through steep and rugged mountains 12 hours every day. This has weakened the strength and health of our mothers. Our husbands have died while searching for food for their families.

.... Strafing of our villages by Iroquois helicopter gunships is an everyday event. Mortar bombardment from the PNG army has destroyed many of our villages and food gardens. On two occasions - 24 and 27 January 1994 - mothers and children were bombarded in their food gardens in the Koromira area by a PNG military plane. The smoke from these bombs makes our skin itchy and sore; the children scratch this itchiness which causes sores on their skins; and these become ulcers that cannot be treated. The chemicals from these bomb explosions have also contaminated our food gardens. Malnutrition is therefore a big problem with our people. We, the women and children, should not be targets of the PNG military campaign. This is an inhuman action.

Mr Chairman Sir, the women of Bougainville appeal to this Commission to find a workable strategy to promote an involvement of all Bougainvillean leaders with Papua New Guinea to open dialogue, to end the sufferings as soon as possible, and to determine the political future of Bougainville. The blockade must be lifted by PNG as a matter of urgency. In line with this Commission's 1993 resolutions, international fact-finding missions must be allowed to visit my people; free movement for all people must be restored; and health services must be immediately restored. Most importantly, there must be an end to the conflict and a negotiated settlement.

Address to the 50th Session of the International Working Group on Indigenous Affairs, United Nations Commission on Human Rights, Geneva, 1994

Conclusion

All Bougainvilleans, irrespective of where they are on the island, are suffering and dying as a result of the war. Their sufferings must not be allowed to continue. People have reached a point where they can no longer endure the criminal torture inflicted upon them. It is in this state of despair that the following recommendations have emerged with a view to ending the suffering.

1. That as a first step the Papua New Guinea government permit Bougainvillean leaders in both PNG-controlled and other areas to seek ways of settling the differences amongst themselves.

2. That the United Nations find a workable strategy to promote dialogue between Bougainvillean leaders and PNG, and to determine the political future of Bougainville.

3. That the blockade be lifted to allow the restoration of health services, education, the free movement of the people, and the rehabilitation and reconstruction of the whole island.

*   This paper is based on a report prepared for the United Nations, Geneva, in January 1994

Reference

Emberson-Bain, 'A. (1993) *Bougainville: Women's voices from a Pacific war zone,* 30 minute radio documentary

Twenty-Two

Militarism and market mania in Fiji*

Kushma Ram

Background

Fiji's post-independence (1970) experiment with multiracial democracy crudely ended in 1987, when its military forces, with the connivance of an ethnic Fijian feudal aristocracy - the Council of Chiefs - removed the first multiracial and labour-led government from power through the force of the gun. The military unleashed a wave of terror aimed at marginalising the ethnic Fijian leaders of the Fiji Labour Party (FLP) and crippling the leadership of the Fiji Indian worker and small-holder cane farming community. Fiji Indians had been brought to the country between 1879 and 1917 to work on the sugar plantations as indentured labourers.

A Fiji Labour Party-led government, of which the powerful, multiracial Fiji Trades Union Congress (FTUC) provided the main support base, was elected to office in April 1987. It represented the first multiracial, working class challenge to the 17-year political reign of a largely (Fijian) chiefly-led and big business-backed Alliance Party. Expatriate commercial interests including powerful multinational companies, and a local business class, had provided the main pillars of support for successive Alliance governments. Contrary to persisting popular myths, the military coups of 1987 took place not because multiracialism had failed, but because it was finally beginning to challenge, with some success, the big business and transnational forces dominating the economy. In fact, there has been evidence of big business collusion in the destabilisation campaign prior to the military coups. The Australian mining company, Emperor Gold Mining Company Ltd, played a part in these political activities[1].

The military upheavals and resulting tensions in Fijian society caused a dramatic downturn in the economy and led to a period of general instability. Tourism collapsed overnight as violence, ethnic tensions and the ugly effects of military rule destroyed the 'romantic' image of the country as an attractive holiday destination. The sugar industry, the backbone of the Fijian economy from the outset of British colonial rule in 1870, ground to a halt as small-holder growers and labourers staged the longest boycott of the sugar cane harvest in Fiji's history to pressure the regime to relinquish power. Unions in Australia and New Zealand swiftly imposed trade bans as a form of pressure. Investor confidence eroded overnight and 1987 saw a massive decline (12%) in gross domestic product (GDP). Investment fell from an average 25 per cent of GDP between 1982 and 1985 to a meagre eight per cent in 1988. Official unemployment increased from seven per cent to well over 20 per cent by early 1988, with only the service sector showing employment gains as a result of large-scale recruitment into the military (Government of Fiji 1994a; FTUC 1990).

A single dawn

A dawn of freedom
glitters on the chains of today
mildewed, rusted, yet senselessly laden
Agonies of yesterday
newly awaken
the memorable break of early a day
from the chain of servitude

A dawn of freedom
strikes on the solitude of a century
sweated, and blooded
And yesterday's dreams
painfully aborted
from a colonial yoke
delivered into new bond, re-newed agony
into new-colonialism

A dawn of freedom
envelops a barren, fertile but land
        unprepared
Cultivated by a century of hate
watered with fear, division and lust
to benefit a few
A century of struggle
and a single dawn of freedom

Kushma Ram

Prior to 1987, Fiji enjoyed moderate economic growth and stability. With a per capita income of approximately $FIJ 1,900, it had moved into the rungs of the top 15 'developing' countries. But under pressure from the International Monetary Fund (IMF) and the World Bank to control the influence of its trade unions over the policy-making process, particularly in light of their success in securing modest wage increases between 1977 and 1983 through the Tripartite Forum, Fiji became the only South Pacific Island state, according to the World Bank, to experience a decline in per capita incomes between 1987 and 1991. The IMF had in fact suggested as early as 1983 that wages in Fiji were 15 per cent too high, criticism that resulted in the government's unilateral imposition of a national wage freeze in 1984. The ramifications of the freeze went beyond its adverse impact on incomes and living standards. It brought to an end an era of industrial relations in which workers had enjoyed some access to state power. The wage freeze and the marginalisation of the trade unions from the policy-making process after 1984 led to the formation of the Fiji Labour Party (FLP) in 1985. Barely two years later, the FLP brought about the first change in political power. Its momentous achievement was, however, to be short-lived.

Post-May 1987 stabilisation

With the country steeped in its deepest political and economic crisis, the military regime took steps to fundamentally transform the national economy. Drastic stabilisation measures were immediately applied. They included a 33 per cent devaluation of the Fiji dollar, an immediate 15 per cent wage cut, severe controls on foreign exchange transactions and movements, affecting even those wishing to migrate permanently, a halt on public infrastructural developments, a freeze on public sector recruitment (with the exception of the military) and numerous other measures including controls on the migration of skilled labour. These and other policies forming part of a long-term structural adjustment of the economy revealed a contemptuous disregard for working people, particularly women.

Structural adjustment

It is significant that it was in the depths of a traumatic political and social crisis, and as the military strengthened its control, that Fiji's government began to implement comprehensive measures to reform the economy according to standard World Bank prescriptions. In contrast to past practice, no pretence of consultation over these policies was made. Fiji's structural adjustment programme included the following:

1. The privatisation of major public enterprises beginning with the corporatisation of the most successful public sector enterprise, Fiji Post and Telecommunications.

2. Corporatisation of other public sector enterprises such as the Fiji Broadcasting Corporation, sections of the Public Works Department, and over 15 other key units (Government of Fiji 1994b).

3. Adoption of user-pay schemes in health, education and other social services. Notably, basic health care was made available without charge during the one-month reign of the FLP-led government in 1987. Since its overthrow, hospital outpatient fees have been reintroduced, and health charges are likely to be increased over the next three years. Public sector corporate bodies like

the Fiji Electricity Authority increased their tariffs by over 30 per cent between 1987 and 1990.

4. The implementation of a tax-free system for export processing enterprises with concessions like 13-year tax holidays, free repatriation of profits and full exemption on local equity requirements. A comprehensive range of incentives designed to lure foreign and local investors into export sectors of the economy included the de facto relaxation of occupational health and safety regulations in the tax-free factories.

5. The removal of import and export licensing and other protective trade barriers, with the professed aim of making Fiji's relatively high-wage manufacturing sector (drinks, cement, paint, confectionery, matches, soap etc.) and other sectors like dairy farming and rice production more competitive with the low-wage economies of Asia.

Removal of economic protection, or the so-called 'levelling of the playing field', has already resulted in production cutbacks in certain domestic sectors. The viability of many industries has been undermined by the dumping of cheap products from Association of South-East Asian Nations (ASEAN) countries. In the absence of fair trade legislation, the country is being exposed to products of an inferior quality, some of which may pose health hazards. Domestic manufacturing industries such as Carlton Brewery, Hume Industries (South Seas) Ltd, Fiji Forest Industries and Rewa Dairy were relatively high-wage areas of the economy with minimum wages close to $FIJ 2.00 per hour. Production cutbacks have lowered not only production levels but also wages and employment levels in such industries. In September 1994, the government announced that it was closing down the Rewa Rice Irrigation Scheme through which over 500 farmers cultivated rice as their sole income-generating crop (*Fiji Times* 8 September 1994).

By 1987, Fiji's rice industry - which has received local investment of over $FIJ 30 million - had achieved 80 per cent self-sufficiency. An industry on which some 50,000 people depend for their subsistence now stands on the verge of collapse in the wake of cutbacks in state support and cheap imports from Thailand and other ASEAN countries. Fiji's Finance Minister has publically stated that the industry will simply have to fold up if it cannot compete! The dairy industry, on which some 25,000 people depend for their livelihoods, is similarly poised to collapse. Both industries, which have traditionally drawn on domestic capital resources, have already witnessed a considerable decline in employment and income levels (Chand et al. 1993).

6. A comprehensive reform of the country's labour laws intended to crush the trade union movement has shifted the basis of industrial negotiations towards enterprise bargaining (so weakening the larger, more powerful unions). The reforms have made it nearly impossible for unions to take effective strike action, and they have banned international solidarity actions and secondary union action taken locally. The reforms have also been aimed at destroying the political potential of the trade union movement.

As part of the reform package, Decrees 18 and 19 of 1991 stipulated a 14-year prison sentence, together with a $10,000 fine for unions and individuals agitating for stop-work actions once a strike was declared illegal[2]. The Minister for Labour was given sweeping powers under these decrees to declare almost any industrial action illegal. On the eve of a massive national strike organised by the FTUC in July 1991, Fiji's President ordered the suspension of the decrees. They nevertheless remain on the statute books. Similar reforms were legislated subsequently, in particular the infamous Decrees 42, 43 and 44 which impose compulsory secret ballots and state supervision for all union elections, strike mandates and other union actions. Secondary action has been branded illegal; and unions can be held liable for production losses due to industrial action[3]. An FTUC complaint with the International Labour Organisation (ILO) Freedom of Association Committee has resulted in a damning critique of the unilateral changes to Fiji's labour laws. The reaction of the Fiji Government was to withdraw from the ILO Conference in 1990 and 1991.

7. The deregulation of wages in 1991, formally removing the national wage guidelines which had worked to the advantage of unorganised and poorly organised sectors (such as the garment trade), which were mainly dominated by women. Until 1984, the Tripartite Forum had set national wage guidelines. A deregulated incomes policy has resulted in severe downward pressure on wages in the manufacturing sector, and in sectors where unions have a marginal presence.

8. A comprehensive reform of taxation which saw the introduction of a general consumption tax (VAT) of 10 per cent alongside a reduction in corporate and personal income tax.

Overall, the policies comprising Fiji's structural adjustment purportedly aimed to enhance exports and competitiveness in the international economy; reduce government deficits and hence external borrowing; improve Fiji's external debt exposure - debt servicing in 1987 grew to 35 per cent of government revenues (Chand et al. 1993); provide a basis for sustained growth without subsidies or other forms of state support; enhance the quality of life in the context of an allegedly stagnant economic environment; and shift the focus of economic development away from the state to the private sector (making no distinction between domestic or multinational capital). Between 1988 and 1990, the foundations of adjustment were firmly laid. This meant that by the time an elected government took office in 1992 under a new racially discriminatory, feudalist and authoritarian constitution, the economic landscape of Fiji had been fundamentally altered. The net results of structural adjustment show how the global neo-liberal free market agenda has compromised the integrity and well-being of a vulnerable economy.

Some broad consequences of structural adjustment

One of the crudest consequences of structural adjustment in Fiji has been the country's transition from a middle-level income country to a low-wage economy in the relatively short period of five years, thereby making it a suitable site for transnational investment. The post-1991 wage deregulation policies have promoted the deterioration of wages in the unskilled and unorganised sectors, where the vast majority of workers are employed and the tax-free enterprises are concentrated. The beneficial effects of a national wage guideline were previously passed on to workers throughout the economy. Since 1991, however, only well-organised sectors such as finance, civil aviation and telecommunications have recorded real wage increases (Ram 1991). In 1992, only 35,000 workers (out of a total 91,000 in wage and salaried employment) or 38 per cent of the workforce were members of trade unions. Of these, only 15 unions (out of a total 35) secured wage increases in excess of six per cent. Significantly, over the previous 12 months, the consumer price index (CPI) hovered at 5.5 per cent. Wage deregulation has exposed workers to the far superior bargaining power of their employers, and for the vast majority has helped lower prevailing wage rates.

Another point to bear in mind is that wage and salaried workers constitute only one-third of the total labour force. The majority of adults are subsistence workers (with no or negligible cash incomes), unpaid homemakers or officially unemployed. Without fixed or regular cash incomes, they nevertheless increasingly depend on the market economy for their subsistence. In assessing the effects of economic adjustment on employment, income levels etc., this structural feature of the labour force needs to be remembered. When consumer prices increase (as they did with the introduction of VAT), or when income levels of workers deteriorate, they directly erode the conditions of life for people in the subsistence as well as the formal sectors of the economy.

Deregulation, as stated earlier, has exposed several primary industries like dairy and rice farming to the possibility of total collapse, and the social costs of adjustment in these two sectors have already become visible. Since 1987, deregulation has also led to a considerable decline in employment in the domestic-oriented areas of the manufacturing sector. Approximately 3,000 jobs have been lost since mid-1987 (FTUC 1990 & Naidu 1994). Workers in these industries enjoyed much better wages and working conditions than those in the tax-free garment industry.

The corporatisation of Fiji's Housing Authority, the principal source of low-cost homes in urban areas, has seriously aggravated the problem of housing low-income earners in urban areas. Over the past two years, a World Bank revision of housing tariffs and loan repayment policies has resulted in the eviction of hundreds of families from low-cost Housing Authority homes. This has exacerbated the squatter problem in the main urban centres, and added a tremendous strain on low-wage families. Severe overcrowding, as a way of cutting housing costs, has also been a visible result of this. Social, health and other consequences of this development will no doubt become more marked over the next few years. More generally, Fiji's housing problem has worsened as a result of escalating house rentals in key urban areas like Suva, Lautoka and Nadi (rising by more than 300% over the past four years).

VAT and the poor

One of Fiji's most significant tax reforms has been the introduction of a 10 per cent consumption tax (VAT) on goods and services. In spite of trade-offs in the form of reduced personal tax (the highest rate being reduced from 47% to 35%), research findings show that about 65 per cent of workers earned below $FIJ 5,000 per year (the tax threshold) in 1990 and were therefore not eligible for income tax reductions. Accordingly, VAT has meant that the majority of workers are simply worse off because it represents an additional (not an alternative) tax. It is essentially a tax on the poorest segment of society. At the other end of the spectrum, those earning above $FIJ 15,000 per year were better off (in absolute terms) because of the lowering of income tax rates.

VAT has compounded the debilitating effects of declining employment and a general fall in incomes in the low-wage sectors. Our surveys have shown that it has had a visibly negative effect on family nutrition and health, the burden of which falls mainly upon women in the household (FWRM 1992). While opposition to the tax from trade unions, the FLP and other community groups has prompted the government to offer some concessions (exemptions for medicine and agricultural implements for example), none of these have yet been brought into effect.

Letter to the Colonel

sir some people are sad
because of your words
and actions
that is why i bring you
this cup of kava
from your neighbour's soil

it contains the tears
of workers, farmers, miners
fisherfolk who go down
to the depths of adopted
seas for food
many have lost their jobs
robbed of opportunities
to make a profit
here, take it anyway
symbol of suffering and sorrow
of women

in the fields
in garment factories
at home where children
cry out their fears and frustration
take it, sir, it is yours

ah, but you see, sir
for some this cup is full
of hope
when you drink it you
will know your victory
like the kava it comes
from the roots
of people's hopes in the land
their collective confidence
will lift you up
their new-found pride
will bloom around you
while they wait
for their duty-bound son
to bury his weapons
and liberate their souls

and by the way, sir
i hope that as you drink this
you will remember
that when the dawn breaks
no one can shut out
the light
       Konai Helu-Thaman

Fiji's tax-free garment industry

The tax-free garment industry - one of the classic showpieces of structural adjustment in developing countries - has provided almost the entire basis for Fiji's post-coup economic recovery. The implementation of the tax-free system in 1988 saw most of the existing garment factories converting to tax-free status. Since then, several enterprises from New Zealand and Australia have relocated to Fiji to take advantage of the 13-year tax holiday and numerous other benefits, together with the guaranteed preferential access into their home markets under the South Pacific Regional Trade and Economic Cooperation Agreement (SPARTECA). A total of 12 large enterprises from the ASEAN region also opened up operations in the country to take advantage of the new incentives as well as guaranteed access into the US, European Community and Australasian markets. It is in these circumstances that the garment industry grew from a $FIJ 2 million export industry into a $FIJ 160 million industry by 1992, with employment rising from 3,000 in 1986 to approximately 9,000 by the end of 1992 (Reserve Bank of Fiji 1992).

However, there is another side to the picture. Over 95 per cent of workers in this showpiece industry are women, many of whom had been laid off from jobs in the relatively high-wage industries of the manufacturing sector after the post-coup economic collapse. It was not until 1991 that the first minimum wage order was legislated for garment workers, following a vigorous domestic and international campaign by women's organisations and the trade unions. The starting wage in the industry was then about $FIJ 1,800 per year, as much as 64 per cent short of the $FIJ 5,000 per annum official (urban) poverty level wage estimated by government. Under the 1991 order, the minimum wage was set. This amounted to no more than 75 per cent of the rate prescribed by a tripartite team in 1982, some ten years earlier (Prasad 1991). It was also only 40 per cent of the prevailing rate in the organised manufacturing sectors.

In 1992, a FTUC study revealed contraventions of even this low minimum wage in 20 per cent of the enterprises surveyed (Prasad 1991). However, not a single prosecution for minimum wage violations has been recorded to date. Nor have there been prosecutions in relation to the widespread breaching of occupational health and safety standards, recorded by both the unions and the government itself. In fact, the industry was given a 12-month grace period in which to comply with health and safety standards laid down in national legislation. Despite the expiry of this period in mid-1990, contraventions continue to be recorded. One of the danger signals for garment workers would seem to be the direct equity stake in the industry held by members of Fiji's current ruling elite[4].

The entry of large numbers of women into one of the lowest wage sectors of the workforce also has major social implications which are only beginning to be recognised. These include the growing incidence of domestic violence and declining nutrition standards amongst children. Household data on women garment workers is currently being compiled by the Fiji Women's Rights Movement. Garment workers are forced to work exceptionally long hours. According to a sample survey, the average working week is 60 hours (compared to the 45 hours/week industrial average). In spite of legislation prohibiting the employment of women after 8 pm, employers operate on a shift basis, with overtime known to continue long after 8 pm. There are known cases of women being given medication to enable them to endure long hours of work. Despite the highly exploitative conditions of work, including the failure of employers to pay overtime or to provide meals or transport to night workers, there has been no attempt by Fiji's political rulers to demand better standards. Instead, they have recommended lifting the 8 pm restriction which is almost certain to pave the way for deteriorating conditions[5].

To date, only seven out of 111 employers in the industry have recognised the Fiji Garment, Textiles and Allied Workers Union (Prasad 1991) and entered into collective agreements. Most have opposed efforts to organise the workforce. Some have even closed operations to pre-empt a compulsory union recognition order, only to reopen under another name a few weeks later, in the same factory. It is highly unlikely that the industry will enjoy a significant degree of unionisation over the next few years, thus ensuring that Fiji's new-found status as a low-wage economy will be preserved.

The garment industry is mainly controlled by expatriate interests that show little sign of any long-term commitment to the economy, and many of their factories would most likely close operations once the SPARTECA preferences wind down. The boom in tax-free factories has not resulted in a construction boom which would be a useful indicator of long-term commitment by foreign investors. Instead, investors have come to Fiji because of its 13-year tax holiday and preferential markets. Indeed, besides the employment it has generated, the contribution of the garment industry to the economy as a whole is insignificant. There are no gains to the economy from corporate tax exemptions. There is no revenue generated for the state through employee taxes because over 95 per cent of workers earn incomes below the tax threshold. There are no duties on imported raw materials or machinery. There are no export taxes. All profits can be repatriated. Investors can raise their initial capital on the domestic financial market at preferential rates. In fact, in a number of ways, the industry represents a burden to the non tax-free economy as it passes on the costs of infrastructure, subsidised land and electricity, and health. Despite these obvious economic

246

disadvantages, the garment industry continues to be heralded as the way of the future. It continues to be projected as the basis for long-term growth and development.

Conclusion

This paper has tried to demonstrate the political context in which Fiji's structural adjustment programmes have been implemented as well as their impact upon the country and its people, particularly women. The social and economic costs of these programmes are proving to be severe, especially for workers, women and children. Adjustment has been imposed upon the people through the barrel of a gun - by an illegitimate regime - with callous disregard for the views and interests of the people. It is worth remembering this context. Equally disturbing is the way in which adjustment has been 'sold' by global financial lords like the World Bank, because this has the potential to undermine the very basis of democracy that we are trying so hard to restore. The challenge before us is therefore not solely concerned with narrow economic rights, but with protecting and advancing fundamental human rights.

*   This is a revised version of a paper presented to the South Pacific Peoples Foundation Conference on Globalisation and Structural Adjustment, Victoria, Canada, in May 1993

Notes

1.   See for example Howard (1991); Robertson & Tamanisau (1989); and Bain & Baba (1990).

2.   The Sugar Industry (Special Protection) (Amendment) (No 3) Decree, No 18, 1991 and the Protection of the National Economy Decree, No 19, 1991 (Fiji Republic 1991a & b).

3.   Industrial Associations Act (Amendment) Decree No 42, 1991; Trade Unions (Recognition) Act (Amendment) Decree No 43, 1991; Trade Unions Act (Amendment) Decree No 44, 1991 (Fiji Republic 1991c, d & e).

4.   For a discussion of the unregulated working environment in the garment industry, including the lack of law enforcement and charges of complicity between the government and the manufacturing lobby, see Emberson-Bain (1992) and Emberson-Bain & Slatter (1993).

5.   See Emberson-Bain & Slatter (1993) for a discussion of the ideology and practice of the night work ban with respect to garment and other women workers.

References

Bain, 'A. and Baba, T. (eds) (1990) *Bavadra - Prime Minister, statesman, man of the people: Selection of speeches and writings 1985-1989,* Nadi, Fiji: Sunrise Press

Chand, G., Prasad, B.C., Reddy, M. and Chand, A. (1993) *The woes of structural adjustment policies: The Fiji government budget,* Research Report Series No.3, November, Suva: Fiji Institute of Applied Studies

Emberson-Bain, A. (1992) 'Fiji: Women, poverty and post-coup pressure' in Robie, D. *Tu galala: Social change in the Pacific,* Sydney: Bridget Williams Books/Pluto Press

Emberson-Bain, 'A. and Slatter, S. (1993) 'Labouring under the law: A feminist critique of employment legislation affecting women in Fiji', unpublished research paper prepared for the Fiji Women's Rights Movement, Suva, Fiji

Fiji Trades Union Congress (1990) 'Submission to the national economic summit', Suva, Fiji

Fiji Times 8 September 1994

Fiji Republic (1991a) *Sugar Industry (Special Protection) (Amendment) (No 3) Decree No 18,* Suva: Fiji Republic Gazette, vol.5, no.37

------- (1991b) *Protection of the National Economy Decree No 19,* Suva: Fiji Republic Gazette, vol.5, no.37

------- (1991c) *Industrial Associations Act (Amendment) Decree No 42,* Suva: Fiji Republic Gazette, vol.5, no.77

------- (1991e) *Trade Unions Act (Amendment) Decree No 44,* Suva: Fiji Republic Gazette, vol.5, no.77

------- (1991d) *Trade Unions (Recognition) Act (Amendment) Decree No 43,* Suva: Fiji Republic Gazette, vol.5, no.77

Fiji Women's Rights Movement (FWRM) (1992) 'Investigation into working conditions for women in employment', unpublished data compiled by FWRM, Suva, Fiji

Government of Fiji (1994b) *Privatisation policy and strategy for Fiji,* Supplement to the 1994 Budget Address by the Minister of Finance and Public Enterprises, Suva, Fiji

Government of Fiji (1994a) *Current Economic Statistics,* Bureau of Statistics, April, Suva: Government Printer

Howard, C. (1991) *Fiji: Race and politics in an island state,* Vancouver, Canada: University of British Columbia Press

Naidu, R. (1994) 'The shackles of SPARTECA' in *The Review,* June

Prasad, S. (1991) 'Survey of Fiji's garment industry', unpublished document prepared for the Fiji Trades Union Congress, Suva, Fiji

Ram, K. (1991) 'Report of pay and working conditions of garment workers in Fiji', unpublished research paper for International Confederation of Free Trade Unions - Asia Pacific Regional Office (ICFTU-APRO)/Fiji Trades Union Congress (FTUC), Singapore

Reserve Bank of Fiji (1992) *News Review,* vol.1

Robertson, R.T. and Tamanisau, A. (1989) 'Fiji, race, class and the military' in *Development and Change,* 20:203-234

Twenty-Three

How democratic is our democracy?

Women and politics in Papua New Guinea

Orovu Sepoe

Introduction

Lack of participation or limited participation by women in politics is a crucial development issue. This is particularly true in the third world (Jahan 1984). But while there is increasing acknowledgment of the fact that, in a comparatively short space of time, some third world women have 'made it' in various spheres of contemporary life, such as formal education, employment and business, this has not generally been so for politics. Certainly, for Papua New Guinea (PNG), women's integration into the political domain as part of post-independence 'development' has not occurred. In politics, it appears that women have to struggle even harder to break through the barrier of male dominance, particularly at the national level. Unlike the bureaucracy, where jobs are offered largely on the basis of formal merit, access to political power through competition in an open political field with men of all calibres and persuasions is proving a much more difficult task.

This is a global phenomenon. Women all around the world have discovered that politics is a no-woman's land. Even among the exceptional women who have made it to the top in politics, it is amazing what proportion of them have done so as 'stand-ins' for their slain or otherwise 'departed' husbands and fathers. Why have women not been successful in entering the highest political decision-making arena? No doubt the answers to this simple, yet difficult, question would be numerous. However, one crucial factor which hinders women is that - compared to men - they have limited access to strategic resources (such as wealth, property, bank loans and, above all, supportive values embedded in the political culture) which determine or at least facilitate success in politics. Only a tiny minority of women manage to brave these obstacles and enter electoral politics. Who are these women candidates? The answer to this question reflects the complex (in particular the class) factors that underlie the political and development processes in PNG.

Women in PNG politics

In September 1975, PNG attained formal independence. The system of government adopted was the Westminster parliamentary model. Today, contrary to experiences elsewhere, for example in Africa, a thriving multi-party system is still intact. In an era when colonialism was internationally despised, and the desire for democracy for all peoples - of all races, colours and creeds - was recognised, the women of PNG received specific mention of their equal status as citizens. In the prevailing egalitarian climate, the Constitution of the newly independent state ushered in a 'national goal of equality and participation' specifically for its female citizens: '... *equal participation by women citizens in all political, economic, social and religious activities'.*

Official calls for increased participation

At both international and national levels, there are calls for greater participation by women in politics. In a recent National Convention for Women in PNG, the so-called 'Madang Declaration' called on the government to nominate at least **one** woman to the national parliament. According to the new President of the National Council of Women - a prominent women's rights activist and former politician - the November 1993 sitting of parliament would see a woman nominee for the first time in PNG's political history; this would witness the implementation of a special section of the Constitution. The bipartisan committee charged with discussing constitutional changes also recommended that regional seats in parliament be reserved for women to contest at every national election. At the international level, the 1993 Commonwealth Heads of Government Meeting called upon governments to make a concerted effort to increase the level of participation of women in the higher echelons of decision making.

(i)   Provincial and local politics

Up-to-date statistical information about provincial- and local-level participation is lacking for the entire country. Despite this, it is possible to form some general impressions about the current situation. At the provincial and local levels of government, participation by women is low. These levels are dominated by conservative elements in our society, making it almost impossible for women to venture into the formal political sphere. However, a handful of women has entered electoral politics as candidates, thereby making some inroads into the centres of power and authority. One case is worthy of special mention since it was a significant historical breakthrough for the women of PNG. In Morobe Province, Mrs Enny Moaitz, who was initially elected as a provincial member, later became the Premier (1988-89), the first woman Premier in the history of provincial government in PNG. Currently, the entire country has only one elected woman provincial member - Laura Martin. Although she failed to get elected in the 1992 national election, upon her second attempt to enter electoral politics at the provincial level, she won comfortably. Laura Martin is a naturalised citizen of PNG and a business woman.

In July 1992, in PNG's Central Province, three women candidates contested the elections. One of them took third place in a field of nine candidates but polled 50 per cent fewer votes than the winning candidate. The other two women polled poorly - fourth out of four candidates and seventh out of eight candidates (*Post Courier* 29 July 1993). Throughout the country, provincial-and local-level participation in electoral politics is generally low compared to performance at the national level.

(ii)   Women in national politics

In 1961, well before independence and in the period prior to national elections, the colonial government appointed Alice Wedega to be a woman representative in the Legislative Council (Lynch 1962). Wedega was a women's rights activist, representing the Territory of Papua and New Guinea at a United Nations Economic and Social Commission for Asia and the Pacific (ESCAP) Conference for Women's Advancement held in New Zealand. In 1972, four women contested. Only one of the four, (now Dame) Josephine Abaijah, was elected to the Central regional seat. This was a very significant breakthrough for women as participants in electoral politics in PNG. However, in terms of influencing decision making for women's advancement, Abaijah's presence was insignificant. Successionist politics interested her more than women's advancement (Griffin, Nelson & Firth 1984).

Since the 1972 elections, PNG has held four national elections, all in the post-independence era. Only three women have won seats. In the first post-independence election of 1977, a total of 10 women candidates contested, including Dame Josephine Abaijah. Only two, Waliyato Clowes (for Middle Fly Open) and Nahau Rooney (for Manus Open), won seats. In the 1982 election, all three - Abaijah, Clowes and Rooney - stood with 14 other women. Only Rooney won her seat, and this was only after a successful appeal in the Court of Disputed Returns. In 1987, Rooney and 17 other women (including Abaijah once again) contested. All women candidates were defeated.

The 1992 Election

(i)   *Candidates*

Of the 1,653 candidates who contested the 1992 election, 16 were women, with 13 of them standing for the 'geographically smaller and less populous' (open) seats (Turner & Hegarty 1987). The beginning of electoral politics in 1964 saw three women, one indigenous and two expatriates, stand whilst in 1968 only one woman contested. 'All polled poorly.' (Lucas 1987). The National Capital District (NCD) regional electorate, with its more developed communication/transport network, and a record of at least one woman candidate in each election since 1977, had two women candidates in 1992, making it an exceptional provincial (regional) seat. In line with past election trends, the greatest number of women stood for seats in the NCD. In other parts of the country, only veterans such as Abaijah considered vying for the larger and more populous provincial seats.

(ii)   *Party Affiliation*

Significantly, not a single woman candidate who contested the election received formal party endorsement. All stood as independent candidates.

(iii)   *Outcome*

Overall, the outcome of the election was disappointing for those who had hoped to see women succeed at the polls. All women candidates were unsuccessful. Just one candidate, the veteran and former member of the House of Assembly (1972-77) and Member of Parliament (1977-82), Josephine Abaijah, secured second place to the winning candidate, although with a large shortfall of 14,700 votes behind the winner. The second-best performance amongst the women candidates was that of another veteran politician, Enny Moaitz, who came fourth out of a total of 19 candidates in the Huon Gulf Open. In the NCD, Margaret Loko performed best amongst the women, coming fifth out of a total of 18 candidates. However, she only polled about half the number of votes of the winning candidate. Altogether the women candidates polled well below 50 per cent of the total number of votes cast for the winning candidates. Most scored less than five per cent of total votes cast in their respective electorates (Electoral Commission of Papua New Guinea 1992a).

(iv)   *Analysis of outcome: Past and present*

As in 1987, the 1992 election turned out to be one without a successful bid by a woman for a seat in the national parliament. A second consecutive electoral defeat for **all** women candidates raises a certain amount of anxiety amongst women activists and advocates. What have women got to do to become accepted as capable of representing voters in the national legislature? What factors account for their poor election performance? I offer two hypotheses.

First, the nature of PNG politics seriously diminishes the chances of women being elected to the highest legislative body in the land. Specifically, the country's political culture emphatically casts women aside as casualties in electoral politics in spite of the constitutional guarantees of mass (male and female) public participation in the political process. Systematically and unconstitutionally, it denies women equal participation in positions of power. Thus, irrespective of the formal constitutional guarantees, certain features of PNG politics adversely affect the chances of women being elected.

Second, women are not a homogeneous category. Differences amongst them abound. There are obvious socio-economic or class differences such as levels of economic attainment, occupation and income, and cultural, ethnic, religious and many more social cleavages which make women just as heterogeneous as any other group in society. The very small percentage of women who contest elections undoubtedly belong to the elite in society - those with relatively high levels of income, who are educated, and who have often held relatively high or powerful positions in the modern, formal sector. It is very unusual to see rural, less-educated, low-income earners standing for national elections.

254

a.   Political culture

The 'National Goals and Directive Principles' of PNG's Constitution have remained largely 'pen and paper' and the 'word' of politicians because of the style of politics which has developed and is still prevalent in the country. A bargaining process characterises the political system. This is essentially pragmatic and opportunist (Saffu 1982). Actors or participants in the political process engage in bargaining in order to gain access to the centre of political power. Amongst the participants, political parties are particularly interesting because of their significant impact on other actors (be these female or male candidates) and the process in general.

In PNG, political parties are extremely unstable; and rarely are they ideological groupings. This is why, since independence, the country has always had coalition governments usually formed by loosely allied political parties, lacking firm policy commitments. In the event that women's issues are raised, this poses a challenge to competing claims from many other interest groups. In the absence of firm policy stands, any actor in the process can voice similar policy issues, or specifically appeal on women's issues, making use of the opportunity to win votes. Thus, opportunism - claiming concern for women's interests and needs - is another aspect of the bargaining political style of PNG. The development of such a political culture has significantly contributed to making casualties of women candidates in electoral politics.

Numbers matter more than policy issues. Whether or not women candidates voice concern for women's issues, those who contest elections are themselves manifestations of these issues. Their participation in the electoral process is in itself a statement about women's presence in a firmly established male domain. Over the years, political parties have expressed concern for (and included) women's issues in their party platforms, but concrete support has been very shallow indeed. The 1992 election provided stark proof of this. None of the women candidates were party affiliates (Electoral Commission of Papua New Guinea 1992). All stood as Independents in 14 electorates. In the electorates they contested, only four of the winners were Independents. The rest who won seats - 10 altogether - were affiliates of the major parties operating in PNG, namely PANGU, the Papua Action Party, the Melanesian Alliance, the National Party and the People's Democratic Party.

It is evident that calculations for possible coalitions begin prior to the elections. A pragmatic process, this (implicitly) projects potential women candidates as liabilities. After all, women are newcomers to politics which has been a man's game throughout PNG's political history. Political parties would, at all costs, avoid the risk of losing power and would maximise their chances of gaining it. Women are inevitably left out. As long as PNG politics remains a numbers game - another consequence of its bargaining style - what difference would it make to have **no** women at all in the countdown towards coalition formation or its maintenance?

b.   Elite politics

The irony of the historical record of women as national politicians is that the highest number of women in parliament (i.e. three) was achieved in the first national parliament, whereas there are none in the fourth post-independence poll. One would expect there to be more women Members of Parliament now.

Why aren't there any women in the current parliament - 17 years after independence?

The political environment of 1977 is significant here. PNG had gained independence just two years earlier. The system was fresh and relatively free of entrenched interests - whether economic, social, intellectual or political. The predominance of a nationalist ideology and the concept of unity meant that sectional interests or other social cleavages became secondary. These interests did not matter much as most people enjoyed a similar standard of living and lifestyle. Politics as a means to rapid wealth had also not become so obvious then. But in PNG today, it takes money and investment to make money, and even to enter politics. And where are the women with thousands of *kina* of their own to enable them to compete? The noticeable absence of women in the nation's highest political offices is a clear indication that secondary or sectional interests, which have become more clearly defined, are now a potent force in the politics of PNG.

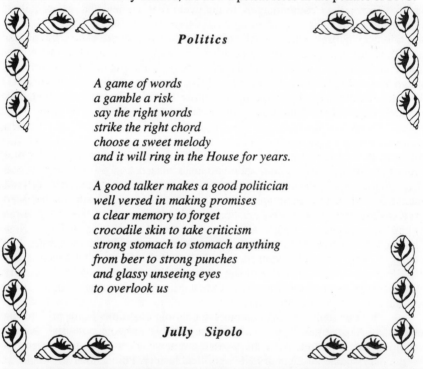

Politics

A game of words
a gamble a risk
say the right words
strike the right chord
choose a sweet melody
and it will ring in the House for years.

A good talker makes a good politician
well versed in making promises
a clear memory to forget
crocodile skin to take criticism
strong stomach to stomach anything
from beer to strong punches
and glassy unseeing eyes
to overlook us

Jully Sipolo

Elites - whether political, economic, social or intellectual - play a crucial role in any third world state. This group of people, who represent only a tiny fraction of the population, takes on leadership roles. Although the nature and size of national elites may differ from one political system to another, the fact remains that they are crucial social forces to be reckoned with. PNG is no exception. Politics, particularly at the national level, is elite business (Saffu 1982). And because electoral politics is conducted Western-style, it is not surprising that only those with knowledge of the formal system are expected to assume leadership roles.

Why should this situation favour men more than women? The majority of participants in electoral politics have been men because 'development' and 'modernisation' have predominantly been male-biased. In terms of participation in formal education, employment, business etc., the male population has advanced further than its female counterpart. Women are newcomers to the modern formal sector, so that only a minority, to date, has received the same level of formal qualifications and experience as men. Hence, the emergence of only a minority of women amongst the elite group in society. Turner aptly makes the point from a historical perspective.

> It was men who acquired the steel axes to lighten their workload, who travelled, who acquired knowledge and skills, and who negotiated with the white men of the colonial administration. Even when 'development' came along, this was taken to be the exclusive business of men (Turner 1990:86).

What this means for women is that because only a minority of their elite are conscious of the gender gap in the political life of the country, it is only these women who make special efforts to be involved in electoral politics. These are the women who are able to verse themselves in the processes and structures of the formal sector. These are the women who decide to contest elections in the hope that their presence will reflect a broader image of women as active participants in politics. Rural women are, therefore, effectively left out of decisions to participate as candidates themselves or to lend support to the elite women who contest. The greatest support base - the rural and non-elite women - is left out of virtually the entire process.

In the 1992 election, this trend of an elite bias in women's advancement became more pronounced. The backgrounds of the candidates show that all have been through the formal educational system, educated to high school or beyond. At least three - Gagari, Aitsi and Gavera - have been exposed to, or have received, university education (Electoral Commission of Papua New Guinea 1992b). As Turner observes,

> Education is universally perceived as a major vehicle for women's advancement, and in Papua New Guinea it has been educated women who have been its staunchest advocates ... Education allows women to participate in the modern world ... When women acquire education they begin to understand and gain access to modern institutions. Jobs, cash income, status, power, new technology and material possessions all come into reach with education (Turner 1990:87-88).

In the political arena, education has certainly become an unofficial criterion for candidacy (Turner & Hegarty 1987:17).

The 1992 election and women's advancement in general have been biased in favour of the country's elite because, as elsewhere, improvements for women in PNG have initially started from the top. Women as a group have become increasingly polarised (Klein 1986). The top layer of women are atypical in that they can be easily differentiated by their educational attainments, labour force participation in previously 'male' fields, income levels etc. The majority of women have fallen well behind. They continue to live largely subsistence lifestyles and await their share of the benefits of modernisation and development.

Who am I?

I was ignored by men
I was regarded as
a child bearer
a pig raiser
and a house keeper.
I stayed at home
and nursed the kids,
I cleaned the house
and fed the pigs,
I wanted freedom
and looked for it
but was beaten
and sent home.

I want love and equality.
I want justice among men,
women and children.

Education has come to my country
Independence has come to my country.
Has freedom come to my country?

I am the mother of the nation.
I am the producer of life.
I build Vanuatu.
Has equality come to my country?

Dorah Obed

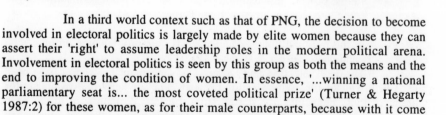

In a third world context such as that of PNG, the decision to become involved in electoral politics is largely made by elite women because they can assert their 'right' to assume leadership roles in the modern political arena. Involvement in electoral politics is seen by this group as both the means and the end to improving the condition of women. In essence, '...winning a national parliamentary seat is... the most coveted political prize' (Turner & Hegarty 1987:2) for these women, as for their male counterparts, because with it come status, extra resources and a host of personal benefits and privileges.

The failure of women to win any seats in the national parliament in 1992 resulted from the fact that these candidates were mostly operating in a vacuum. A simple question can illuminate the point. Are non-elite women interested in electoral politics? Perhaps as voters, but most unlikely as candidates. Even as voters, it is unlikely that they would vote for women candidates, since electoral strategies of this kind are not usually collectively determined by women.

The decision of elite women to participate in politics is itself rarely a collective decision or strategy, but rather a personal or individual choice. A significant point is that elite women are themselves a divided group, and their efforts to achieve equal political rights seem to have been defeated (as evident in the election results) by their own internal conflicts[1]. In the NCD, for example, two women - Loko and Gavera - contested the same regional seat, while two others - Hayes and Debessa - stood for the Moresby North West Open.

Conclusion

The fact that all the women who contested the 1992 election were defeated does not necessarily mean a failure on their part. It is once again the politics of PNG which has failed women. At this point in time, however, we must recognise the fact that not all women in PNG share the view that women must gain political power at the national level, or for that matter at lower levels of government either. Perceptions, attitudes and behaviour differ between and within sections of our society due to differences in custom, religion, economic and educational status etc. We must acknowledge this diversity. Societal differences are difficult to overcome and the struggle for equality must therefore be recognised as a long-term and continuous one.

Increasing the number of women with formal education and in business will ensure greater levels of participation by women in politics, and not just in elite politics. It has the potential to engage a larger number of Papua New Guinean women in the political process. Greater participation in these spheres of modern life will help reduce the vast differences that exist today between the elite and non-elite women of PNG. What is important, from my point of view, is the need for an awareness and education programme (aimed at both men and women) which would penetrate all sections of our society. This might help to reshape the more conservative conscience and the perceptions of the population at large. It would seem to be essential to enhancing the quality of the political sphere, although it is by no means the only option available. Organisation and forward planning are also necessary. Who should take up this task? Women themselves, but certainly with the support of the state and the entire society.

There is much evidence then to show that politics in Papua New Guinea has been, and still is, male-dominated. Although women are active participants in non-formal decision making, the same cannot be said of the formal centres of power. Some inroads were made during the first decade after independence, especially by elite women, but generally speaking PNG women are still a long way from exerting influence on a continuous basis. That there are no women in the national parliament today, and only one elected woman member in one of the 21 provinces, says it all. For a large majority of rural women, formal political participation other than voting is beyond their grasp. All told, the style of politics that has developed in the country poses a major obstacle to women's greater participation both in the political arena and development process at large. It limits their ability to influence who governs and how (Hague & Harrop 1987), and so to encourage more equitable and sustainable forms of development. This political isolation of women, along with that of other less-advantaged people in our society, is a weakness in our liberal democratic system of government. The absence of (meaningful) mass participation in the political process raises questions about the accountability and legitimacy of government.

Notes

1.   Occasional 'collisions' amongst elite women illustrate this point. See *Post Courier* 18 September 1991 & 10 December 1992.

References

Electoral Commission of Papua New Guinea (1992a) *Papua New Guinea national election 1992, total votes polled by candidates,* Papua New Guinea

------- (1992b) *1992 national election candidates bio-data,* Papua New Guinea

Griffin, J., Nelson, H.N. and Firth, D.G. (1979) *Papua New Guinea: A political history,* Australia: Hienemann Educational

Hague, R. and Harrop, M. (eds) (1987) *Comparative government and politics: An introduction,* 2nd ed., Haindsmill, United Kingdom: Macmillan

Jahan, R. (1984) Participation of women in politics' in *Social Development Newsletter*, United Nations Economic and Social Commission for Asia and the Pacific (ESCAP), no.10, April-July

Klein, E. (1986) 'Gender politics from consciousness to mass politics' in *Socialist Review*, vol.16

Lucas, L. (1987) *Electoral Commissioner of Papua New Guinea National Elections 1987 Report*, Report to the Fourth National Parliament, 5 August

Lynch, C.J. (1962) *Appointed members in the Legislative Council for Papua and New Guinea*, Papua New Guinea

Post Courier 29 July 1993

Saffu, Y. (1982) 'Aspects of the emerging political culture in Papua New Guinea' in *The politics of evolving political cultures in the Pacific Islands*, Utah, U.S.A.: Institute for Polynesian Studies, Brigham Young University

Turner, M.M. (1990) *Papua New Guinea: The challenge of independence*, Australia: Penguin Books

Turner, M.M. and Hegarty, D.W. (1987) *The 1987 national elections in Papua New Guinea*, Occasional Paper, no.6, Canberra: Australian Institute of International Affairs, Australian National University

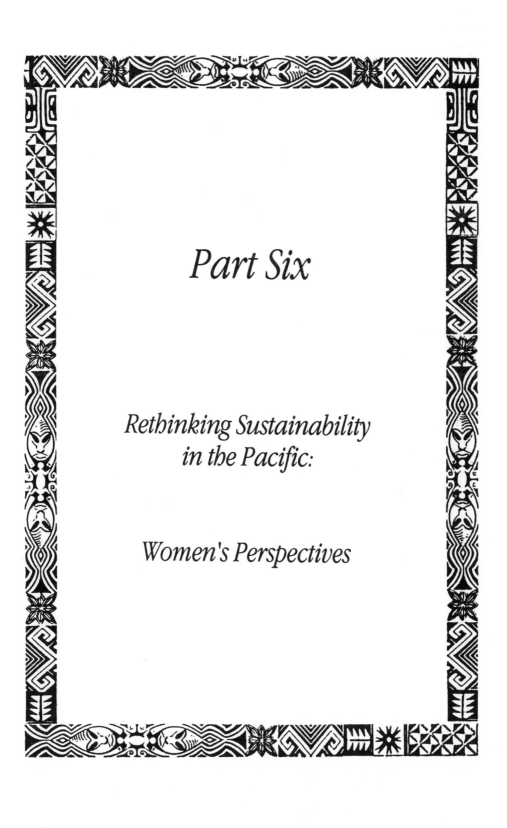

Part Six

Rethinking Sustainability in the Pacific:

Women's Perspectives

Twenty-Four

The politics of sustainable development in the Pacific*

Vanessa Griffen

Introduction

The idea of sustainable development does not have wide currency in the South Pacific. Perhaps a few academics, environmentalists and the ecology-minded have an understanding of the term. The idea of alternative development, meaning an alternative to the present market-oriented capitalist economies dominating the Pacific, has been voiced by a wide range of sources over a number of years. Women, anti-nuclear and independent Pacific movements, church groups and individuals or groups involved in research in the Pacific region, have long debated 'development' and how it is affecting the Pacific. Not all discussions of development, however, have necessarily questioned the fundamental social, political and economic structures that produce inequalities, uneven development, increasing poverty and environmental degradation in Pacific societies.

I argue here that challenges to the inequitable, profit-motivated and materialistic development presently promoted by most Pacific Island governments need to be made by groups representing a range of concerns such as the environment, social injustice, women's participation, labour and land issues, if we are to redirect the kinds of development promoted by Pacific Island governments.

A people-centred sustainable development

A genuine commitment to sustainable development will not come from governments on the whole, but from people. For it is people, increasingly concerned about their own impoverishment, positions of social disadvantage, and the misuse of national resources, who are genuinely likely to support the idea of sustainable development.

The official promotion of sustainable development from above in the United Nations, through international organisations, regional organisations, national governments and by national political leaders will not carry weight until people and governments are involved in more participatory decision making over the use of the world's resources - physical, financial and human. It is necessary that an awareness of social injustice also become part of decision makers' thinking on sustainable development. In considering social justice questions, issues of intra-national, inter-regional and international exploitation also become pertinent. Sustainable development is not just an environmental issue where contributing social, economic and political factors are recognised for the purposes of organising international opinion to protect the world's resources. The politics of 'unsustainable' development must also be recognised.

In too many countries of the world, particularly the third world, women's groups, environmental groups, people's movements, groups within the established churches concerned with social justice, trade unions, and political parties with critical platforms on development, have had their activities in various ways repressed by national governments and those at the head of the existing power structures (often backed by the military, foreign governments and conservative traditional, religious and social elements in the society). The ideas of sustainable development will appear within the official documents of these same governments, particularly for international consumption, but sustainable development, which essentially requires a motivation for change in current development philosophies, can only come from those groups and categories in society most in need of sustainable development choices. Further, sustainable development will only come from alternative groups: those left out or marginalised in society by the present growth-oriented development promoted by most governments and supported by political leaders, the privileged elite of bureaucrats and other profit-inheritors of the system.

Sustainable development in the Pacific

The idea of sustainable development, particularly as published officially in the Brundtland Commission's Report, will undoubtedly be expressed in development plans or country paper presentations at international forums. In fact, however, the current development strategies adopted by most South Pacific Island governments are heavily oriented towards successfully coping with the conditions set by the dominant capitalist economy. The common view is that South Pacific countries have few resources and require overseas aid to boost their small island economies. Promotion of foreign investment in the Pacific and the utilisation of island resources for the maximum economic gain are common objectives of most island governments. Concern for the environment is being expressed nationally and regionally (most notably through the South Pacific Regional Environmental Programme [SPREP]), but official awareness of the contradiction between environmental concerns and the obvious market-oriented thrust of economic development policies is not evident. Cautions on the depletion of Pacific Island resources are voiced simultaneously with continued signing of agreements with foreign and local companies for exploitation of these same resources.

Pacific governments' opposition to environmental damage tends to be more easily expressed when the blame rests outside the region (e.g. damage to fisheries caused by Japanese and Taiwanese companies engaged in driftnet fishing) than when depletion is based on national government decisions allowing the exploitation of important resources (forestry reserves, for example, in Papua New Guinea (PNG), Fiji and the Solomon Islands). The easier condemnation of damage caused by outside interests is partly due to the long history of environmental exploitation of the Pacific by foreign powers: from the use of islands in Micronesia in the North Pacific for United States nuclear weapons testing in the 1950s to the present use of atolls in the South Pacific for French nuclear testing (atmospheric tests in French Polynesia began in 1966 and were conducted underground in the early 1970s after protests by Pacific Island peoples and governments).

The disregard for marine life and Pacific livelihoods by foreign driftnet fishers and the destruction of chemical weapons by the United States on Johnston Atoll are other examples of continuing negative use of the Pacific environment by nations outside the region. The Pacific Islands, north and south, continue to be considered as dumping grounds for nuclear and/or chemical wastes. In Belau, in Micronesia, a proposal for a toxic waste incinerator to destroy wastes from Australia and South-East Asia has the support of the Minister of State, even though water and land pollution are likely (*Pacific News Bulletin* February 1991:1-2,6).

Critique of Pacific policy

Criticisms of decisions by Pacific Island governments on the use of natural resources are nevertheless beginning to emerge. In the Kingdom of Tonga, which is a constitutional monarchy, a small core of people's representatives challenged a government scheme to sell Tongan passports to foreigners as a means of earning foreign exchange, supposedly for national benefit. They queried the development scheme, its constitutionality and, more importantly, the land use and development implications for land-scarce Tonga of an influx of foreign passport holders.

While this case of a popular challenge to a government decision on the use of national resources can be cited, the norm is that there are few broadly-based challenges to the development choices being made by Pacific Island leaders and governments, even where quite serious damage or loss of resources is involved. In Tonga, while the passport scandal continues, the royal leadership still considers setting up an oil refinery (*Pacific Islands Monthly* March 1991:34) and building a low-grade nuclear reactor (costing $US 12 million) as possible revenue-earning measures. The Crown Prince has dismissed fears of problems caused by a nuclear reactor, arguing that any nuclear waste from the reactor would be sent overseas to be reused in nuclear recycling (*Pacific News Bulletin* April 1991:14). A well-known Tongan educator recently described the Tongan passport dispute as an example of *palangi* (European, white, foreign) politics'[1].

Pacific environmental protests or calls for accountability, democratic processes, the involvement of women and alternative development options with wider distribution of benefits are similarly often dismissed. Ironically, the 'protection of culture' and conservation of Pacific values and identity are given as reasons for dismissing critical voices - indigenous or otherwise - that query political, social or economic development in the Pacific. Democratic processes have been labelled 'foreign', 'Western' and 'inappropriate' by the traditional leadership/elite opponents of popular calls for accountable, participatory political systems. Yet many Pacific countries have indigenous examples of consultative decision making which also include women, for example, in decisions on land use, cultivation and conservation. Furthermore, principles of sustainable development have been understood and practised in many Pacific societies for some time and these principles are being forgotten (Clarke 1990:233-253).

Samana (1988:41-57) gives an example of a more participatory and democratic decision-making structure from the community level upwards worked out by popular participation in constitution making in Morobe Province in PNG. This model of community involvement in decision making and development was unfortunately denied when Morobe Province was compelled to adopt the structure of provincial government set up by the national government of PNG. Pacific women in a series of regional meetings have stressed the need for participation in decision making, a different approach to 'development' and better use of the environment and resources in the Pacific (Griffen 1976 & 1990). From these examples, we can see that calls for sustainable development, participatory decision making and democratic structures are not necessarily foreign in origin.

Government unreliability

In Papua New Guinea, landowners in May 1989 closed down the Bougainville copper mine (which opened in 1975 and is the largest open-cut copper mine in the world) because of the damage to the environment caused by the mine and landowners' discontent over benefits received from mining. The mine is 2.5 kilometres across and 400 metres deep and has left 3000 hectares destroyed by tailings (Standish 1989). Demands for compensation and closure of the mine led to a protracted confrontation between the Bougainville Revolutionary Army and the PNG government forces. The closure of the mine has produced harsh conditions at many levels - the challenge of landowners, the loss of earnings, the use of force on both sides, the PNG government's cessation of medical and other services to the island and the continuing hopes and failures of peaceful negotiation - and all point to the high cost of economic development decided over the wishes of the people whose resources are being used. Taylor (1990:14-15) notes that the matrilineal social structure in Bougainville was also ignored when mining negotiations began years ago, thereby excluding women who are the actual landowners.

There are other examples from PNG of people's protests against development decisions. In the Southern Highlands, landowners are in dispute over the Hides gas project which is 95 per cent owned by British Petroleum (*Pacific Islands Monthly* March 1991:36). This is intended to provide electricity for the Porgera gold mine nearby rather than as a development project for people in the area. Competing landowners' groups are demanding compensation but not necessarily attempting to remove the project[2]. The Lihir gold mine in New Ireland Province is similarly being disputed by landowners (King 1991:49).

Examples abound of government support and involvement (sometimes complicity) in continuing to jeopardise the environment and quality of life for Pacific Island peoples. Forestry reserves are traded in return for small compensation to landowners and receipt of lease payments, and without noticeable regard to the world alert on the problems of deforestation. In Fiji, a newspaper article sometime ago announced that landowners would get one-third of the net profits from a $FIJ 75 million timber agreement being negotiated by an Australian-based company which would operate in a joint venture with local landowners to exploit timber resources over the next 20 years. The Fiji company would supply 500,000 cubic metres of logs over 20 years. There was a promise of joint responsibility for reafforestation. The Native Land Trust Board, the Ministry of Forestry, the Fiji Trade and Investment Board and the Reserve Bank of Fiji were all to be involved in facilitating the project if it was finally approved (*Fiji Times* 30 April 1991). There was no evidence of conservationist opinion having been sought, nor a sustainable development philosophy in the proposal.

In Papua New Guinea, the Barnett Commission of Inquiry into Aspects of the Forestry Industry (1987-89) concluded that the forestry industry in Papua New Guinea is out of control (King 1991:50). The extent of the destruction was squarely attributed to a number of cooperating indigenous/local/national forces:

A magnificent resource is being devastated by foreign interests
in corrupt collusion with local and national political notables,
senior civil servants and comprador businessmen - and in the
process the livelihood and well being of entire communities of
traditional landowners are being set at naught (King 1991).

267

The exploitative activities of logging companies, once allowed a foothold in the country, are well documented. King (1991:51) records the often damaging results:

> ...in Papua New Guinea an industry which earns a modest 70m *kina* in export revenue has totally devastated the timber resources and greatly damaged the ecology and agricultural prospects of one province (New Ireland)...

The suppression of the Barnett Report[3] by the PNG government raises an important point that cannot be ignored in any discussion of sustainable development: political repression of any sources of criticism, exposure, challenges or protests in support of sustainable development where these obstruct the activities of foreign and local business interests.

In Barnett's report, senior government ministers and civil servants were accused of corruption and fraud[4] Barnett's description of the scene in the forestry industry in PNG conveys that the *modus operandi* is not one of protection but destruction of the environment:

It would be fair to say, of some of the companies, that they are
now roaming the country side with the self-assurance of robber
barons, bribing politicians and leaders, creating social
disharmony and ignoring laws in order to gain access to, rip out
and export the last remnants of the provinces' valuable timber
(Barnett quoted in King 1991).

Some island governments, for example Kiribati, have taken a more
critical view of foreign investment and aid, determining to carefully select aid to
ensure that only those projects most needed by and beneficial to the country are
accepted. Across the South Pacific, however, there is evidence of economic
development still oriented towards material income (gross domestic product or
GDP) where cash crops, forestry exploitation and tourism are strongly promoted.
Income disparities and worsening health and nutritional status have been noted
(Thaman 1988). It is evident, however, that a general divide between expanding
urban centres and rural areas exists across the South Pacific where better facilities,
services and chances of employment are considered to be located in the urban
centres. Rural development projects intended to redress imbalances are still
considered the solution.

In the Pacific, there is a need for philosophical and political challenges
to the existing power structures if sustainable development is to become more
widely known and achievable. Support for groups and individuals publicising and
working for alternative development will be more helpful than international
appeals to governments to consider more environment-friendly but nevertheless
market-oriented development. The sustainable development philosophy does not
identify capitalist development, the profit motive, government promotion of
foreign investment and the activities of transnational companies as part of the
problem.

In considering development in the Pacific in the next century, it seems
more than ever urgent that a range of support movements for alternative
development need to emerge and gain political strength if sustainable development
is to be a philosophy practised by Pacific Island states. The connections between
powerful foreign states and Pacific Island dependency cannot be ignored. Political
leaders and local elites are unlikely to be the source of change or challenges to
current development thinking. They have an investment - economic and political -
in the short-term benefits of 'unsustainable' development. The philosophy of
sustainable development, which must mean more than 'economic growth without
ecological disaster', will have to come from people in the Pacific. Changes to the
existing power structures are necessary if alternative views of development are to
be expressed in national development priorities and policies.

Popular support and pressure for sustainable development

Pressure for sustainable development is more likely to come from a
number of different non-government groups and organisations. The anti-nuclear
movement, environmental groups outside and within the region, Pacific women's
organisations, church groups, trade unions and possibly a reactivated student
movement, are sources of support for sustainable development.

The regional anti-nuclear network developed in the 1970s to lobby
against French nuclear testing expanded its brief to include concern for

militarisation of the Pacific and independence struggles. However, the movement has not evolved its own indigenous Pacific expertise and drive for environmental protection and conservation (see Naidu 1988:185-195). Its concerns for a nuclear-free and independent Pacific (the movement was renamed the Nuclear Free and Independent Pacific Movement [NFIP]) have not broadened into concern about the actions of post-independence Pacific Island governments in overuse and abuse of Pacific Island resources. The issue of sustainable development as a fundamental condition for an independent Pacific in the 21st century is a needed element in the NFIP movement. Environmental concerns have continued to be expressed by non-island members of NFIP. Pacific activists have supported anti-colonial and indigenous minority struggles for two decades, without developing a critical response to the exploitation of Pacific Island resources by foreign and local companies with the support of independent Pacific governments.

A regional non-government environmental action group, the South Pacific Action Committee for Human Ecology and the Environment (SPACHEE) based in the University of the South Pacific, does provide a central point for expert knowledge on environmental issues and has worked to raise government and popular awareness of environmental issues. However, its stress on the physical environment and scientific explanation, and the tendency to limit its audience to like-minded academic and government experts does not give it popular appeal. It is an important NGO in providing monitoring and information on environmental problems[5]. It has been successful in its alerts on environmental and ecological problems in the Pacific and its newsletter provides some sharing of information.

A more promising development is the creation of community-oriented environmental awareness organisations with programmes that are educational and more participatory at a local, community level. The Fiji Council for Social Services (FCOSS) has set up a Community Environment Awareness Committee (CEAC) which has planned a series of activities and projects emphasising environmental care by the community in urban centres and outlying areas. On the western side of Viti Levu in Fiji, the Lautoka Environmental Action Group (LEAG) has also been formed.

A link between the community, those in power making decisions affecting the environment, and powerful interests exploiting resources without concern for development effects, also needs to be made. The communication of concerns and community problems may produce change but it must also be anticipated that there can be indifference, neglect or repression (indirect or direct) of opposing views. This fact is often ignored: sustainable development will involve a struggle of opposing views and practices, and conflict and repression at many levels may be the response.

Women's contribution to the environment

Pacific women's groups have for a long time been involved in articulating views on development, the environment and the health of future generations. They remain an important and unrecognised resource for community knowledge, action and awareness for sustainable development. The marginalisation of these groups by present development strategies and women's subordinate position in society have meant the suppression of women's interest in, and comments on, development. A women's workshop in Papua New Guinea in 1989 called for a new form of development for the Pacific: development that would sustain peoples and cultures based on people's own experiences and visions[6]. The regional women's network that has been established in the Pacific since 1975 is a forum for debate and action for sustainable development. For this to be effective, Pacific governments will need to recognise and incorporate Pacific women's perspectives on development.

Individuals in groups working within the churches have also been involved in raising development issues and concerns. The churches have played a critical role in supporting calls for changes in government decisions where adverse social effects are anticipated or have resulted. They have played a part in the anti-nuclear movement in the Pacific and have raised issues of unequal distribution and poverty caused by development (Barr 1990).

Non-government organisations such as environmental and anti-nuclear groups, women's organisations and the churches are the most likely sources of pressure for sustainable development in the Pacific. A sustainable development philosophy may provide the ideological link between these various groups, and be a means of mobilising a broadly supported popular movement for alternative development in the region. Democratic political processes and participatory decision making will facilitate a peaceful solution to pressures for change. Even if a repressive, conservative reaction by the powerful is the response to such a movement, the politics of sustainable development cannot be ignored.

271

* This paper was presented at the Society for International Development, 20th World Conference 'One world or several: Towards a strategy for growth, sustainability and solidarity in an interdependent world', Amsterdam, The Netherlands, 6-9 May 1991 and subsequently published in *Development* 1991:3/4, Society for International Development, Rome.

Notes

1. Talk by Futa Helu at the University of the South Pacific, Suva, Fiji, 29 April 1991.

2. It would be wrong to romanticise the actions of landowners in opposing such developments. In many cases, their objective is to extract a greater share of the earnings and/or compensation from the government in return for use of their resources. In the Hides Gas Project, the Kikari Landowners Development Association is claiming K35 million (PNG *kina*) from the project developers (*Pacific Islands Monthly* March 1991:22).

3. Only two of the report's nine volumes were printed and none of them are now publicly available in PNG. A 60-page summary of the report is available from Asia Pacific Action Group in Tasmania, Australia. Barnett himself was assaulted and seriously injured during the course of his inquiry (King 1991; *Pacific News Bulletin* April 1991:11).

4. One of the Ministers implicated in the report was the Deputy Prime Minister.

5. See for example *SPACHEE Environmental News Alert* (1989) on oceanic driftnet fishing (Thaman & Murti 1989).

6. Pacific Workshop organised by the Women's Programme, Asia and Pacific Development Centre, Kuala Lumpur and the Division of Women's Affairs, Papua New Guinea, October 1989.

References

Antrobus, P. (1991) 'Women's world: Realities and choices', paper presented at the Fourth Interdisciplinary Congress on Women, Hunter College, City University of New York, New York, June 3-6

APDC Newsletter (1989) 'Gender-sensitivity in development planning implementation and evolution', vol.8, no.3, pp.8-9

Barr, K.J. (1990) *Poverty in Fiji*, Suva, Fiji: Fiji Forum for Justice, Peace and the Integrity of Creation

Bryant, J. (1988) 'The role of women's organizations in environmental education', paper presented at the Fourth Regional Women's Conference, Suva, Fiji

---------- (1990) 'Assistance in human resources development for improvement of shelter and settlements planning in small island developing countries of the Pacific', paper presented at the Consultative Meeting of National Experts in Human Settlement of Small Pacific Island Countries of the Pacific, Port Vila, 3-6 October

Clarke, W.C. (1990) 'Learning from the past: Traditional knowledge and sustainable development in *The Contemporary Pacific,* vol.2, no.2

Fiji Times 30 April 1991

Findlay, T. (1990) 'Green vs Peace? The Johnston Atoll controversy' in *Pacific Research,* Australian National University, vol.3, no.2, May, pp.3-7

Goodman, D. (1991) 'Severing chains of foreign dependence' in *Fiji Times,* 13 February

Griffen, V. (1976) *Women speak out: Report of the Pacific Women's Regional Conference, Suva, Fiji, October 1975,* Suva: Pacific Women's Association

---------- (1990) *Women, development, empowerment: A Pacific feminist perspective,* Kuala Lumpur, Malaysia: Asia and Pacific Development Centre

King, P. (1991) 'Redefining South Pacific security' in Thakur, R. *The South Pacific: Problems, issues and prospects,* New Zealand: MacMillan in association with the University of Otago

Naidu, V. (1988) 'The Fiji Anti-Nuclear Movement: Problems and prospects' in Walker, R. and Sutherland, W. (eds) *The Pacific: Peace, security and the nuclear issue,* United Nations University Studies on Peace and Regional Security, London: Zed Press

Nisbet, I. (1991) 'Some justice at long, long last' in *Pacific Islands Monthly,* March, pp.20-21

Pacific Islands Monthly (1991) 'Affluent but unemployed', March, p.22

---------- (1991) 'Economic boost for Banabans', March, p.34

---------- (1991) 'Oil refinery finance sought', March, p.34

---------- (1991) 'PNG gas project obstructed', March, p.36

Pacific News Bulletin (1990) 'Tongan political reform', April

---------- (1991) 'Belau update', February

---------- (1991) 'Kanaky: The ever-present threat of immigration', February, p.15

---------- (1991) 'Mururoa: Educating the French', February, p.11

---------- (1991) 'New Bougainville Accord', February

---------- (1991) 'Ban toxic wastes', April, p.14

---------- (1991) 'Crown Prince: Nuclear power', April, p.14

---------- (1991) 'The Barnett Report: A Summary of the Report of the Commission of Inquiry into Aspects of the Timber industry in Papua New Guinea', April

Samana, U. (1988) 'People's cultural groups and political power' in Samana, U. *Papua New Guinea: Which way?,* Melbourne: Arena Publications

SPACHEE Environmental News Alert (1989) no.1, January

SPACHEE Newsletter (1991) 'A look at US plans to incinerate chemical weapons on Johnston Atoll', vol.4, no.1, January, pp.2-3

---------- (1991) 'Australian plans for hazardous and industrial waste disposal in the Pacific', vol.4, no.1, p.6

---------- (1991) 'Environmental groups around Fiji', vol.4, no.1, January

Standish, B. (1989) 'Bougainville: Undermining the state in Papua New Guinea', Foreign Affairs Group, Department of the Parliamentary Library, Canberra, Australia, October

Taylor, M.M. (1990) 'Papua New Guinea and the aquatic continent' in *Ms.* magazine, November/December, pp.14-15

Thaman, R.R. (1988) 'Health and nutrition in the Pacific Islands: Development or underdevelopment?' in *Geojournal* 16:2:211-227

Thaman, R.R. and Murti, R. (1989) 'Oceanic drift gillnet fishing: A threat to our fisheries' in *SPACHEE Environmental News Alert* no.1, South Pacific Action Committee for Human Ecology and the Environment, University of the South Pacific, Suva, Fiji

Va'a Leatuailevao, R. and Teaiwa, M. J. (1988) *Environment and Pacific women: From the globe to the village,* Suva: Fiji Association of Women Graduates in association with The Institute of Pacific Studies, University of the South Pacific

Walker, R. and Sutherland, W. (eds) (1988) *The Pacific: Peace, security and the nuclear issue,* Tokyo: United Nations University Studies on Regional Peace and Security, London: Zed Press

William, I. (1991) 'Where phosphate and time are running out' in *Pacific Islands Monthly,* March, pp.19-20

---------- (1991) 'Islands' big pitch at climate conference' in *Pacific Islands Monthly,* March, p.54

Twenty-Five

Putting people first

Noumea Simi

Political forces inevitably influence the management and outcomes of development, and Western Samoa is no different in this respect from other Pacific countries. In all cases, development continues to be affected by the experiences of shared colonial pasts as well as present-day realities including aid dependence, global market uncertainties and the politics of traditional cultures. Despite the complexities of these forces, and the difficulties they sometimes pose for Pacific Island states, political processes can be mobilised in creative ways; and they can and should be instrumental in purposefully bringing about positive social change rather than simply being a point of entry to the realms of national power and prestige, or a platform to satisfy the wishes of individual political parties and their supporters.

Western Samoan development cannot be transplanted from elsewhere. It is a process of transformation that should be anchored in local structures and values and which should grow out of the harmonious interaction of a stable economy, and its particular social and political institutions, all working to promote national goals and objectives. Economic growth is important to securing development, and in turn requires favourable conditions for technological advancement and capital accumulation. However, it is equally important that non-economic considerations such as the values and norms of the general population, the quality and accountability of our country's leadership, and the ability of our political system to direct the processes of socio-economic change in accordance with the expressed needs of our society are taken into account in the long-term interests of promoting democratic and meaningful development.

So-called developing countries, including most Pacific Island states, are now being directed to face the challenge of balancing economic growth with equity. More specifically, the recent call by the aid donor community, and the much-publicised annual Human Development Reports of the United Nations Development Programme (UNDP), are encouraging us to put a 'human' face on development. For decision makers in the Pacific, a region where traditional cultures have always assumed that the interests of the community were paramount, there is a little confusion as to what the targets of their (development) efforts are, if not people!

As developing countries, we cannot afford to waste scarce resources. Hence efficiency is a key prerequisite of economic management, especially given the demands of competing in the world economy. The pursuit of economic efficiency should, however, go hand in hand with a concern for social justice; that is, a concern to build development upon the principles of equity and people's needs. We can never be self-sustaining if our societies do not possess a spirit of social justice.

Policies aimed at improving the status of women are seen as a measure of a country's commitment to development with equity. A gender-sensitive approach to development is politically necessary. It is also a basic condition for sustained social and economic progress. It requires changes in all societies, particularly in those where traditional perceptions of women as inferior to men still prevail. A 'people-centred' approach to development will work to weaken such perceptions and bring about changes for the better in social attitudes towards women.

The responsibility to develop processes that will reconcile the requirements of efficiency and equity lies with each individual country. Many countries in the Pacific do not have adequate administrative and technical capabilities to meet the demands of development oriented towards the global economy. This is evident in the high proportions of expatriate personnel in our bureaucracies and in aid programmes heavily weighted towards technical assistance: The question often asked is whether this is the most effective way to use assistance under aid programmes. To this question, we might add another. Is the problem really a lack of skills or are development projects too heavily based on concerns for economic growth and efficiency at the expense of our people's needs, wants and skills?

There should be more careful and discriminating selection in the development activities pursued by our regional governments. Selection should be based on the resources, capabilities and skills that we have, and the ways in which we can make the most productive use of them. At a time when we are facing constraints as a result of external pressures and natural calamities, there is clearly a need for innovative development approaches that take full advantage of the creativity of our own people.

Political Complex

He was much too ladylike
Much too soft in manner
his hold of his audience much too quiet
with his much too put on Oxford accent
in his put down message
that women should remain in the home.
'If I could I would
I would stay home and
do just that ...'
His Bali dancer fingers twirled
Caressing his desire to bear children
For a second he was like a spider
spinning his gossamer finery
around patterns of his venomous abuse
'I respect women I married one
Why oh why do they want to be men?'
The women boiled the men chuckled
goading confrontation
A woman feigning immunity to the assail
volunteered to soothe his agony
'Life is a unity of partners
that gives birth to development
Give man technology
give woman opportunity
let development grow'
The lady-like gentle man
fingered his macholess tie
and gazed through the studious lenses
of his professionalism
wondering where god went wrong
in his blueprint of creation.

Noumea Simi

Twenty-Six

At the dawn of the 'Pacific century':
A place for Pacific feminism

Arlene Griffen

And they shall beat their pots and pans into printing presses
And weave their cloth into protest banners
Nations of women shall lift up their voices with nations of
other women
Neither shall they accept discrimination any more

Mary Chagnon

Since the publication of Ester Boserup's classic work, *Women's Role in Economic Development* (1970), in which she prefaces her analysis with the observation that, in the ever-growing literature on economic development, reflections on the particular problems of women are 'few and far between', much has been done to write women into this particular story as well as to document the story of women and development in general. This collection of essays by Pacific women provides a unique Pacific contribution to this continuing, vitally important, now global debate.

A summary consideration of these perspectives of Pacific Island women on development in the Pacific region may be enlightened in the first place by some knowledge of similar perspectives and the circumstances of their manifestation in other parts of the world which may have affinities with the Pacific Island region. Only the Caribbean region commends itself in this regard, sharing as it does with the Pacific a long history of European colonialism and many of its economic and socio-political ramifications in a post-colonial small island national context. Thus, a brief survey of women in development in the

Caribbean in the last few decades can be instructive for its parallels with women in development in the Pacific during the same period.

In her overview of women in development programmes in the Caribbean resulting from the initiatives of the 1975 International Women's Year and the ensuing United Nations Decade for Women (1975-1985), Peggy Antrobus of Barbados observes that, with the qualified exceptions of Jamaica (1975) and Grenada (1979), no Caribbean government

> perceived these Women in Development programmes as integral parts of their development programmes. Their establishment of national machinery for the integration of women in development reflected for the most part an indifferent tokenism. The programmes which emerged were consequently influenced by the perceptions, strengths and priorities of the existing women's organizations and by the particular background of the persons selected to head the special units (Antrobus 1988:38).

The exceptional example of Grenada under the unfortunately short-lived government of Maurice Bishop deserves further explication here because of its exemplary qualities for emulation. Merle Hodge of Trinidad, in an inspirational paper on the few success stories of people's participation in Caribbean development, cites the Grenada of this period as the Caribbean's singular, glowing example of this phenomenon:

> For a system of community and national development which is based on the premise that the development process **begins** with empowering people to run their own affairs, we have to look at what was attempted in the Grenada Revolution, 1979-1983 ... Grenada represented a new departure in development in the English-speaking Caribbean - an attempt to reverse our history of dependence and to truly empower the ordinary people of the society. It is no wonder that America's 'rescue mission' to this country [after Bishop's assassination in 1983] included the uprooting of the system of popular democracy and the firm reinstatement of cockfight politics (Hodge 1986:109, 116).

Peggy Antrobus also emphasises the unique example of Grenada in the central place given to women in development programmes there during the Bishop years:

> Grenada's experience deserves special mention. An integral part of the Grenada Revolution of 1979 was the attention given to women, youth, farmers and workers. A National Women's Organisation (NWO) was formed in 1979 and a Ministry of Women's Affairs established. The NWO and the Ministry worked closely to mobilise women for national development, to raise consciousness on issues affecting women and to ensure that a number of steps were taken to improve and change the situation of women in the country. **In many ways the Grenada experience under the People's Revolution-**

ary Government ... demonstrated what is possible when the issue of women's status is part of a process of social transformation. It presented an alternative approach to women and development, an approach which recognises the existence of oppressive structures and relationships and their linkages to persistent poverty and the marginalization of the majority of the population (Antrobus 1988:40; my emphasis).

To continue the overview of Caribbean women in development programmes in the last few decades, Peggy then describes how Caribbean women's thinking changed over these years from an 'uncritical acceptance of the separate goals of Equality, Development and Peace in 1975 [reflecting the priorities of the three global groupings at the time: the first world advocating equality; the third world, development; the Eastern bloc, peace] to an increasingly critical search for alternative approaches which would acknowledge and accommodate the fact that intricate links interconnected the three goals (Antrobus 1988:36).

Much of this critical re-search was the product of feminist analyses of Caribbean development issues. Through these analyses, Peggy continues:

> women began to perceive the parallel between their experience of powerlessness, alienation, dependency and inequality in countries of different social, political, cultural and economic characteristics, and the structured powerlessness of Third World countries in relation to the 'developed' countries of the North - both of those of the East as well as of the West. Feminist theorists began to suggest that an understanding of women's inequality may be the key to an understanding of the inequality of other groups based on race, class and different levels of development. The issue of power emerged as central to an understanding of the goals of Equality, Development and Peace (Antrobus 1988:45-6).

However, the positive contribution of feminism to the development debate was not necessarily unanimously acknowledged or supported. Peggy refers to the predicament arising out of some of the 1975 Mexico City debates, of the negative portrayal of feminism and feminists as 'irrelevant and divisive to women in development' (Antrobus 1988:46). Another Caribbean feminist, Rhoda Reddock of Trinidad, corroborates this:

> For us Caribbean women, in recent times the struggle to define our womanness as well as our Caribbeanness has, especially in the 1960s and 1970s, been fraught with demands that we deny and reject any feminist consciousness or the need for a feminist struggle. Feminist consciousness and action preceded the actual coining of the word. This was so not only in Europe, but in all parts of the world where women (at rare times with the support of men) have sought to challenge the subordination and exploitation that have to varying degrees been the history of most women (Reddock 1990:61-61).

Reddock defines 'feminism very simply as the awareness of the subordination and exploitation of women in society and the conscious action to change that situation' (Reddock 1990:62). Despite the hostility towards feminism, Peggy Antrobus can still emphasise as a major achievement of the Decade the emergence of 'Third World feminists, activists, researchers and policy makers' who recognised that feminism is not monolithic and who asserted that women can only play a vital role for the good of their societies when change is based on a theory of development which embraces it (Antrobus 1988:46).

Similarly, in the Pacific, at the 1987 'Women, Development and Empowerment Workshop' held in Fiji, the women participants from various Pacific Island countries showed in their debates over feminism and its relevance and definition for Pacific women that the issue still generated at least as much controversy as it had at the first 1975 Pacific Women's Conference also held in Fiji. In canvassing their negative and positive attitudes to the term in the process of working towards a Pacific definition, the group advanced the following as part of the list of 'positives':

> Pacific women needed to develop a feminist ideology to analyse the wider issues of women's struggles, which were important to them as women and as Pacific people - for example, all forms of dominance, social inequalities, and the role and influence of institutions such as the church ... Having a feminist perspective would influence the questions Pacific women asked about institutions and enable women to challenge conditions and cultural practices that contribute to their oppression (Griffen 1989:21).

Whilst it is clear that there are historically- and culturally-specific differences in detail to be acknowledged in the formulations of these definitions and theories, the acknowledgement that remains a constant to all definitions of feminism is of the fundamental issue of a 'woman's place' which is integrally embedded in social life. Thus, changes and disruptions to a 'woman's place', whether by the agency of feminism or not, must potentially have ramifications for the rest of society and the structures of power that operate within it.

Another third world feminist, Chandra Talpade Mohanty, likewise acknowledges the imprudence of generalisations about 'third world feminisms'. But she is also persuasive in her emphasis of the links in the different histories and struggles of third world women against racism, sexism, colonialism, imperialism and monopoly capital which can point to the goal of forging a commonality across differences, to an 'imagined community' of third world oppositional struggles

> '[I]magined' not because it is not 'real' but because it suggests potential alliances and collaborations across divisive boundaries, and 'community' because in spite of internal hierarchies within third world contexts, it nevertheless suggests a significant, deep commitment to ... 'horizontal comradeship' (Mohanty 1991:4).

282

The contributions in this collection bear cogent and often poignantly-impassioned witness to the fact that there are indeed far more commonalities than there are differences in the life experiences, aspirations and struggles of women in our Pacific community. The genesis and existence of the collection exemplify that these commonalities can provide a strong foundation on which to build a pan-Pacific feminism to work explicitly for the holistic development and well-being of our region and to support implicitly similar feminist endeavours beyond our shores. For what we have in common can help to overcome the tyrannies of the physical, socio-cultural and ideological distances that come between us. Our commonalities can empower us to strengthen the bonds of horizontal comradeship necessary for a united front against the very real threats that face us and our environment in these closing years of what has been a century of momentous, challenging and yet also life-threatening changes.

Furthermore, the contributions in this collection exemplify the recognition feminism gives to the importance of writing, in its various forms, as a means of producing vital knowledge for feminism's use. Thus the discourses of the academic theorist, the sociologist and the political scientist are here accorded equal rights and importance with the words of the poet and the ambassador, the mother and the worker, the activist and the documentarist. Side by side and together, these Pacific women's words cogently and coherently voice some of the most important concerns, aspirations, hopes and fears of our region. Within and beyond our shores, they support and share in a feminist vision of

> a world where inequality, based on class, gender, and race is absent from every country, and from the relationships among people and countries ... where basic needs become basic rights and where poverty and all forms of violence are eliminated ... where massive resources now used in the production of the means of destruction will be diverted to areas where they will help to relieve oppression, both inside and outside the home (Antrobus 1988:47).

This visionary feminism encompasses a concept of social transformation that, as part of the eventual liberation of all women, will change all human relationships for the better. Although centrally about women, their experiences, their conditions and environment, feminism is therefore also fundamentally about men, and about positive social and developmental change.

The voices of women have long been raised, both individually and collectively, in calls for equality, justice and peace. At this momentous time of the closing of an old, and the dawn of a new, and Pacific, century, let us hope and urge that the perspectives of Pacific Island women, such as those voiced in this collection, will be listened to with the considered attention that they surely merit, yet for too long have been denied.

References

Antrobus, P. (1988) 'Women in development programmes' in Mohammed, P. and Shepherd, C. (eds) *Gender in Caribbean development,* Kingston, Jamaica: University of the West Indies, Mona Campus, Women and Development Studies Project

Boserup, E. (1970) *Women's role in economic development,* New York: St. Martin's Press

Reddock, R. (1990) 'Feminism, nationalism, and the early women's movement in the English-speaking Caribbean (with special reference to Jamaica and Trinidad and Tobago)' in Cudjoe, S. (ed.) *Caribbean women writers. Essays from the first international conference,* Wellesley: Callaloux Publications

Griffen, V. (ed.)(1989) *Women, development and empowerment,* Kuala Lumpur, Malaysia: Asia and Pacific Development Centre

Mohanty, C. et al. (eds) (1991) *Third world women and the politics of feminism,* Bloomington and Indianapolis: Indiana University Press

A note on contributors

Authors

Vina Ram Bidesi, from Fiji, teaches in the Ocean Resources Management Programme at the University of the South Pacific. She has a research interest in fisheries socio-economics, fisheries resource management and development, and women in fisheries. She is a member of the Women and Fisheries Network.

'Atu Emberson-Bain, a Tongan-born Fiji national, is a graduate of Oxford University and holds a Ph.D in history from the Australian National University. She is a researcher and activist on labour, development, mining and women's issues and is the author of *Labour and Gold in Fiji* published by Cambridge University Press (1994). She has an interest in making video and radio documentaries.

Peggy Fairbairn-Dunlop is from Western Samoa and teaches at the University of the South Pacific School of Agriculture at Alafua, Western Samoa. She holds a Ph.D from Macquarie University, is a 'one-time planter', and is currently Acting Pro-Vice Chancellor and Head of School at Alafua.

Arlene Griffen, from Fiji, is a Lecturer in post-colonial literature at the University of the South Pacific. She produced the first extended feminist critique of Pacific literature for her MA thesis at London University, and is currently completing a feminist critique of Pacific and Caribbean literature for a Ph.D at Macquarie University, New South Wales. She has a continuing research interest in Pacific women writers.

Vanessa Griffen, from Fiji, holds a Ph.D from Sydney University in politics and is a Senior Lecturer in the History/Politics Department at the University of the South Pacific. She is a writer, activist (with a long background in both the nuclear-free and independent Pacific and women's movements), and producer/ editor of educational materials on development and women's issues. She has a special interest in women's health.

Ruby Mirinka is a Bougainvillean health educator and former Matron of Arawa Hospital on the Island of Bougainville.

Cita Morei is a Belauan activist who has been centrally involved in the struggle to retain her country's nuclear-free Constitution.

Susanna Ounei-Small, from Ouvéa in Kanaky, has been actively involved in the struggle for Kanak independence since 1969. She is a founding member of the PALIKA Party and the USTKE trade union. She is currently working as an Assistant Director (decolonisation desk) of the Pacific Concerns Resource Centre in Suva.

Kushma Ram, from Fiji, is an Assistant Director (development desk) with the Pacific Concerns Resource Centre. She has worked in both the labour movement (the Fiji Trades Union Congress) and the women's movement (the Fiji Women's Rights Movement) in Fiji and has carried out research on the working conditions of Fiji garment workers.

Nahau Rooney, from Manus Island in Papua New Guinea, is a former Minister of Justice in the Papua New Guinea government.

Orovu Sepoe, from the Gulf Province in Papua New Guinea, is a Lecturer in Political Theory with the Department of Politics and Administrative Studies at the University of Papua New Guinea. She holds a Masters Degree in politics from the University of Warwick, in the UK.

Premjeet Singh is a Teaching Assistant in the Department of History/Politics at the University of the South Pacific. She is currently completing a Masters thesis on the relationship between NGOs in Fiji and aid donors.

Claire Slatter teaches Politics at the University of the South Pacific. From Fiji, shẹ has a background in the anti-nuclear, women's and labour movements and has been engaged in research on, and analysis of, women's employment and post-coup economic and labour policies. She is a founding member of DAWN and is the Pacific representative on DAWN's Steering Committee.

Laura M. Torres Souder is from Guam. She holds a Ph.D from the University of Hawaii where she completed her thesis on the Chamorro women of Guam. She currently teaches at the University of Guam and undertakes consultancy work.

Isabella Sumang is a Belauan activist who has long been in the forefront of the political and legal struggle to retain Belau's anti-nuclear Constitution.

Konai Helu Thaman is a Tongan educationist and poet who has been teaching since 1974 at the University of the South Pacific where she is a Reader in the Department of Education and Psychology. She holds a Ph.D in education and has published widely in the areas of curriculum development, education and culture, cultural literacy and tourism. She has published four collections of poetry.

Yvonne Underhill-Sem is a Cook-Island born geographer/anthropologist who is currently pursuing doctoral studies at the University of Waikato on the social and economic reproduction of women in the Pacific. Since 1991 she has been teaching in the Geography Department as well as doing research and consultancy work in Papua New Guinea, the Cook Islands and Palau on climate change, structural adjustment policies and population issues.

Poets

Déwé Gorode has.long been a prominent political activist in the struggle for an independent Kanaky. An intellectual, teacher and poet, she has published a collection of poems entitled *Sous les Cendres des Conques* (Edipop, Les Editions Populaires, Noumea). The poems used in this book have been taken from that collection.

Vanessa Griffen has written and published several short stories. Her poem 'White Ashes' was published in *Asian and Pacific Women's Resource and Action Series - Environment* (Asia and Pacific Development Centre, Kuala Lumpur, 1992).

Grace Mera Molisa is from Vanuatu. She has published a number of collections of poetry. The poems used in this book are taken from *Black Stone* (Mana Publications, Suva, 1983) and *Who Will Carry the Bag?* (Vanuatu National Council of Women, Port Vila, 1990).

Cita Morei's poem was published in Marjorie Crocombe et al. (eds) *Te Rau Maire: Poems and Stories of the Pacific* (Tauranga Vananga, Ministry of Cultural Development, Rarotonga, 1992).

Dorah Obed's poem was published in *Who Will Carry the Bag?* (Vanuatu National Council of Women, Port Vila, 1990). She is from Vanuatu.

Teresa M. Pasilio is a poet and civil servant from Tokelau. Her poetry has been published in Mana Publications, Suva. She currently works in the Office for Tokelau Affairs in Apia, Western Samoa.

Saili Paulo is a poet from Tokelau.

Kushma Ram has published poetry in Kamlesh Prakash (ed.) *Struggle on Jahajibhai: A Collection of Poetry from and about the Children of Indenture* (Fiji Youth and Students League, Suva, 1989). One of her poems used in this book has been taken from that collection.

Vaine Rasmussen, from the Cook Islands, is an economist at the South Pacific Commission in Noumea. She has published her work in Mana: *A South Pacific Journal of Literature and Language.* The poem used in this book was published in Marjorie Crocombe et al. (eds) *Te Rau Maire: Poems and Stories of the Pacific* (Tauranga Vananga, Ministry of Cultural Development, Rarotonga, 1992).

Noumea Simi, from Western Samoa, is a senior civil servant in the Ministry of Foreign Affairs in Western Samoa. Most of her poems selected for this book have been taken from her collection *Sails of Dawn* (Samoa Observer NZ Ltd, Apia, 1992).

Caroline Sinavaiana holds a Ph.D and is a Lecturer in Literature and Language at the American Samoan College in Pago Pago, American Samoa. A poet and story-teller, she has published in Marjorie Crocombe et al. (eds) *Te Rau*

Maire: Poems and Stories of the Pacific (Tauranga Vananga, Ministry of Cultural Development, Rarotonga, 1992). She read the poem used in this book in Barbados at the opening of the NGO Islands Forum which accompanied the First Global Conference on the Sustainable Development of Small Island Developing States. The poem was subsequently published in *The Barbados Advocate* (25 April 1994).

Jully Sipolo is a well-known and widely published Solomon Island poet. The poems used in this book have been published in the collections *Praying Parents* (University of the South Pacific Centre, Honiara, 1986) and *Civilized Girl* (Mana Publications, 1981).

Claire Slatter's poem, 'To Djubelly', was published in Arlene Griffen (ed.) *With Heart and Nerve and Sinew: Post-coup writing from Fiji,* (Suva, 1990).

Konai Helu Thaman is a well known poet who has published widely. Her poems in this book have been previously published in her own collections, *Lagakali* (Mana Publications, Suva, 1981) and *Kakala* (Mana Publications, Suva, 1993).

Makarita Vaai, from Western Samoan, is Centre Director at the University of the South Pacific Centre in Nauru. Her poem 'Pinnacles' was published in Marjorie Crocombe et al. (eds) *Te Rau Maire: Poems and Stories of the Pacific* (Tauranga Vananga, Ministry of Cultural Development, Rarotonga, 1992).

Momoe Malietoa Von Reiche, from Western Samoa, is a well-known poet. She has published four volumes of poetry, including *Solaua - a Secret Embryo, Pa'a Alimago on Wet Days, Alaoa* and *Tai - Heart of a Tree.*

288

We meet once again in good health
under the fetau tree.

A flock of birds
a little weary, but
grateful and glad.
A flock of birds
from the nests
of Moana Pacifica
Pacific Ocean
13,000 miles hence
13,000 miles back
a belt of miles
around Maina Earth
our planet
our egg.

We fly here
joining other flocks of birds
from other oceans
Caribbean Atlantic
Mediterranean Indian and Pacific
north and south

Each bird
each one of us
bringing twigs
leaves
bits of blue
plastic
whatevah!
to make a new nest
together
a leafy womb
enfolding our progeny
the ovum we will make
together
born from our union
born from our struggle
born from communion.

Our leaves and twigs
made of heart
muscle
and bone.
Our song
born in ocean and
weaned on struggle.
Strong clear voices
singing:
we have arrived!

we are here.
we declare ourselves.
we announce our presence.
we tell our own stories...

Caroline Sinavaiana
Excerpt from Village of Hope: By the River of Babylon

DATE DUE			
GAYLORD			PRINTED IN U.S.A.